PHILOSOPHICAL

ESSAYS

HANS JONAS

PHILOSOPHICAL

ESSAYS

From Ancient Creed
To Technological Man

PRENTICE-HALL, INC., *Englewood Cliffs, New Jersey*

192
J76

Library of Congress Cataloging in Publication Data

JONAS, HANS, 1903–
    Philosophical essays: from ancient creed to
technological man.
    CONTENTS: Technology and responsibility: reflections
on the new tasks of ethics.—Jewish and Christian
elements in philosophy: their share in the emergence of
the modern mind.—Seventeenth century and after: the
meaning of the scientific and technological revolution.
[etc.]

    1. Philosophy—Addresses, essays, lectures.
I. Title.
B29.J595   192   73-22168
ISBN   0-13-662221-6

© 1974 by PRENTICE-HALL, INC., *Englewood Cliffs, N.J.*

10   9   8   7   6   5   4   3   2   1

Printed in the United States of America

PRENTICE-HALL INTERNATIONAL, INC., *London*
PRENTICE-HALL OF AUSTRALIA, PTY. LTD., *Sydney*
PRENTICE-HALL OF CANADA, LTD., *Toronto*
PRENTICE-HALL OF INDIA PRIVATE LIMITED, *New Delhi*
PRENTICE-HALL OF JAPAN, INC., *Tokyo*

FOR ADOLPH LOWE
My Watchful Critic and Friend

Acknowledgments

With two exceptions, the essays in this volume have appeared in print during the years from 1965 to 1973. Some have undergone revision and enlargement of varying extent for their republication here. Acknowledgment is gratefully made to the publishers who have kindly granted permission to reprint the articles in question.

I wish to thank Dr. Adolph Lowe and Dr. Robert Heilbroner for their helpful advice regarding the order and title of this collection.

Leon R. Kass, M.D., provided valuable observations on the unpublished manuscript on Biological Engineering, which were gratefully heeded by me. The many debts of gratitude I owe to my colleagues of the Institute of Society, Ethics, and the Life Sciences for the benefits I derived from collaborating with them can be only collectively acknowledged here.

I wish to thank my assistant, Mr. Richard Rainville, for his diligence in preparing the manuscript for the printer and checking my proofreading.

Contents

PART TWO

ORGANISM, MIND, AND HISTORY

PART THREE

RELIGIOUS THOUGHT
OF THE FIRST CHRISTIAN CENTURIES

Introduction

Custom decrees that an author who collects a variety of essays into one volume prefaces it with a few words of justification for doing so. Somewhat more than this ritual is required where the variety of subjects is such as the table of contents of this volume exhibits at a glance. My apologia on the following pages is intellectual as well as biographical. The latter aspect cannot be avoided, as it tinges the former with that irreducible element of contingency from which a century like ours did not spare the life of the intellect. In spite of this intrusion of biographical accident, I hope to make a preliminary case for some unity of philosophical purpose that holds together the wide thematic spread of these pieces written over the last decade.

Having been formed during the 1920s in the school of such teachers as Husserl, Heidegger, and Bultmann, I began my own scholarly work in the field of early Christian and late classical thought. My first book was on Augustine's struggles with the problem of free will in the course of the Pelagian controversy,[1] and for many years thereafter all my theoretical energy was absorbed by the phenomenon of Gnosticism and its role in the world of declining Antiquity. I had committed myself to a comprehensive, perhaps overambitious analytic and synthetic task which was destined never to be completed (not to this day, anyway) in its

---

[1] *Augustin und das paulinische Freiheitsproblem* (Göttingen: Vandenhoeck & Ruprecht, 1930; 2nd ed. 1965).

initially conceived scope. The first volume[2] saw publication in 1934, in the Germany which I had left the year before, and not until twenty years later was it followed by a second volume,[3] whose appearance had been announced as imminent on the cover of the first. For from that time on, historical events too well known to require narration here intervened in the destiny of the work, not only regarding the prospects of its eventual publication in my native land, but also regarding my ability to complete it under the adaptive demands of a new life in what was then Palestine. Still, the work stayed with me throughout the years prior to World War II; and within the small but intense world of Jerusalemite academia, I was pretty much stamped as a specialist in this field. How much more so—with the apocryphal career of the German book—on the then remote European stage, I was to learn only later.

Five years of soldiering in the British army in the war against Hitler ushered in the second stage in my theoretical life. Cut off from books and all the paraphernalia of research, I had to stop work on the Gnostic project perforce. But something more substantive and essential was involved. The apocalyptic state of things, the threatening collapse of a world, the climactic crisis of civilization, the proximity of death, the stark nakedness to which all the issues of life were stripped, all these were ground enough to take a new look at the very foundations of our being and to review the principles by which we guide our thinking on them. Thus, thrown back on my own resources, I was thrown back on the philosopher's basic duty and his native business—thinking. And while living in tents and barracks, being on the move or in position, tending the guns or firing them, all the reductive primitivism and ordered waste of the soldier's life in a long war are most unfavorable to scholarly work, they do not prevent, are even eminently conducive to thinking—and thinking to the point—when there is a will to it.

The results of my re-thinking of the fundamentals during those seemingly unending years set my philosophical task for the next two decades. The few major truths I then perceived and began to draw conclusions from were these:

(a) that the dominant line of philosophy in which I had been brought up in Germany, namely the idealism of consciousness—whether in the form of neo-Kantianism, phenomenology, or existentialism, brothers under the skin in their exclusive focus on mentality—exposed no more than the tip of the iceberg of our being and left submerged the broad organic basis on which the miracle of mind is perched;

(b) that this was the heritage of Cartesian dualism, which had split reality into *res cogitans* and *res extensa* (what the then to me unknown

---

[2]*Gnosis und spätantiker Geist* I (Göttingen, 1934; 2nd ed. 1954; 3rd ed. 1964).
[3]*Gnosis und spätantiker Geist* II (Göttingen, 1954; 2nd ed. 1966).

Alfred North Whitehead had called "the bifurcation of nature"), and whose continued hold, in one form or another, over all subsequent theorizing had prejudged the ontological question from its roots;

(c) that philosophy's retreat into the mental half of the dichotomy—which left all of "nature" to victorious science and substituted epistemology of natural science for the philosophy of nature whose very idea had been renounced—not only was a scandal of philosophy in itself, but also vitiated its work in the residual field of its choice (or captivity);

(d) that, therefore, revising the dualistic premise, and first of all rethinking the problem of dualism itself, had become a foremost duty of philosophical critique; and, as to its positive task,

(e) that the *organism* with its insoluble fusion of inwardness and outwardness constituted the crucial counterevidence to the dualistic division and, by our privileged experiential access to it, the prime paradigm for philosophy of concrete, uncurtailed being—indeed the key to a reintegration of fragmented ontology into a uniform theory of being.

For practical purposes, it followed from these propositions that, short of achieving the last and still too distant goal, an ontological interpretation of organic being, transcending the hardened dichotomies of the past, was clearly the indispensable first step to it. For philosophy, strange to say, this was almost virginal soil! Clearly also, the execution of this first step would lead beyond the anthropocentric confinement of most modern philosophy into the living kingdom of which man is a part. On its historical side, the task involved a critique of past theories predicated on dualism which would yet have to save the abiding truths which dualism had gained for thought during its epochal sway. On the systematic side, it demanded a serious but not servile attention to the teachings of natural science, especially biology. Thus a compelling program of long range was taking shape. With this sketch of theoretical points, I ask leave to return to the narrative.

Impatient for the new task, convinced also that twelve years of inquiry into a historical subject were enough for a philosopher's apprenticeship, I returned to civilian life determined to leave my Gnostic studies behind where the accident of war had interrupted them, and to devote the coming years wholly to the working out of the philosophy of organism whose outlines I had conceived and begun to jot down during the pregnant intermezzo. I soon learnt that escape from an earlier beginning is not lightly permitted by the world and can never be complete for internal reasons as well. The first reminder came before I had even doffed the uniform, when I moved into devastated Germany with the occupying forces (making true, by the way, the vow with which I had left twelve years before: never to return except as the soldier of a conquering army). In the deeply moving reunion with the untainted few,

I was told of the impact that the first volume of *Gnosis und spätantiker Geist* had achieved during those dark years, without benefit of public reviewing, completely unknown to me, beyond any expectations of mine, and also far beyond the specialist limits of the topic. This was gratifying news—and, incidentally, a demonstration of the probably more general truth that a book can make its way, as it were, behind the official jury's back. But the almost impassioned appeals from such revered men as Bultmann and Jaspers to go on with the work and deliver the promised Part II tempered the gratification with a serious conflict of loyalties to tasks—to an old contract and a new commitment, the former's strength added to by the tempting trap of success. A more superficial but tenacious byproduct of the last was the increasingly apparent fact that in the eyes of international scholarship my name had become identified with Gnosticism. Once bestowed, such a label sticks with wonderful adhesiveness; and while it does not obligate the subject of the extraneous consensus, it can lead to curious encounters with the imposed image—to the point of outright incredulity that the Hans Jonas of the later studies in philosophical biology is the same as the Jonas of the Gnosis. The noncomical side of this pattern was that, with its implied expectation and even reproach, it fed the pangs of conscience to which the real conflict of loyalties gave cause anyway. In short, from those first postwar encounters on I knew that I would have to serve my new commitment under the shadow of an unredeemed I.O.U. From my own side there is to be added that the new resolve had by no means relegated the fascination of the earlier subject to the memory of a youthful infatuation, or lessened my conviction of its philosophical relevance; also, that I was anything but unresponsive to the challenge of the massive new text discoveries which from the late 1940s (just when I wanted to say goodbye) to this day keeps the fellowship of Gnosis scholars throughout the world in thrall. Even secret philosophical connections of this unlikely topic with my new interests emerged in the latters' pursuit. To the last, as yet cryptic, remark I shall return later when I make the plea of internal unity. The present is no more than a biographical explanation of the multiplicity which the reader will find in this book, and which on that count alone might well be accidental. But the fact that he will find, among essays none of which appeared before 1965, a whole group falling into the area that was meant to be abandoned in 1945, tells that the reported conflict of loyalties led to compromises, whose history would be too tedious to relate, but whose outcome is documented in my publication record before as well as after the date from which the present collection takes off.

At any rate, until the mid-sixties it was the elaboration of the insights or intimations of the war years which occupied the center stage of my theoretical efforts; except for the said compromises (i.e., intermittent returns to the earlier field), Organism was their unifying theme. But no sooner had this found its first approximation to a systematic statement in my book, *The Phenomenon of Life* (1966)—the sum of studies that had been appearing singly from 1950 on—than a new set of problems began to take hold of my philosophical attention: the moral challenges of modern technology. Again I cannot resist indulging in an autobiographical digression.

I had returned from the war experience and the nightmare preceding it in an optimistic frame of mind as to the condition of the world about to emerge from the holocaust. Humanity, so it seemed to me, had passed through a crisis which, at its excessive and totally unacceptable price, would still have the effect of a catharsis, at least of a calm after the storm. It was the illusion that crushing one supreme evil, after it had taken its terrible course, would halt the public power of evil in general, if only by sheer exhaustion, for a goodly time to come. Of the better things mankind could now turn to I held good hopes—paradoxically derived from the most frightening technological bequest of the war. I still vividly remember a talk I had with Karl Jaspers shortly after the dropping of the atomic bombs (toward whose one-time military necessity the soldier of many years was duly hardened), in which I outlined what I anticipated as the turn in human affairs that the peaceful use of atomic energy would usher in. Nothing less than a new civilization of leisure, with vast humanistic potentials, arose before my eyes from the prospect of unlimited mechanical power—a radical change, and for the better, from mankind's inherited problems and goals. "Sehr schön," said Jaspers, considering, "sehr schön!" For once I succumbed to the spell of the Baconian utopia and expected, if not salvation, at any rate a great furtherance of the human good, at the least a novel chance, a new scope for freedom, from technology.

Such gratuitous hopes could be left to themselves. As to the modest anticipation of a becalmed sea, I had for years, in the relativity of such judgments, no reason to question the temporary leave from world history for which the needs of my contemplation had asked. For one who had gone through the horrors of the thirties and forties and had to live the rest of his days under the shadow of Auschwitz, the stalemate of the Cold War was tame stuff indeed. Even of the precarious nuclear deterrence, I took a cool view—whether from judicious soberness or blunted sensitivity. For while I had no illusions about the power of reason in the governance of human affairs, I set great store, with old Hobbes, in the wholesome power of naked fear; and although one underestimates at his peril the magnitude of human stupidity and its capacity for disaster, one may still give the comforting odds to fear of the vividly imminent extreme. So far, luckily, this somewhat somberly placid view has not been refuted by events, which of course does not prove it right or even commendable.

What recalled me from theoretical detachment to public responsibility and set a new task to my philosophizing—surely the last, considering my age—was the growing realization of the inherent dangers of technology as such—not of its sudden but of its slow perils, not of its short-term but of its long-term threats, not of its malevolent abuses which, with some watchfulness, one can hope to control, but of its most benevolent and legitimate uses which are the very stuff of its active possession. The later sixties of this, our fateful century, saw the emergence of the most acute, internal crisis of the Baconian ideal, compared with which all former, external challenges by romantics, traditionalists, or malcontents had been child's play.

As this has meanwhile impressed itself so much on the public mind, there is no need for me to spell out the issues that here raise their heads; the mere mention of the ecological complex on the one hand, of human, especially genetic, "engineering" on the other, is sufficient. While for the first it is not prima facie obvious that it concerns philosophy (which it does), it is most evident for the second. For here, where norms for the use of the optional new powers are called for, an image of Man must provide their nonarbitrary basis; and with the eclipse of revelation, this image is the sole responsibility of philosophy. Here also, the link with the philosophical anthropology into which any philosophy or organism worth its salt must issue, and thus with my preceding theoretical theme, is manifest enough. But the most obvious fact is that meeting the challenges of technology is a matter for ethics; and with the unprecedented novelty of some of those challenges, for which no previous ethics has prepared us, this entails a search for principles that enable us to deal with issues mankind never had to deal with before. Thus it has come about that since the late sixties I find myself—by a transition from "theoretical" to "practical" reason enforced by the very pressure of events and even more of possibilities colossally looming on the horizon—engaged in questions of ethical theory and finally in a quest for the foundations of an ethics adequate to the matters on which we now or soon have to decide. Lately this has led me into the first stages of writing a book on technology and ethics, which for some years to come will stop any piecemeal presentations of mine in the long-favored form of essays. Given the epistemological, skeptical creeds of our time, the venture sounds, and indeed may turn out to be, quixotic; but it is my last call to arms, with no more choice but to follow it than the physical one over thirty years ago and, of course, with no more assurance of success. Be that as it may, this seemed to me the moment to gather the essays published over the last seven or eight years, in which the new theme makes its appearance but still overlaps with the other two of my theoretical career, into one volume tristructured according to the distinct subject matter of those stages. And herewith I turn to the promised attempt to show the internal bond that links the disparate subjects to one another beyond the biographical bond just reported.

This is easily done for the two later themes. Their mutual connection has already been indicated with the mention of philosophical anthropology and is plausible enough in itself. The fact alone that the new problems have to do, *inter alia*, with the integrity of our organic being, and that, of the integrity (or proper "good") of anything, we can have an informed idea—and a possible norm—only if the nature to be guarded, saved, or improved, is known, provides one substantive link between the theory of organism and the ethics of technological intervention. This is a link extended backwards from the ethical interest to the cognitive support needed by it. But there is a deeper link in the independent, intrinsic forward thrust of organic theory itself toward an ethical completion. In fact, *The Phenomenon of Life* explicitly projected this outstanding completion in its Epilogue, where I state:

> We opened this volume with the proposition that the philosophy of life comprises the philosophy of organism and the philosophy of mind. At its end, and in the light of what we have learned, we may add a further proposition, implied in that first one but setting a new task: a philosophy of mind comprises ethics—and through the continuity of mind with organism and of organism with nature, ethics becomes part of the philosophy of nature. . . . Only an ethics which is grounded in the breadth of being, not merely in the singularity or oddness of man, can have significance in the scheme of things. It has it, if man has such significance; and whether he has it we must learn from an interpretation of reality as a whole. But even without any such claim of transhuman significance for human conduct, an ethics no longer founded on divine authority must be founded on a principle discoverable in the nature of things, lest it fall victim to subjectivism or other forms of relativity. However far, therefore, the ontological quest may have carried us outside man, into the general theory of being and of life, it did not really move away from ethics, but searched for its possible foundation.

When I wrote those words, I was only dimly conscious of the possibility that what I delineated as a theoretical task—the continuation of the ontological argument into ethics—might through the course of human affairs be made an ethical duty itself. Indeed, the tide of things most nonphilosophic forced my hand and overruled the hesitation of not feeling ready yet (or ever) for that most demanding task. Having now plunged into it (not without some prodding from the friend to whom this book is dedicated) I am well aware that, for good or ill, its

execution puts to the test the earlier work on organism on whose findings it must draw.

Not equally plain is the connection of either or both of these themes
with Gnosticism. But even here, one link at least must have suggested
itself to the informed reader in the concept of *dualism* which figured so
large in the story of what led to, and is involved in, a philosophy of
organism. Gnosticism had been the most radical embodiment of dualism
ever to have appeared on the stage of history, and its exploration provided a case study of all that is implicated in it: the split between self
and world, man's alienation from nature, the latter's metaphysical devaluation, the cosmic solitude of the spirit and the ensuing nihilism of
mundane norms, the general style of extremism—all these had been
acted out in that deeply agitated play. The analogical "modernity" of
ancient Gnosticism, or the hidden "Gnosticism" in the modern mind,
had struck me early and been propounded already in 1952 in a special
essay.[4] To the extent that the intellectual and existential conditions engendered by modern science, with which the philosophy of organism
has to cope, are related to the dominion of dualism, the gnostic paradigm, in which everything stands out with the sharpness of unblushing
naiveté, proved an enlightening help. Another link, extending across
the second into the third stage of my work, may be termed "crisis."
This is so much a catchword for the contemporary situation that its
pertinence to the technological syndrome needs no elaboration. Here
again, the age of Gnosticism is the classic case of a human crisis on a
large historical scale, and similar considerations hold for the relevance
of its lesson to the present crisis of Western man—thus also to any
groping for an ethics in response to it—as applied in the case of dualism. Actually, "Man in Crisis" was among the first titles suggested for
this collection, and discarded only for fear of shrillness.

Herewith I rest my case. Ultimately it is for the reader to decide
whether the essays collected here do speak with a common voice, not
only of their author but also, less directly perhaps, of their multiple
subject matter. The sequence in which they are presented reverses the
chronological order of their subjects as well as of their authorship.
I had first adopted the "natural" order. Although there is not much to
choose between the two alternatives, I finally decided (mindful of the
Aristotelian distinction between what is first in knowledge and first in
things) that the reader should be allowed to make his way from the
proximate and topical to the remote in time and knowledge, rather than
having sprung on him at the outset things distant and alien to him.

---

[4]"Gnosticism and Modern Nihilism," in *Social Research* 19 (1962); later added
as Epilogue to the second edition of *The Gnostic Religion* (Boston: Beacon Press,
1963). A German version is included in my book *Zwischen Nichts und Ewigkeit*
(Göttingen, 1963).

PART ONE

SCIENCE,
TECHNOLOGY,
AND ETHICS

1.
Technology and Responsibility: Reflections on the New Tasks of Ethics

All previous ethics—whether in the form of issuing direct enjoinders to do and not to do certain things, or in the form of defining principles for such enjoinders, or in the form of establishing the ground of obligation for obeying such principles—had these interconnected tacit premises in common: that the human condition, determined by the nature of man and the nature of things, was given once for all; that the human good on that basis was readily determinable; and that the range of human action and therefore responsibility was narrowly circumscribed. It will be the burden of my argument to show that these premises no longer hold, and to reflect on the meaning of this fact for our moral condition. More specifically, it will be my contention that with certain developments of our powers the *nature of human action* has changed, and since ethics is concerned with action, it should follow that the changed nature of human action calls for a change in ethics as well: this not merely in the sense that new objects of action have added to the case material on which received rules of conduct are to be applied, but in the more radical sense that the qualitatively novel nature of certain of our actions has opened up a whole new dimension of ethical relevance for

Originally presented as a plenary address to the International Congress of Learned Societies in the Field of Religion held in Los Angeles, September 1972, and included in *Religion and the Humanizing of Man*, ed. James M. Robinson (Council on the Study of Religion, 1972). Subsequently published in *Social Research* 15 (Spring 1973).

which there is no precedent in the standards and canons of traditional ethics.

I

The novel powers I have in mind are, of course, those of modern *technology*. My first point, accordingly, is to ask how this technology affects the nature of our acting, in what ways it makes acting under its dominion *different* from what it has been through the ages. Since throughout those ages man was never without technology, the question involves the human difference of *modern* from previous technology. Let us start with an ancient voice on man's powers and deeds which in an archetypal sense itself strikes, as it were, a technological note—the famous Chorus from Sophocles' *Antigone*.

Many the wonders but nothing more wondrous than man.
This thing crosses the sea in the winter's storm,
making his path through the roaring waves.
And she, the greatest of gods, the Earth—
deathless she is, and unwearied—he wears her away
as the ploughs go up and down from year to year
and his mules turn up the soil.

The tribes of the lighthearted birds he ensnares, and the races
of all the wild beasts and the salty brood of the sea,
with the twisted mesh of his nets, he leads captive, this clever man.
He controls with craft the beasts of the open air,
who roam the hills. The horse with his shaggy mane
he holds and harnesses, yoked about the neck,
and the strong bull of the mountain.

Speech and thought like the wind
and the feelings that make the town,
he has taught himself, and shelter against the cold,
refuge from rain. Ever resourceful is he.
He faces no future helpless. Only against death
shall he call for aid in vain. But from baffling maladies
has he contrived escape.

Clever beyond all dreams
the inventive craft that he has
which may drive him one time or another to well or ill.
When he honors the laws of the land and the gods' sworn right
high indeed is his city; but stateless the man
who dares to do what is shameful.

(lines 335–370)

This awestruck homage to man's powers tells of his violent and violating irruption into the cosmic order, the self-assertive invasion of nature's various domains by his restless cleverness; but also of his building—through the self-taught powers of speech and thought and social sentiment—the home for his very humanity, the artifact of the city. The raping of nature and the civilizing of himself go hand in hand. Both are in defiance of the elements, the one by venturing into them and over-powering their creatures, the other by securing an enclave against them in the shelter of the city and its laws. Man is the maker of his life *qua* human, bending circumstances to his will and needs, and except against death he is never helpless.

Yet there is a subdued and even anxious quality about this appraisal of the marvel that is man, and nobody can mistake it for immodest bragging. With all his boundless resourcefulness, man is still small by the measure of the elements: precisely this makes his sallies into them so daring and allows those elements to tolerate his forwardness. Making free with the denizens of land and sea and air, he yet leaves the encompassing nature of those elements unchanged, and their generative powers undiminished. Them he cannot harm by carving out his little dominion from theirs. They last, while his schemes have their shortlived way. Much as he harries Earth, the greatest of gods, year after year with his plough—she is ageless and unwearied; her enduring patience he must and can trust, and to her cycle he must conform. And just as ageless is the sea. With all his netting of the salty brood, the spawning ocean is inexhaustible. Nor is it hurt by the plying of ships, nor sullied by what is jettisoned into its deeps. And no matter how many illnesses he contrives to cure, mortality does not bow to his cunning.

All this holds because man's inroads into nature, as seen by himself, were essentially superficial, and powerless to upset its appointed balance. Nor is there a hint, in the *Antigone* chorus or anywhere else, that this is only a beginning and that greater things of artifice and power are yet to come—that man is embarked on an endless course of conquest. He had gone thus far in reducing necessity, had learned by his wits to wrest that much from it for the humanity of his life, and there he could stop. The room he had thus made was filled by the city of men—meant to enclose, and not to expand—and thereby a new balance was struck within the larger balance of the whole. All the well or ill to which man's inventive craft may drive him one time or another is inside the human enclave and does not touch the nature of things.

The immunity of the whole, untroubled in its depth by the importunities of man, that is, the essential immutability of Nature as the cosmic order, was indeed the backdrop to all of mortal man's enterprises, including his intrusions into that order itself. Man's life was played out between the abiding and the changing: the abiding was Nature, the changing his own works. The greatest of these works was the city, and on it he could confer some measure of abidingness by the laws he made for it and undertook to honor. But no long-range certainty pertained to this contrived abidingness. As a precarious artifact, it can lapse or go astray. Not even within its artificial space, with all the freedom it gives to man's determination of self, can the arbitrary ever supersede the basic terms of his being. The very inconstancy of human fortunes assures the constancy of the human condition. Chance and luck and folly, the great equalizers in human affairs, act like an entropy of sorts and make all definite designs in the long run revert to the perennial norm. Cities rise and fall, rules come and go, families prosper and decline; no change is there to stay, and in the end, with all the temporary deflections balancing each other out, the state of man is as it always was. So here too, in his very own artifact, man's control is small and his abiding nature prevails.

Still, in this citadel of his own making, clearly set off from the rest of things and entrusted to him, was the whole and sole domain of man's responsible action. Nature was not an object of human responsibility— she taking care of herself and, with some coaxing and worrying, also of man: not ethics, only cleverness applied to her. But in the city, where men deal with men, cleverness must be wedded to morality, for this is the soul of its being. In this intra-human frame dwells all traditional ethics and matches the nature of action delimited by this frame.

II

Let us extract from the preceding those characteristics of human action which are relevant for a comparison with the state of things today.

1. All dealing with the non-human world, i.e., the whole realm of *techne* (with the exception of medicine), was ethically neutral—in respect both of the object and the subject of such action: in respect of the object, because it impinged but little on the self-sustaining nature of things and thus raised no question of permanent injury to the integrity of its object, the natural order as a whole; and in respect of the agent subject it was ethically neutral because *techne* as an activity conceived itself as a determinate tribute to necessity and not as an indefinite, self-validating advance to mankind's major goal, claiming in its pursuit man's ultimate effort and concern. The real vocation of man lay elsewhere. In brief, action on non-human things did not constitute a sphere of authentic ethical significance.

2. Ethical significance belonged to the direct dealing of man with man,

including the dealing with himself: all traditional ethics is *anthro-pocentric*.

3. For action in this domain, the entity "man" and his basic condition was considered constant in essence and not itself an object of reshaping *techne*.

4. The good and evil about which action had to care lay close to the act, either in the praxis itself or in its immediate reach, and were not a matter for remote planning. This proximity of ends pertained to time as well as space. The effective range of action was small, the time-span of foresight, goal-setting and accountability was short, control of circumstances limited. Proper conduct had its immediate criteria and almost immediate consummation. The long run of consequences beyond was left to chance, fate or providence. Ethics accordingly was of the here and now, of occasions as they arise between men, of the recurrent, typical situations of private and public life. The good man was he who met these contingencies with virtue and wisdom, cultivating these powers in himself, and for the rest resigning himself to the unknown.

All enjoinders and maxims of traditional ethics, materially different as they may be, show this confinement to the immediate setting of the action. "Love thy neighbor as thyself"; "Do unto others as you would wish them to do unto you"; "Instruct your child in the way of truth"; "Strive for excellence by developing and actualizing the best potentialities of your being *qua* man"; "Subordinate your individual good to the common good"; "Never treat your fellow man as a means only but always *also* as an end in himself"—and so on. Note that in all these maxims the agent and the "other" of his action are sharers of a common present. It is those alive now and in some commerce with me that have a claim on my conduct as it affects them by deed or omission. The ethical universe is composed of contemporaries, and its horizon to the future is confined by the foreseeable span of their lives. Similarly confined is its horizon of place, within which the agent and the other meet as neighbor, friend or foe, as superior and subordinate, weaker and stronger, and in all the other roles in which humans interact with one another. To this proximate range of action all morality was geared.

III

It follows that the *knowledge* that is required—besides the moral will —to assure the morality of action, fitted these limited terms: it was not the knowledge of the scientist or the expert, but knowledge of a kind readily available to all men of good will. Kant went so far as to say that "human reason can, in matters of morality, be easily brought to a high degree of accuracy and completeness even in the most ordinary intelligence";[1] that "there is no need of science or philosophy for knowing what man has to do in order to be honest and good, and indeed to be wise and virtuous. . . . [Ordinary intelligence] can have as good hope of hitting the mark as any philosopher can promise himself";[2] and again: "I need no elaborate acuteness to find out what I have to do so that my willing be morally good. Inexperienced regarding the course of the world, unable to anticipate all the contingencies that happen in it," I can yet know how to act in accordance with the moral law.[3]

Not every thinker in ethics, it is true, went so far in discounting the cognitive side of moral action. But even when it received much greater emphasis, as in Aristotle, where the discernment of the situation and what is fitting for it makes considerable demands on experience and judgment, such knowledge has nothing to do with the science of things. It implies, of course, a general conception of the human good as such, a conception predicated on the presumed invariables of man's nature and condition, which may or may not find expression in a theory of its own. But its translation into practice requires a knowledge of the here and now, and this is entirely non-theoretical. This "knowledge" proper to virtue (of the "where, when, to whom, and how") stays with the immediate issue, in whose defined context the action *as the agent's own* takes its course and within which it terminates. The good or bad of the action is wholly decided within that short-term context. Its moral quality shines forth from it, visible to its witnesses. No one was held responsible for the unintended later effects of his well-intentioned, well-considered, and well-performed act. The short arm of human power did not call for a long arm of predictive knowledge; the shortness of the one is as little culpable as that of the other. Precisely because the human good, known in its generality, is the same for all time, its realization or violation takes place at each time, and its complete locus is always the present.

IV

All this has decisively changed. Modern technology has introduced actions of such novel scale, objects, and consequences that the framework of former ethics can no longer contain them. The *Antigone* chorus on the *deinotes*, the wondrous power, of man would have to read differ-

---

[1]Immanuel Kant, *Groundwork of the Metaphysic of Morals*, preface.
[2]*Op. cit.*, chapter 1.
[3]*Ibid.* (I have followed H. J. Paton's translation with some changes.)

ently now; and its admonition to the individual to honor the laws of the land would no longer be enough. To be sure, the old prescriptions of the "neighbor" ethics—of justice, charity, honesty, and so on—still hold in their intimate immediacy for the nearest, day by day sphere of human interaction. But this sphere is overshadowed by a growing realm of collective action where doer, deed, and effect are no longer the same as they were in the proximate sphere, and which by the enormity of its powers forces upon ethics a new dimension of responsibility never dreamt of before.

Take, for instance, as the first major change in the inherited picture, the critical *vulnerability* of nature to man's technological intervention —unsuspected before it began to show itself in damage already done. This discovery, whose shock led to the concept and nascent science of ecology, alters the very concept of ourselves as a causal agency in the larger scheme of things. It brings to light, through the effects, that the nature of human action has *de facto* changed, and that an object of an entirely new order—no less than the whole biosphere of the planet— has been added to what we must be responsible for because of our power over it. And of what surpassing importance an object, dwarfing all previous objects of active man! Nature as a human responsibility is surely a *novum* to be pondered in ethical theory. What kind of obligation is operative in it? Is it more than a utilitarian concern? Is it just prudence that bids us not to kill the goose that lays the golden eggs, or saw off the branch on which we sit? But the "we" that here sits and may fall into the abyss is all future mankind, and the survival of the species is more than a prudential duty of its present members. Insofar as it is the fate of *man*, as affected by the condition of nature, which makes us care about the preservation of nature, such care admittedly still retains the anthropocentric focus of all classical ethics. Even so, the difference is great. The containment of nearness and con- temporaneity is gone, swept away by the spatial spread and time-span of the cause-effect trains which technological practice sets afoot, even when undertaken for proximate ends. Their irreversibility conjoined to their aggregate magnitude injects another novel factor into the moral equation. To this take their cumulative character: their effects add them- selves to one another, and the situation for later acting and being be- comes increasingly different from what it was for the initial agent. The cumulative self-propagation of the technological change of the world thus constantly overtakes the conditions of its contributing acts and moves through none but unprecedented situations, for which the lessons of experience are powerless. And not even content with changing its beginning to the point of unrecognizability, the cumulation as such may consume the basis of the whole series, the very condition of itself. All this would have to be co-intended in the will of the single action if this is to be a morally responsible one. Ignorance no longer provides it with an alibi.

Knowledge, under these circumstances, becomes a prime duty beyond anything claimed for it heretofore, and the knowledge must be commensurate with the causal scale of our action. The fact that it cannot really be thus commensurate, i.e., that the predictive knowledge falls behind the technical knowledge which nourishes our power to act, itself assumes ethical importance. Recognition of ignorance becomes the obverse of the duty to know and thus part of the ethics which must govern the ever more necessary self-policing of our out-sized might. No previous ethics had to consider the global condition of human life and the far-off future, even existence, of the race. Their now being an issue demands, in brief, a new concept of duties and rights, for which previous ethics and metaphysics provide not even the principles, let alone a ready doctrine.

And what if the new kind of human action would mean that more than the interest of man alone is to be considered—that our duty extends farther and the anthropocentric confinement of former ethics no longer holds? It is at least not senseless anymore to ask whether the condition of extra-human nature, the biosphere as a whole and in its parts, now subject to our power, has become a human trust and has something of a moral claim on us not only for our ulterior sake but for its own and in its own right. If this were the case it would require quite some rethinking in basic principles of ethics. It would mean to seek not only the human good, but also the good of things extra-human, that is, to extend the recognition of "ends in themselves" beyond the sphere of man and make the human good include the care for them. For such a role of stewardship no previous ethics has prepared us—and the dominant, scientific view of *Nature* even less. Indeed, the latter emphatically denies us all conceptual means to think of Nature as something to be honored, having reduced it to the indifference of necessity and accident, and divested it of any dignity of ends. But still, a silent plea for sparing its integrity seems to issue from the threatened plenitude of the living world. Should we heed this plea, should we grant its claim as sanctioned by the nature of things, or dismiss it as a mere sentiment on our part, which we may indulge as far as we wish and can afford to do? If the former, it would (if taken seriously in its theoretical implications) push the necessary rethinking beyond the doctrine of action, i.e., ethics, into the doctrine of being, i.e., metaphysics, in which all ethics must ultimately be grounded. On this speculative subject I will here say no more than that we should keep ourselves open to the thought that natural science may not tell the whole story about Nature.

V

Returning to strictly intra-human considerations, there is another ethical aspect to the growth of *techne* as a pursuit beyond the pragmatically limited terms of former times. Then, so we found, *techne* was a measured tribute to necessity, not the road to mankind's chosen goal— a means with a finite measure of adequacy to well-defined proximate ends. Now, *techne* in the form of modern technology has turned into an infinite forward-thrust of the race, its most significant enterprise, in whose permanent, self-transcending advance to ever greater things the vocation of man tends to be seen, and whose success of maximal control over things and himself appears as the consummation of his destiny. Thus the triumph of *homo faber* over his external object means also his triumph in the internal constitution of *homo sapiens*, of whom he used to be a subsidiary part. In other words, technology, apart from its objective works, assumes ethical significance by the central place it now occupies in human purpose. Its cumulative creation, the expanding artificial environment, continuously reinforces the particular powers in man that created it, by compelling their unceasing inventive employment in its management and further advance, and by rewarding them with additional success—which only adds to the relentless claim. This positive feedback of functional necessity and reward—in whose dynamics pride of achievement must not be forgotten—assures the growing ascendancy of one side of man's nature over all the others, and inevitably at their expense. If nothing succeeds like success, nothing also entraps like success. Outshining in prestige and starving in resources whatever else belongs to the fullness of man, the expansion of his power is accompanied by a contraction of his self-conception and being. In the image he entertains of himself—the potent self-formula which determines his actual being as much as it reflects it—man now is evermore the maker of what he has made and the doer of what he can do, and most of all the preparer of what he will be able to do next. But not you or I: it is the aggregate, not the individual doer or deed that matters here; and the indefinite future, rather than the contemporary context of the action, constitutes the relevant horizon of responsibility. This requires imperatives of a new sort. If the realm of making has invaded the space of essential action, then morality must invade the realm of making, from which it had formerly stayed aloof, and must do so in the form of public policy. With issues of such inclusiveness and such lengths of anticipation public policy has never had to deal before. In fact, the changed nature of human action changes the very nature of politics.

For the boundary between "city" and "nature" has been obliterated: the city of men, once an enclave in the non-human world, spreads over the whole of terrestrial nature and usurps its place. The difference between the artificial and the natural has vanished, the natural is swallowed up in the sphere of the artificial, and at the same time the total artifact, the works of man working on and through himself, generates a "nature" of its own, i.e., a necessity with which human freedom has to cope in an entirely new sense. Once it could be said *Fiat justitia, pereat mundus*, "Let justice be done, and may the world perish"—where "world," of course, meant the renewable enclave in the imperishable whole. Not even rhetorically can the like be said anymore when the perishing of the whole through the doings of man—be they just or unjust—has become a real possibility. Issues never legislated on come into the purview of the laws which the total city must give itself so that there will be a world for the generations of man to come.

That there *ought* to be through all future time such a world fit for human habitation, and that it ought in all future time to be inhabited by a mankind worthy of the human name, will be readily affirmed as a general axiom or a persuasive desirability of speculative imagination (as persuasive and undemonstrable as the proposition that there being a world at all is "better" than there being none): but as a *moral* proposition, namely, a practical *obligation* toward the posterity of a distant future, and a principle of decision in present action, it is quite different from the imperatives of the previous ethics of contemporaneity; and it has entered the moral scene only with our novel powers and range of prescience.

The *presence of man in the world* had been a first and unquestionable given, from which all idea of obligation in human conduct started out. Now it has itself become an *object* of obligation—the obligation namely to ensure the very premise of all obligation, i.e., the *foothold* for a moral universe in the physical world—the existence of mere *candidates* for a moral order. The difference this makes for ethics may be illustrated in one example.

VI

Kant's categorical imperative said: "Act so that you *can* will that the maxim of your action be made the principle of a universal law." The "can" here invoked is that of reason and its consistency with itself:

Given the existence of a community of human agents (acting rational beings), the action must be such that it can without self-contradiction be imagined as a general practice of that community. Mark that the basic reflection of morals here is not itself a moral but a logical one: The "I *can* will" or "I *cannot* will" expresses logical compatibility or incompatibility, not moral approbation or revulsion. But there is no self-contradiction in the thought that humanity would once come to an end, therefore also none in the thought that the happiness of present and proximate generations would be bought with the unhappiness or even non-existence of later ones—as little as, after all, in the inverse thought that the existence or happiness of later generations would be bought with the unhappiness or even partial extinction of present ones. The sacrifice of the future for the present is *logically* no more open to attack than the sacrifice of the present for the future. The difference is only that in the one case the series goes on, and in the other it does not. But that it *ought to go on*, regardless of the distribution of happiness or unhappiness, even with a persistent preponderance of unhappiness over happiness, nay, even of immorality over morality[1]—this cannot be derived from the rule of self-consistency *within* the series, long or short as it happens to be: it is a commandment of a very different kind, lying outside and "prior" to the series as a whole, and its ultimate grounding can only be metaphysical.

An imperative responding to the new type of human action and addressed to the new type of agency that operates it might run thus: "Act so that the effects of your action are compatible with the permanence of genuine human life"; or expressed negatively: "Act so that the effects of your action are not destructive of the future possibility of such life"; or simply: "Do not compromise the conditions for an indefinite continuation of humanity on earth"; or most generally: "In your present choices, include the future wholeness of Man among the objects of your will."

It is immediately obvious that no rational contradiction is involved in the violation of this kind of imperative. I *can* will the present good with sacrifice of the future good. It is also evident that the new imperative addresses itself to public policy rather than private conduct, which is not in the causal dimension to which that imperative applies. Kant's categorical imperative was addressed to the individual, and its criterion was instantaneous. It enjoined each of us to consider what would happen *if* the *maxim* of my present action were made, or at this moment already were, the principle of a universal legislation; the self-consistency or inconsistency of such a *hypothetical* universalization is made the test for

[1]On this last point, the biblical God changed his mind to an all-encompassing "yes" after the Flood.

my *private* choice. But it was no part of the reasoning that there is any probability of my private choice *in fact* becoming universal law, or that it might contribute to its becoming that. The universalization is a thought-experiment by the private agent to test the immanent morality of his action. Indeed, real consequences are not considered at all, and the principle is one not of objective responsibility but of the subjective quality of my self-determination. The new imperative invokes a different consistency: not that of the act with itself, but that of its eventual *effects* with the continuance of human agency in times to come. And the "universalization" it contemplates is by no means hypothetical—i.e., a purely logical transference from the individual "me" to an imaginary, causally unrelated "all" ("*if* everybody acted like that"); on the contrary, the actions subject to the new imperative—actions of the collective whole— have their universal reference in their actual scope of efficacy: they "totalize" themselves in the progress of their momentum and thus are bound to terminate in shaping the universal dispensation of things. This adds a *time* horizon to the moral calculus which is entirely absent from the instantaneous logical operation of the Kantian imperative: whereas the latter extrapolates into an ever-present order of abstract compatibility, our imperative extrapolates into a predictable real *future* as the open-ended dimension of our responsibility.

VII

Similar comparisons could be made with all the other historical forms of the ethics of contemporaneity and immediacy. The new order of human action requires a commensurate ethics of foresight and responsibility, which is as new as are the issues with which it has to deal. We have seen that these are the issues posed by the works of *homo faber* in the age of technology. But among those novel works we haven't mentioned yet the potentially most ominous class. We have considered *techne* only as applied to the non-human realm. But man himself has been added to the objects of technology. *Homo faber* is turning upon himself and gets ready to make over the maker of all the rest. This consummation of his power, which may well portend the overpowering of man, this final imposition of art on nature, calls upon the utter resources of ethical thought, which never before has been faced with elective alternatives to what were considered the definite terms of the human condition.

a. Take, for instance, the most basic of these "givens," man's mortality. Who ever before had to make up his mind on its desirable and *eligible* measure? There was nothing to choose about the upper limit, the "threescore years and ten, or by reason of strength fourscore." Its inexorable rule was the subject of lament, submission, or vain (not to say foolish) wish-dreams about possible exceptions—strangely enough, almost never of affirmation. The intellectual imagination of a George Bernard Shaw and a Jonathan Swift speculated on the privilege of not having to die, or the curse of not being able to die. (Swift with the latter was the more perspicacious of the two.) Myth and legend toyed with such themes against the acknowledged background of the unalterable, which made the earnest man rather pray "teach us to number our days that we may get a heart of wisdom" (Psalm 90). Nothing of this was in the realm of doing and effective decision. The question was only how to relate to the stubborn fact.

But lately, the dark cloud of inevitability seems to lift. A practical hope is held out by certain advances in cell biology to prolong, perhaps indefinitely extend the span of life by counteracting biochemical processes of aging. Death no longer appears as a necessity belonging to the nature of life, but as an avoidable, at least in principle tractable and long-delayable, organic malfunction. A perennial yearning of mortal man seems to come nearer fulfillment. And for the first time we have in earnest to ask the question "How desirable is this? How desirable for the individual, and how for the species?" These questions involve the very meaning of our finitude, the attitude toward death, and the general biological significance of the balance of death and procreation. Even prior to such ultimate questions are the more pragmatic ones of who should be eligible for the boon: persons of particular quality and merit? of social eminence? those that can pay for it? everybody? The last would seem the only just course. But it would have to be paid for at the opposite end, at the source. For clearly, on a population-wide scale, the price of extended age must be a proportional slowing of replacement, i.e., a diminished access of new life. The result would be a decreasing proportion of youth in an increasingly aged population. How good or bad would that be for the general condition of man? Would the species gain or lose? And how *right* would it be to preempt the place of youth? Having to die is bound up with having been born: mortality is but the other side of the perennial spring of "natality" (to use Hannah Arendt's term). This had always been ordained; now its meaning has to be pondered in the sphere of decision.

To take the extreme (not that it will ever be obtained): if we abolish death, we must abolish procreation as well, for the latter is life's answer to the former, and so we would have a world of old age with no youth, and of known individuals with no surprises of such that had never been before. But this perhaps is precisely the wisdom in the harsh dispensation of our mortality: that it grants us the eternally renewed promise of the freshness, immediacy and eagerness of youth, together with the supply of otherness as such. There is no substitute for this in the greater accumulation of prolonged experience: it can never recapture the unique privilege of seeing the world for the first time and with new eyes, never relive the wonder which, according to Plato, is the beginning of philosophy, never the curiosity of the child, which rarely enough lives on as thirst for knowledge in the adult, until it wanes there too. This ever renewed beginning, which is only to be had at the price of ever repeated ending, may well be mankind's hope, its safeguard against lapsing into boredom and routine, its chance of retaining the spontaneity of life. Also, the role of the *memento mori* in the individual's life must be considered, and what its attenuation to indefiniteness may do to it. Perhaps a nonnegotiable limit to our expected time is necessary for each of us as the incentive to number our days and make them count.

So it could be that what by intent is a philanthropic gift of science to man, the partial granting of his oldest wish—to escape the curse of mortality—turns out to be to the detriment of man. I am not indulging in prediction and, in spite of my noticeable bias, not even in valuation. My point is that already the promised gift raises questions that had never to be asked before in terms of practical choice, and that no principle of former ethics, which took the human constants for granted, is competent to deal with them. And yet they must be dealt with ethically and by principle and not merely by the pressure of interest.

b. It is similar with all the other, quasi-utopian powers about to be made available by the advances of biomedical science as they are translated into technology. Of these, *behavior control* is much nearer to practical readiness than the still hypothetical prospect I have just been discussing, and the ethical questions it raises are less profound but have a more direct bearing on the moral conception of man. Here again, the new kind of intervention exceeds the old ethical categories. They have not equipped us to rule, for example, on mental control by chemical means or by direct electrical action on the brain via implanted electrodes —undertaken, let us assume, for defensible and even laudable ends. The mixture of beneficial and dangerous potentials is obvious, but the lines are not easy to draw. Relief of mental patients from distressing and disabling symptoms seems unequivocally beneficial. But from the relief of the *patient*, a goal entirely in the tradition of the medical art, there is an easy passage to the relief of *society* from the inconvenience of difficult individual behavior among its members: that is, the passage from medical to social application; and this opens up an indefinite field with grave potentials. The troublesome problems of rule and unruliness in modern mass society make the extension of such control methods to non-medical categories extremely tempting for social management. Numerous questions of human rights and dignity arise. The difficult question of preempting care versus enabling care insists on concrete answers. Shall we induce learning attitudes in school children by the mass administration of drugs, circumventing the appeal to autonomous motivation? Shall we overcome aggression by electronic pacification of brain areas? Shall we generate sensations of happiness or pleasure or at least contentment through independent stimulation (or tranquilizing) of the appropriate centers—independent, that is, of the objects of happiness, pleasure, or content and their attainment in personal living and achieving? Candidacies could be multiplied. Business firms might become interested in some of these techniques for performance-increase among their employees.

Regardless of the question of compulsion or consent, and regardless also of the question of undesirable side-effects, each time we thus bypass the human way of dealing with human problems, short-circuiting it by an impersonal mechanism, we have taken away something from the dignity of personal selfhood and advanced a further step on the road from responsible subjects to programmed behavior systems. Social functionalism, important as it is, is only one side of the question. Decisive is the question of what kind of individuals the society is composed of— to make its existence valuable as a whole. Somewhere along the line of increasing social manageability at the price of individual autonomy, the question of the worthwhileness of the human enterprise must pose itself. Answering it involves the image of man we entertain. We must think it anew in light of the things we can do to it now and could never do before.

c. This holds even more with respect to the last object of a technology applied on man himself—the genetic control of future men. This is too wide a subject for cursory treatment. Here I merely point to this most ambitious dream of *homo faber*, summed up in the phrase that man will take his own evolution in hand, with the aim of not just preserving the integrity of the species but of modifying it by improvements of his own design. Whether we have the right to do it, whether we are qualified for that creative role, is the most serious question that can be posed to man finding himself suddenly in possession of such fateful powers. Who will be the image-makers, by what standards, and on the basis of what knowledge? Also, the question of the moral right to experiment on future human beings must be asked. These and similar questions, which demand an answer before we embark on a journey into the unknown, show most vividly how far our powers to act are pushing us beyond the terms of all former ethics.

VIII

The ethically relevant common feature in all the examples adduced is what I like to call the inherently "utopian" drift of our actions under the conditions of modern technology, whether it works on non-human or on human nature, and whether the "utopia" at the end of the road be planned or unplanned. By the kind and size of its snowballing effects, technological power propels us into goals of a type that was formerly the preserve of Utopias. To put it differently, technological power has turned what used and ought to be tentative, perhaps enlightening, plays of speculative reason into competing blueprints for projects, and in choosing between them we have to choose between extremes of remote effects. The one thing we can really know of them is their extremism as such—that they concern the total condition of nature on our globe and the very kind of creatures that shall, or shall not, populate it. In consequence of the inevitably "utopian" scale of modern technology, the salutary gap between everyday and ultimate issues, between occasions for common prudence and occasions for illuminated wisdom, is steadily closing. Living now constantly in the shadow of unwanted, built-in, automatic utopianism, we are constantly confronted with issues whose positive choice requires supreme wisdom—an impossible situation for man in general, because he does not possess that wisdom, and in particular for contemporary man, who denies the very existence of its object: viz., objective value and truth. We need wisdom most when we believe in it least.

If the new nature of our acting then calls for a new ethics of long-range responsibility, coextensive with the range of our power, it calls in the name of that very responsibility also for a new kind of humility—a humility not like former humility, i.e., owing to the littleness, but owing to the excessive magnitude of our power, which is the excess of our power to act over our power to foresee and our power to evaluate and to judge. In the face of the quasi-eschatological potentials of our technological processes, ignorance of the ultimate implications becomes itself a reason for responsible restraint—as the second best to the possession of wisdom itself.

One other aspect of the required new ethics of responsibility for and to a distant future is worth mentioning: the insufficiency of representative government to meet the new demands on its normal principles and by its normal mechanics. For according to these, only *present* interests make themselves heard and felt and enforce their consideration. It is to them that public agencies are accountable, and this is the way in which concretely the respecting of rights comes about (as distinct from their abstract acknowledgment). But the *future* is not represented, it is not a force than can throw its weight into the scales. The non-existent has no lobby, and the unborn are powerless. Thus accountability to them has no political reality behind it yet in present decision-making, and when they can make their complaint, then we, the culprits, will no longer be there.

This raises to an ultimate pitch the old question of the power of the wise, or the force of ideas not allied to self-interest, in the body politic. What *force* shall represent the future in the present? However, before *this* question can become earnest in practical terms, the new ethics must find its theory, on which do's and don'ts can be based. That is: before the question of what *force*, comes the question of what *insight* or value-knowledge shall represent the future in the present.

IX

And here is where I get stuck, and where we all get stuck. For the very same movement which put us in possession of the powers that have now to be regulated by norms—the movement of modern knowledge called science—has by a necessary complementarity eroded the foundations from which norms could be derived; it has destroyed the very idea of norm as such. Not, fortunately, the feeling for norm and even for particular norms. But this feeling becomes uncertain of itself when contradicted by alleged knowledge or at least denied all sanction by it. Anyway and always does it have a difficult enough time against the loud clamors of greed and fear. Now it must in addition blush before the frown of superior knowledge, as unfounded and incapable of foundation. First, Nature had been "neutralized" with respect to value, then man himself. Now we shiver in the nakedness of a nihilism in which near-omnipotence is paired with near-emptiness, greatest capacity with knowing least what for. With the apocalyptic pregnancy of our actions, that very knowledge which we lack has become more urgently needed than at any other stage in the adventure of mankind. Alas, urgency is no promise of success. On the contrary, it must be avowed that to seek for wisdom today requires a good measure of unwisdom. The very nature of the age which cries out for an ethical theory makes it suspiciously look like a fool's errand. Yet we have no choice in the matter but to try.

It is a question whether without restoring the category of the sacred, the category most thoroughly destroyed by the scientific enlightenment, we can have an ethics able to cope with the extreme powers which we possess today and constantly increase and are almost compelled to use. Regarding those consequences imminent enough still to hit ourselves, fear can do the job—so often the best substitute for genuine virtue or wisdom. But this means fails us towards the more distant prospects, which here matter the most, especially as the beginnings seem mostly innocent in their smallness. Only awe of the sacred with its unqualified veto is independent of the computations of mundane fear and the solace of uncertainty about distant consequences. But religion as a soul-determining force is no longer there to be summoned to the aid of ethics. The latter must stand on its worldly feet—that is, on reason and its fitness for philosophy. And while of faith it can be said that it either is there or is not, of ethics it holds that it must be there.

It must be there because men act, and ethics is for the ordering of actions and for regulating the power to act. It must be there all the more, then, the greater the powers of acting that are to be regulated; and with their size, the ordering principle must also fit their kind. Thus, novel powers to act require novel ethical rules and perhaps even a new ethics.

"Thou shalt not kill" was enunciated because man has the power to kill and often the occasion and even inclination for it—in short, because killing is actually done. It is only under the *pressure* of real habits of action, and generally of the fact that always action already takes place, without *this* having to be commanded first, that ethics as the ruling of such acting under the standard of the good or the permitted enters the stage. Such a *pressure* emanates from the novel technological powers of man, whose exercise is given with their existence. *If* they really are as novel in kind as here contended, and if by the kind of their potential consequences they really have abolished the moral neutrality which the technical commerce with matter hitherto enjoyed—then their pressure bids to seek for new prescriptions in ethics which are competent to assume their guidance, but which first of all can hold their own theoretically against that very pressure. To the demonstration of those premises this paper was devoted. If they are accepted, then we who make thinking our business have a task to last us for our time. We must do it in time, for since we act anyway we shall have some ethic or other in any case, and without a supreme effort to determine the right one, we may be left with a wrong one by default.

2.
Jewish and Christian Elements in Philosophy: Their Share in the Emergence of the Modern Mind

We are used to distinguishing between the Judaeo-Christian and the Graeco-Roman strains in the Western tradition. It is a unique feature of the civilization which evolved in Europe in post-classical times that it encompassed in its very constitution this dual bequest from Mediterranean antiquity. There is, to my knowledge, no analogue to this fact in any of the major civilizations of mankind; it has profoundly shaped ours. The inner tension it created, the enormous arc of the polarity that had to be spanned and acted out in a long gigantomachy of competing commitments, may well account for some of the uniqueness which today sets "Western man," the heir of this historic toil, apart from anything that elsewhere appeared on this globe. The reflective and retrospective consciousness of this complexity of our roots is with us at least since Hegel, and the very fact of such historical self-analysis is among the phenomena unique to our civilization (thus itself subject to that analysis). In the light of this ongoing genetic appraisal of European mentality, both components of the historical duality that went into its making must appear

Originally presented as the Third Lentz Lecture at the Colloquium on Judaism and Christianity held at the Harvard Divinity School in October 1967. Published in *Commentary* 44 (Nov. 1967) with the title "Jewish and Christian Elements in the Western Tradition." A revised version appears in *Creation: The Impact of an Idea*, ed. Francis Oakley and Daniel O'Connor (New York: Schibner's, 1969). The present, annotated text is the definitive version.

as integral to our heritage, and without either of them in our past our present could not be understood.

The duality does not stop here. Its members again, it will be noted, are expressed in composite, hyphenated terms: "Judaeo-Christian," "Graeco-Roman"—complexities within complexity, tensions within tension. It is with the first of these pairs that we propose to deal, and in the philosophical arena only. That is to say, we wish to treat of the respective roles of Jewish and Christian "motifs" insofar as they were transplanted from their native soil of faith to the field of philosophical thought. But this field itself inevitably brings into play the other half of the larger complexity, seeing that philosophy as such is the eminently "Greek" entry in the historical contest, and any move onto its grounds means an encounter with the pagan-classical side. Thus the confrontation of "Jewish" and "Christian" we have in mind, by being undertaken in terms of their impact on philosophy, is placed in the setting of the larger confrontation of why they both form but one side. This larger confrontation, in one or another of its many aspects, is a familiar theme, but the narrower one between Jewish and Christian elements within one of the two battle lines is not. We depart from the usual pattern when we intend to speak, not of Judaeo-Christian elements, but of Jewish and Christian elements, in the Western philosophical tradition.

I

Such an attempt immediately raises two questions which must be dealt with before we can deal with the topic proper. In what sense, if any, can Jewish and Christian elements be *separated* in a consideration of our Western tradition? And in what sense can either or both be considered as falling inside the *philosophical* tradition? These questions need some explaining themselves.

Regarding the first question, Judaism and Christianity in themselves are distinctly separate, to be sure; but when considering them as elements of the Western tradition, we must bear in mind that Christianity alone, or almost alone, transmitted the Jewish share—simply by what it contained of Judaism in its own, original constitution, or by what it later appropriated from it into its own armory when both had their encounter with philosophy. Thus if Jewish elements are to be found in the history of Western thought, they are Christian elements there, and our theme which calls for a confrontation of them in this medium seems to collapse at the outset. It seems to collapse into the well-worked theme of the Judaeo-Christian elements in Western thought, with the hyphen de-

noting an indissoluble connection—as indissoluble indeed as the connection between the Old Testament and the New in the Christian body
itself.

The second question must be asked irrespective of whether we deal
with this hyphenated whole or with either of its members: how can any
of them become part of philosophy? Since, on their own testimony,
they are based on revelation, while philosophy is based on reason, can
the former really enter the latter—can religion enter philosophy without
disrupting it or forsaking itself? If the answer were to be No, the history
of Jewish-Christian, or Jewish and Christian, influence on philosophy
would be nothing but a history of trespass and mutual adulteration. Such
elements of them that actually found their way into philosophy would
be there not by right but by encroachment; they would be non-philo-
sophical elements within philosophy, and the study of them would
constitute a merely historical rather than a genuinely philosophical task.
We should then be speaking, in fact, not of elements in philosophy, but
of interference with philosophy.

Yet, to philosophy (to take up this question first), even the experience
of encroachment, including the eventual overcoming of it, would itself
be a philosophical experience. Unlike the interference of ordinary interest, power, or prejudice, which touches philosophy only at its outskirts and becomes at most a matter for philosophical tactics, the claim
of revelation to the highest truth, and to the most important truths with
which philosophy itself is concerned, touches philosophy at its core and,
in a real encounter, must affect its whole strategy. The totality of the
claim as such, even apart from the particular *content* of the revealed
truths, imposed *questions* and perspectives on philosophy which it would
otherwise not have faced, and which were destined to outlive the answers
that philosophy at first obediently accepted from revelation. And even if
"Christian philosophy" or "Jewish philosophy" is finally recognized to
be a contradiction in terms, the very recognition and assimilation of *this*
truth would be a philosophical feat, and one that leaves philosophy different and more self-knowing than it was before. Its reflection, e.g., on the
scope and limits of rational knowledge was infinitely radicalized through
the confrontation with revealed truth. This and similar radicalizations,
forced on philosophy by the exacting coexistence with revelation,
changed the whole climate of philosophizing. Philosophy could not but
try to match the unconditional spirit of its rival. That is one reason why
later philosophy lacks the composure, the spirit of moderation, characteristic of ancient philosophy.

All this, however, though it makes the relation of faith and philosophy
a philosophically relevant one, still does not make Jewish-Christian

ideas themselves elements in the philosophical universe, except as a dialectical counterpoint or irritant in its discourse. But something more occurs in the course of the religious-philosophical dialectics than the imposition of alien themes on philosophy, and more than the subsequent self-assertion and perhaps radicalization of an otherwise unaltered philosophy. Since philosophy is the work of living men, the humanity of the philosopher, insofar as it partakes in a common heritage of faith, asserts itself in his philosophizing: as a result, certain ideas, motifs and choices of revealed religion pass over, open or concealed, into the patrimony of philosophy itself and—eventually dissociated from their origin in revelation and its authority—become genuine parts of the modified philosophical landscape. This happens even where a philosopher, like Descartes, does his utmost to strip his thought of all presuppositions.

What I am speaking of is not the insinuation of extraneous ideas into philosophy through the all-too-human psychology of the philosopher. I am speaking of the legitimate continuation, in the medium of philosophy, of existential insights and emphases whose original locus was the world of faith, but whose validity and vitality extend beyond the reaches of faith. Some basic concept of man and world speaks through the Word of God and hence informs the understanding of man as a general premise that will underly even his worldly philosophizing. And it will be at home there, by rights and not by stealth; it may even come fully into its own there. This would be an instance of the "cunning of Reason." In this sense of an assimilation which may be transforming enough to make us speak of a secularization of originally religious thought, one can meaningfully look for Jewish or Christian elements in a philosophy that need not therefore be a Jewish or a Christian philosophy, or indeed a religious philosophy at all.

This answer to one of our preliminary questions, viz., in what sense one can speak of Jewish-Christian elements in philosophy, still leaves unanswered the other question, viz., whether in the context of Western thought Jewish and Christian aspects can be considered apart and, as our title suggests, as alternative to each other. Strictly speaking they cannot, for the reason noted before. When the Western world constituted itself a Christian world, Christianity gained something of a monopoly in mediating the Jewish heritage through its own derivative Jewishness; and once this situation prevailed, authentic Judaism had little opportunity to exert its influence independently and directly. Where this nevertheless happened, as in the marked influence of Arabic-Jewish thinkers on Latin Schoolmen, or in the brief spurt of Cabbalistic interests in the Renaissance, it was a Christian choice which determined the reception, and a

Christian amalgam in which it resulted. This being the case, we must, for our purpose, accept the Jewish theme mainly in the form in which Christianity transmitted it. As it was through the Church that Jewish teaching, however partially, was impressed on the West, so it was mainly in the Christian embrace that it also entered the orbit of Western philosophy. If, then, we reclaim it there for the Jewish side, we must realize that we are somehow splitting the phenomenon of Christianity down the middle. We do violence to the consciousness of a past age when we divide what was indivisible to it: the one sacred truth of the Christian creed.

One justification for such a (quasi-Marcionitic) procedure lies in the fact that in their *philosophical* reception, with which we have to do, the fortunes of the two halves of the Christian whole were markedly different: while the "Jewish" half was thematically close enough to the terms of natural theology to fall, at least as an issue, within the philosophical domain, the other half tended to defy philosophical assimilation and to compel its recognition as suprarational mystery. This becomes apparent if we understand by the "Jewish" half whatever Christianity still has in common with Judaism—historically speaking, what it retained of it in its own teaching—and as specifically Christian what it has beyond it and all to itself. For the sake of brevity we can identify the former by the concept of Creation, the other by the concept of Incarnation. Having made this distinction, we can see at once the reason for the different philosophical fortunes of the two halves. The doctrine of creation and all that flows from it, with its obvious bearing on natural theology and even on the concepts of nature and of man, *had* to be taken up by philosophy, whether affirmatively or negatively. On the other hand, the doctrines of the Trinity, incarnation, and salvation were more alien to the established themes of philosophy to begin with; and since they defied rational discourse, they could be considered to lie beyond its pale as mysteries of faith.

In short, the *rational* status of the two components of the Christian complex, and therefore their suitability for philosophical assimilation, were *intrinsically unequal*. The propositions of the one were more germane to philosophy than those of the other. We shall therefore not be surprised by the seemingly paradoxical finding that in a Christian intellectual universe it was the Jewish component which had the major philosophical impact. In fact, as far as I can see, it was not before Hegel's theory of the absolute Spirit, its alienation and self-consummation through history, that the theme of incarnation found major expression in philosophy—and then only by the boldest transmutation.

The last example raises the problem of recognition. Spread out before

our historical glance lies the Western philosophical tradition.[1] It is complex, and we look in it for elements of a particular, nonphilosophical
provenance. How recognize them as such in their philosophical transformation? Some cases are obvious, because they could not have arisen
in philosophy except under the pressure of theological doctrine, which
moreover is explicitly referred to. Such, e.g., is the subject of "creation"
directly, and indirectly the whole cluster of topics deriving from its introduction into philosophy. Even there, the farther offshoots of the seed
may not show the connection at a glance. Other cases are more subtle
to begin with, as they devolve from the total spirit rather than from any
particular dogma of revelation. To this category belongs, e.g., the
emphasis on the will as against the intellect, or the status of the particular and the individual.

Thoughts in philosophy do not as a rule carry passports certifying
their place of birth; and the philosophical career of immigrants from
religion may even be more than just anonymous: it may be masked and
concealed. On the other hand, not every declared concordance with
sacred truth, nor even appeal to its authority, proves origin from that
source: it can be—and sometimes is—expedient rhetoric. To spot our
quarry we have, in fact, two clues that promise to supplement each other.
The primary one, of course, must come from a knowledge of the theological tradition in terms of its plainly identifiable themes. But a subsidiary one can be independently provided by the philosophical tradition
itself: Viewing Western philosophy against its pre-Christian past, we
note what in its later picture stands out as heterogeneous from this
autochthonous background. Since all pre-Christian philosophy was
Greek, the prescription in effect means that everything substantially non-
Greek in later philosophy, everything palpably at odds with the classical
heritage, invites a prima facie presumption, subject to further examination, of its being Jewish-Christian in origin. We are aware of the risky
and in a way prejudging nature of this clue, as there is no telling what
the evolution of philosophy might not have brought forth autonomously,
without the intervention of Christianity: an ignorance besetting all the
large "ifs" and "if-nots" in history. However, the clue is no more than
heuristic; and in its most modest understanding, our presumption would
already be satisfied if Jewish-Christian influence had merely been instru-

---

[1]By this and the related term of "Western philosophy" we always mean what
began with the re-emergence of philosophy—after the interval of the "dark ages"—
first in the Islamic-Jewish orbit and then (at the turn of the millenium) in the
Christian West. This was a new beginning, characterized from the first by the tension of reason and faith, with which all later European thought is continuous.
Accordingly, the Trinitarian speculations, by Neoplatonic means, of a Pseudo-
Dionysius and Scotus Erigena, which lack that tension, lie chronologically and sub-
stantively outside the "tradition" so defined.

mental in fostering a philosophical development which, for all we know, would eventually have taken place "by itself."

II

Let us turn first to the cardinal and most obviously Jewish theme thrust on Western philosophy by Christian faith, the theme of creation, and to that aspect of it on which so much philosophical controversy centered: the teaching that the world had a beginning in time. Classical philosophy—Neoplatonic as well as Aristotelian—had taught its eternity, i.e., its co-eternity with the supramundane principle that in philosophy corresponds to the God of religion. At first glance, the difference between the two views seems to be about the past only and to have no bearing on the conception of the existing nature of things. But in truth it profoundly affects this conception. The encounter with the biblical doctrine of creation brought to light what the philosophical doctrine of the eternity of the world really meant. Making the latter antithetically a doctrine of the *non*createdness of the world changed it from being *the* philosophical view into being a particular philosophical view of the world. In turn, the encounter with the original philosophical view elicited from the biblical doctrine its latent implications concerning the whole nature of reality and made these (though not the unassimilable doctrine of creation itself) at home in philosophy as an alternative, no less philosophical, theory of the world. Seen from the long perspective of modernity, it can be said that the challenger, in a purely secular garb, eventually prevailed over the classical view, philosophy's native child.

What was the philosophical meaning of the classical view that the world is eternal? We may summarize it in the following eight points:

(1) The sensible world is in some sense (variously specified in various systems) an extension of the divine nature. That is to say, it is itself a mode of divine being, even if a derivative and diminished mode.

(2) The nexus of derivation is one of necessity. That is to say, the world is a necessary consequence of the divine nature, and this in the double sense that it exists because the divine exists, and it exists as it is because the divine nature is what it is. In short, the existence as well as the essence of the world are necessitated by the existence and the essence of God.

(3) The necessity of the world's *existence* entails co-eternity with God. Given the eternity of divine being, the world as its accompaniment or expression cannot at any time not be; thus it cannot have a beginning or an end (though the things *in* the world can either be or not be and thus have a beginning and an end).

(4) The necessity of the world's *essence* means that its *order*, deriving from the divine nature, is as external as its existence, deriving from the divine reality. The fullness of the proposition that the world cannot not be, is that it cannot be *other* than it is.

(5) That the world cannot be other than it is, holds only insofar as God himself cannot be other than he is. The necessity of the world's essence is predicated on the necessity of God's essence—the eternity of the former on the immutability of the latter. Thus God has an essence or nature if the world has one, and a nature of the kind which intrinsically excludes mutability.

(6) Intrinsic impossibility of "being otherwise" pertains to logical or rational necessity. Thus if God is the primary locus of necessity, he must be pure reason or intellect. This indeed *is* the divine nature.

(7) Accordingly, the "essential" necessity of the world is equivalent to its rationality, i.e., to what it possesses of rationality, and is apprehended in knowledge. The rational necessity of the world is a qualified one, while the divine rationality is unqualified. The qualified rationality of the physical order, thus open to knowledge, i.e., the degree of its intrinsic intelligibility, is the measure of its divinity—and indeed the inductive path to the conception of pure divinity.

By now it is clear that the thesis of the eternity of the world, far from being a mere assertion of temporal fact, involves a whole ontology from which it derives. By the terms of this ontology it is intimately connected with the theses that God has a nature; that this nature is pure intellect and thus enjoys the immutability of intrinsic necessity; and that the world's lesser nature has the relation of analogy, similitude, or image to the divine original, measured by the world's intelligibility.

(8) This brings us to the final point. Terms like "similitude" and "degree" suggest that God and world are members of a continuum in which God is the summit of a scale that comprises degrees of approximation to his absolute norm. The system of being, to which God himself belongs, is thus a hierarchy with intermediate levels between the minimum and the maximum, between grossest matter and purest form. Thus a pervading homogeneity of being unites Man, Nature and God.

All this is involved in the doctrine of the eternity of the world. Upon this integrated scheme of theory burst the biblical doctrine of creation, which posited a temporal beginning of the world. What conceptual adjustments did its acceptance enforce on the philosophical stage? Just as the tenet of the eternity of the world symbolized a whole metaphysic, so the tenet of its temporal beginning served as a mere symbol for the wider and truly philosophical issues that were latent in the idea of creation as such and were brought to light in the debate on the temporal issue. It would be too much to say that the dialectics promoted by those issues crystallized into an alternative metaphysics—there was an antimetaphysical agent in the very nature of the biblical position; but it is true to say that it led to the erosion of classical metaphysics and in its outcome changed the whole character of philosophy.

To put it as briefly as possible, the biblical doctrine pitted contingency against necessity, particularity against universality, will against intellect. It secured a place for the "contingent" within philosophy, against the latter's original bias. If we add to this the divorce of mind and nature which followed from the Jewish-Christian separation of God and world and eventually led to the specifically modern division of philosophy into human and natural philosophy, we need not fear that we are exaggerating when we say that the consequences of the encounter between the biblical and the classical views were immense.

When that encounter had to all intents and purposes run its course, and philosophy was just turning to new tasks, Francis Bacon pointed out that it was "heathen opinion," i.e., ancient philosophy, which had supposed the world to be the image of God, while "sacred truth," i.e., Scripture, had denied this honor to the world and reserved it to man, declaring the world to be God's handiwork only and not his image.[2] I leave it an open question whether this appeal to sacred truth in advocacy of the new philosophy, which aimed at the subjection of nature to man, was sincere or rhetorical. But I do suggest that it was indeed the long impact of that "sacred truth" on philosophical thought which in the end made this new direction of philosophy possible—and therewith, for better or for worse, the modern mind. Clearly, the very idea of Jewish monotheism implied a certain demotion of the world compared with pagan nature worship, and much of prophetic energy had been expended in hammering home the truth that no part of the world was divine and that all its parts, with the sole exception of man, were equally different from their maker. This essential equality of createdness, later radicalized by the addition "from nothing," implicitly did away with any natural gradations towards God and thus with the idea of a cosmic hierarchy.

However, we are ahead of our story. Philosophy drew this final, levelling consequence of the biblical position only at the end of a long process of erosion of classical metaphysics, which it inherited—first in its Neoplatonic, later in its Aristotelian forms—when it resumed its life in the Middle Ages. Let us go back to those beginnings. When philosophy reappeared after the interval of its postclassical eclipse, it was under

---

[2]Francis Bacon, *The Advancement of Learning*, Book II (*The Philosophical Works*, ed. J. M. Robertson) p. 91. I have discussed this passage more fully in *The Phenomenon of Life*, pp. 192–93. Compare also *ibid.*, pp. 71–72.

the entirely new constellation which the advent of the great religions of revelation had created, and in which the received doctrine of the eternity of the world had lost the innocence of a mere proposition of theory: it had become a challenge flung by reason at faith. The challenge was taken up by those champions of faith who undertook to meet reason on its own ground and became philosophers themselves. As such, they looked at the *nature of the world* whose eternity or createdness was in question.

It was the aspect of *contingency* against that of necessity, and concomitantly that of divine *will* versus divine intellect, on which the philosophical argument of the "creationists" focused first. And the first to do so were the latest converts to monotheism, the Moslems—more uncompromising on the issue in its original Jewish purity than the prescholastic Christian thinkers from Augustine over Dionysius Areopagiticus to John Scotus (Erigena), who stayed in close alliance with Neoplatonic emanationism which could be naturally adapted to Trinitarian thought. Arabic thinkers, beginning with the Kalam (ninth century and after), dwelt on the logical nondeducibility, the refractory factuality, of the structure and concrete manifoldness of the world. If the world, so they argued, came forth with necessity from the divine essence, as the philosophers claim (e.g., in the doctrine of emanation), then it must, in plan and in detail, be deducible from first intellectual principles.[3] But it cannot be so deduced. Its constitution cannot be demonstrated a priori. Everything, from the color of a blossom to the order of the stars, could as well—that is to say, without contradiction—be other than it actually is. The nature it actually has represents a choice from among all the possible alternatives; strictly speaking, from an infinite range of possibilities. But choice is a matter of the will. Thus the logical evidence of the world is more in accord with its having been called forth by the free spontaneity of divine will than with its having emanated or otherwise derived from the divine essence. God could have willed the world to be other than it is, or not have willed it at all. And the world itself proclaims its createdness by its intrinsic contingency. It is to be noted that the "contingency" here argued concerns less the particular existence of things—where classical philosophy had located contingency—than their generic properties and their total configuration, which classical philosophy had regarded as necessary.

In this argument of the Kalam, an immanent character of worldly being is made to yield testimony for the transcendent fact of creation. To this extent, it is a philosophical argument. But in this form, it is destructive of knowledge and thus of philosophy itself, for it makes each particular at each moment the creature of a divine will that is bound by

---

[3]See Julius Guttmann, *Philosophies of Judaism*, trans. by R. J. Zwi Werblowsky (New York: Holt, Rinehart and Winston, 1964), p. 168.

no general law. It deprives the created things of any nature and force of their own and thus of all explanatory connection among themselves. Only God's arbitrary pleasure saves each from instant relapse into nothingness.

The skeptical import of this extreme view can be seen clearly in al-Ghazali's (1058–1111) critique of causal knowledge by which he buttresses the theological attribution of causality to God alone and the denial of it to things. In a remarkable anticipation of Malebranche and Hume, he argues that the connection of so-called cause and effect, that is, of one thing following upon another, is not a necessary, i.e., intelligible, connection. No one thing really entails another; none in fact has active power. All that is known is the succession of things, and since its grounding is not to be found in what antecedes at each time, nor within the physical series at all, it must be sought in the sole power of God. The evidence of nature itself is purely positive and nonrational, thus showing up its basic contingency. This indeed renders a science of nature, which must be a science of causes, impossible.

This "Humean" skepticism was to find its "Kantian" answer. It was Maimonides (1135–1204) who lifted the consideration of contingency onto a higher plane, which combined contingency of the whole with necessity among its parts. Although he, too, stressed the rational inexplicability of the variety in the given cosmic structure (e.g., in the number and motions of the celestial spheres[4]), which in his view, too, points to a fiat of divine will,[5] he does not take al-Ghazali's skeptical road. To Maimonides, Aristotelian and creationist at the same time, the world is a coherent whole governed by laws—the laws of Aristotelian physics—which concretely determine what is necessary and possible within it. Thus there *can* be a science of nature, and the mere abstract possibility of logical (i.e., non-self-contradictory) alternatives does not lessen the cogency of such a science. But those laws themselves, from which everything else follows in rational order, are not logically deducible in turn, nor are they rationally self-evident. They, the ultimate conditions of the given cosmic reality, must be accepted as pure fact, as must the particular layout of the macrocosmic framework in which they operate.[6] Contingency, in other words, is shifted from the single existences to their principles, from the conclusions to the premises of the cosmic syllogism, with the latter retaining its internal necessity once its terms have been granted. Compared with the Kalam idea of the "arbi-

[4]*Guide of the Perplexed* II, 19.
[5]*Ibid.* II, 22. Points to—but does not prove it. Without the teaching of revelation we could not, according to Maimonides, draw a *conclusion* from the fact of mundane contingency to an act of divine will.
[6]J. Guttmann, *op. cit.*, p. 167ff.

trary" choice of the actual from an infinite number of possibles, this can be expressed by saying that not each item (as in the Kalam) but their total set represents such a choice. God, as Thomas Aquinas later put it, freely selected for realization *this* from all the possible worlds.[7] But a world, of course, is a determinate order.

This Maimonidean synthesis saved both the Aristotelian rationality of the universe and the biblical nonrationality of its origin; and in a way it prepared the modern approach. However, since Maimonides recognized the validity of Aristotelian physics, he was compelled to face the Aristotelian proofs for the eternity of the world, derived from that physics. It is here that Maimonides evolves his profound doctrine of the relative scope of all reasoning that makes use of laws of nature. Reflecting on the logical nature of such reasoning, he argues as follows. Although for every motion within the universe it is true (as Aristotle has taught) that its beginning involves the transition from potency to act, which is itself a motion preceding the motion that is to begin, and so *ad infinitum*; and although it is true that all becoming presupposes matter, so that a coming-to-be of matter itself would presuppose another matter, and so forth again *ad infinitum*—it is not true that these laws, valid for things within the world, can be extended to apply beyond the world, e.g., to the relationship of the world as a whole to God. The laws in question do indeed specify the internal conditions of the system we call the world, among them the conditions of all becoming within the world, but they have nothing to say about the coming-to-be of that system itself.[8]

This is the first enunciation of a principle concerning the area of pertinence of natural categories and the limits of their speculative use, which was to find its final formulation in the philosophy of Kant. Thus was the long self-examination of speculative reason brought under way. Nothing short of the encounter with creationist faith and its surpassing demands on speculation could have compelled reason to as relentless a probing of itself and its possible range as that on which medieval thought launched it under this impulsion.

Kant still used the question of a temporal beginning or non-beginning of the world as one of the metaphysical issues on which the failure of a reason that oversteps its competence is made manifest. It is to be noted,

---

[7] *Summa theol.* I, qu. 25, art. 5–6.

[8] *Guide* II, 17–18; cf. Guttmann, *op. cit.*, p. 165ff. To Maimonides, the issue was in principle not so much whether the world has or has not a temporal beginning, but whether it follows with necessity from the being of God or was freely created by him. The decision for the latter alternative then *involves* for him also that for a beginning in time, since he considers the compromise, proposed by some thinkers —to assume an eternal activity of the divine will resulting in an eternal procession of the world from God—as a mere glossing over of the opposition between necessary consequence and free creation.

however, that in Kant, "contingency" is relocated once more: from the principles of nature it is shifted to the principles of knowledge. To put it differently: the rational limitation imposed by createdness now resides in the finite nature of the knowing subject rather than in the nature of finite things. The tradition had seen in man's theoretical faculty his eminent title of being "in the image of God," for notwithstanding all the difference between the created and the uncreated, the finite and the infinite, man's intellect was considered to be of a kind with absolute intellect. According to Kant, however, it is precisely the *theoretical* intellect which bears the main burden of createdness by being unaccountably cast in a particular mold. If man is "in the image of God" it is because of his *practical* reason, that is, his *will*, in which his potential of moral perfection resides: the self-determination of the will is his only remaining point of contact with the absolute. As we shall presently see, the line of reasoning puts Kant closer to the "voluntarist" line of medieval thought that culminated in Duns Scotus, than to the "intellectualist" line represented by Maimonides and Aquinas.

To come back to Maimonides, his strictures on the scope of natural reason fall on friend and foe alike: he acknowledges that the disproof of Aristotelian arguments for the eternity of the world does not prove the alternative of "creation from nothing," but merely gives it logical eligibility. Generally, in regard to the truths of revelation, reason, and demonstrate no more than that they are not repugnant to reason, and perhaps that they have an edge when it comes to probability or plausibility. In this form, with some variation as to the exact drawing of the line, the idea of a demarcation of the domains of faith and reason was taken over by the Christian West.[9]

Here a word about Thomas Aquinas is in order. In the matter of creation Aquinas went beyond Maimonides' critical caution. By distinguishing between "from" nothing (*ex nihilo*) and "after" nothing

---

[9]First by Albertus Magnus (1206?–1280), founder of Christian Aristotelianism, who made extensive use of Maimonides' work. Especially in the critique of the arguments for the eternity of the world he took over whole chapters from the *Guide of the Perplexed*. To him, too, creation is a temporal act; he rejects the Aristotelian proofs of an eternal existence of the world, but like Maimonides considers the arguments for a temporal beginning as not stringent, though as "better" than the contrary ones (*Phys.* VIII, tr. 1, c. 13). "The beginning of the world through creation is not physical, nor can it be proved physically" (*ibid.*, c. 14): it is an article of faith that transcends reason. But whereas in this question reason at least has a role in weighing the arguments on both sides and clearing the ground for the decision of faith, in regard to the doctrine of the Trinity and the dogmas connected with it, Albertus came to a complete sundering of the two domains, placing those Christian truths par excellence entirely outside the scope of rational or philosophical theology: "By the connatural light one cannot rise up to the knowledge of the Trinity and the incarnation and the resurrection" (*Summa theol.* I, tr. I. *qu.* 1, *ad.* 2). In all this, his great pupil Thomas Aquinas—a Dominican like himself—followed him.

(*post nihil*) he separated the question of creation as such from that of a temporal beginning (a separation which Maimonides had considered but rejected): whether or not the world had a beginning in time (*post nihil*), Aquinas too held to be beyond rational decision and to be answered by revelation only; but creation "from" nothing, regardless of time, he included among the demonstrable truths, on a par with those concerning God's existence and attributes. Thus he widened the scope of natural theology: createdness to him is a demonstrable property of worldly being. At the same time, the realm of the nondemonstrable was swelled by those Christian mysteries—Trinity, original sin, incarnation, resurrection, etc.—about which Jewish and Islamic thought did not have to concern themselves. Thus the extension of the rational domain by Aquinas did not entail a contraction of the suprarational one, or a lessening of the chasm between the two. On the contrary, the mystery character of the peculiarly Christian doctrines led to a greater tension between reason and faith than the mere "Jewish" part of revelation required. Indeed, when Thomas says[10] that "through natural reason we can know that about God which pertains to the unity of his essence, but not that which pertains to the distinction of his persons," he is, in effect, spelling out the different rational status of the "Jewish" and the "Christian" elements of the Christian faith. The former are at most beyond rational proof (as they are for Maimonides); the latter are "suprarational" in a sense that bears a suspicion of their being contrary to reason; showing that they are not that, is the best that reason can do for them. Consequently, there is merit in the faith that holds on to them in the teeth of such rational strain; and this assigns a priority (*principalitas*) to the *will* whose lead the intellect follows when it assents to those propositions.[11] We thus observe, in spite of Aquinas' own unifying spirit, a sharpening of the dialectics between reason and faith in the Christian universe of discourse. The peculiar *scandalon* of the Christian faith, to use Pauline language, radicalized the confrontation and led to more extreme consequences also inside philosophy than the Jewish context alone would have compelled. These we shall encounter in Duns Scotus.

III

Let us return once more to the subject of creation. It will have been noted that the argument from contingency—which alone we have con-

[10]*Summa theol.* 1, qu. 32, art. 1, ad 3.
[11]*Ibid.* II–II, qu. 2: art. 1, ad 3; art. 2; art. 9–10.

sidered so far—finds the sign of "createdness" in a *negative* rather than a positive feature of the world: in the absence of that rational necessity which according to classical doctrine it should have. It would appear, then, that "createdness" implies a certain devaluation of that which has this attribute; and this indeed was the tendency of creationist arguments in the grand debate with the classical position. Here we may pause to reflect that from the stand we moderns have reached in the matter—faced as we are with the extreme success of that devaluation and the complete loss of the classical counterposition against which it was directed—it would seem that now the "world" rather needs some rehabilitation of metaphysical status, if ever it is again to be connected with the idea of a divine origin in *any* sense. The situation was opposite at the stage in Western history we are describing; then the world had to be diminished in status so as to be brought into that relation with a divine origin which the doctrine of creation demanded. For the relation it demanded was such that, with the utter dependency of the made from the maker, it would yet not involve the communication of *divine properties* from the cause to the effect; and in the light of this requirement, traditional philosophy had clearly overvalued the world. The diminution of status then set in motion has meanwhile, with a momentum it has somewhere gathered on the way, run its full course, and we may well be today on the point where some backswing of the pendulum might be in order.[12]

Even more manifest than in the argument from contingency does this "negativity" become in the insistence of creation *"from nothing,"* whose philosophical significance we must now probe, especially since it was not really demanded by the biblical text and thus represents more or less a philosophical choice. Why this insistence, so commonly found—though also contradicted—among Moslem, Jewish, and Christian thinkers alike? In general, of course, it falls into the observed pattern of "putting the world in its place." That which is called into being from sheer nothingness is totally dependent on its transcendent cause not only for its origin but also for its continued existence. By reason of its "natural priority,"[13]

---

[12]As a final comment on the argument from "contingency," let us note the logical limitation given with its negative nature. Its strength lies in what it disproves: the rationally necessary character of the world, not in what it thereby wants to establish: the creation by divine fiat—for which it merely makes room as a likely alternative. But when all is said, this alternative is optional and could be dropped when no longer urged by faith; and it could be dropped *without a return* to what it was meant to replace. This is what eventually happened, and this is what we are left with.

[13]Aquinas, *Summa theol.* I, qu. 45, art. 1, ad. 3. On creation from nothing, and the power of the "nothing" in the nature of created things, see already Augustine, *Confess.* XII, 7: "not out of Thyself, for then they would be equal . . . to Thee;

the "nothing" looms in the very heart of things, ready to reclaim them at every moment, were it not for their continual re-creation—the renewal of the original fiat—by God. This is the extreme of negativity with which the doctrine of creation imbues mundane being. But this very extreme, in true dialectical fashion, brings to light the positive aspect in the reappraisal of being which the idea of creation caused in philosophy. We can discover it by turning to that ingredient in the doctrine of "creation from nothing" which directly relates it to the philosophical tradition, namely the negation of preexistent matter.[14] Why is this negation important, apart from the motive of homage to divine omnipotence? Scriptural authority did not compel it. Indeed, the opening sentences of Genesis almost suggest a primordial, chaotic matter as preceding the work of creation, or could easily be construed in that sense; and Plato's *Timaeus*, so highly esteemed in the Middle Ages, had certainly shown the *philosophical* compatibility of an external "receptacle" (the prototype of Aristotelian "matter") with the concept of a divine creator. Why then invite a philosophical battle which on both counts could be avoided?

One answer to this question can be given in terms of the received philosophical doctrine of matter and form, which gave rise to the following, very subtle argument.[15] If matter were pre-given, creation would consist in the imparting of form to it; God, in that case, would be the principle of form, which means, intellect; but form is universal, as is intellectual knowledge: thus God, being the author of the universal only and not of the particular in creation, would not know the particulars; and thus there would be no individual providence. If there is to be individual providence, and its condition, divine knowledge of particulars,

---

. . . therefore, out of nothing didst thou create heaven and earth"; *De civ. Dei,* XIV, 11: "only in a nature created out of nothing" can there be vice; *ibid.* XII, 25: "if He were, so to speak, to withdraw from created things His creative power, they would straightway relapse into the nothingness in which they were before they were created." Aquinas follows Augustine in conceiving the conservation of the world as a constant operation of the divine creative cause: *Contra gent.* III, 65; *Summa theol.* I, qu. 104, *art.* 1–2. Descartes still holds to this view.

[14]The createdness of matter was, to my knowledge, first explicitly asserted in the 3rd century by Origen (*De principiis,* II, c. 1,4), and Augustine implies it in his strong emphasis on the creation "out of nothing" (see note 13). The Jewish (like the Islamic) thinkers of the Middle Ages were divided on the issue. Gabirol, still a Neoplatonist, derives both matter and form from God; but only the forms originate in his will and express the divine spontaneity, while matter emanates from his nature and expresses its necessity (see Guttmann, *op. cit.,* pp. 100ff.). Maimonides, as we have seen, firmly asserts the creation from nothing, while Gersonides after him as firmly denies it and (like Averroes) argues that matter is not derivable from God, but preceded his creation (see note 16).

[15]The subtlety of medieval thought is another product of the intellectual strain which the tension of faith and reason imposed on a thinking committed to both. Of this whole chapter in Western history one might say what Nietzsche said of Pascal: "Consider what opposites had to be united there!"

then matter, as the principle of individuation, must be divinely created too, or, it must be as directly an object of the divine will as are the forms.[16] Thus for the sake of particular providence, which is so vital to both Judaism and Christianity for the individual's relation to his God, *creatio ex nihilo* had to replace or to recast the "essentialist" form-matter ontology of the past.

The philosophically relevant effect of this line of thought is that it changes the whole ontological status of individual existence. And here we can see how utter negativity in one respect turns into utter positivity in another. Against the background of nothingness from which it is called forth, individual being assumes a rank of primacy which all ancient philosophy had denied it. To be called forth from nothing and to exist only by constant renewal of this act, assures each individual of the immediate interest of the creative cause and so makes it interesting in itself. The divine attention required individually for their mere existing gives the single things their own truth and a corresponding claim on the attention of knowledge. This changed approach benefits both the knower and the known, the human subject and the things of the world as his potential objects: both, in their ultimate particularity as willed by God, have gained a status in the conceptual scheme of things which they had not enjoyed before. As Maimonides put it: all parts of creation are with equal authenticity intended by the divine will; all therefore are ends in themselves.[17] When, in the later Middle Ages, this train of reasoning was joined by the mighty tide of nominalism, which itself was actuated by a similar concern with individuality, Petrus Aureoli (in the 14th century) could say that "it is nobler to know the thing individuated . . . . than to know it through the abstract and universal mode."[18]

[16]About God's knowledge of particulars, see Maimonides, *Guide*, III, 20; about particulars being intended by the creator for their own sake, see note 17. The connection between the doctrine of matter and that of providence is best shown in the anti-Maimonidean argument of Gersonides (1288–1344), who indeed concluded from the postulate of preexistent (uncreated) matter—to which he was led by his more orthodox Aristotelian (Averroist) position–the impossibility of individual providence: see Guttman, *op. cit.*, pp. 213–15. The dualism of matter and form on which Gersonides based his doctrine of creation, and its necessary corollary that divine knowledge can encompass only the general order of forms, made this conclusion inevitable—just as from Maimonides' doctrine of a *creatio ex nihilo* it necessarily follows that God, as the Creator of the universe, also knows all its particulars.

[17]See *Guide*, III, 13, e.g.: "There does not exist a final end, but only the Will alone. . . . It should not be believed that all the beings exist for the sake of the existence of man. On the contrary, all the other beings too have been intended for their own sakes and not for the sake of something else. . . . In respect to every being He intended that being itself" (trans. Pines, p. 452); "all that exists was intended by Him, may He be exalted, according to His volition. And we shall seek for it no cause or other final end whatever" (*ibid.*, p. 454).

[18]Petrus Aureoli, *In sent.* 1, p. 816bC, as cited in R. Drieling, *Der Konzeptualismus in . . . Petrus Aureoli* (Münster, 1913), p. 193, note 1.

It would be tempting to show, but can be no more than indicated here, how these changes also affected the whole concept of *matter*, with consequences that reach into the beginnings of modern science. From a mere, abstract complement of form, it becomes a thing in its own right—its creation opposing it to the *nihil* with the absolute difference of existence, compared to which all differences of essence become relative. For creation by God surely means production into reality. Thus matter, if created by God, must have a positive, actual being of its own and cannot be merely the potency for something else to be, the empty possibility of becoming. Called forth "from nothing," it must be something, *aliqua res actu*, as Duns Scotus says.[19] This change in ontological status, closely related to that of the individual, prepared matter for the role it was to play in the modern theoretical scheme.

IV

In our discussion, we have repeatedly come upon the concept of the "will." This is indeed the common denominator in which the different aspects of the idea of creation meet and in which they fully reveal their positive—and explosive—side. Will is equally the principle of the contingent and of the particular. It chooses for being what could also not be; it chooses this thing rather than another; and it chooses, in the first place, that there be anything at all. Will is directed toward existence, while its choice may be guided by essence. Its results share in the uni-

[19]Duns Scotus, *De rerum princ., qu. 7, art. 1, n. 3.* He also held that there is no matter besides the "first," but only this in its different determinations: *materia prima est idem cum omni materia particulari* (*ibid., qu. 8, art. 4, n. 24*). "Here I return to the position of Avicembron," says Duns Scotus: the Avencebrol whom Albertus and Aquinas had opposed. Little did Duns Scotus—a confirmed enemy of the Jews, who even justified coercion by the secular power to bring about their conversion to the Church—suspect that the authority on which he based himself was the Jew Ibn Gabirol, whose songs were chanted in the liturgy of the Synagogue. A later (but apparently independent) example for the revision of the concept of matter is found in the Jewish philosopher Crescas (ca. 1340–1410), whose critique of the fundamental concepts of Aristotelian physics foreshadows in several respects the modern philosophy and science of nature (cf. J. Guttmann, "Chasdai Creskas als Kritiker der aristotelischen Physik," *Festschrift zum 70. Geburtstag Jakob Guttmanns*, Leipzig, 1915, pp. 28–54; and H. A. Wolfson, *Crescas' Critique of Aristotle*, Cambridge, Mass., 1929; both authors note the sometimes startling parallels with Galileo and Giordano Bruno). Crescas arrives at an entirely new concept of body. The common substratum of the four elements is a basic matter which *requires no form for its existence* but is capable of *actual existence by itself*. Matter thus becomes, from a mere potentiality for being, an independent, primary *corporeal* substance, which is only further specified through the forms of the particular elements (Hasdai Crescas, *Or Adonai* I, 2.7; cf. Guttmann, *Philosophies of Judaism*, p. 227 [unfortunately, the English translation is here marred by several faulty renderings of Guttmann's text]).

queness of its own decision: they are "this," and "this once," and un-exchangeably themselves. Pure intellect, the principle of the necessary and the universal, cannot determine the transition from essence to existence, from universal to particular, from the eternal to the temporal. This is why, from the first, creationist theology interposed divine will and its freedom between divine wisdom and divine power, and increasingly emphasized will among the attributes of God. And this emphasis on the divine will was soon reflected in the emphasis on man's will—first as the respondent of God's will, which in his commandments addresses itself to will more than to anything else in man; then increasingly as the dominant attribute of man himself. The theological doctrine of God's attributes engendered, or at least encouraged, a philosophical doctrine of man's attributes.

It is beyond the scope of this essay to trace the rise of the Western metaphysics of the will, whose roots were Jewish-Christian, and whose anti-Christian culmination we behold in Nietzsche and in modern existentialism. But it is worth pointing out that the vigor of its growth is a fruit of the encounter between the Jewish-Christian and the Greek standpoints: without the dialectical stress against the essentialist-intellectualist *parti pris* of traditional philosophy, there would hardly have arisen a theory of the primacy of the will—with all the consequences such a theory entails.

Although no account can be attempted here, we may at least chart a few points on the road of this Western voluntarism. It had, in fact, two distinct points of departure: on the one hand, Augustine's stress on the will in *man*, as the ultimate locus of the drama of sin and salvation; on the other, the Jewish-Islamic stress on the will in *God*, as the first principle of creation and individual existence. It was the fusion, in later medieval thought, of these two strains, the theological and the anthropological, or, the metaphysical and the psychological, or, as we may also say, the objective and the subjective, which terminated in the powerful ascendency of voluntarism in the West. In terms of the attribution of lineage adopted for our purposes, the one represents the more Jewish, the other the more Christian, contribution to what finally emerged. The Jewish factor can be identified as such by its connection with the idea of creation, as well as by its prior appearance in the Arabic-Jewish orbit; we have dealt with it as much as space permits. The Christian, Augustinian factor, bound up with the mysteries of original sin, faith and grace, was in itself less directly "philosophical" in import; but the enormous stress it laid on the inner dimension interpreted in volitional terms could not fail to shape the general self-consciousness of man, and through it indirectly the philosophical interpretation of man.

It is not that the subjective aspect is missing on the Jewish side. The freedom of the human will, as the counterpart of divine justice, was consistently argued by the Jewish thinkers, often in opposition to the determinism of their Islamic contemporaries. But freedom of the will need not mean its primacy; and on Jewish premises there is no reason for "radical" voluntarism, that is to say, for focusing the total essence of man in the unfathomable doings and events of his will. Nor, in Jewish thought, is the eternal salvation of the individual soul the total object of divine concern; nor, for that matter, did the moderate Jewish suspicion of nature ever reach anything like the radical distrust of nature that went with the dualistic mood of Christianity. We may note here that Judaism, radical as it could be on occasion, is not intrinsically wedded to extremism. But the "Cross" is an extreme conception to begin with; and in the Pauline version adopted by Augustine, it centers all of eschatology in the personal reenactment of this extremity of divine death and resurrection by each individual will. This was one existential meaning that could be given to the doctrine of Incarnation. To summarize: although both voluntarism and individualism, as we have seen, were native to the Jewish position in its confrontation with the Hellenic one, we find both— and the issues they posed—immeasurably sharpened in the Christian ambient. There they tend to assume an either-or quality, and this, together with the heavy accent on the subjective sphere, may well be the specifically Christian share in the philosophical transformation of those themes.

As to individualism, its battle was fought and won in the struggle of nominalism with realism, that long medieval conflict over the status of universals which is very much part of our story but can only be alluded to here. Voluntarism, though naturally congenial to nominalism, found its most powerful statement independently of it in Duns Scotus, greatest in the succession of Augustinians that countered the Aristotelian synthesis of Aquinas.

Duns Scotus claims the primacy of the will on both the human and the divine plane. On the human plane, this means that will exercises dominion over the intellect.[20] Will determines the otherwise neutral thought to the contemplation of this or that object; and when thought in turn determines volition by its insights, it does so in the service of the overarching will that activates it from the first. Will, in other words, sets intellect its task, causes it to act, employs it for its end. It is thus first in the order of causes and of actuality. Instead of the "active *intellect*" of Aristotelianism, we have the "active will" as the principle moving the

---

[20]*Voluntas imperans intellectui est causa superior actus eius. Intellectus autem, si est causa volitionis, est causa subserveins voluntati (Oxon. IV, d. 49, quaest. ex latere, n. 16).* Scotus here follows Augustine and diverges from Thomas Aquinas.

otherwise passive intellect. And willing in turn has no other cause but itself; it is free in radical indeterminacy.

Together with this elevation in rank goes a vast extension of the area where the will must make its decisions unaided by the intellect. Scotus' list of what is rationally undemonstrable engulfs most of the propositions of natural theology, which together with the specifically Christian mysteries are now referred to faith—a mode or state of the will. And this is no mere epistemological and temporary stopgap function of the will, to be superseded in a future consummation: Beatitude itself is placed by Scotus in the volitional sphere, not as by Aquinas in the intellect. This shift breaks with a millenial tradition that had understood consummation to consist in a state of knowledge.[21]

On the other hand, what the intellect has lost at the transcendent end, it has gained at the opposite end of the spectrum. It can know the individual in its individuality.[22] This is possible only when form, the object of knowledge, is no longer identified with the universal, and individuation is not attributed to mere matter. Since individual existence, as the "ultimate reality,"[23] is a perfection and not a defect, there must be a formal principle of individuality for each individual, its "thisness" (*haecceitas*) which completes its general essence, its "whatness" (*quiditas*): the latter is incomplete without it. Thus the principle of individuation is placed in the ideal sphere itself, that is to say, in the heart of things. Aristotle, too, had regarded the individual existent, namely "form enmattered," as the "primary substance." But in terms of knowledge only the form counts, and the individual is just an instantiation of this universal form—i.e., of the species as the sharable "what"—to which matter adds nothing intelligible. The matter that individuates remains extraneous to the essence. Duns Scotus, on the contrary, postulates a *"form of individuality"* as a necessary, internal constituent of concrete essence. He thus, in effect, assigns to each individual its own form: general "whatness" complemented by unique "thisness"—e.g., *humanitas* complemented by *Socratitas*.[24] However, we are concerned with the

[21]Duns Scotus, *Rep.* IV, d. 49, qu. 2, n. 20. Here again, Crescas' thought takes a very similar road in the disengagement from Aristotelian intellectualism, cf. Guttman, *op. cit.*, pp. 235–36.

[22]The intellect forms the general concepts by abstraction, but as well apprehends the singular: *De rer. princ.*, qu. 13, art. 3, n. 28–33.

[23]*Realitas ultima: Oxon.* II, d. 3, qu. 6, n. 15.

[24]*Loc. cit.* The individual difference is the last form to which no other can be added; and this *haecceitas* (not matter) is the principle of individuation. Leibniz later went one step further when he completely individualized "essence" as such: there *are* only individual essences, each the law of a unique career of being, implicit in the "monad" that represents that one essence. Duns Scotus, incidentally, by means of the formal *haecceitas*, just managed to stay in the "realist" camp and

subject of the will rather than the subject of knowledge, and we return to this theme.

Even more pregnant with philosophical consequences than the primacy of will over intellect in man is Duns Scotus' doctrine of the primacy of will in God. It is absolutely sovereign, itself the sole cause of his willing, and not bound by any rules other than those of logic. Accordingly, the laws of nature and of morality are as they are by mere decree of this will and could as well be otherwise: "His will is the supreme rule."[25]

Let us just consider what this doctrine implies as to the nature of the *moral* law. Almost at the beginning of the philosophical tradition, Socrates (in Plato's *Euthyphro*) raises the question of whether "the holy" is holy because it is pleasing to the gods, or whether it is pleasing to the gods because it is holy. The issue at stake in the question was the intrinsic nature of "holiness" and the like, and first of all the question whether or not there *is* such a "nature" independent of anyone's pleasure and choice. In Socrates' case the answer could not be in doubt. Given the many gods, and the frequent disagreements among them, the knowledge of what is holy and unholy, honorable and dishonorable, right and wrong, cannot be derived from the accidents of such pleasure and displeasure, even though they be divine; on the contrary, divine pleasure and displeasure must be based on, and if need be judged by, the knowledge of what is right and wrong in itself—a knowledge obtainable on its own. The implication is that there are essences of these things, binding in their validity even on the gods; or, that there is a realm of truth entirely outside the realm of power. The Socratic answer stood up for over a thousand years of "essentialist" tradition in Western philosophy.

Monotheism somewhat altered the conditions of the question. With the many gods gone, the question now affected the conception of the omnipotence of the one God, which would be less than absolute if limited by the laws of eternal reason. And so Duns Scotus, having reversed the classical order by which the will in God was subordinated to his intellect, and therefore determined by its immutable verities, concludes that the biblical commandments are morally valid because he willed them, not that he willed them because they are morally valid.[26] The goodness of anything apart from God consists in its being willed by Him. And in

---

could avoid crossing the line into nominalism, on the brink of which his whole theory hovers.

[25]*Voluntas sua est prima regula: Oxon.* IV, *d.* 46, *qu.* 1, *n.* 6.

[26]. . . *ideo est bonum, quia a Deo volitum et non e converso: Oxon.* III, *d.* 19, *qu. un., n.* 7; cf. I, *d.* 44, *qu. un., n.* 2: *ideo [Deus] sicut potest aliter agere, ita potest aliam legem statuere rectam, quia si statueretur a Deo, recta esset.* . . .

virtue of God's absolute power, another moral order would also be possible.

What is of importance for the subsequent evolution of thought is the connection here established between value, will, and power. The will to posit values, and the power to make them law, are jointly at the bottom of all operative norm. When linked to divine wisdom, this source of moral law is still in safe hands which man can trust. Nevertheless, the meaning of law as such has changed, and the reference to God's purely positive will and power becomes its sole available ground. God's wisdom is inscrutable; what His will is has been revealed to faith. But when that ground vanishes, as it does with the vanishing of faith, there is only *man's* will and power to ground any norm or law. In the Socratic answer, the commandments would stand even without God, based as they are on intelligible essences; in the Scotist answer, radicalized by the subsequent victory of nominalism, they collapse without God unless another will steps in and takes over their guardianship. Man inherits the role of creator and guardian of values, with no light to guide his choice, since he is not wise and has no vision of eternal wisdom on which to draw. This is a profoundly paradoxical outcome of what had begun as pious self-abnegation and a giving of all honor to God. First the ancient distinction between laws valid "by nature" (therefore immutable) and laws "instituted," (therefore mutable) was obliterated by the creationist-volitionist creed for which everything was "instituted," and the distinction became that between divine and human institution. Then this distinction in turn, when its creedal support was withdrawn and its divine term vanished, collapsed into the remaining, human term, and man's law-giving alone, immersed in the flux of his being, was left in possession of the field. This was the potential dynamite in the Scotistic-plus-nominalistic turn with which the Middle Ages passed over into the Modern Age.

Many obvious, and not so obvious, lines extend from these considerations to salient phenomena of later philosophy, down to our own, post-Christian era. One may think of the Baconian nexus of knowledge and power and the kingdom of man; of the Cartesian *ego* and the suspicion of the deceiving demon; of Nietzsche's will to power; and of the philosophy of Heidegger. But in this connection one must also remember Kant's majestic effort to synthesize voluntarism and rationalism. That synthesis appears in the categorical imperative (surely of Hebrew vintage), grounded in the autonomy of the moral will (a transformed Christian conception), but objectively valid because this will is itself reason and thus universal (a classical conception).

The case of Kant shows, what the examination of other thinkers would show as well, that the original, classical-intellectualist source of the philosophical tradition never ceased to flow and to provide the mainstream into which the Jewish-Christian catalysts injected themselves. The last great reassertion of that tradition was at the same time the grandest bid at reconciliation with the other side: Hegel's dialectical system, which at the very moment when the Christian source began to dry up (and the classical perhaps as well), at last gave philosophical room to the one distinctly Christian teaching which philosophy had never ventured to assimilate before: the doctrine of the incarnated God. Admittedly, the doctrine is not easily recognized in the eschatological philosophies of history into which Hegel and his successors metamorphosed it. This dazzling aftermath to our subject—the ultimate secularization of a theology—would require a separate essay. Here I can only indicate my unargued opinion that, all Jewish messianism notwithstanding, the idea of history as a self-operative vehicle of redemption is much more of Christian than Jewish provenance. One may see in it a transmuted form of the Holy Spirit doing his work through man in the interval between incarnation and the second coming.

If, in looking back over the road we have taken, we find that the attempted differentiation between "Jewish" and "Christian" elements did not always lead to sharply drawn lines, this is only what was to be expected in the nature of the case. But whatever may be the verdict on the particular attributions proposed, one truth should have impressed itself on us through the examples we have adduced with all the hazards of selective evidence: that the shadow which these past things cast is long indeed and—even as they recede—still lies upon our present scene. And perhaps our discussion has enabled us to see better how it is due to a unique historical configuration, the meeting of Athens and Jerusalem, each itself a unique fact, that Western mankind has taken a road so different from that of any other civilization. To the accident of this meeting (though not to it alone) we can trace the unique combination of rationalism and voluntarism, generalism and individualism, theory and activism, of which we have yet to decide whether it is a blessing or a curse, but through which, to the vexation of ourselves and the world, we have become what we are.

3.
Seventeenth Century and After: The Meaning of the Scientific and Technological Revolution

I

We live in a revolution—we of the West—and have been living in one for several centuries. We are naming its central agency when we call it the scientific-technological revolution. Having begun as a "provincially" European event, it has by now become global. In its progress it reshapes the external conditions of our being—that is, the world we live in; it thereby reshapes the ways of our living; and finally—or perhaps first—it reshapes the modes of our thinking. In brief, what is being revolutionized is man's environment, behavior, and thought. This has been under way for a long time. Do "revolution" and length of time go together in our concepts? We speak of revolution when the change in question—a collective change in human affairs—is radical in nature, comprehensive in scope, and concentrated in time: the last characteristic setting revolution off from evolution. Radicalism of a change means that it involves the very foundations of that which changes, not merely its surface; comprehensiveness, that it affects a broad spectrum of life manifestations, not merely an isolated phenomenon. The third criterion is one of tempo and style rather than of substance: that dramatic quality which change gains only with concentration in time. While evolution

An earlier version of this essay was published in *Philosophy Today* 15 (Summer 1971), with the title "The Scientific and Technological Revolutions."

spreads itself over long periods and proceeds by imperceptible degrees, the word "revolution" suggests to us a certain suddenness of onset and violence of progress. This is more than a morphological trait: its subjective side is that those caught up in the change *experience* it is a break with the past, as overturning the established order of things, even replacing any established order with the condition of change itself, and consequently as unsettling their lives. To be thus perceptible is of the essence of revolution. This felt "violence" of change (not identical with the physical violence that attends political revolutions in particular) is, then, very much a function of the mere speed of change: even the most profound and far-reaching change, affecting all the things we named, if only slow enough, is not considered a revolution.

But what is fast, what slow? What interval of time is long, what short? By what standard do we measure? Is not the difference between slow and fast, and thus between evolution and revolution, entirely relative and therefore arbitrary? Relative it is, but not arbitrary. For it is relative to something itself absolute, to a natural unit of measurement: the individual human life span, the length of a generation. And this is a good test that anyone can make when his times comes: If a man in the fullness of his days, at the end of his life, can pass on the wisdom of his accumulated experience to those who grow up after him; if what he has learned in his youth, added to but not discarded in his maturity, still serves him in his old age and is still worth teaching the then young— then his was not an age of revolution, not counting, of course, abortive revolutions. The world into which his children enter is still *his* world, not because it is entirely unchanged, but because the changes that did occur were gradual and limited enough for him to absorb them into his initial stock and keep abreast of them. If, however, a man in his advancing years has to turn to his children, or grandchildren, to have them tell him what the present is about; if his own acquired knowledge and understanding no longer avail him; if at the end of his days he finds himself to be obsolete rather than wise—then we may term the rate and scope of change that thus overtook him, "revolutionary." Adopting this standard—the only natural one for the finite and mortal beings that we are— it is meaningful and entirely legitimate to speak of a revolution going on through generations and even centuries, which is precisely what we do when we date the state of revolution we live in, variously, from the First World War, the Industrial Revolution, the French Revolution, and ultimately from the rise of the new science and cosmology in the sixteenth and seventeenth centuries with which it all began—truly a revolution of secular scale. To be sure, the pace of events during those centuries was not always as breathtaking as it is now, and the spectacular, exponential acceleration of the whole movement is a fairly recent fact. But this movement was revolutionary from its inception, by its intrinsic nature, and it periodically spawned new, sudden turning-points of the briefer and more concentrated kind customarily termed "revolutions," which in retrospect we recognize as parts, as critical phases of the ongoing movement which is a revolution in its entirety.

Let us turn back once more to the initial statement of what characterizes a revolution. We said that it is a collective change in human affairs which is radical, comprehensive, and of a certain rapid pace; and we said that it concerns man's environment, behavior, and thought. One qualification is missing here. In order to be termed a revolution, the change must be man-made, it must ultimately have its source in ourselves. We would not honor with the name of "revolution" a change in human affairs brought about by some cosmic event, a sudden change in climate, or anything of that kind. We must be subjects, agents, of the change, however much we may also be the objects of it. We inevitably become the objects, of course, if the subjective change is effective, i.e., if it turns into practice and thus affects the conditions of life. The works of man recoil upon himself, and it is of the nature of things human that in collective terms the agent becomes the creature, perhaps the victim, of his action.

To say that the revolution originates in man is to say that it originates in thought. It may even at first be a revolution of thought purely and for thought's own sake, a metamorphosis of looking at things, long before it becomes one of action too, of dealing with things. This is indeed the sequence of the scientific and technological revolution to which these reflections are devoted. The scientific revolution changed man's ways of thinking, *by* thinking, before it materially changed, even affected, his ways of living. It was a change in theory, in world-view, in metaphysical outlook, in conception and method of knowledge. It did not at first—and for a long time—concern itself with the realm of practice, even though some of its most eloquent philosophical prophets assigned to it this role early enough: that assignment itself was in the realm of thought. That modern science as such started with hardly any technological intent is clear from the fact that it started mainly with the astronomer's reform of *cosmology*, and the cosmos, the stellar universe, does not lend itself to manipulation. Technology, historically speaking, is the delayed effect of the scientific and metaphysical revolution with which the modern age begins. The theoretical change alone merits the name of a revolution in its own right, even without this later, revolutionizing effect.

That effect, however, was far from accidental, or extraneous to the cause. The technological turn later given to the speculative revolution was somehow in the cards from the beginning, as those early philo-sophical prophets more clearly perceived than the scientific pioneers themselves. The very conception of reality that underlay and was fos-tered by the rise of modern science, i.e., the new concept of *nature*, contained manipulability at its theoretical core and, in the form of ex-periment, involved actual manipulation in the investigative process. Not that Galileo and others undertook their experiments with practical intent: their intent was to gain knowledge; but the *method* of knowledge itself, by the active intercourse with its object, anticipated utilization for prac-tical ends (and it is only surprising, in retrospect, how long it took the actual step to be taken on any large scale). Technology was thus implied as a *possibility* in the metaphysics, and trained as a *practice* in the pro-cedures, of modern science. Its eventual emergence into the extra-theoretical sphere of vulgar utility, as an instrument of power on the broadest public scale, was no more than drawing the conclusion from the intellectual premises which the scientific revolution had established. This being the case, the present global technology of man has itself a meta-physical side to it besides the more obvious practical one. The meaning of the technological revolution is thus part of, indeed the completion of, the metaphysical meaning of the scientific revolution. It is the meta-physics of science come into the open.

Before turning to the beginnings themselves one other remark on the sequence as a whole is in order. If the revolution started in thought, then it started in freedom and as an exercise of human freedom. Its first trail blazers, men like Copernicus, Galileo, Descartes, were a select few who came by their novel conception in acts of independent insight and personal decision. To their lot it fell to break old habits of thought and overturn long established views. These first innovators, thus, not only caused a revolution by what they did—they were revolutionaries by what they were. But the more their outlook became common property, the more there accrued an irresistible compulsion to the movement which they had started, and its later protagonists, born into it by histor-ical fate, no longer entered it by free choice. When, in addition, the technological factor came into play, changing the external conditions of life, a self-feeding necessity was set up which, from without as it were, took increasingly possession of the process; with this added actuator, the movement continuously gathers new momentum, carrying its carriers along as its appointed instruments. Thus while the revolution was started by revolutionaries, it is now continued, although still a revolution, by the orthodox. What began in acts of supreme and daring freedom has set up its own necessity and proceeds on its course like a second, deter-minate nature—no less deterministic for being man-made.

II

My contention here is, to repeat it once more, that the *theoretical* beginnings—what we may call the ontological breakthrough occurring at the onset of the modern age and laying the foundations on which the edifice of modern science was reared—was the all important event. To understand this event historically, we do well to turn our minds back to the sixteenth and seventeenth centuries. It was a time not only pregnant with change but also conscious of it, with a will for it, and with the polemical animus that turns against the old in the name of the new and hails the break with the past. A sign of this spreading mood is the currency of the word "new," which from the sixteenth century on we encounter all over Europe (and much earlier in Italy) as a commendatory epithet. That "novelty" is a recommendation is by no means the rule in the history of cultures; in fact, it was itself a signal and perhaps unique novelty. In the Graeco-Roman world, for instance, which of all former ages is most akin to modernity in so many respects, the highest recommendation for a view, a maxim, a truth was its reputed antiquity. The poets and seers of old, the sages of Egypt and Babylon, the myths of one's own past or of the still remoter past of the East, were called to witness for the truth of contemporary teaching. This hardly cramped the style of intellectual innovation, as the allegorical method could extract almost any desired meaning from the veiled evidence of the past.[1] But novelty was no recommendation, rather the opposite, and its appearance was generally shunned. It certainly was almost never openly professed. This, and the corresponding appeal to antiquity, are found in many epochs. Even advanced civilizations, which owed their height to a history of bold innovations from their archaic beginnings, tended to hide this aspect of their genesis. Antiquity served as the stamp of confirmation on the value and truth of beliefs about the nature of things. The source of truth lies with the ancestors who were nearer to the gods and more attuned to the undimmed voice of the world. Their truth has stood the test of time; it has to be recaptured because they spoke in riddles; but truth itself is old and well weathered. Rarely before the onset of the modern age is novelty invoked in favor of a venture or a vision.

This changed profoundly at the time when the Middle Ages drew to a close. An increasing use of the commending label "new" for an increas-

[1]About the mainly "conservative" intent of allegory, see H. Jonas, *The Gnostic Religion* (Boston: Beacon Press, 1963), p. 91.

ing variety of human enterprises—in art, action, and thought—marks the great turn. This verbal fashion, serious or frivolous as the case may be, tells us a number of things. A weariness, even impatience, with the long-dominant ways of thought and life, an irreverent and revisionist spirit, betray themselves in the elevation of the word to an adjective of praise. Respect for the wisdom of the past is replaced by the suspicion of hardened error and by distrust of inert authority. Together with this goes a new mood of self-confidence, the heady conviction that we moderns are better equipped than the ancients—certainly better than our immediate predecessors—to discover the truth and improve many things.

The confidence that the new is more likely than not to represent an improvement over the old goes with a new appraisal of the ages of man. Up to that time it was natural to believe that in looking back into the past we look into a perspective of greater age and maturity. We late-comers are the heirs of more inspired times, the recipients of a wisdom so much "older" than ourselves. A strangely persuasive, perspectival illusion was at work in this belief: What comes to us from the remote past has acquired the superiority of great age by the fact that it has been transmitted for so long, and the age of the thing transmitted is somehow transferred to the source that produced it. It was a curiously startling discovery of the obvious when the sixteenth and seventeenth century moderns contended that we moderns are the older ones; that mankind in times past was younger, thus more prone to the errors of childhood; that greater maturity was on our side, and that we, taught and dis-enchanted by the errors of the past, are better fitted to tackle the questions of nature and man.

Thus emerges the novel evaluation of *modernity as an asset*. Instead of being depreciated as the lot of epigones, it is extolled as the chance for us to break the ancient idols and start mankind on its true road. A rising tide of distrust of historical authority, and indeed of all authority in matters of truth, joins itself with a confidence of contemporary man in his power to go it alone, and to discover truth and value by his own lights. This twin combination of distrust and self-confidence puts the revolutionary stamp on the movement of thought that started in its sign. The break with the past as such was partly overlaid by the enlistment of the remoter past of classical Antiquity, then eagerly rediscovered, as an ally in the break with the immediate past of the Middle Ages. But important as was the lesson of pre-Christian, secular Antiquity in the early stages (and much that was forgotten had simply to be relearned), in the end its heritage too was included in the general verdict on the past, and the great masters of the revolution, once it had become fully conscious of itself, could discard the crutches of the Ancients with sovereign disdain. "That wisdom which we have derived principally from the Greeks is but the boyhood of knowledge," Francis Bacon said at the opening of his *New Organon*.

What is truly unique, however, is that the break was not a one-time event where innovation occurs only at the beginning. In all the other great breaks in history, among them the greatest of all, the irruption of Christianity into the ancient world, the authority of the revolutionary founders soon hardened into a new orthodoxy. The break at the beginning of the modern age embodied a *principle* of innovation in itself which made its constant further occurrence mandatory. As a consequence, the relation of each phase to its own preceding past—itself a phase of the revolution—remained that of critique and overcoming for the sake of further advance. In the sign of permanent progress, all history becomes what Nietzsche later called "critical history." This, as we have suggested, may be a kind of "orthodoxy" itself, that is, a settled routine, but it surely is a very dialectical kind. It made the revolution permanent, irrespective of whether its agents were still revolutionaries.

III

How this came about is a story involving many things besides the history of science. The movement that remade thought from its foundations was not an isolated event but had a background commensurate in breadth with its own dimension in depth. We cannot go here into the manifold aspects of the crisis that attended the transition from medieval to modern man. Among them are the rise of the cities which eroded the feudal order, the concurrent rise of national monarchies, the expansion of trade, the spreading of information through the printing press, the maritime voyages of discovery which widened the physical and mental horizons. . . . Widening the horizons, and in rather abrupt manner, was the general signature of the age. From the relatively closed compass of Christian Europe, Western man moved into the expanding world of modern enterprise and global politics. External and internal barriers were breaking down everywhere. New outlooks, often confused, were born, and paid their toll of infant mortality. With the broadened ethnological knowledge of humankind in the variety of its beliefs and customs—matched in the historical dimension by the new knowledge of the Classics—came a new skepticism concerning the validity or inevitability of one's own inherited ways (*vide* Montaigne). Every province of human affairs came to be affected by these changes, and at the center the conception which man held of himself and his relation to the universe. The

discovery of the autonomous individual—of his worldly glory in the
Italian Renaissance, of his religious conscience in the Northern Reformation—elevated personal insight and judgment to unprecedented
authority. In exchange, almost everything else became insecure. To try
out new ways became natural.

In the midst of this ferment of many liberations and gropings, appeared the book that ushered in the scientific revolution: Copernicus'
On the Revolutions of the Celestial Orbs. It is not amiss to remember
that the same year, 1543, saw the publication of Vesalius' *On the Fabric
of the Human Body*. The fact is symbolic of the two sides of the scientific
revolution as it eventually took shape: the macrocosmic and the micro-
cosmic, the abstract and the concrete, the mathematical and the empirical,
construction and observation—the unifying conception of the total
scheme of things and the differentiating perception of particular detail.
But it is not surprising that of these two sides it was the first which
proved to be the effectively revolutionary factor in the revolution: revolutions always are what they are by their abstract component. Let us
now look at the main traits of this metamorphosis of speculative thought.

Taking as known the direct content of Copernicus' feat in astronomy
—the replacement of the geocentric by a heliocentric system through
the hypothesis of a double, axial and orbital, movement of the earth,
with the resultant simplification of theory compared to the cumbersome
Ptolemaic scheme—we fix our attention on certain implications of the
new theory which were not at all in its inventor's mind, but which
inevitably led to a new physical cosmology far beyond any merely
mathematical reinterpretation of astronomical data. Let us consider these
three: (1) the necessarily implied proposition of the homogeneity of
nature throughout the universe; (2) the absence of a solid architecture
of the universe to account for its orderliness; and (3) its probable infinity, by which it ceased to be a "whole" or a "cosmos" in the sense of a
determinate entity.

1. The entirely novel conception that nature is the same everywhere,
be it heaven or earth, followed from the non-geocentric cosmology by
the simple fact that the earth had become a "star" itself, viz. a planet,
and by the same token the planets had become "earths." Instead of
enjoying a nobler, more refined and sublime type of being, they were
instances of the same physical reality as the one we are familiar with
on this gross, material, heavy earth. Thus, with one stroke, the essential
difference between the terrestrial and celestial spheres, between sub-
lunar and stellar, corruptible and incorruptible nature vanished: and with
this, the idea of *any* natural order of rank lost its most telling support

in the visible scheme of things. If not even the universe in its majesty is a hierarchical order, if the heavens themselves are assimilated to earth, then nature as such may not be a hierarchial principle at all and not bestow privileges of sublimity anywhere. The newly interpreted evidence of the universe pointed to its being homogeneous throughout.

This homegeneity means, to begin with, that the universe is everywhere composed of the same kind of matter—the same substance: this would in due course lead to the more far-reaching postulate that it is also everywhere subject to the same laws. The first notion alone had to overcome deep-seated habits of thought, sanctioned by the tremendous authority of Aristotelian teaching. It was the main burden of Galileo's telescopic observations of the heavenly objects to lend visual proof to the argument of substantial sameness and confute the Aristotelians on this point (and by implication on the larger issues of cosmology). If there are mountains and valleys on the moon and spots on the sun; if the planets are seen as disks (showing that they are spherical bodies of differing magnitudes) and Venus as subject to phases (showing that it shines with reflected light)—then the eye can see what reason must infer from the Copernican theory: that the astronomical objects are material bodies in space of no "purer" substance than other bodily things. To us, who have long been accustomed to thinking of "heavenly" bodies in no other way and have actually seen men walking on the moon, it is not easy to appreciate the spectacular impact which this first ocular display of physical detail had not only on the direct issue, viz., the material nature of the stars, but on the verification of the total world-hypothesis from which it was but one marginal inference—and one hardly contemplated by Copernicus himself. In the case of the sun spots, incidentally, observation here exceeded the inference from theory, which directly extended only to the nature of the planets, as companions of the earth: the sun, in the original "heliocentric" scheme, occupied a qualitatively unique position as the ruling center (which to Kepler assumed almost mystical significance) and was therefore exempt from the physical generalization otherwise invited by the theory in its initial form. Equally so was the sphere of the fixed stars, the outermost circumference of the world cavity, which had been removed to extremes of distance from the solar family at its core, so that all of its former bonds to our world were cut (as discussed below). But this very disconnection, as we shall see, instead of offering a refuge to qualitative diversity, eventually resulted in the inclusion of sun and stars in the unifying argument.

Anticipating this result, we may add already the functional complement to the "substantial" aspect of homogeneity. If made of the same substance throughout, as suggested by the substantial sameness of earth and planets, the universe can reasonably be expected to obey the same laws in all its parts. This would mean that the same physics applies to the heavens that is found to operate on earth. There was, of course, little point in stressing this inference before there was a physics to make good the promise it held out. But once the laws of motion were discovered, through the combination of abstract reasoning and terrestrial experiment which Galileo's genius initiated, their extrapolation to the celestial world —to *everything* in the world—followed naturally from the implied homogeneity of the "Copernican" universe. With the triumphal success of this extrapolation in Newton's feat, the "mathematical" construction of Copernicus and Kepler was at last vindicated as a physical cosmology. The identical laws holding throughout the universe turned out to be the laws of mechanics.

2. Let us consider now the second of the three implications of the Copernican revolution we have set out to explicate: the dissolving of the solid cosmic architecture which had guaranteed the orderly working of the Aristotelian-Ptolemaic universe. Laws of motion indeed became a necessary desideratum to explain the orbits of the planets when those moving celestial objects were no longer thought to be attached to re-volving orbs. The discarding of such "orbs" or "spheres" followed from a theoretical development somewhat more complicated than the one we have just discussed. First we must recall the function of these time-honored constructs of earlier cosmology.

The concept of heavenly spheres is closely connected with the axiom that all cosmic motion is circular. This idea, originally impressed on the imagination by the visible revolution of the star-studded night sky around the celestial pole, had gained the quality of a metaphysical prin-ciple and become wedded to ideas of perfection which were associated with the geometrical properties of the circle. Such excellence alone was thought fitting for the most perfect part of corporeal nature. The two a priori requirements, therefore, which every cosmic motion—as distinct from sublunary motions—had to satisfy were circularity of path and uniformity of speed. But only the diurnal motion of the total sky, i.e., the collective revolution of the fixed stars, fulfilled this double require-ment directly and visibly. It alone also presented the immediate appear-ance of a great hollow sphere revolving about an invisible axis drawn through the poles. The irregular motions of the planets, with their "stations" and "retrogradations," were only indirectly, by an ingenious multiple combination of eccentrics and epicycles, brought into conso-nance with the general axiom. Complicated as the resulting system was, it generally succeeded in saving the phenomena with fair accuracy. But beyond this calculatory aspect, the system had this important physical aspect that it required *force* merely to account for the fact of motion and not for its shape: the latter followed simply from the shape of movable *structures*, endowed with just one "degree of freedom." Whatever rides on the circumference of a wheel or axially rotating sphere cannot but describe a circular path. Thus, given a certain spatial order of cycles, and cycles mounted on cycles (etc.), conceived like rigid bodies; and given one continuous impulse, imparted to the outer sphere by the First Mover and hence transmitted down the system through the concentric spheres, nothing more is required to produce the path of any particular star in all its complexity. Since it was not the moving force, but the form of the structures moved, that defined the form of particular movement, one efficient cause sufficed to eternally supply the motion as such: the rest followed from the coeternal matrix of differentiating structures on which it acted. Thus no dynamics of interacting forces was called for, merely a geometry of constraining forms. In other words, the "physics" of the heavens is not a kinetics, but an architectonics with one basic form—circularity—"natural" to the heavens as such and reserved to them alone.

This solid architecture of the cosmos dissolved in the wake of Copernicus' reinterpretation of celestial mathematics. Copernicus himself, still clinging to the axiom of circularity, could not yet dispense with a system of cycles and epicycles (though greatly diminished in number) to account for the astronomical facts. But the opaque, earthlike, no longer ethereal bodies into which the planets had changed, were ill fitted for the continued association with transparent spheres that were to carry them around. And the fixed stars, since *their* motion had become merely apparent, no longer stood in need of a vehicle at all; so at least the outer sphere, the original model of all the postulated spheres, had lost its raison d'être—which was that of all spheres, viz., to be the vehicle of stellar movement. The immobilized Great Sphere was thus the first to become theoretically redundant: it so happened that in historical fact— since it did not *contradict* theory—it was the last to go. With it went the venerable idea of the vaulted heaven—another of the many victims which Copernican doctrine extracted from the appearances of sense.

The death blow was dealt to the concept of spheres as such by Kepler's discovery of the elliptic orbits. It was a threefold deathblow: to the axiom of circularity, to the axiom of uniformity, and to the total conception of a structured world space. The first follows from Kepler's first law of planetary motion (the law of the ellipse) and requires no explanation. The second follows from the second law (the law of areas), stating the variation of orbital velocities between the maxima at perihelion and the minima at aphelion. The third follows from both together; no combination of uniformly revolving, rigid structures would yield for any point this combination of elliptic path with the required asymmetric variation of speed. Whatever was to be done about the outer sphere—and Kepler himself, from a dislike of infinity, still held to it—for the planets it was obvious that they were attached to nothing. The inescapable conclusion was that they were independent bodies, moving freely through empty, featureless space. And the inescapable question arose: What, then, holds them in their orbits and determines their varying velocities?

Already Kepler himself felt the weight of this novel question arising from his discoveries, and groped for an answer. The law of areas clearly pointed to a force directed toward the sun and dependent on distance from it. From there on, the quest for *causes* of motion, that is, for a dynamics that would *explain* the empirically discovered, purely descriptive laws—that would furnish their common *why*, and in direct application would yield the particular movement of each planet as a *causal* necessity—became the order of the day. It had to wait for Newton to reach its goal.

3. A third unpremeditated consequence from Copernican doctrine—with a far more than physical significance—was the extension of the world to infinity. It was set in motion almost immediately after the appearance of the new theory, in response to one of the earliest objections raised against it. The failure of any trace of a parallax to be detected in the fixed stars, which should be there as counterpart to the alleged annual revolution of the earth, either refuted the notion of a moving earth altogether, as the anti-Copernicans contended, or it put those stars at such a distance as to make the effect of the earth's motion unobservable: which was the rejoinder of the Copernicans. This sounds like a mere technical, upward revision of cosmic magnitudes. But this is a case where quantity turns into quality. Given the enormous length of the diameter of the *orbis magnus* (the earth's orbit around the sun), the observational zero value of any triangulation from this truly cosmic base to the outer sphere called for an almost unimaginable lengthening of the radius of that sphere—to a magnitude which no longer bore any relation to former beliefs about the size of the universe. According to those former beliefs, the cosmos—closed, though of quite imposing dimensions—presented a well-proportioned distribution of entities occupying the space between the earth and the outer limit. Now, with the leap in dimensions, this outer limit, becoming implausible itself as an *entity* in its monstrous magnification, presided over the immense emptiness of a cavity in whose center huddled the solar system. And since

this great sphere, the locus of the fixed stars, had already lost its other and more convincing role, that of diurnal revolution, little was needed for the final step to deny its bounding role as well—that is, to discard it altogether, and to pass from the closed to the open universe. Thus, what started as an embarrassment to theory (the missing parallax) led by its immanent logic to a profound change of world view. It must be said that the first, momentous steps toward infinity were taken under duress and without exuberance.

Exuberance, however, was soon to seize upon the half-finished thought and sweep it to its bold conclusions. Where the astronomers moved warily, the impatience of the visionary forged ahead and with one stroke translated all the latent potentials of the Copernican hypothesis into a majestic, new, intoxicating vista of the infinite universe. It is in essentials still ours. I speak of Giordano Bruno, who proclaimed the infinity of the world not as a concession to be made to the exigencies of theory, but as an inspiring and liberating revelation which alone was in keeping with the inner nature of things.[2] This only martyr of the scientific revolution, himself not a scientist, became the prophet of "the decentralized, infinite and infinitely populous universe" (Lovejoy). Stated briefly, Bruno realized, and drew together, the following implications of the new astronomy, one or the other of which had singly found some lower-keyed statement before.

a. When looking at the night sky, we do not look at a confining vault but into the depth of infinite space.

b. The luminaries seen there are not at an equal radius—however large—from the earth, but are scattered ad infinitum through this depth.

c. Even the nearest of them is so distant (*vide* the argument of the parallax), that its mere visibility and apparent size[3] requires us to assign it a real size comparable to that of the sun.

d. The stars *are* indeed suns and—since their space is the same as ours and conditions are alike everywhere—must be thought as attended by planets as well, too small in size and luminescence to be seen from our distance.

e. The universe therefore consists of worlds upon worlds in infinite multitude, and abounds with life and immanent creativity.

f. The universe has no center: its infinity is the coequal company of all the infinitely numerous bodies which it contains. Each of these is the center of its own surrounding space, but none has a privileged position

[2] I refer the reader to Alexander Koyré's beautiful book, *From the Closed World to the Infinite Universe* (Baltimore: The Johns Hopkins Press, 1957).

[3] To the naked eye (and still to the earliest telescopes) the fixed stars have some angular dimension.

with respect to the whole. (Bruno thus abolished the shortlived cosmic centrality which the *sun* had just gained through Copernicus in replacing that of the earth, and which the great Kepler still upheld a generation later in express opposition in Bruno's rush into infinity.)

g. The world space itself is a homogeneous void, though pervaded by invisible forces (conceived by Bruno in rather magical terms), through which there is universal communication among the dispersed worlds, and their multiplicity fuses into unity. (Bruno thus did not wait for Kepler's laws to do away with any remnant of a structural architectonics of world space: in principle, his vision had left only a dynamics—still to be specified—to provide the ordering necessity for the scattered pluralism in the unstructured void.)

h. The infinity of the universe, far from contradicting the nature of creation (which was of necessity finite to medieval-theological thought, as infinity befits God alone), is on the contrary the necessary and only adequate expression of the infinity and perfection of the creative cause, which totally expresses itself in its product, is constantly at work within it—is indeed not distinct from it.

This enumeration of objective doctrine conveys nothing of the hymnic tone, the almost inebriated mood, with which Bruno propounded it through the length and breadth of a Europe girding itself for the longest religious war in its history. This burning spirit greeted the opening of the universe like the crumbling of prison walls, as an outer infinity congenial to the infinity in man. It is only fair to add that in the following century, with a chillier air, a very different voice was heard in response to the—by then no longer controversial—infinity of the physical universe. "Cast into the infinite immensity of spaces of which I am ignorant, and which know me not, I am frightened"—thus Pascal expressed the contrary mood it may elicit, the mood of cosmic solitude. Bruno, lonely among men, welcomed cosmic infinitude as the revelation of a divine superabundance of reality and something kindred to himself; Pascal shrank from it and felt the loneliness of mankind in an alien universe. But whatever the response, the cosmos and man's place in it had changed beyond recognition.

IV

The new cosmology called for a new physics but did not provide one itself. It offered a new image of the universe but no explanation of it. It showed, by an ingenious combination of hypothesis, observation, and mathematical construction, how the macrocosmos "looks" and what motions its bodies describe, but not why they do so—i.e., what *causes* operate in that universe. The major structures of the world system had decisively changed, but nothing in the Copernican system as such, or in Kepler's refinement of it, or in Bruno's widening of its perspective to infinity, decided anything on the modus operandi of this revised totality. In brief, the new cosmology presented the shape of things, but by itself gave no account of the working of things. Its acceptance was thus at first left to the powerful appeal of its mathematical, rational, and imaginative qualities. Neither Copernicus nor Kepler could answer *physical* questions concerning the nature of their universe. Copernicus did not even ask them; Kepler felt the need for them, but for lack of an adequate physics his search for causes could find no satisfactory answer. His laws were descriptive and marvellously accurate in that respect, but not explanatory. His attempted explanations remained groping. He did, however, conceive the idea of a *vis motrix* (moving force) for his planets emanating from the sun; and he had proclaimed that measurable quantity was the essence of reality, and measurement the key to its secrets. And Bruno had grasped that motion and change rather than immutability were the truth of this universe, and that forces must provide the bond for its scattered multiplicity in unstructured space.

The one thing clear to all was that Aristotelian physics no longer applied to the altered scheme of things. Movements were no longer explained by forms of order; instead, the form of movement had to be explained by the action of forces. But about them the heavens were silent; their spectacle did not tell its secret. For the celestial bodies can only be contemplated, not experimented with; and contemplation alone will not disclose the play of forces. Terrestrial mechanics must come to the aid of the celestial spectacle. It could do so because the new homogeneity of nature would extend the findings of any local mechanics into limitless space. The actual development of such a mechanics itself was entirely independent of that of astronomy and is eminently associated with the name of Galileo.

While the most dramatic of Galileo's many feats concerned his championing of the Copernican cause and the telescopic discoveries that butressed it, his really decisive contribution to the rise of modern science was the laying of the foundations of a science of motion—a general "kinetics." This involved—apart from a new *method* of analysis and verification—a radical reframing of the very concept of motion, which—if less spectacular—was no less revolutionary in its long-term results than the reform of cosmology. Let us briefly remember how motion had been understood before.

In Aristotelian physics, motion was subsumed under the ontological category of *change*. That is to say, locomotion is one species of the genus "change," namely change of place (as distinct from change of quality, quantity, and substance). "Place" itself, in this view, *is* something, and for a body to be in a certain place is to be in a certain condition. When it moves to another place, a change occurs, and while it moves, a continuous sequence of changes occurs—as many changes as there are places traversed: which means an infinite number of changes, because of the infinite divisibility of the spatial continuum. But any change, according to the basic principle of causality, requires the operation of a *cause* as the sufficient reason for the change to occur, whereas the absence of change, the persistence of a given condition, requires no cause. *Ergo*, any process of motion, being a serial passage from place to place, and thus a series of changes, requires during its whole duration the continual renewal of the motive power, i.e., the constant activity of an agent cause (in modern parlance: a continuous input of energy).[4]

The corollary of this conception of movement as change is that *rest* is the natural state of a body, in which it will persist unless caused by an active principle to move. This is precisely what the *inertia* of bodies here means: the concept of inertia is fulfilled in the state of rest only. As applied to motion, it means that without the added supply of motive energy the motion will cease. Motion itself, the opposite of rest, is not a cause; it has a cause. Rest, on the other hand, has no cause: it is its own cause in the absence of any active cause.

I know of no simpler way to state the conceptual revolution in kinetics associated with Galileo (though in historical fact it was prepared by various prior steps), than to say that he removed motion from the category of change and made it understood as a *state* equivalent, in regard to cause, to the state of rest. Not the principle of causality, or of sufficient reason, as such was changed (let alone discovered), but the subject to which it applies: not the idea that every change must have a sufficient cause, but the idea of what constitutes a change. The import of this innocent-looking intellectual turn is so profound and so fraught with consequences that it calls for some elaboration.

---

[4]The fuller and more strictly Aristotelian statement of this argument would have to include the following. Each of the changes of which the whole movement is composed involves a passage from potency to act (which is not the same as the passage from one point of space to another: it underlies it). The mobility of every body means the potentiality it possesses of being in a place other than it is. But this is a passive potency whose actualization requires the activity of an agent cause. (This agent cause may be external or internal: it is internal in animate bodies, and in all bodies insofar as they are not in their "natural" place toward which they have an intrinsic tendency.) Thus any process of motion, as it involves a constantly repeated passage from potency to act corresponding to the serial change of place, requires for its sustainment a constant actuator.

Motion, so it is contended, is as much the "state" of a body as is rest. Its continuation therefore is not a repetitious change but the retention of a given state and, as such, no more requires a cause than does the retention of rest (except if retention of a state be itself counted among the "causes," as indeed it can, as we shall see). What requires a cause is the change from motion to rest, or from rest to motion, or a change in motion itself. But what is a change in motion? This question can only be answered by reference to what defines the sameness of motion, its *unaltered* state.

A motion is defined by velocity and direction. Unaltered (uniform) velocity means that equal distances are covered in equal times; unaltered direction means progression in a straight line. Thus unaltered motion means uniform rectilinear motion. And the new proposition is that a moving body will continue to so move unless interfered with by an outside force. The elementary terms in both of those two defining aspects of motion—in velocity and direction—are space and time: both can be so combined in a geometrizing arithmetic that a given motion at a given moment is defined by a determinate quantity made up of these two terms. It is then a change in this quantity which constitutes a change of the motion, and the quantity of the change, again measured in terms of space and time, is a measure of the force that caused it. Thus any increase or decrease in velocity, and any change in direction, betrays the action of a force *added* to the force that keeps the body on its uniform rectilinear course: but the initial "force" to which the addition is made remains operative in the compound with its own unaltered quantity —i.e., the new motion is a composite of several motions.

V

All this is far from obvious. In fact, all appearances are on the side of the opposite, Aristotelian view. In our common experience, bodies do come to rest when the force propelling them ceases to act: the wagon does stop moving when no longer pulled or pushed; and the pulling or pushing, when done by us, is felt to produce the motion from moment to moment. Nor is there anything obvious about a circular motion not being a simple, unitary act. The Galilean revolution has this in common with the Copernican revolution that it replaces the testimony of the senses with an abstraction that directly contradicts but indirectly grounds it. Such an abstraction—and a highly artificial one—is the concept of a quantity of motion as an invisible object, treated like an abiding unit that can be combined with other such units, added to or subtracted from them, much as static, numerable entities can. It leads directly to the cardinal, no less artificial, concept of composite motions whose ultimate elements are simple motions, viz., uniform rectilinear motions. In particular, an accelerated motion (e.g., in free fall) is the cumulative sum of continuous increments of motion produced by the continuous operation of a force (e.g., gravity) which is at any moment a *new* cause (as to Aristotle was the force causing the mere continuation of a motion). And likewise, any curvilinear motion is a composite of at least two motions, a tangential and a radial, of which the first represents mere persistence in a state, and the second the continuous incremental input of new force— i.e., again "acceleration" (even if the resultant translatory velocity is uniform). Furthermore, the effect of any "single" input of force, once its work is done, can only be uniform rectilinear motion in which the increment and the antecedent are fused (as after the impact of one billiard ball on another). Or, the motion of a body at any one, infinitesimal moment of its progress is uniform rectilinear motion, and so the total (e.g., parabolic) trajectory can be conceived as the composite of an infinite number of "simple" (tangential) motions with varying values. Its "law" is then the law of the *variation*, which can be computed from the forces at work—as the forces in turn can be inferred from the geometrical properties of the path.

Finally, in a last step of abstraction, the duality velocity-direction which defines motion, when considered with respect to force and the changes produced by it, reduces to one single datum vis-à-vis the concept of *acceleration* to which in turn all possible *changes* of this datum reduce: increase as well as decrease of velocity, as well as any change of direction, can equally be represented as different values of "acceleration." And velocity (absorbing "direction" into its concept) comprises *rest* among its possible values simply as the zero value: the concept of "inertia" extends as a constant magnitude over all those values. All this is set in a *neutral*, homogeneous space continuum which knows of no privileged directions, and it concerns bodies with no preference for specific places, differing—with respect to mechanics—only in certain quantitatively specifiable magnitudes.

This novel conceptual scheme—whose novelty and boldness cannot be overstated—was clearly one grand prescription for the mathematical analysis and synthesis of motions (what was first called the "resolutive" and the "compositive" methods). Motions, being resultants, could be resolved into their simple components and, vice versa, constructed from them. Three important developments promoted by the new conceptualization should be noted here.

The first is the geometrizing of nature and consequently the mathematization of physics. Kepler, Galileo, and Descartes were equally convinced (though for different ostensible reasons) that geometry is the true language of nature and must therefore also be the method of its investigation, which is to decode its sensuous message. This growing conviction was raised by Descartes to the dignity of a metaphysical principle when he split reality into the two mutually exclusive realms of the *res cogitans* and the *res extensa*—the world of mind and the world of matter: the latter is in its essence nothing but "extension"; therefore nothing but determinations of extension, i.e., geometry, are required for a scientific knowledge of the external world. (The defect of this overstatement was that it left no room for the concept of energy, which is an "intensive" rather than a purely "extensive" term: Leibniz and others set out to remedy this defect of Cartesian extremism.)

Secondly the program of an analysis of motions necessitated a new mathematics, of which Descartes' analytical geometry was only the first step. The reduction of a complex motion to simple motions involves, as we have seen, breaking it down to infinitesimal portions (any curvilinear motion being a composite of an infinite number of tangential motions which, of course, must be conceived as infinitesimal): the answer to the mathematical task thereby posed was the infinitesimal calculus, invented simultaneously (or almost so) by Leibniz and Newton.

Thirdly, the conceptual analysis of motions permitted an actual dissociation of its component parts in suitably set up *experiments*: it thus inspired an entirely new method of discovery and verification, the experimental method. It must be realized that the controlled experiment, in which an artificially simplified nature is set to work so as to display the action of single factors, is *toto coelo* different from the observation, however attentive, of "natural" nature in its unprocessed complexity, and also from any nonanalytical trying-out of its responses to our probing interventions. It essentially differs, in one word, from *experience* as such. What the experiment aims at—the isolation of factors and their quantification—and is designed to secure by the selective arrangement of conditions, *presupposes* the theoretical analytic we have described; and it repays theory by its results. Galileo's inclined plane, which made the vertical component in the motion of the balls clearly distinguishable from the horizontal, is a classical example of such analytic experiment.

VI

It only remains to draw one last inference so as to have this account of the conceptual revolution terminate in a full-fledged mechanics of nature. To use abridged labels, it means completing the Galilean with the Newtonian record. There recurred in our account one term which is obviously crucial but is not a geometrical term and not resolvable into purely geometrical, i.e., space-time, terms; the concept of "force." It lurks in the concepts of both acceleration and inertia. We may define (measure) a force by the magnitude of acceleration which it can impart *to a given body*; or we may define the inertia of a body (i.e., its "force" of resisting a change in its state of motion or rest) by the magnitude of acceleration that can be imparted to it *by a given force*. In either case we have geometrized the action of force through the concept of acceleration, which is constituted of space-time magnitudes purely, and have thereby "defined" the force in question—acting force in one case, resisting force in the other. But in either case we have a nongeometrical referent in the definition as a primitive datum (*a given body*) alternative to its counterpart in the other definition (*a given force*): what remains primitive datum (*definiens*) in one is defined in the other, and vice versa; and we cannot geometrize both data together in one definition without falling into an empty circle. In other words, the dynamic account is incomplete without a concept of the "intensive" order added to those of the "extensive" order. This clearly concerns the mysterious concept of force, and more particularly, in the case of inertia, the seat of force. The slowly emerging concept of *mass* filled the desideratum. Although Newton simply defined it as "the quantity of matter," it actually denotes in its physical function a *dynamic* quantity, viz., the quantity of inertia—a magnitude independent (not a variable) of size, shape, place, motion, temperature or any of the variables by which we may otherwise determine the being of a body. "Mass" in short denotes a *power* somehow identical with the essence of matter—which thus becomes an *ens realissimum* in its own right, with respect to whose stubborn, primary invariance all other determinations become shifting and secondary. This is worlds apart from the Aristotelian scheme of substantial forms, qualities, accidents (etc.) determining an indifferent "prime matter" which becomes "real" only insofar as thus determined. It also is vastly different from ancient atomism which, lacking in its concept of matter this dynamic aspect of "mass," could never evolve into a physics.

Since inertia (= "quantity of matter"), when conjoined with motion, yields momentum, i.e. kinetic energy, it follows that mass, space, and time—or, with the last two united in one term, *mass and acceleration*— are the sufficient terms for a mechanics of impact; and through the equation of mass with weight also for a mechanics of attraction, viz., of terrestrial motions involving free fall. This joint mechanics is thus constituted by two geometrical (formal) quantities, space and time, and one nongeometrical quantity, mass, the last of which represents the core reality; but all three are *quantities*, subject to the simple law of numerical addition.

What Newton then achieved by transforming the merely terrestrial concept of "weight" (as a force directed to the center of the earth) into the universal concept of "gravitation" (as a force acting between all bodies in strict correlation with mass and distance) was to extend the unitary mechanics of "mass and acceleration" to the limits of the universe. "Mass" here assumed a doubly dynamical meaning, matter thus becoming the seat of *two* forces—inertia and gravitation—whose conjunction and equivalence in one entity (so that one can alternate with the other in defining a given mass) remained the unexplained mystery of Newtonian physics. But mystery or not, by its irrefutable evidence the celestial orbits were assimilated to the trajectories of terrestrial missiles: astronomy and ballistics had become branches of one and the same science. For the epistemologist we may add that this science of nature represented the union of a priori with a posteriori elements: while space, time, and motion *in abstracto* present a pure mathematical manifold for a priori construction, inertia and gravity, the dynamical ingredients of mass (and the same goes for the electromagnetic forces discovered later) fall as to their existence and their actual values in the realm of irreducible empirical fact; the gravitational constant, e.g., is a purely empirical magnitude. Insofar was Descartes' excessive rationalism rectified. But those empirical constants operate in the mathematical continuum, their values expressible in its terms, and so physics could be mathematized *with* these rationally recalcitrant facts.

VII

After this analytical summary of the direct conceptual content of the theoretical revolution in dynamics, a brief metaphysical evaluation of it is in order. We said at one point that what the innovation was originally about was not the time-honored principle of causality per se, but the conception of change. We must now add that the altered conception of what constitutes a change, i.e., an *effect*, naturally reacted on the conception of what constitutes a *cause*. Now, "change" had been redefined as acceleration of mass, and to this its primary form all (phenomenally) other kinds of change—such as qualitative change—must be reduced. Accordingly, "cause" is redefined as that which imparts (or resists) acceleration—i.e., as *force*, whose *sole effect* is acceleration (or its negative), and whose magnitude is precisely measured by the amount of acceleration it imparts to a given mass: and to this, its primary form, all (phenomenally) other kinds of "causes" must be reduced. From this simple correlation, extraordinary physical as well as metaphysical consequences follow.

First of all, with the quantifiability of all changes in nature, the cause-effect relation has become a quantitative relation, namely that of strict *quantitative equivalence* of cause and effect. To be the sufficient cause for an event means to be sufficient in quantity for the quantity of change which that event represents, i.e., of equal quantity. The presence of such a quantity is therefore the sole—necessary as well as sufficient—cause for the effect: its antecedence is to be postulated when the latter is the given; contrariwise, the succeeding of the latter is to be deduced (predicted) when the former is the given. Consequently, any physical state can be represented as a determinate configuration of masses and forces from which the next state follows necessarily and—more important—can be computed rigorously by a calculus of the represented magnitudes, if all of them are known.

However, to the last qualification there must be added this one: *unless* in the interval new magnitudes of this sort—forces or masses—appear spontaneously *ex nihilo* or given ones vanish into nothing. *That this does not, nay cannot, happen* follows in no way logically from the new system of concepts themselves; but it is their necessary metaphysical corollary, for without it, i.e., with the possibility of physical magnitudes appearing and disappearing, the assertion of quantitative equivalence and of computability remains vacuous. The *constancy* of matter and energy (or matter-plus-energy) is therefore an indispensable axiom of modern science. In its implied negative aspect it means the denial of the possibility of any nonphysical, e.g., spiritual, cause intervening in the physical course of things—in short, the denial of the possibility of *miracles*, which in the last analysis involve either creation or annihilation. That they themselves would be proceeding from a cause, e.g., the will of God (thus complying with the general principle of sufficient reason), does not make them any the more reconcilable with the new idea of causality in nature, which demands that every physical event be accounted for by purely physical, i.e. material, antecedents in the quantitative sense we have described. This exclusion of miracles, generally and tacitly held at least as a methodological assumption, Spinoza alone of the philosophers of the new creed—its *enfant terrible*—had the boldness or indiscretion to spell out as a metaphysical certainty.[5]

---

[5]And a metaphysical proposition it is: Kant's later, ingenious (one is tempted to say cunning) attempt to transform it into an *epistemological* proposition, whereby the impossibility of miracles means that they cannot be "experienced," thus evading the metaphysical issue, remains as far below Spinoza in metaphysical straight-forwardness as it is above him in subtlety. The attempt, incidentally, is a failure. For it is simply not true that a sudden emergence "from nothing" of a substance or

But just such a "miracle," by the terms now defined, would be the most ordinary initiation of an external change by an act of *human*, no less than by one of divine, will, because this would start a new causal train "from nothing" as far as physical antecedents are concerned: and the new metaphysics of science showed its determination by braving the clash with this our most immediate and common experience (viz., that we are authors of our actions from purpose and design) and by going to extravagant lengths of metaphysical construction so as to be able to relegate this basic experience to the realm of mere appearance. Here the fideistic quality of the new stance comes into the open, as both assertions—that of "subjective" experience, and that of "objective" science which denies it—are equally beyond proof or disproof.

Thus not only intervention by a transcendent, extramundane cause but also any intramundane mental causality is ruled out. Things do not stop there. Ruled out from the mundane universe are, together with the causal efficacy of *human* purpose, *end-causes* of any kind—i.e., *teleology* as such which, in whatever attenuated analogy of striving and satisfaction it is conceived, must share with human purpose a transmaterial, quasi-mental aspect. That Nature is devoid of even the most unconscious bias toward goals, and of the formative power to serve it—that final and formal causes are struck from its inventory and only efficient causes left, follows simply from the principle of quantitative equivalence and invariance in cause-effect relations which is the distinguishing mark of

---

force, or any *exceptional* violation of the constancy laws, would explode the ordered totality of our "experience" and reduce its unity to a shambles. True, it would be a startling and disconcerting experience, but then, miracles are supposed to be startling and disconcerting. The simple truth is that the concept of rules (other than logical) is perfectly compatible with the concept of exceptions therefrom; and should they happen, they would be experienceable precisely *as such*, i.e., against the background of prevailing rule. Admittedly there can be no science of the exceptions (since science is concerned with the rules), but whoever claimed that there is a science of miracles? Only when "experience" is *defined* as (and thereby restricted to) the context of that which conforms to universal rules throughout and thus is indefinitely open to scientific correlations, is it true—but also trivial—to say that miracles do not fall within "experience": it is a tautological statement. Such a tautology does not take one off the metaphysical hook. In honest fact, the conviction that miracles never happen is as much a "faith" as is the belief that they may happen. The former is superior only as an injunction to always *seek* for a natural explanation—which the latter may tempt one to neglect (Spinoza's argument of the *asylum ignorantiae*). However, the injunction itself means that what *seems* to be a miracle must not be accepted as such: but that "seeming" itself is an experience, and the confidence that it will eventually be disproved is only a posteriori vindicated. The exclusion of miracles is thus a veritable article of faith in the metaphysics of science: so much so that (as shown in the next paragraph) it is pitted against a class of "miracles" nobody can deny to constantly experience himself—without this fact, of course, proving their truth, for there can be deceptive experience.

the "determinism" of modern science. This determinism must not be confounded with any premodern beliefs in fate, predestination, predetermination, and the like. It actually is opposed to them because it excludes the future-reference indicated in the prefix pre-. It means that always and only the immediate antecedent determines the next instant, that there are no long-term trends toward something, but only a transfer of the mass-energy sum from moment to moment, and the *vis a tergo* of this propagation—in short, no pull of the future, only the push of the past.

VIII

The plain picture of classical, Newtonian mechanics here drawn, whose prime data were nothing but mass and acceleration, was later, especially from the nineteenth century on, made more complex by the addition of electromagnetism, radiating energy, atomic valency, nuclear forces, molecular structure. Though a far cry from the simplification of the original "matter and motion" formula of Descartes, the more advanced scheme in all its enormously increased subtlety still adheres to the basic postulates of quantitative cause-effect equivalence assured by constancy laws, the linear transfer of given mass-energy magnitudes through the progression of time, and the consequent fitness of mathematical computation to all natural phenomena. For the foundation of the technological approach, which is predicated on these postulates, the original simplification sufficed to provide the essential condition. Its delineation therefore also suffices for our purpose. Let us further spell out some of its implications, speculative and methodological, which prepared the ground for the technological revolution.

The concept of the one, neutral, quantitative world stuff of which reality is essentially made is matched, so we found, by the concept of the sameness of the laws that govern this spread of bodies through space and determine their changes: *one set of laws* is sufficient for *all* phenomena. There are no different orders or classes of things calling for the application of different types of laws and thus for different modes of knowledge. The *reduction* of every type of phenomenal change to one basic set of laws means, of course, reduction to those laws which govern the basic level of reality, viz., pure matter distributed in space, bodies interacting according to their geometrical configuration. These laws are the laws of mechanics, and the idea of the world machine arises. It is to be noted that it preceded the machine age.

For the gain of calculability the cosmic mechanism paid with certain losses that are entailed by its *negative* aspects. Of these we mentioned the discarding of the idea of a hierarchical order and the denial of teleology. Nature is not a place where one can look for ends. Efficient cause knows no preference of outcomes: the complete absence of final causes means that nature is indifferent to distinctions of value. It cannot be thwarted because it has nothing to achieve. It only proceeds—and its process is blind. Its "necessity" is not that of compulsion but the mere absence of alternatives to the type of inter-connection by which all things operate—and by which they can be known. Thus the object of knowledge—the whole ceaseless drama of creation, be it the universe, terrestrial nature, or living things—is divested of any "will" of its own. The regularity which makes it knowable makes it meaningless at the same time. With the last trace of anthropomorphism expunged, nature retains no analogy to what man is aware of in himself, namely, that one direction is preferred to another and that outcomes make a difference, some being fulfillments and others failures. In the working of things there are no better or worse results—indeed there is no "good" or "bad" in nature, but only that which must be and therefore is. Again Spinoza was the first to pronounce this pitiless truth.

From this follows that there is nothing terminal in nature—and thus no "results" at all, other than the stage just reached at the moment which we happen to consider. None of the formations that make their appearance in the ongoing transactions, no passing configuration more than another, has a claim to representing the appointed terminus of a natural process. Whatever comes to be has only the validity of happening to be the consequence of what likewise happened to be a consequence before. The solar system itself, which Newton still looked upon as a definitive, created order when he analyzed the mechanics of its working, was later (by Kant and Laplace) conceived to have originated by the same mechanics from some unordered primal state: according to the basic nature of the causality involved in its genesis no less than in its function, it represents not an achievement, a "realization," but merely a dynamic equilibrium that has worked itself out in the long sequence of interactions among the elements. A different initial distribution of these would have resulted in a different solar system or none at all—and the overall system of nature as a balance of forces would be none the worse for it. There is nothing providential in the disposition of planets that in fact did evolve, and in that of the earth in particular with its suitability for life. Some configuration had to arise, and from the random concurrence of many causes it happened to be this.

Now this concept that all formations in nature are in a certain sense "accidental," though "necessary" in terms of their causal antecedents, that there is nothing intentional or terminal in whatever arises, applies in the Darwinian extension of Newtonian physics also to the *life* forms, not excluding *man*. What holds for the structures and entities of inanimate nature: that they are the consequence of a history of aggregate mechanics that goes on beyond them to ever new configurations of matter, so that any given configuration is nothing but a point of passage to another and yet another, and none the expression of an idea at work— this pattern was extended by Darwinism to the sphere of the living world. There, too, a certain continuous mechanics operates, whose seemingly stable effects astound us by their complexity and functional subtlety; and among these unplanned products, elaborate beyond any justification of need, are we ourselves—we who harbor purpose, intention, preference, love and hate, joy and grief. But that which brought this about, us and all the other living creatures, is not affected by any of those feelings nor motivated by an inner direction toward them. No creative urge is satisfied, no aiming finds or misses its mark. It just so happened that in the protracted interplay of random mutation and natural selection there emerge forms upon forms, and the fact that man is among them is a mere oddity. Speaking cosmically and in terms of mere natural categories, there is nothing in nature, conceived as a great automatism of indifferent forces, which predisposed it toward this event, and no interest was invested in its coming to pass. Let us now turn to the bearing of all this on the fostering of the technological attitude.

IX

What has neither will nor wisdom and is indifferent to itself solicits no respect. Awe before nature's mystery gives way to the disenchanted knowingness which grows with the success of the analysis of all things into their primitive conditions and factors. The powers that produce those things are powerless to impart a sanction to them: thus their knowledge imparts no regard for them. On the contrary, it removes whatever protection they may have enjoyed in a prescientific view. The implication this has for man's active commerce with the equalized manifold is obvious. If nature sanctions nothing, then it permits everything. Whatever man does to it, he does not violate an immanent integrity, to which it and all its works have lost title. In a nature that is its own perpetual accident, each thing can as well be other than it is without being any the less natural. Nature is not a norm (which to Aristotle it was), and a monstrosity is as natural as any "normal" growth. There is only the extrinsic necessity of causal determination, no intrinsic validity of its results.

Furthermore, if nature is mere object and in no sense subject, if it is devoid of "will," then man remains as the sole subject and the sole will. The world, after first having become the object of man's knowledge, becomes the object of his will, and his knowledge is put in the service of his will. And the will, of course, is a will for power over things. The heavens no longer declare the glory of God; but the materials of nature are ready for the use of man.

This is one train of reasoning that shows how the scientific revolution was intrinsically ready for the technological turn given to it later. Other, less spiritual and more technical aspects of the new science pointed the same way. I mention two, the role of analysis and that of experiment. The analysis of any complex phenomenon into its simplest geometrical, material, and dynamical factors is tantamount to finding out how even the most sophisticated natural entity comes about—is *brought* about— from the collocation of primitive components. But knowing how a thing is made up of its primitive elements leads of itself to knowing how one can make it up oneself out of those elements. The passage from analytical knowledge to making, i.e., to providing the requisite components and manipulating them so as to secure the desired results—the passage, in short, from analysis to synthesis is open on principle whenever the former is completed in a given case. And so is the passage from experiment as a means of knowledge to applied science as a means of use. Practice in the service of theory, which is what experiments are, is readily converted into theory, in the service of practice, which by now most of "science" almost automatically becomes.

Nevertheless, logical consequence that it was from the new scientific conception of the universe, foretold and urged by such philosophical exponents of it as Bacon and Descartes—in the actual course of history it took technology rather long to seize upon this momentous potential. Not for almost two centuries did the two streams join and effectively interpenetrate.

X

It is a common misconception that the evolutions of modern science and modern technology went hand in hand. The truth is that the great, theoretical breakthrough to modern science occurred in the seventeenth century, while the breakthrough of mature science into technology, and thereby the rise of modern, science-infused technology itself, happened in the nineteenth century. What happened in between?

The question involves the impact which science may have had on technology or vice versa. Let us begin with mechanics, the oldest branch of modern science. As a theory, it meant preeminently celestial mechanics, with such very general terrestrial applications as the understanding of free fall, ballistic trajectories, and the like—in short, phenomena exemplifying the general laws of kinetics. As to man-made *machines*, their example was used in theoretical discourse to illustrate cosmic (and sometimes biological) mechanics: but the theory of cosmic mechanics was not used for the designing of machines. Descartes, for the purpose of illustrating matters of theory, showed particular interest in automata. Such as existed in his time were not for work but for the amusement of court society, the one exception being clocks, the favorite example in certain deterministic speculations and later in the description of the whole universe. The clock also was the first case where findings of the new theory of mechanics were applied to the improvement of an existing, practically important mechanism (in the introduction of the pendulum by Huyghens). This was technologically applied theory, but the mechanism in question itself is for a *cognitive* purpose, viz., measuring time, and not for performing work. The same goes for most of the inventions closely related to the progress of knowledge, notably the optical instruments, which were *for* rather than *from* the progress of scientific theory. All instruments of this class—chronometers, telescopes, microscopes, to which may be added the compass—whether used in the furtherance of theory or for practical ends, were in themselves "theoretical" rather than "practical" implements in that their function was cognitive, and not that of effecting physical change.[6] Only gunpowder, among the crucial technical innovations of the modern beginnings, falls into the latter class, and its "invention," like that of the compass, was entirely "unscientific"; both found their theories only centuries later. For the long first phase of the growth and perfection of classical mechanics, it generally holds that the artificial that happened to be there served to further the understanding of the natural, and not the scientifically understood natural to promote the inventive expansion of the artificial.[7]

[6]They were in fact called "philosophical instruments," also "metaphysical instruments." James Watt in his youth was apprenticed to the trade of philosophical-instrument maker (he later worked as a mathematical-instrument maker). There is a nice symbolism in the fact that the philosophical-instrument maker became the first maker of the new, nonphilosophical, power-generating and work-producing machine.

[7]There are, of course, exceptions to this rule. The barometer, e.g., (again a "cognitive" instrument) was wholly a product of scientific theory. Suction pumps anteceded and stimulated the science that explained them, but then the new mechanics, doing away with the *horror vacui*, benefited their further development; and it is similar with the whole field of hydraulics. This does not materially alter the main point that classical mechanics arose, as a purely theoretical enterprise, independently of a machine technology and in turn did not lead to one in straight course.

What is true for mechanics holds even more for the younger and more slowly evolving branches of natural science. The investigation of magnetism and electricity, with all its theoretical progress, remained entirely nonpractical until the second half of the nineteenth century. (The only practical application before that was Benjamin Franklin's lightning rod.) Thermodynamics, far from influencing the initial evolution of thermal machines, had to wait for their arrival to come into being—*vide* the persistence of the search for a *perpetuum mobile* into the nineteenth century. And the steadily growing sciences of zoology, botany, mineralogy, geology, had in nobody's mind any conceivable technological application: they were descriptive, classificatory, and historical. Only when the first two were by geneticism transformed from morphological into causal systems and subsumed under the norms of classical mechanics (in a bold extension of its terms), could the idea of a science-informed biological technology arise. This is happening just now, in the latter half of our twentieth century. Any field of natural knowledge, so it seems, has to be assimilated to physics before it becomes amenable to a scientific technology. Thus for chemistry too, its nineteenth century transformation into a branch of physics was required to set a systematic chemical technology afoot. Medicine alone, and naturally, was always an intimate fusion of theory and practice, and the increasingly scientific inquiries into the human body were never undertaken without regard to their use in the art of healing (and indeed never by other than medical men). To the extent, then, that medicine can be called a "technology" (a moot point), evolving modern medicine would be the first case of a scientific technology.[8]

The last, somewhat special case apart, we may sum up that science did not significantly inspire technology before the nineteenth century, while receiving some help from it in the form of investigative instruments. Technology itself moved forward in those centuries on its own. It had been making strides since the Middle Ages and continued to do so without the aid of science. Wind- and watermills, improved sailing vessels and sailing techniques, compass, loom, gunpowder, canon, metal alloys, deep mining, porcelain—inventions were made in many fields before and after the advent of the new physics, with little if any impact of this event on the rate and kind of inventions. Engineering regained and then surpassed the level it had reached in later Roman times, and a general machine-consciousness developed (wonderfully and precosciously displayed by Leonardo da Vinci) unknown to the ancient

---

[8]Descartes, in his curious concern with health, had wished for this and indeed regarded the conquest of disease and the lengthening of life as the principal fruit to be expected of the new science of nature.

counterpart. But not before the industrial revolution did the *alliance of science and technology*—of the knowledge of nature and the art of invention—come about which Leonardo and Bacon had anticipated.

Bacon's is a classical case of the combination of prescience and blissful ignorance which seems to be necessary for mortal man to entertain a grand vision. His vision was that the new knowledge of nature will make man master over his environment. Bacon's grasp of the nature of this knowledge itself, untouched by the spirit of Galilean analysis, was strangely imperfect, and his own prescriptions would never have led to the results he expected from them. Yet, in a kind of prophetic anticipation of what was to come much later, he proclaimed that knowledge is power, and that it is the aim of knowledge to advance man's earthly estate, to conquer human "necessity and misery" by subjecting nature to his more complete use. With this vision went the belief that man's power over nature would end men's power over men, as this would become redundant through the wealth which conquered nature would yield for all. Bacon is thus the first of a new breed of philosophers (the *philosophes*) whose *optimistic* creed—the creed of progress—challenged the pessimistic wisdom of all previous philosophy and religion. Some pessimism had always tinged the assessment of man and of the prospects of his enterprises by the thinkers of the past. Optimism, as confidence in man, in his powers and his natural goodness, is the signature of modernity. No pleader of a revolution can afford to suspect the revenges which nature—human and environmental—may hold in store, in the immense complexity of things and the unfathomable abyss of the heart, for the planner of radical change. We act blindly, and such is our condition that even the light of knowledge becomes a means of our blindness. We late-comers, tasters of the bitterness of the Baconian fruit, smitten with the wisdom that comes after the fact, may just be moving, with the burden of science on our shoulders, into a humbler, postmodern age. The science we take with us will still be that which Bacon, unsuspecting of the darker consequences, was the first to conceive of as a utilitarian tool of civilization, a collective enterprise of society, institutionalized, organized, split up into subcontracted tasks, its results fit for the production of wealth and the destruction thereof, for the furtherance of life and the annihilation thereof. Bacon, and the still naiver innocents after him, failed to remember the simple Aristotelian insight (with which the "pessimistic" Leonardo was still deeply imbued) that any science is of contraries—of the object and its opposite: if of good, then also of evil, if of building, then also of destroying, if of health, then also of disease, if of life, then also of death: from which alone it would seem to follow that only in the hands of angels would the power of science be sure to be for the good only. Even there, Lucifer comes to mind.

XI

Modern technology, in the sense which makes it different from all previous technology, was touched off by the industrial revolution, which itself was touched off by social and economic developments entirely outside the theoretical development we have been considering. We need not deal with them here, except for saying that they determined the first distinctive feature of modern technology, namely the use of artificially generated and processed natural forces for the powering of work-producing machines. In this respect, the steam engine signified a radical departure from all former methods of saving human labor through animal traction, wind, and water. Other objects were added to this initial one as the new technology progressed, and the sequence of its stages reflects to some extent the development of the physical sciences on which technology increasingly drew.

1. As mechanics was the first form in which natural science had emerged, so the first stage of technology ushering in the industrial revolution was what we may call the *mechanical* stage. Its products were machines made of rigid parts and powered by the mechanics of volume expansion under heat—thus operating with the familiar solids and forces and on the familiar dynamical principles of classical mechanics. Their predominant use was in the manufacturing of goods and their transportation. The goods were the same as those hitherto produced manually. Changed was the mode of their production and therewith the whole condition of human labor; unchanged at first were the products themselves, which were the conventional ones of pre-industrial society, cloth in particular. Yet, a new class of goods was added to the conventional ones: the machines themselves, which had to be produced, thus giving rise to a new, specifically "mechanical" and predominantly metallurgical industry.

One cannot say that this initial stage of modern industrial technology depended in any decisive manner on the contemporary condition of physics. Much of its apparatus was designed by craftsmen with little succour from science. James Watt, it is true, was a keenly scientific mind, and the inventions that went into his steam engine were the result of much theoretical knowledge and reasoning. But nothing like the advanced mathematical techniques by which Newtonian celestial mechanics had been refined at the hands of such eighteenth century thinkers as Euler, Lagrange, and Laplace, was required for the calculations he had to carry out. Generally, in the first stages of modern technology, the engineer was an empiricist with a knowledge of materials and of the

broad rules of statics and dynamics, with no need for the degree of
sophistication which pure theory had attained by that time.[9]

This changed radically with the coming-of-age of the two younger
sciences of chemistry and electromagnetics, which all by themselves
originated their own, novel arts of large-scale utilization. The respective
technologies, springing as it were from Jupiter's head, without the inter-
mediary of any of Vulcan's pretheoretical crafts, were thus the first
wholly science-generated (and henceforward science-guided) technologies
in the history of mankind. They led, moreover, into entirely new *directions* of technological advance, with objects unanticipated *in kind* by the
human crafts of the past. Opening up hitherto unknown domains for
manipulation and possible artifacts, these new technologies became goal-
setting rather than merely goal-serving: they made the very possibility
of such goals known before even their desirability could be conceived,
whereas all previous technology, whether stationary or progressing, had
been in the service of familiar goals, and even the inventor used to work
toward objectives always thought of and desired. Now for the first time,
discovery and invention *preceded* not only the power but the very will
for what they made possible—and imposed the unanticipated possibilities
on the future will. Compared with this, even the steam engine had been
conventional.

2. There is little to choose in point of chronological precedence between chemical and electrical technology as they arose side by side in
the latter half of the nineteenth century, and we take chemistry first
for mere reasons of theoretical convenience. Chemical industry, then, is
in our survey the first case of an industry really originating from scientific discoveries; and in it, scientific and industrial-technological progress,
hitherto apart, came together definitively and inseparably. Here for the
first time the scientific laboratory and the manufacturing plant, that is,
small-scale investigation and large-scale application, became parts of one
intertwined venture—and by no means with unilateral dependence of
the practical on the theoretical side. Increasingly the tasks of research
were set by the interests of industry, and even when not directly undertaken in their service, the idea of applicability was never far from the
researcher's mind. In other words, scientific experiment here ceased to
be a purely theoretical activity, and the hidden practical implication
which its manipulative aspect always had beyond the cognitive one came
to the fore.

[9]Anyone who has admired Thomas Telford's (1757–1834) magnificent suspension
bridge across the Menai Straits in Wales (begun in 1820), and then learns how little
theory and scientific calculation went into its construction, must be struck by the
relative independence, at this stage, of bold technological achievement from scientific
underpinning.

This is not the only novelty of chemical technology. There is a significant difference between mechanical and chemical technology in the *depth* of man's intervention in the working of nature. In the chemical stage, man does more than construct machinery from natural materials and use natural forces as sources of power. In chemistry he changes the *substances* of nature and even comes to synthesize substances which nature never knew. At first—e.g., in the dye, fertilizer, and pharmaceutical industries—the older idea that art imitates nature, reinforces nature, or provides substitutes for it, seemed still to hold. But with the advent of molecular engineering man assumed a more sovereign role, involving a deeper meddling with the patterns of nature—indeed a redesigning of such patterns. We now are in an age where by imposed dispositions of molecules, substances can be made to specification—substances nature might produce but in fact does not produce. Man steps into nature's shoes, and from utilizing and exploiting he advances to creating. This is more than merely shaping things. Artificiality enters the heart of matter.

Also, technology here changes not merely the mode of production but the nature of the products themselves. With its new, synthetic substances, it introduces things unknown before into daily use and thoroughly refashions the habits of consumption. This is the general course of technology, which can be observed in its "mechanical" branch as well: starting as a labor-saving method with the multiplication of conventional goods, it later added machines themselves to the consumer goods with which men lead their lives.

3. The growth of artificiality is even more pronounced in *electrical* technology. Here the dependence on science in the very conception of the "object" to be dealt with is complete. The "matter" of chemistry is still the concrete, corporeal stuff of our natural experience; and chemical practice has at least a prescientific forerunner in all the combining, refining, and other processing of natural substances which had been practiced as far back as pottery, metallurgy, and wine-making go in the history of mankind. Also, scientific chemistry evolved in an intimate, reciprocal relationship of theoretical and practical progress. By contrast, there just was no experience of such a thing as electricity, let alone any dealing with it, before science discovered and investigated it; and even then utilization had to wait until theory was to all intents and purposes complete. The mere technique of the generation, distribution, and kinetic transformation of electrical power calls for the full armor of sophisticated theory. Electrical technology is thus the first that was wholly and *unilaterally* science-generated. Its industrial purpose, to be sure, was originally no different from that of the first, "mechanical" stage of modern

technology represented by the steam engine: to supply *motive power* for the propulsion of machines.[10] But whereas heat and steam are familiar objects of sensuous experience, and their force is bodily displayed in nature, electricity is an abstract entity, disembodied, immaterial, unseen;[11] and to all practical intents, viz., as a manipulable force, it is entirely an artificial creation of man.

4. The height of abstraction is reached in the passage from electric to *electronic* technology, where purpose changes as well. In terms of technique, it is the difference between high and low tension engineering; in terms of purpose, the difference between power and communication engineering. In its theoretical as well as its practical aspects electronics marks a genuinely new phase of the scientific-technological revolution. Compared with its subtlety, as also the delicacy of its apparatus, everything which came before seems crude—and almost "natural." To "imitate nature" had been one of the watchwords of the early pioneers. When Leonardo grappled with the problem of human flight, when Bacon envisaged nature "commanded by being obeyed," when Descartes spoke of machines yet to be invented—they liked to think of this as a systematic imitation of nature by man (of her methods, to be sure, not her products). As the technological revolution progresses with an ever increasing artificiality of its means as well as its ends, the image becomes more and more obsolete. To appreciate the point, take a look at the man-made satellites now in orbit. In one sense, they are indeed an imitation of celestial mechanics—Newton's laws finally verified by cosmic experiment: astronomy, for millenia the most purely contemplative of the physical sciences, turned into a practical art! Yet, astonishing as it is, the astronomic "imitation," with all the power and finesse of techniques that went into it, is the least interesting aspect of those entities. Their true interest lies in the instruments they carry

---

[10]Electricity is itself generated by motive power, whose original source again is either heat, conventionally produced by the burning of fossil fuels, or the gravity of water, whose level differential in turn stems from solar heat: from these primitive forms of physical activity, heat and motion, electricity is derived, and into them it is reconverted when doing work. It is thus an artificially interposed link in the chain of energy transformations and *not yet* an aboriginal source of power (which it may yet become). Since also the fossil fuels are stored-up solar energy, this is still today the ultimate source of all the power that runs our tellurian technology. Atomic energy is just beginning to make a dent in this monopoly. Up to now, in its nonexplosive use, it reaches the desired electrical stage still via the primitive, intermediate stage of heat and the mechanical power generated by it; but this need not be the last word in power technology.

[11]This created amusing legal problems at first, and special legislation had to be enacted to bring the tapping of power lines, where no corporeal object is carried away, under the concept of "theft."

through the voids of space—and there is nothing in all nature which even remotely foreshadows the kind of things that now ride the heavenly spheres. Man's imitative "practical astronomy" merely provides the vehicle for something else with which he sovereignly passes beyond all the models and usages of known nature. Electronics indeed creates a range of objects imitating nothing and progressively added to by pure invention. And no less invented are the ends which they serve. Power engineering and chemistry for the most part still answered to the natural needs of man: for food, clothing, shelter, locomotion, and so forth. Communication engineering answers to needs of information and control solely created by the civilization itself which made this technology possible and, once started, imperative. The novelty of the means continues to engender no less novel ends—both becoming as necessary to the functioning of the civilization that spawned them as they would have been redundant for any former one. Computers or radars would have been condemned to idleness had they somehow been dropped into the world of only one hundred years ago. Today's world can no longer do without them.

Compared with the extreme artificiality of our technologically constituted, electronically integrated environment and corresponding habits, the Greek *polis*—this supreme work of collective "art" wrested from nature in the first flowering of Western man—has almost the naturalness and intimacy of an organic fact. For this reason, alas, its wisdom is lost to us and its paradigm no longer valid. Technology is stronger than politics. It has become what Napoleon said politics was: destiny.

XII

There may be in the offing another, conceivably the last, stage of the technological revolution. When we check what sciences have successively contributed to it—mechanics, chemistry, electronics, and, just beginning, nuclear physics—we notice the absence of one great branch of natural science: biology. Are we, perhaps, on the verge of another—conceivably the last—stage of that revolution, based on biological knowledge and wielding an engineering art which, this time, has man himself for its object? This has become a theorectical possibility with the advent of molecular biology and its understanding of genetic programming; and it has been rendered morally possible by the metaphysical neutralizing of man. But the latter, while giving us the licence to do as we wish, at the same time denies us the guidance for knowing what to wish. Since the same evolutionary doctrine of which genetics is a cornerstone has deprived us of a valid image of man, the actual techniques, when they are ready, may find us strangely unready for their responsible use. Our being, if a mere *de facto* outcome of evolution, enjoys no definitive and defining essence, by whose light—if visible to us—we could choose or reject suggested engineering goals; or whose acknowledged though un-defined presence would at least hold us to respect for a *status quo* which our ignorance must take to embody that hidden essence. The anti-essentialism of prevailing theory surrenders our being to a freedom without norms. Thus the technological call of the new microbiology is the twofold one of physical feasibility and metaphysical admissibility. Assuming the genetic mechanism to be completely analyzed and its script finally decoded, we can set about rewriting the text. The specifications for the rewriting can come from any quarter, interest, or well-meaning belief of the hour. I do not know how close we are to the capability. Biologists vary in the estimate of its imminence. Most seem to expect its eventual arrival, few to doubt the right to use it; but no one can contend that we *must* use it. Under no Baconian pressure of coping with human necessity, which justified all previous technology, biological engineering—of the melioristic or creative sort—would be wholly gratui-tous. So we *could* desist. But, judging by the rhetoric of its prophets, the idea of taking our evolution into our own hands is intoxicating even to men of science, who should know better. In fact, no science is needed to tell us that "to navigate by a landmark tied to your ship's head is ultimately impossible."[12] Imagination boggles at what this Pandora's box might release. Speaking for myself, I fear not the abuses by evil power interests: I fear the well-wishers of mankind with their dreams of a glorious improvement of the race.

In any case, the idea of making-over Man is no longer fantastic, nor interdicted by an inviolable taboo. If and when *that* technological revolu-tion occurs, if technological power is really going to tinker with the central and elemental keys on which life will have to play its melody in generations of men to come (perhaps the only such melody in the uni-verse), then a reflection on what is humanly desirable and what should determine the choice—on "the image of man," in short—becomes an imperative more urgent than any ever inflicted on the understanding of mortal man. Philosophy, it must be confessed, is sadly unprepared for this—its first cosmic—task.

[12]Donald M. McKay in *Man and His Future*, a Ciba Foundation Volume (London, 1963), p. 286. See also C. S. Lewis, *The Abolition of Man* (New York: Macmillan, 1947) pp. 69ff.

4.
Socio-Economic Knowledge
and Ignorance of Goals

In a recent symposium "on economic knowledge," held in honor of a distinguished economist,[1] I was given the task of commenting on a subject that hovers somewhat on the margin of the economist's scientific interest, as "scientific" is nowadays understood, but which cannot fail to be central to his personal concern: the cognitive status of "ends" and, correlatively, the possible "objective" validation of the choices which

An earlier version of this essay was published in *Economic Means and Social Ends*, ed. Robert L. Heilbroner (Englewood Cliffs, N.J.: Prentice-Hall, 1969), with the title "Socio-Economic Knowledge and the Critique of Goals."

[1]The economist in question is my friend, Professor Adolph Lowe, whose book *On Economic Knowledge: Toward a Science of Political Economics* (New York: Harper & Row, 1965) was the subject of two interdisciplinary symposia held in New York in February and March 1968, at the New School for Social Research. At the second meeting, philosophers joined the social scientists in discussing questions of principle raised by Lowe's theory, and the present essay is, with minor alterations, the text of my contribution. Even where no explicit reference is made, the discourse is much related to Professor Lowe's ideas, written and unwritten, and more generally to the mode of thought they represent. My deep indebtedness to his thought remains undiminished by whatever critique is stimulated in the pursuit of the mutually shared theoretical goal.

My commentator at the symposium was Professor Abraham Edel, whose enlightening critical paper, "Ends, Commitments, and the Place of Ignorance," is included in *Economic Means and Social Ends*, the volume containing the papers of both symposia. Although Professor Lowe's concluding Rejoinder to his critics as well as the Edel paper both deserve to be taken account of by me in the open-ended discussion (of which my essay can be no more than a stage), nevertheless I have here let my original statement stand, as indeed I still stand by it in its essentials.

economic policy must make among them to set the terminal goals of its planning. On this matter our economist, in unison with most of his confreres, taking a leaf from the book of natural science, entertains the stance of austere abstention which nineteenth century positivism has made an axiomatic part of the scientific creed: value judgments have no place in scientific discourse; they are "unscientific"; science by its very terms cannot take the step from the "is" to the "ought." To this rule the theoretical economist feels as bound as his elder brother, the physicist; but unlike him he does so with regret. For the economist is aware that he deals after all with a sphere of activities inherently governed by ends. He is moreover aware that of late this sphere has come into a "freedom of choice"—not formerly enjoyed—among a plurality of possible, i.e. optional, goals beyond the mandatory, basic goal of mere subsistence; and that these goals are of such a kind that their realization, transcending the purely economic terms, must affect the total condition of man. He must be aware, therefore, that criteria of desirability among competing goals are all the more needed the more open the choices become and the more far-reaching the decisions to be made (with the need becoming more urgent still as choosing between the alternatives, optional as they are, is itself not optional at all): knowing all this, the economic theorist feels yet constrained to deny to his own science, to economic knowledge, the power to provide such criteria of choice and thus the authority to say "yes" or "no" to any ends proposed, excepting, of course, verdicts on mere feasibility. To the question, then, whether economic knowledge is to be the master or the servant of economic policy, the arbiter of its goals or their executor, the purist's answer is: the latter. It is the answer of scientific asceticism, observed for the sake of the purity of economics as a science. As such, it has to pronounce on means only, not on ends.

Still, the particular purist I had to comment on does not think that the determination of goals must therefore remain a matter of mere fancy, power interest, or chance. What none of the "positive" sciences of man—economics, political science, sociology, anthropology, psychology, biology—can provide, philosophy (happily, or alas, not a "science," yet a species of knowledge) is expected to provide: a knowledge of the "good life," objective criteria of choice based on such knowledge, a justification of ends, ultimate and intermediate. The following composite quotation fairly expresses the position I was supposed to respond to.

> Technological progress has greatly reduced the traditional pressures which left room for one state of economic welfare only. It is granting us for the first time "freedom of choice" [among a variety of feasible goal alternatives. We are thus required to make] specific decisions on

ends, for which no economic mechanism offers any criteria. [Economic policy] cannot be derived from intraeconomic considerations. It is the political or social philosopher who alone can vindicate the ends. . . . In a society of increasing wealth, decisions on welfare become his explicit business.[2]

In other words, goals, with respect to their comparative worth or obligatory claim, are not objects of economic knowledge and not to be adjudicated by it; but they are objects of philosophical knowledge, whence economics may borrow them as "givens," as "hypotheses" for its own reasoning. It was in this spirit of economic modesty and faith in philosophy that I, a non-economist and presumed philosopher, was asked to deal with the cognitive status of ends and values and, on the basis of what that status is found to be, with the question of valid approbation and condemnation of goals. It is the hoary question of a science of the "good" and the "bad," the "better" and the "worse," for man.

I

Let me say right away that I must, on behalf of philosophy, reciprocate the modesty and disclaim the competence so generously accorded. The historical record clearly discourages the expectation that philosophers can demonstrate a *summum bonum*, the ultimate purpose of man, an absolute scale of values, the authority of "oughts," and the like. Nor should economics (or political science, for that matter) be permitted to wash its hands of those questions entirely and, by shifting responsibility for them to the misty court of "philosophy," leave undone that part of the theoretical task—this side of the unattainable absolute—which in fact it can do, which does fall within its terms, and which therefore is part of its own business. Here indeed the so-called philosopher—that is, the thoughtful outsider—simply by being less immersed in the technicalities of the field, less encumbered (less intimidated, I might say) by its conventions than the insider, and therefore freer to reflect on principles, may be in a position to rectify the opinion of itself which a science such as economics develops by internal consensus, and perhaps to show that its limitations in the matter of judging goals are not quite as narrow as those which its own presently accepted rigorism or defeatism enjoins on its practitioners.

1. This at least is the main and not overly ambitious purpose I set

[2]Adolph Lowe, "The Normative Roots of Economic Values," *Human Values and Economic Policy*, ed. Sidney Hook (New York: New York University Press, 1967), pp. 177–78.

myself in this paper: to argue that a definite goal-commitment is constitutive for the economic field as such and therefore implicitly under-
written by any theory of the field; that from this built-in fundamental
commitment, some criteria for the evaluation of economic goals derive
which are entirely germane to economic knowledge at its most scientific;
and that their application goes a long way beyond the primitive, choice-
less goal of mere subsistence, extending well into the sphere of that
latter-day freedom of choice where our purist sees the economist resigned
to agnosticism and to awaiting instruction from the holders of power or
metaphysical truth. Thus, returning the compliment, the philosopher
returns the task where it belongs: to economic knowledge itself. At least
concerning what should *not* be—what goals ought to be resisted—the
economist may be able to speak with the authority of his theory: no
small matter in the uniquely modern situation where the "no" can become more important than the "yes" in answering the massive offer of
possible goals with which our novel powers besiege our "freedom of
choice."

2. So far my message, as one of normative duty and competence, will
seem to be cheering, in that it widens the conception of economic knowledge beyond the restrictive conception of its mere factual or instrumental
assignment. But, alas, my second purpose will be to suggest where the
real difficulty lies: *not* in determining the criteria for choosing among
goals, where the scientific purist sees it, but in providing the matter for
the *application* of those criteria—namely, valid anticipations of the final
state to which any long-term macro-goal will lead under the novel conditions of total and global impact. In other words, the real trouble, as I
see it, is our scientific inadequacy—more than just a temporary inadequacy—to the task of representing, with anything like demonstrative
or even inductive certainty, the alternatives between which the choices are
to be made, if they are to be between ultimate effects and not merely
proximate advantages.

"Instrumental analysis" seems to assume that, since the projected
terminal state is of our own designing, conceived and specified by us,
we should surely know it. Having laid down its terms ourselves, we are
at least certain what it is we are offering for acceptance or rejection,
agonizing as thereafter the choice may be, and difficult as may be the
task of devising the means for its implementation: the latter alone will
be our theoretical problem. It will be my contention that this assumption
that we know the final state by defining it through some select features
relevant to our choice—an assumption taken over from mechanical
engineering—is unwarranted in the field in which the economist must
make his projections. And since the adequately defined "final state" is
to function as the initial datum, as the "known" in the deductive-instru-

mental analysis, my contention means that this analysis will in turn be vitiated if its premise, the goal state (whose availability to knowledge the "instrumentalist" must take for granted), is in fact elusive. I may add that with the same principle of "total impact" operating all along the line, each deductive link (destined, in reverse order, to become an instrumental step, but representing in itself a total state of the system *at the time*) will be rendered equally doubtful in terms of *its* total effect.

What it comes to is that, in the last resort, the directed and "controlled" alternative is cognitively little better off than the "automatically" self-realizing one. In either case the "terminus"—whether projected for planning or merely expected from the observed trend of events—is spotlighted for our vision out of a darkness of collateral unknowns with which it is inextricably intertwined, unlike the terminal states of isolable and repeatable physical sequences. We *could*, I say, judge rationally end-states and decide their order of preferability *if* we had their full measure, but we haven't and are reduced to imaginative guessing. And when, on a guess, we do decide for any controlled target-alternative, we cannot gauge the full implications of our own progressive, mediating acts of control and thus predict with certainty their consequences.

This view of the state of affairs almost reverses that of the economic positivist. It places within "economic knowledge" what according to him transcends it—viz., standards for goal selection even without knowledge of the ultimate good (here the metaphysician is no better off than he)— and it doubts what he is confident of—namely, the competence of existing social science both to represent goal states adequately and to deduce the intermediate, instrumental states cogently. This skeptical reasoning, of course, applies only to the long-range, large-scale goal perspectives which our self-propelled technological powers press on us with their inherent trend to go "all the way," to carry each possibility to its extreme conclusion; and it is these quasi-utopian, quasi-eschatological perspectives, rather than the measured alternatives of our short-range, deliberate planning, that are the "goals" about which we will someday have to decide before they decide about us.

3. The paradox of our having to decide about ends we don't understand, about hypothetical and incompletely specified, yet unavoidable alternatives, will prompt some concluding surmises on the cautionary rather than "instrumental" role of economic theory and policy in our journey into the unknown.

II

I will now go step by step over the ground staked out in the preceding statement of purpose and try to argue the conclusions provisionally summarized there. What I have first to deal with is the alleged gulf between scientific truth and ends, obviously related to the concept of "value-free science" that is axiomatic to the social scientist as it is to the scientific fraternity as a whole. "It is intuitively obvious," writes Adolph Lowe, "that such a discussion [viz., concerning the choice of an economic macro-goal] will carry us beyond the realm of facts and factual relations into the region of value judgments—a region in which discursive think-ing, and thus scientific inquiry as the modern mind understands it, can-not by themselves offer final answers."[3] Well, not final, perhaps, but what science offers final answers on anything? Does "not final" amount to "none at all?"

1. Let us clarify the relation of values and ends (or goals); they are by no means the same, although they are often confused. We will begin with ends. An end is that for whose sake a thing exists and for whose produc-tion or preservation a process takes place or an action is undertaken. Thus a hammer exists for hammering, a digestive tract for digesting and thereby keeping the organism alive and in good shape; walking is done to get somewhere; a court of law sits in order to administer justice. Note that the ends or goals said in these cases to define the things or actions in question do so independently of their status as values, and that the statement of these ends does not involve value judgments on my part. I may deem a state of nature without hammers preferable to a state of civilization where nails are driven into walls; I may deplore the fact that lions are not vegetarians and therefore disapprove of digestive systems geared to the carnivorous mode of sustenance; I may think it better for people to stay where they are instead of always going elsewhere; I may take a dim view of any justice dispensed by courts of law—in brief, I may consider all those ends as worthless in themselves; nevertheless, I would still have to acknowledge them as the ends of the objects in question, considered on their own terms, *if* my description of them has been cor-rect. Adopting, as it were, the "point of view" of the objects themselves, I may then proceed from the recognition of their intrinsic ends to judg-ments on their greater or lesser adequacy for the achievement of those ends, and I may speak of a better or worse hammer, digestive condition, locomotive performance, or judiciary institution. These, indeed, are value judgments, but they are surely not based on value-decisions or goal-choices of my own: they are derived from the being of the objects them-selves, based on our understanding of them, not on our feelings about them. Thus we can form the concept of a specific "good" and its opposite and the grades in between for different entities and contexts of entities—provided that, and to the extent that, we can recognize "ends" as prop-erly belonging to the nature of the things themselves.

[3]See *Economic Means and Social Ends*, p. 18.

2. And here, of course, arises the first and most sweeping challenge to the claim of an objective value-knowledge: Can we rightly attribute ends to the nature of things? Of any things, if not of all things? As is well known, the answer was "yes" for a long time with the full backing of natural philosophy, and it increasingly has become "no" with the rise of modern natural science and *its* philosophy. Our query, of course, raises the problem of teleology. In the long-dominant Aristotelian view, the things of nature were activated by principles of goal-direction discernible in their normal modes of operation. This was most obviously so, of course, in the animate sphere, but by hypothesis also in inanimate nature; and again not only for each class of entities according to its specific nature, but also for their totality—i.e., the universe as a system of self-sustaining order assuring the balanced coexistence of its parts. In terms of such a view, it was possible to speak of realization, approximation, and frustration of natural ends; of perfection and imperfection; and of a rank order among those ends according to value criteria derived from the teleological stratification of the system itself. The "good," in other words, and the distinction of lesser and greater goods, had a foundation in the knowable nature of things—i.e., in their particular natures and the nature of the whole.

To be sure, even such a theory of reality leaves "man the knower" free to dissociate himself from the value-decision (as it were) of the universe, to counter it with his own, and in *his* order of preference, e.g., to set ignorance over knowledge, feeling over thinking, unconsciousness over consciousness, inanimate over animate existence, disorder over order, not-being over being. In the exercise of his right to dissent, he is free to entertain the wholesale conviction, *"Drum besser wärs, dass nichts entstünde."*[4] But this is the exercise of a private right and does not mate-

---

[4]This indubitable possibility points indeed to some sort of transcendence of value over all facts—an ultimate arbitrariness or freedom in value-*option* (even vis-à-vis a universe whose facts do embody value). No argument can establish that being is better than not-being, or refute the contention that God had better not created the world. There is no demonstrable reason why there should be anything rather than nothing—nor, of course, why there should be nothing rather than something. This undemonstrability—or lack of self-evidence—extends even to the value of value as such, i.e., to the proposition that it is a good already that the distinction between what is (or would be) good and what is not can be made at all, no matter whether an instance of the former can be actually found. It is the proposition that for anything existing to be open to the difference of value is better than to be indifferent to it: that to be *able* to be in *either* a better *or* worse state is better than such a distinction not to be predicable of it at all. Of this proposition, too, I say that it is neither demonstrable nor self-evident, but that it is an *ex nihilo* originative option for difference against indifference (with which its object is *de facto* established, viz., as the value difference between difference and indifference). For if this proposition were evident, the worth of being over nothing were evident as well, since only being offers the opportunity for making at least *that* distinction and with it already realizing value—even if in the negative mode of exposing being as indifferent, and

rially alter the cognitive situation. Once he has registered his dissent from without, and so long as he does not contest the *facts* of the Aristotelian universe, the theoretician must still, *within* its object-field, abide by its evidence and assess degrees of the good and the success or failure of natural activities on *its* terms—i.e., according to its intrinsic system of ends *as perceived*, even if not approved. Without endorsing these ends (or indeed their very principle), he should yet arrive at the same evaluations as he who, in addition to perceiving, also endorses them. The qualified value verdicts *ex hypothesi* ("given this universe . . .") should not differ from the verdicts delivered absolutely in the case of personal identification. This would then be a pure case of separation between subjective and objective value judgments—i.e., between my own preferences and the immanent standards of the object; it would be a "value-free" science deferring to an object which by its teleological nature is not value-free at all and therefore demands of the knower the consideration of value as integral to his knowledge. This holds independently of whatever answer be given to the rather outsized question concerning the universal nature of things: it simply says that with objects *of a certain type*, provided there are any such objects, descriptive theory turns of itself into normative theory. The question is: Are there such objects?

3. The crucial concept here is that of "ends," without which the concept of norm and objective value would be meaningless. The story of how, since the anti-Aristotelian beginnings of modern science, "ends" have come to be thrown out of the scientific account of reality, indeed of our very idea of reality, is too well known to need retelling. Suffice it to recall that first, in Galilean–Newtonian mechanics, inanimate nature was purged of teleological principles and, stripped down to "efficient" causality, was left alien or neutral to value. Then, with Darwinism, the same thing happened to animate—i.e., organic—nature, the original home ground of final causes and the paradigmatic object of teleological understanding. Working with the mere mechanics of random mutations and natural selection, Darwinian evolution made reason out of the "folly" (as Voltaire had still called it) "to deny that the eye is made to see, the ear to hear, the stomach to digest": precisely this *is* denied, and we are

---

that as something bad: it then has produced the good of my making the right value judgment in finding it wanting, the value of missing the possibility (let alone the existence) of value—a paradoxical enough vindication of what stands thus convicted, but a vindication nonetheless. On the other hand, if I deny the value of difference over indifference (i.e. the value of value), I have not necessarily denied the value of being over not-being: Spinoza asserted being to be indifferent to the distinction of good and bad; and yet *being as such* was to him the value *per se*, and thus quantity of being (i.e. power) the measure of—"value." In fact, the assertion of total and absolute indifference—nature's and my own—is probably absurd, since making it entails a breach in it.

bidden with all the authority of Science to look upon seeing, hearing, digesting, and, in sum, "living," as *de facto* functions, but not purposes, of structures that came about without the causality of purpose. And so we have to strike the "digestive tract" from our sample list of teleological entities.

At this point we may briefly stop to survey the different meanings of "value-free" that have emerged in our discussion. In the expression *"wertfreie Wissenschaft,"* it means an injunction, an "ought" addressed to the scientist: that he should not allow the values of his own option to intrude into and color his reading of the evidence and his reasoning about the evidence. This is nothing but the ideal and duty of objectivity, and on this there are no two opinions. But beyond this self-evident rule, "value-free" may also express a theoretical proposition concerning the nature of things or what is knowable about things. It then implies that not only should the scientist keep from importing his own values into the subject matter; he also should not expect value-information from the subject matter. Neither as prejudgments nor as resultant judgments do values have a place in the universe of science. It is only a secondary .point, making little difference in the practical effect, whether this is to be understood as an ontological or an epistemological statement. In the first and prevalent sense, the object itself is claimed to be value-free— that is, alien or neutral to value; this means, when extended to *all* objects, that "value" in its very being is merely subjective and has no objective status whatsoever. In the more cautious epistemological sense, the proposition is skeptical rather than dogmatic, contending that values, whatever their ontological status, cannot be known (i.e., demonstrated or even defined) scientifically, and for this "agnostic" reason they are assigned to the sphere of mere belief.

4. In any case, it is the propositional (not just the admonitory) meaning of "value-free" which we see emerge with the progressive ejection of "ends" from the field of natural science. With regard to "nature" itself, we saw this movement culminating in Darwinian biology. From there the story goes on into the behavioral sciences. Fortunately, we need not follow it any further; nor need we take a stand on whether this goal-indifferent view of nature is the definitive truth. We can afford to grant it summarily without prejudging our particular subject. For whatever the final word about the status of ends in the scheme of things (and it surely has not been spoken yet), when it comes to the type of thing exemplified in our initial sample list by "court of law"—i.e., when it comes to *human institutions*—there is no room to doubt that these institutions have been brought about by the causality of purpose and are kept alive by that causality alone. Ends are indeed their *raisons d'être*, and how well they serve them is a consideration wholly germane to their

nature—a nature *defined* by a "what for." Here we have no choice but to accept the "subjective" aims, with which "in view" they were instituted and are being operated, as "objectively" constitutive of their existence and essence. Not even the meaning of their names could be explained without reference to the "what for." Economics falls in this category. As an instituted system of human activities, it has its inherent goal or goals and is subject to evaluations of its adequacy to serving those goals.

I do not believe that on this truism there is disagreement with economists or any other social scientists; nor is there disagreement on what is at least the first inherent goal of the economic sphere: the provisioning of its members with the physical goods necessary to sustain their lives or, at the very least, to sustain the collective life composing the economic sphere itself. The problem begins with the situation created by modern technology, viz., the (allegedly) assured *solution* of this primary provisioning task and the expanding *latitude* for goals and goal alternatives (and applicable methods) *no longer determined* by the dictates of natural necessity. This situation of freedom produces practical anarchy in the selection of goals and epistemological anarchy in the evaluation of them. It is the problem, bless our hearts, of affluence.

5. This point has engaged the particular attention of Professor Adolph Lowe, and his discussion of it leads up to an intriguing coincidence between the question of goals and that of determinism, i.e., between the chances for economic theory to be scientifically predictive and its chances to be normatively prescriptive. Former pressures, so he argues, endowed the economic process with a quasi-mechanical determinacy which permitted economic theory to approximate the logical form of natural science and its predictive power. At the same time, the one "categorical imperative" of economic activity, which theory could not but affirm, viz., subsistence, provided an unquestionable intra-economic norm for evaluating that activity in given instances and, if need be, for prescribing to it its proper course. With the emancipation from those pressures through technological progress, both predictive and prescriptive certainty vanished: under the conditions of excess productivity the economic process lost its constraining determinacy, and thereby economic theory its purported likeness to physics. And the monism of the one imperative goal which was as normatively binding on theory as it was actually dominant in practice, gave way to a pluralism of elective goals, for which—as they transcend the only goal which economics validates *per se*—economic theory fails to provide criteria.

Thus far Professor Lowe's reasoning. If correct, it means, alas, that economic theory enjoyed normative competence when it did not need it—viz., when circumstances saw anyway to the observance of the "ought" and even, through their deterministic mechanics, guaranteed the automatic implementation of its goals in the final outcome; and that it lost normative competence just when it began to really need it—viz., when goals became elective, and circumstances no longer by their objective causality acted in lieu of human choice. I do not raise the question whether there ever really was—as economic liberalism assumed —such a "pre-established harmony" between causality and the good, in virtue of which economic science *eo ipso* coincided with economic wisdom (as prescriptive knowledge of ends) and in which by the same token wisdom was practically redundant because unwisdom (or laissez faire) led to the same effect. My concern is with the new dispensation where both the monism of effect and that of goal are gone, the passing coincidence between them (if ever it existed) is ended, and knowledge concerning the intrinsic good of ends, now anything but redundant, is deemed to fall outside economic knowledge altogether.

I now propose to argue that in fact there is more normative competence (and thus responsibility) left to rational theory in the new situation than this picture suggests, or, put differently, that the original and incontestable "categorical imperative" of the economic realm, properly understood in its implications, remains logically effective in yielding criteria for goal selection even after the seeming fulfillment of its primary goal.

III

To state the obvious, let us first recall that the fact of economics is grounded in the primary biological fact that we live by *metabolism* and are thus creatures of need. But by saying "need" I am already naming something more than a mere "fact"—i.e., more than the physical truth that food, oxygen, etc., are causally necessary for organic existence to go on and must therefore be provided *if* it is to go on. I am saying that this going on is "willed" by the organic subject, with no "if" about it, since "to be" for the subject is to be engaged in the business of ensuring its being through metabolism: and that *therefore, because* of the involvement of *interest*, the necessary means to that effect (i.e., to keeping up the metabolic process) assume for it the quality of "needs."[5] Their pursuit thus expresses the basic self-affirmation of life, which—because it is

---

[5]On "need" as a biological category, see the remarks in Essay 9, Section V, and in my book *The Phenomenon of Life: Toward a Philosophical Biology* (New York: Harper & Row, 1966), pp. 83ff. and 101ff.

not simply assured, but requires metabolism—becomes a purpose in itself. This purposive affirmation, an a priori "option," underlies all economic activity as the pervading commitment of the whole field, and its acknowledgment is the tacit premise of economic theory. Whatever the private misanthropic leanings of the individual thinker, he has *qua* economist adopted this affirmation without which there would be no economic life. Thus economic theory embodies from the outset the transfactual element of endorsing what is itself another transfactual element—viz., interest in being. In that sense it is in value-consent with its subject, reaffirming its intrinsic affirmation.

Next, still elaborating the obvious, we remember that "provisioning" requires "providence," i.e., looking and planning ahead. Here again economic theory, bound by the initial affirmation, must endorse the imperative, "Be provident," and judge economic actions in its light. But here the questions arise: provident for whom? and how far ahead? Pondering these questions, we realize how inappropriate the Robinson Crusoe model is for representing even the most elementary economic situation, not so much because of the absence of companions—and thus of the whole aspect of cooperation, exchange, and distribution, important as this is—but because of the absence of children and thus of a relevant time dimension and of responsibility for the future. Surely there would be no economic life to speak of without care for the offspring. The needs of terminal individuals could be attended to in a makeshift manner. Crusoe, or even a whole company of shipwrecked sailors, could live from hand to mouth and have to answer only to themselves if they chose to emulate the grasshopper rather than the ant. "Let us eat and drink, for tomorrow we are dead," is a perfectly eligible maxim for mortals without a future; but with newborns rising and the unborn waiting in the wings, the "we" has an indefinite time spread, and "tomorrow" means an ever extending future. The self-affirmation of need, then, includes affirmation of this continuity, and this means *responsibility*.

Thus it must be stressed that metabolism is only half of the biological premise underlying economic life; the other half is reproduction. Through this counterpoise to mortality, with its powerful commitment, a horizon of self-transcendence is added to the reference of need and interest: self-preservation is widened into preservation of progeny; needs beyond one's own become an integral part of concern; and with the unique length of human childhood and dependency, what would otherwise be short-range and merely optional providence in the service of self-interest becomes long-range providence enjoined by responsibility.

That we name reproduction alone as the biological source of responsibility may provoke the objection that economic life knows also of responsibility for the well-being of one's contemporaries irrespective of future generations. True, but this can easily be reduced to self-interest, which requires the functioning of the other cooperants in the economic process (including that of the most exploited and despised) and thus the protection of the condition for their doing so: no independent source is needed for this "rational" responsibility. But the clearly selfless responsibility for the long-term future, from which one stands to reap no possible return, cannot be thus derived: it constitutes a genuine dimension of its own that has its own foundation as irreducible as that of self-interest. If this is a consolation to the positivist, we may add that in the last analysis "self-interest" (the instinct of self-preservation) is no less mysterious or "irrational" a fact than is care for the offspring.[6]

Now "responsibility" surely is a transfactual, normative category, and we claim that it is as germane to economics as is "self-interest." Both have the dignity of immanent principles. Stating them, we are saying more than that people, as a matter of fact, wish to stay alive and wish their children to stay alive; and more than that, in fact, they act to provide for both. Our contention is twofold: that "responsibility," deriving from the fundamental *fact* of reproduction, is as *constitutive* of the economic sphere as is (by general admission) "self-interest" or "need," deriving from the fundamental fact of metabolism; and that therefore it

[6]Friedrich Schiller put the irreducibility of these *two* forces succinctly in the lines: "*Einstweilen, bis den Bau der Welt/ Philosophie zusammenhält,/ Erhält* sie [*scil. Natur*] *das Getriebe/ Durch Hunger und durch Liebe.*" (Meanwhile, until philosophy conducts the worldly symphony, *nature* through hunger and through love ensures that all creation move.) My contention is that economics as an art is designed precisely and basically to subserve these two basic drives: hunger and reproductive love—just as medicine is designed to serve health. The fact that either can also be used for the opposite (as any art can be used for the opposite of its destination) does not, of course, in the least invalidate what their true object is—*and* that of their supportive sciences. Professor Lowe thinks otherwise. "If Hitler (so he writes in his Rejoinder to my argument) had decided in 1945 to bring about the final *Götterdämmerung*, the complete destruction of the German people and land, then the task of the economist *qua* economist, unmoved by extrinsic considerations, would have been to help in doing so most efficiently" (op. cit., p. 196). This is the same as saying that the builder *qua* builder practices his knowledge as truly in a demolition job as in a construction job. Or that medical science does not *as such* subscribe to life, but is merely "by extrinsic considerations" moved to pay somewhat more attention to the means of fostering than to those of destroying it.

Incidentally, my case for economics is *stronger* than that for medicine or house-building since, unlike these, it is not a consciously invented art, whose goal may be arbitrarily changed, but an inevitable pursuit arising from the human condition—a pursuit engendering its own art, which then must be judged by the adequacy to, or at least compatibility with, the basic *end* inherent in the activity itself *of* which it is the art, and of which the respective science is the theory. In all these species of knowledge, where the object is not simply "there" but in its primary *esse* is constituted by human concern and nonexistent without it, the equation with natural science rests on an ontological confusion.

is as *normative* to the economist for the evaluation of economic behavior and the critique of economic goals as "need" is usually agreed to be.

The scientific economist may balk at this. While he will hardly dispute the claims for need and self-interest, which indeed have a long and honorable standing in classical theory, he will tend to regard "responsibility" as a category imported from the moral sphere, not indigenous to economics *per se*, and therefore not scientifically entitled to normative use in economic theory *qua* economic. He may be willing to grant that people do wish their children to stay alive, besides wishing to stay alive themselves, and he will count this in with the various actual motivations to be reckoned with in explaining and predicting economic behavior; but under the individualistic or atomistic tradition of his craft he will shy away from admitting that this "wish" or commitment is integral to the economic purpose and thus binding upon it.

Nevertheless, he surely must admit that this commitment was originative of the economic purpose in historical fact. The initial economic unit, the family, owes its rationale to the rearing of the young; no economic order of any elaboration could conceivably have evolved without it or, once evolved, make sense without continuing devotion to its own regenerative perpetuity. Thus on purely *descriptive* grounds the economist must accord to trans-individual providence and responsibility the status of being at the root of economic reality, and must acknowledge them as being of its very essence; however, when he does, he must also accord them the *prescriptive* status of providing an intra-economic principle of valid *judgments* on economic policy, including the choice of goals. Where the *raison d'être* of a field is teleological in its nature, as is the case here, its recognition assumes of itself normative force.

IV

How fruitful is this principle for the setting or critique of economic goals? Perhaps we can find out by first asking how far into the future responsible providence extends. This depends on the causal scope of our actions and the attainable reach of our rational foresight. Both of these were formerly small and have lately become tremendously enlarged. This alone suggests that we now have more to say on economic goals—viz., long-term goals—than any former age. The mere size and "totalistic" style of our ventures under the aegis of technology force us to face their remote outcome conjoined with all the collateral effects. In these conditions the principle of responsible providence operates not so much in the positive prescription as in the critical examination of goals— practically as a principle of restraint. There is no dearth of goals in the modern situation of unbound powers clamoring for actualization, nor is there a dearth of means; what now claims our attention are the dangers lurking in the actualization of the goals and the uses of the means.

The a priori object of an unconditional economic imperative is the continued possibility of the economic system itself: not necessarily of the given system, but of a viable economy as such. This was hardly a consideration in former times. With all the ups and downs of capricious nature, the good old Earth could be trusted to endure and to regenerate the conditions for future life, even patiently to repair the follies of man. Modern technology has changed this radically. Thanks to it, we live in an era of enormous and largely irreversible consequences of human action, in an era of what I call the total and global impact of almost any of the courses we embark upon under the conditions of technological might; and we must anticipate that these courses, once set in motion, will run self-propelled to their extremes. In these circumstances, the otherwise abstract obligation to preserve for posterity the conditions necessary for an economy as such, turns into a fairly concrete principle for normative judgment—i.e., for approval or rejection of policies. The *a priori* imperative whose positive form might be, "Act so that the effects of your action are compossible with the permanence of an economic order," is for purposes of critical application better expressed in the negative equivalent, "Act so that the effects of your action are not destructive of the possibility of economic life in the future," or simply, "Do not compromise the conditions for an indefinite continuation of some viable economy."

This, I submit, is a relevant, nontrivial, and highly topical rule for decision-making (or decision-checking) in the novel state of our affairs. It is, of course, reminiscent of Kant's "categorical imperative." I cannot properly discuss the logical relationship here, but I may point out at least some of the differences.[7] Kant's imperative enjoins us to consider what would happen *if* the maxim of my present action were made a universal law; the self-consistency or inconsistency of such a *hypothetical* universalization is made the test for my *private* choice. But it is no part of the reasoning that there is any probability of my private choice in fact becoming universal law—indeed, real consequences are not considered at all, and the principle is one not of objective responsibility but of the subjective quality of my self-determination. Now the criterion of consistency seems at first to be similar in our imperative. But there the "universalization" is by no means hypothetical—i.e., a purely logical transference from the individual "me" to an imaginary, causally un-

[7] Here I may be forgiven for repeating some statements made in Essay 1. Actually, they are prior here and were later utilized in the other context.

related "all" ("*if* everybody . . ."); on the contrary, the actions subject
to our imperative have their universal reference in their actual scope of
efficacy—they "totalize" themselves in the progress of their momentum
and thus are bound to terminate in shaping the universal dispensation
of things.

Furthermore since this concerns things that will eventuate "in the long
run," there is the *time* horizon, which is entirely absent in the instantaneous logical operation of the Kantian imperative; whereas the latter extrapolates into an ever-present order of abstract compatibility, our
imperative extrapolates into a predictable real *future* as the open-ended
dimension of our responsibility.

Finally, "consistency" here takes in the interplay of all the conditions
making up the final situation under the vast complexity of "the real": it
involves foresight saturated with empirical content, requiring the fullness of our factual knowledge, and thus escapes the often-noted vacuity
of the Kantian consistency rule. The rule that economics must watch
over its own continued possibility is therefore decidedly nontrivial. Before illustrating this by some hypothetical applications, I wish to reiterate
its claim to normative authority: the new imperative embodying the principle of responsibility (new, because the occasion for it has only recently
arisen) is as unconditionally self-validating as was the immediate-sub-
sistence imperative of pretechnological economy that is allegedly being
superannuated through success (I wonder for how long?); it fills the
vacant place of the latter with a long-range criterion pertinent to the
goal-indulgence of our technologically powered success economy. Its
concrete application is, of course, to our interaction with nature, into
which our economic pursuits precipitate us on an unprecedented scale
and in ever increasing depth; and "nature" here includes human nature
together with the animate and inanimate environment.

Everyone can think for himself of the kind of issues which arise here,
and which the economist is duty-bound to make his business, unaccus-
tomed as he may be to them. That they are the economist's business follows both from the fact that they originate in economic practice actually
under way (and assumed as a datum in his own projective reasoning)
and from the fact that they will recoil upon the economic possibilities
confronting the inheritors of the present run of things. In this connection
one thinks first of the physical side—i.e., of the whole intricate ecological
complex, now decisively affected by what man, in the pursuit of his
economic goals, is doing to his terrestrial environment. The large-scale
perspectives opening up here are very much in the public mind these days
and can only be called alarming. Biologists and physicists warn of an
"ecological crisis" which this planet is approaching under our steward-

ship and "which may destroy its suitability as a place for human society." Already, so Professor Barry Commoner holds, the environment is being placed under stress "to the point of collapse." I resist the temptation of dwelling on the impressive examples and arguments advanced in support of this apocalyptic view. They range from outright despoliation over pollution to the very endangering of the earth's oxygen supply. The points to be emphasized are (1) that since such anticipated and by no means fanciful developments have an indubitably economic causation as well as a final economic effect, the economist is concerned with them; (2) that the challenge they pose qualitatively exceeds the more traditional question of exhaustion or preservation of local resources; and (3) that in facing this challenge there is nothing "value-free" about economic science: on the contrary, the principle of responsibility for future life, indigenous to economics, becomes the source of categorical, normative judgment.

V

To take one imaginary example, suppose that a proposed rate of industrial growth, perfectly feasible and desirable in itself, involves a rate of fuel-burning that brings into play the so-called greenhouse effect —i.e., the trapping of thermal radiation under a carbon dioxide layer that forms in the upper atmosphere. Suppose that calculations show that this in time will raise terrestrial temperatures to a point where the polar ice caps begin to melt; and that once started, this is an irreversible and self-acccelerating process with the end-result (ignoring all other consequences of the climatic change) of raising the ocean level enough to submerge vast continental areas on this globe, thus leading to incalculable catastrophe in economic as well as other respects. Surely then, with such a prospect demonstrated as certain or highly probable, the simple imperative that no economic policy is right whose eventual outcome defeats the prime purpose of all economy will bid the economist to place a normative interdiction on the policy in question whatever its intermediate benefits may be even over a considerable interval of time.

This is a relatively simple case involving the plain alternative of physical preservation or ruin; it can be decided without regard to any specifically *human* qualities whose presence or absence may affect the viability of the economic order that either promotes or suppresses them. Even here, though, the decision-maker himself must muster more than correct information and clear thinking; he must exercise the moral virtue of resisting the lure of immediately desirable results in deference to the command of long-range responsibility. To sacrifice proximate expediency to the consideration of what will be when we are no more is in itself a moral stance, implying a sense of commitment and strength of self-denial. We claim that these are intrinsic in the meaning of the economic undertaking as such and therefore invokable as "oughts." And the lengthened range of our responsibility, a *novel moral horizon*, is precisely the normative correlate to the entirely novel lengthening of the effective range of our projects and of the theoretical range of our foresight. This much, then, of the *exercise* of "human value" beyond the merely cognitive is implicit in the adequate practice of economic theory, even where, as in our example, no *consideration* of human values beyond the physical enters into the goal-decision itself.

This, however, is the case when we include *human* nature in the "nature" affected by our projects, and when we remember that man himself is among the "economic resources" which must be kept intact and functional. We then are forced into considerations of a subtler kind, as in the following example—again a hypothetical one. Suppose that technically a state of "full automation" is possible which would abolish work for the overwhelming majority of the population, and that therefore a process now initiated toward this target would terminate in a state where humanity consisted mainly of taskless state pensioners, "employed" to consume. Further suppose that for such a state to endure, a high degree of orderliness and "good behavior" would be required of its beneficiaries. Finally suppose that psychology or neuropathology—or generally the "science of man"–can show that the very state of affairs which requires this condition precludes it: for instance, that mass idleness of this sort, the lack of function, purpose, and structuring through work, must give rise to forms of anomie or even collective insanity which would wreck the system—in brief, that the latter is self-contradictory in that it demands a maximum of rationality while fostering a maximum of irrationality. Here again, the theoretical economist must advise against a course that would lead to this contradiction. Scientific insight will of itself become normative. (Whether it will be listened to is an entirely different matter. I personally believe that the warner would be doomed to a Cassandra role.)

One could think of more sophisticated and perhaps more likely examples of this kind—e.g., that the system will predictably dry up the source of *knowledge* on which it rests by failing to regenerate the delicate, intellectual, and partly ascetic virtues necessary in the all-important scientific-technocratic elite. The point is that the human condition in all its breadth, and therewith the consideration of "human values," form a legitimate part of hardheaded economic reasoning, because of the kind of goal states toward which economic developments nowadays move either by design or by their own self-propagating direction.

True, those human values do not figure *per se* in this reasoning—i.e., with their own authentic claims, but merely as part of the criterion of viability—i.e., of the question, "Does it work?" But "viability" here has become rather a comprehensive concept in which the technical aspect of consistency and compatibility tends to merge with the humanistic aspect of man's well-being. For there is some reason for being confident that, *understood in this breadth*, the criterion of "compatibility" will safeguard, along with the functional viability of the system, also the conditions for possible human wholeness. To express it the other way around: we may not unreasonably assume that by *avoiding* the one-sided extremes of the goals that lead to functional self-contradiction, we shall also avoid the crippling distortion of man and keep at least the human potential intact. The chances for preserving the integrity of that potential may well coincide with the precepts of sober economic wisdom.

One may object that these precepts are of a restraining or prohibiting kind only, telling us what not to do, but not what to do. True, but it is at least a beginning. We may remember that even the Ten Commandments are mostly "don't's" and not "do's." Moreover, the negative emphasis fits the modern situation, whose problem, as we have seen, is an excess of powers to "do" and thus an excess of offers for doing. Overwhelmed by our own possibilities—an unprecedented situation, this— we first of all need criteria for rejection. Perhaps we cannot know what the *summum bonum* is, but we can surely know, when presented with it, what a *malum* is. We recognize evil even when ignorant of the good. Thus, granted that heightening and enhancing life is the goal, on economic and other terms, we may well be uncertain what constitutes such "heightening" according to the true idea of man; but we are not uncertain of what constitutes a stunting of man's image or a mutilation of its very base. Thus I do not think that in the case of economics there is really such a schizophrenia between the economist as a scientist and the economist as a person as is sometimes asserted; there is a convergence between intra-scientific and human norms, and no lack of objects for a legitimate "yes" and "no" *valid by both at once*.

VI

But what if the assumption of such a convergence is over-optimistic? If, indeed, functional viability of the most outrageous kind can be bought precisely with the *right kind* of distortion of man and the right kind of mutilation of the human substance? In our theoretical argument we must not overlook the possibility that scientifically armed "human engineering" can credibly promise to tailor man to the requirements of the system and (e.g., by biological and other intervention) to produce the *stunted* humanity required, à la Huxley's *Brave New World*, for the smooth functioning of a projected economic-technological order. Then, instead of disruptive mass insanity (whose prospect might almost be a relief), we would have the adaptive reduction of the sons of Man to behavioral automata that fit the automation of their world. The viability criterion would thus be satisfied—by a caricature of man, to be sure, but still satisfied. Suppose *this* to be demonstrably possible and durable: then our imperative, with its test of mere viability, would be powerless to protect human inviolateness, and the economist—revolting as the picture may be to him—would have *no intra-economic* (i.e., purely *functional*) veto to raise.

Still, the performance of the economist's analytic and synthetic task is not without import for the cause of the values threatened in this perspective. It is his task, after all, to *draw* the picture, to *fill in* all its features beyond the few specified by the policy-makers—that is, to work out what is collaterally involved in the actuality of the goal—prior to the instrumental question of how to achieve it. He cannot shun this task by retiring behind the official terms of his discipline, by pleading that such and such aspects of the picture are not his job, but the physicist's, the biologist's, the sociologist's, the psychologist's. As the compound situation is indivisible, economics is "interdisciplinary" by its nature, and recent developments have merely added to the variety of disciplines the economist must enlist in the execution of his own reasoning—in our case, in the elaboration of the state embodying the projected goal. Having drawn the picture with their help, the economist can show it to the policy-makers and say to them: you can have your target only as part of a package; this is what goes with it, this is what the eventual goal state will look like. Do you want *that*? Given the fact that there is a greater certainty and consensus on what is undesirable than on what is desirable, on the *malum* than on the *bonum*, scientific knowledge can here be of service to concerns beyond its own jurisdiction—if only it is radical and comprehensive enough in its projections and shows far enough ahead where we are moving.

VII

And here comes the rub: Can it really do so? The supposition in the preceding considerations was that we do have the requisite factual knowledge. In my examples there recurred the phrase, "Suppose that it can be shown . . . ," referring to what biology, psychology, sociology, etc., can predict. But can they predict these things? I am afraid not, except very tentatively and always controversially. The normative strength I spoke of rests on predictive strength—i.e., on the validity of the extrapolation presenting us with the terminal states. But such extrapolations in social science, unlike those in astronomy, mechanics, or physics, can at best be persuasive. A penumbra and then an outer darkness of collateral conditions surround the little segment which our extrapolation can spotlight out of the total. What this total will be, we can only find out by letting the thing come to pass; after that, we have retrospective predictions, knowing now, in the light of the result, how it came about (somewhat like the biologist's knowledge of past evolution).

Note that it is the specification of the *goal* state itself, as the correlative, complete "environment" of the proposed target condition, which involves us in a predictive task antecedently to the whole *instrumental* level—i.e., to means-ends prediction. There lies the problem for the *application* of our imperative. The reason for the predictive weakness of all social science (quite apart from the open question of indeterminacy and free will) is the fact that with man and history one cannot make small-scale, repeatable model experiments in lieu of the "real thing." For it is not the isolated causal strand in which we are interested, but precisely the totality of the large-scale, complex conditions, and the only laboratory for testing hypotheses about *this* is reality itself—i.e., history in its true dimensions and true time span. For here numbers, configurations, and durations are not only quantitative but qualitative variables. The molecule remains the same whether it is in the company of few or many; whether it has gone through this or that thermal motion, been part of this or that chemical compound, whether for a short or a long time, in this sequence or that, here or there, often or once. Because of this invariance, we can create for it small-scale, purified, repeatable, experimental situations from which valid generalizations can be drawn. This is not so in the social sciences, whose objects lack this substantial insensitivity to circumstances. There the purified, vicarious paradigms do not work.

Where, then, shall the social scientist get his "empirical generalizations"? From past history? Even if it has something to teach about its own recurrent patterns, its generalizations would no longer hold for us. For the basic novelty of our condition is this: Whereas the agricultural revolution with which civilization began, followed by the urban revolution, established a *fact* which lasted substantially unchanged for several millenia, the scientific–industrial–technological revolution of the modern age did not establish a fact but started a *movement* which continuously creates new facts that always carry in themselves the germ of their own overcoming.[8] But a sequence of unprecedented and nonrepetitious change—which is what we are living in—simply offers no basis for empirical generalizations of any extended scope. And extended scope is precisely what we need today and did not need before.

Such is the inductive side of the matter. The deductive side would look no better, even if the logical premises for it were given. For even supposing that the sequence of novelty is in ultimate truth deterministic, and moreover, that all the single, operative causalities and the laws of their combination were known—in short, if computation were possible "in principle," the order of complexity to be dealt with would defy all human computation. Nothing less than *total* projection will do here for relevant prediction, with integration of all the interacting factors that will compose the future state—human and extra-human, material and mental, natural and institutional, rational and emotional, biological and technological (this last, incidentally, means anticipating future inventions—i.e., making them now). This is clearly a task which no existing science can handle and probably none ever will. The computer that could process all the data combined would have to be of cosmic dimensions, so mathematicians assure me. In fact, of course, we would have neither all the variables to be put into that monster computer nor the sophistication to program it. (Not to mention the paradox that, since the computation is undertaken in order to enable us to change its result—i.e., to offer us alternatives—we have introduced an anti-deterministic element into a purportedly deterministic scheme.)

Returning once more to the inductive side, I repeat that only the full-scale "experiment" would be valid in yielding the desired "empirical generalization": full-scale in numbers, span, and above all *time*, which is a prime reality in human affairs. But we cannot experiment with mankind. When we have run our experiment, the deed is done and we cannot return to the initial state. Its having been done creates a new condition. We may be wise after the fact (e.g., find that it should not have been done), but it cannot be undone; history is unrepeatable and we cannot start over again. Our knowledge would come too late. Our generalization would be good only for a repeat performance of the universe.

VIII

Where does that leave our imperative, which we found to be non-trivial indeed and of indubitable validity in itself, but which we now

---

[8]See Essay 3, pp. 45–47 and p. 51.

have also found to be of uncertain applicability, since its theoretically compelling application requires a certainty of foreknowledge which we lack. If the projection of the total end-state can at best be hypothetical and must always be elliptic, the normative decision the economist is to make will lack strict scientific cogency. It cannot be more valid than the forecast on which it is built. It may still be as persuasive as the forecast itself, and since we are dealing with the best-informed extrapolations that can be had, this persuasiveness can be great indeed. But even the best-informed extrapolations, shot through with guesswork as they are, are contestable and will be contested by disinterested and interested opinion alike. Worse still, the mere appeal to the incontestable fact that "we don't really know" can be used as a license to try out the critical course anyway if its short-range advantages are tempting enough. Here then the principle of long-range responsibility requires that *the fact of ignorance be incorporated in the imperative itself*, and that the normative role of the economist become wedded to the Socratic role of stressing our ignorance. In the face of the quasi-eschatological situations toward which the potentials of our economic–technological processes point, ignorance of the ultimate implications becomes itself a reason for responsible restraint.

The forethought of our ancestors could, in the general shroudedness of the future and with the modest causal scale of their doings, get by with Mr. Micawber's pious expectation that "something will turn up": no use to worry our heads with the very distant, the future will take care of itself, our grandchildren will cross the bridge when they come to it. We cannot afford the Micawber attitude anymore. For we live under a new dispensation and a new responsibility. By the mere scale of its effects, modern technological power propels us into goals of a type that was formerly the preserve of Utopias.[9]

There is, however, one wisdom left to us: that of realizing the inadequacy of our foreknowledge to the scope of our actions. The imperative that incorporates this realization bids us to be cautious—i.e., to forgo a use of our power which, for all we know, may lead to runaway effects of excessive and ungovernable magnitude. Accordingly the economist's normative role is to warn of *eschatological situations as such*, and thus of policies apt to lead to them. Armed with all the tentative knowledge of what could be, yet unable to predict what *will* be, he will have to counsel against courses too pregnant with extreme possibilities.

In conclusion, then, we have this to say about the rational, normative critique of goals. Our "imperative," founded upon the principle of re-

[9]Essay 1 deals with this intrinsically "utopian" aspect of contemporary technology and with the dilemma it creates for us of needing a wisdom for its wielding which its very outsize and spell prevent us from having.

sponsibility, and in its straightforward form supposing our knowledge of consequences, must be adapted to the fact that this responsibility now extends into the unknown. The first mortal sin in economic policy is *"après nous le déluge"*; the second, to *risk* the possibility of deluge for our grandchildren on the excuse of ignorance ("Who knows what unforeseen remedies will appear in time?"). The knowledge of our ignorance, plus the knowledge of the *possibilities* we might be setting in play (this indeed is a knowledge), should beget the corollary imperative: Do not gamble with goals that are too big—and so resist the drift toward them. For although there may, in principle, be cases of good eschatological "terminals"—i.e., a desirable millennium—the chances for apocalyptic ones are immeasurably greater. Thus, in the present state of our affairs, and for some time to come, an advisable principle for normative decision may well be: healthy fear of our own "Promethean" power.

5.
Philosophical Reflections on Experimenting with Human Subjects

Experimenting with human subjects is going on in many fields of scientific and technological progress. It is designed to replace the over-all instruction by natural, occasional and cumulative experience with the selective information from artificial, systematic experiment which physical science has found so effective in dealing with inanimate nature. Of the new experimentation with man, medical is surely the most legitimate; psychological, the most dubious; biological (still to come), the most dangerous. I have chosen here to deal with the first only, where the case *for* it is strongest and the task of adjudicating conflicting claims hardest. When I was first asked[1] to comment "philosophically" on it, I had all the hesitation natural to a layman in the face of matters on which experts of the highest competence have had their say and still carry on

Originally published in *Daedalus* 98 (Spring 1969), and in its present revised version, with a comment by Arthur J. Dyck, in *Experimentation with Human Subjects*, ed. Paul A. Freund (New York: Braziller, 1970).

[1]The American Academy of Arts and Sciences invited me to participate in a conference on the Ethical Aspects of Experimentation on Human Subjects, sponsored by the Academy journal *Daedalus* and the National Institutes of Health. The conference was held September 26–28, 1968, in Boston, Massachusetts, and all papers were subsequently published in *Daedalus*. A previous conference of the same title and under the same auspices is documented in *Proceedings of the Conference on the Ethical Aspects of Experimentation on Human Subjects*, Nov. 3–4, 1967 (Boston; hereafter called *Proceedings*).

their dialogue. As I familiarized myself with the material,[2] any initial feeling of moral rectitude that might have facilitated my task quickly dissipated before the awesome complexity of the problem, and a state of great humility took its place. The awareness of the problem in all its shadings and ramifications speaks out with such authority, perception, and sophistication in the published discussions of the researchers themselves that it would be foolish of me to hope that I, an onlooker on the sidelines, could tell those battling in the arena anything they have not pondered themselves. Still, since the matter is obscure by its nature and involves very fundamental, transtechnical issues, anyone's attempt at clarification can be of use, even without novelty. And even if the philosophical reflection should in the end achieve no more than the realization that in the dialectics of this area we must sin and fall into guilt, this insight may not be without its own gains.

I. The Peculiarity of Human Experimentation

Experimentation was originally sanctioned by natural science. There it is performed on inanimate objects, and this raises no moral problems. But as soon as animate, feeling beings become the subject of experiment, as they do in the life sciences and especially in medical research, this innocence of the search for knowledge is lost, and questions of conscience arise. The depth to which moral and religious sensibilities can become aroused over these questions is shown by the vivisection issue. Human experimentation must sharpen the issue as it involves ultimate questions of personal dignity and sacrosanctity. One profound difference between the human experiment and the physical (beside that between animate and inanimate, feeling and unfeeling nature) is this: The physical experiment employs small-scale, artificially devised substitutes for that about which knowledge is to be obtained, and the experimenter extrapolates from these models and simulated conditions to nature at large. Something deputizes for the "real thing"—balls rolling down an inclined plane for sun and planets, electric discharges from a condenser for real lightning, and so on. For the most part, no such substitution is possible in the biological sphere. We must operate on the original itself, the real thing in the fullest sense, and perhaps affect it irreversibly. No simulacrum can take its place. Especially in the human sphere, experimentation loses entirely the advantage of the clear division between

[2]Since the time of writing this essay (1968), the literature on the subject has grown so much that listing what was then available to me would be of no more than historical interest.

vicarious model and true object. Up to a point, animals may fulfill the proxy role of the classical physical experiment. But in the end man himself must furnish knowledge about himself, and the comfortable separation of noncommittal experiment and definitive action vanishes. An experiment in education affects the lives of its subjects, perhaps a whole generation of schoolchildren. Human experimentation for whatever purpose is always *also* a responsible, nonexperimental, definitive dealing with the subject himself. And not even the noblest purpose abrogates the obligations this involves.

This is the root of the problem with which we are faced: Can both that purpose and this obligation be satisfied? If not, what would be a just compromise? Which side should give way to the other? The question is inherently philosophical as it concerns not merely pragmatic difficulties and their arbitration, but a genuine conflict of values involving principles of a high order. May I put the conflict in these terms. On principle, it is felt, human beings *ought not* to be dealt with in that way (the "guinea pig" protest); on the other hand, such dealings are increasingly urged on us by considerations, in turn appealing to principle, that claim to override those objections. Such a claim must be carefully assessed, especially when it is swept along by a mighty tide. Putting the matter thus, we have already made one important assumption rooted in our "Western" cultural tradition: The prohibitive rule is, to that way of thinking, the primary and axiomatic one; the permissive counter-rule, as qualifying the first, is secondary and stands in need of justification. We must justify the infringement of a primary inviolability, which needs no justification itself; and the justification of its infringement must be by values and needs of a dignity commensurate with those to be sacrificed.

Before going any further, we should give some more articulate voice to the resistance we feel against a merely utilitarian view of the matter. It has to do with a peculiarity of human experimentation quite independent of the question of possible injury to the subject. What is wrong with making a person an experimental subject is not so much that we make him thereby a means (which happens in social contexts of all kinds), as that we make him a thing—a passive thing merely to be acted on, and passive not even for real action, but for token action whose token object he is. His being is reduced to that of a mere token or "sample." This is different from even the most exploitative situations of social life: there the business is real, not fictitious. The subject, however much abused, remains an agent and thus a "subject" in the other sense of the word. The soldier's case is instructive: Subject to most unilateral discipline, forced to risk mutilation and death, conscripted without, perhaps against, his will—he is still conscripted with his capacities to act, to hold his own or fail in situations, to meet real challenges for real stakes. Though a mere "number" to the High Command, he is not a token and not a thing. (Imagine what he would say if it turned out that the war was a game staged to sample observations on his endurance, courage, or cowardice.)

These compensations of personhood are denied to the subject of experimentation, who is acted upon for an extraneous end without being engaged in a real relation where he would be the counterpoint to the other or to circumstance. Mere "consent" (mostly amounting to no more than permission) does not right this reification. Only genuine authenticity of volunteering can possibly redeem the condition of "thinghood" to which the subject submits. Of this we shall speak later. Let us now look at the nature of the conflict, and especially at the nature of the claims countering in this matter those on behalf of personal sacrosanctity.

II. "Individual Versus Society" as the Conceptual Framework

The setting for the conflict most consistently invoked in the literature is the polarity of individual versus society—the possible tension between the individual good and the common good, between private and public welfare. Thus, W. Wolfensberger speaks of "the tension between the long-range interests of society, science, and progress, on one hand, and the rights of the individual on the other."[3] Walsh McDermott says: "In essence, this is a problem of the rights of the individual versus the rights of society."[4] Somewhere I found the "social contract" invoked in support of claims that science may make on individuals in the matter of experimentation. I have grave doubts about the adequacy of this frame of reference, but I will go along with it part of the way. It does apply to some extent, and it has the advantage of being familiar. We concede, as a matter of course, to the common good some pragmatically determined measure of precedence over the individual good. In terms of rights, we let some of the basic rights of the individual be overruled by the acknowledged rights of society—as a matter of right and moral justness and not of mere force or dire necessity (much as such necessity may be adduced in defense of that right). But in making that concession, we require careful clarification of what the needs, interests, and rights of society are, for society—as distinct from any plurality of individuals—is

[3]Wolfensberger, "Ethical Issues in Research with Human Subjects," *World Science* 155 (Jan. 6, 1967), p. 48.
[4]*Proceedings*, p. 29.

an abstract and, as such, is subject to our definition, while the individual is the primary concrete, prior to all definition, and his basic good is more or less known. Thus the unknown in our problem is the so-called common or public good and its potentially superior claims, to which the individual good must or might sometimes be sacrificed, in circumstances that in turn must also be counted among the unknowns of our question. Note that in putting the matter in this way—that is, in asking about the right of society to individual sacrifice—the consent of the sacrificial subject is no necessary part of the *basic* question.

"Consent," however, is the other most consistently emphasized and examined concept in discussions of this issue. This attention betrays a feeling that the "social" angle is not fully satisfactory. If society has a right, its exercise is not contingent on volunteering. On the other hand, if volunteering is fully genuine, no public right to the volunteered act need be construed. There is a difference between the moral or emotional appeal of a cause that elicits volunteering and a right that demands compliance—for example, with particular reference to the social sphere, between the *moral claim* of a common good and society's *right* to that good and to the means of its realization. A moral claim cannot be met without consent; a right can do without it. Where consent is present anyway, the distinction may become immaterial. But the awareness of the many ambiguities besetting the "consent" actually available and used in medical research[5] prompts recourse to the idea of a public right conceived independently of (and valid prior to) consent; and, vice versa, the awareness of the problematic nature of such a right makes even its advocates still insist on the idea of consent with all its ambiguities: an uneasy situation either way.

Nor does it help much to replace the language of "rights" by that of "interests" and then argue the sheer cumulative weight of the interest of the many over against those of the few or the single individual. "Interests" range all the way from the most marginal and optional to the most vital and imperative, and only those sanctioned by particular importance and merit will be admitted to count in such a calculus— which simply brings us back to the question of right or moral claim. Moreover, the appeal to numbers is dangerous. Is the number of those afflicted with a particular disease great enough to warrant violating the interests of the nonafflicted? Since the number of the latter is usually so much greater, the argument can actually turn around to the contention that the cumulative weight of interest is on *their* side. Finally, it may well be the case that the individual's interest in his own inviolability is

[5]See M. H. Pappworth, "Ethical Issues in Experimental Medicine" in D.R. Cutler, ed., *Updating Life and Death* (Boston: Beacon Press, 1969), pp. 64–69.

itself a public interest, such that its publicly condoned violation, irrespective of numbers, violates the interest of all. In that case, its protection in *each* instance would be a paramount interest, and the comparison of numbers will not avail.

These are some of the difficulties hidden in the conceptual framework indicated by the terms "society-individual," "interest," and "rights." But we also spoke of a moral call, and this points to another dimension—not indeed divorced from the social sphere, but transcending it. And there is something even beyond that: true sacrifice from highest devotion, for which there are no laws or rules except that it must be absolutely free. "No one has the right to choose martyrs for science" was a statement repeatedly quoted in the November, 1967, *Daedalus* conference. But no scientist can be prevented from making himself a martyr for his science. At all times, dedicated explorers, thinkers, and artists have immolated themselves on the altar of their vocation, and creative genius most often pays the price of happiness, health, and life for its own consummation. But no one, not even society, has the shred of a right to expect and ask these things in the normal course of events. They come to the rest of us as a *gratia gratis data*.

III. The Sacrificial Theme

Yet we must face the somber truth that the *ultima ratio* of communal life is and has always been the compulsory, vicarious sacrifice of individual lives. The primordial sacrificial situation is that of outright human sacrifices in early communities. These were not acts of blood-lust or gleeful savagery; they were the solemn execution of a supreme, sacral necessity. One of the fellowship of men had to die so that all could live, the earth be fertile, the cycle of nature renewed. The victim often was not a captured enemy, but a select member of the group: "The king must die." If there was cruelty here, it was not that of men, but that of the gods, or rather of the stern order of things, which was believed to exact that price for the bounty of life. To assure it for the community, and to assure it ever again, the awesome *quid pro quo* had to be paid over and over.

Far should it be from us to belittle, from the height of our enlightened knowledge, the majesty of the underlying conception. The particular *causal* views that prompted our ancestors have long since been relegated to the realm of superstition. But in moments of national danger we still send the flower of our young manhood to offer their lives for the continued life of the community, and if it is a just war, we see them go forth as consecrated and strangely ennobled by a sacrificial role. Nor do we make their going forth depend on their own will and consent, much as we may desire and foster these. We conscript them according to law. We conscript the best and feel morally disturbed if the draft, either by design or in effect, works so that mainly the disadvantaged, socially less useful, more expendable, make up those whose lives are to buy ours. No rational persuasion of the pragmatic necessity here at work can do away with the feeling, a mixture of gratitude and guilt, that the sphere of the sacred is touched with the vicarious offering of life for life. Quite apart from these dramatic occasions, there is, it appears, a persistent and constitutive aspect of human immolation to the very being and prospering of human society—an immolation in terms of life and happiness, imposed or voluntary, of the few for the many. What Goethe has said of the rise of Christianity may well apply to the nature of civilization in general: *"Opfer fallen hier, / Weder Lamm noch Stier, / Aber Menschenopfer unerhört."*[6] We can never rest comfortably in the belief that the soil from which our satisfactions sprout is not watered with the blood of martyrs. But a troubled conscience compels us, the undeserving beneficiaries, to ask: Who is to be martyred? In the service of what cause and by whose choice?

Not for a moment do I wish to suggest that medical experimentation on human subjects, sick or healthy, is to be likened to primeval human sacrifices. Yet something sacrificial is involved in the selective abrogation of personal inviolability and the ritualized exposure to gratuitous risk of health and life, justified by a presumed greater, social good. My examples from the sphere of stark sacrifice were intended to sharpen the issues implied in that context and to set them off clearly from the kinds of obligation and constraint imposed on the citizen in the normal course of things or generally demanded of the individual in exchange for the advantages of civil society.

IV. The "Social Contract" Theme

The first thing to say in such a setting-off is that the sacrificial area is not covered by what is called the "social contract." This fiction of political theory, premised on the primacy of the individual, was designed to supply a rationale for the *limitation* of individual freedom and power required for the existence of the body politic, whose existence in turn is for the benefit of the individuals. The principle of these limitations is that their *general* observance profits all, and that therefore the individual observant, assuring this general observance for his part, profits by

---

[6]"Victims do fall here, /Neither lamb nor steer, / Nay, but human offerings untold." —*Die Braut von Korinth.*

it himself. I observe property rights because their general observance assures my own; I observe traffic rules because their general observance assures my own safety; and so on. The obligations here are mutual and general; no one is singled out for special sacrifice. Moreover, for the most part, *qua* limitations of my liberty, the laws thus deducible from the hypothetical "social contract" enjoin me from certain actions rather than obligate me to positive actions (as did the laws of feudal society). Even where the latter is the case, as in the duty to pay taxes, the rationale is that I am myself a beneficiary of the services financed through these payments. Even the contributions levied by the welfare state, though not originally contemplated in the liberal version of the social contract theory, can be interpreted as a personal insurance policy of one sort or another—be it against the contingency of my own indigence, be it against the dangers of disaffection from the laws in consequence of widespread unrelieved destitution, be it even against the disadvantages of a diminished consumer market. Thus, by some stretch, such contributions can still be subsumed under the principle of enlightened self-interest. But no complete abrogation of self-interest at any time is in the terms of the social contract, and so pure sacrifice falls outside it. Under the putative terms of the contract alone, I cannot be required to die for the public good. (Thomas Hobbes made this forcibly clear.) Even short of this extreme, we like to think that nobody is entirely and one-sidedly the victim in any of the renunciations exacted under normal circumstances by society "in the general interest"—that is, for the benefit of others. "Under normal circumstances," as we shall see, is a necessary qualification. Moreover, the "contract" can legitimize claims only on our overt, public actions and not on our invisible, private being. Our powers, not our persons, are beholden to the common weal. In one important respect, it is true, public interest and control do extend to the private sphere by general consent: in the compulsory education of our children. Even there, the assumption is that the learning and what is learned, apart from all future social usefulness, are also for the benefit of the individual in his own being. We would not tolerate education to degenerate into the conditioning of useful robots for the social machine.

Both restrictions of public claim in behalf of the "common good"—that concerning one-sided sacrifice and that concerning the private sphere—are valid only, let us remember, on the premise of the primacy of the individual, upon which the whole idea of the "social contract" rests. This primacy is itself a metaphysical axiom or option peculiar to our Western tradition, and the whittling away of its force would threaten the tradition's whole foundation. In passing, I may remark that systems adopting the alternative primacy of the community as their axiom are naturally less bound by the restrictions we postulate. Whereas we reject the idea of "expendables" and regard those not useful or even recalcitrant to the social purpose as a burden that society must carry (since their individual claim to existence is as absolute as that of the most useful), a truly totalitarian regime, Communist or other, may deem it right for the collective to rid itself of such encumbrances or to make them forcibly serve some social end by conscripting their persons (and there are effective combinations of both). We do not normally—that is, in nonemergency conditions—give the state the right to conscript labor, while we do give it the right to "conscript" money, for money is detachable from the person as labor is not. Even less than forced labor do we countenance forced risk, injury, and indignity.

But in time of war our society itself supersedes the nice balance of the social contract with an almost absolute precedence of public necessities over individual rights. In this and similar emergencies, the sacrosanctity of the individual is abrogated, and what for all practical purposes amounts to a near-totalitarian, quasi-communist state of affairs is *temporarily* permitted to prevail. In such situations, the community is conceded the right to make calls on its members, or certain of its members, entirely different in magnitude and kind from the calls normally allowed. It is deemed right that a part of the population bears a disproportionate burden of risk of a disproportionate gravity; and it is deemed right that the rest of the community accepts this sacrifice, whether voluntary or enforced, and reaps its benefits—difficult as we find it to justify this acceptance and this benefit by any normal ethical standards. We justify it transethically, as it were, by the supreme collective emergency, formalized, for example, by the declaration of a state of war.

Medical experimentation on human subjects falls somewhere between this overpowering case and the normal transactions of the social contract. On the one hand, no comparable extreme issue of social survival is (by and large) at stake. And no comparable extreme sacrifice or foreseeable risk is (by and large) asked. On the other hand, what is asked goes decidedly beyond, even runs counter to, what it is otherwise deemed fair to let the individual sign over of his person to the benefit of the "common good." Indeed, our sensitivity to the kind of intrusion and use involved is such that only an end of transcendent value or overriding urgency can make it arguable and possibly acceptable in our eyes.

V. Health as a Public Good

The cause invoked is health and, in its more critical aspect, life itself —clearly superlative goods that the physician serves directly by curing and the researcher indirectly by the knowledge gained through his experiments. There is no question about the good served nor about the evil fought—disease and premature death. But a good to whom and an evil to whom? Here the issue tends to become somewhat clouded. In the attempt to give experimentation the proper dignity (on the problematic view that a value becomes greater by being "social" instead of merely individual), the health in question or the disease in question is somehow predicated of the social whole, as if it were society that, in the persons of its members, enjoyed the one and suffered the other. For the purposes of our problem, public interest can then be pitted against private interest, the common good against the individual good. Indeed, I have found health called a national resource, which of course it is, but surely not in the first place.

In trying to resolve some of the complexities and ambiguities lurking in these conceptualizations, I have pondered a particular statement, made in the form of a question, which I found in the *Proceedings* of the earlier *Daedalus* conference: "Can society afford to discard the tissues and organs of the hopelessly unconscious patient when they could be used to restore the otherwise hopelessly ill, but still salvageable, individual?" And somewhat later: "A strong case can be made that society can ill afford to discard the tissues and organs of the hopelessly unconscious patient; they are greatly needed for study and experimental trial to help those who can be salvaged."[7] I hasten to add that any suspicion of callousness that the "commodity" language of these statements may suggest is immediately dispelled by the name of the speaker, Dr. Henry K. Beecher, for whose humanity and moral sensibility there can be nothing but admiration. But the use, in all innocence, of this language gives food for thought. Let me, for a moment, take the question literally. "Discarding" implies proprietary rights—nobody can discard what does not belong to him in the first place. Does society then own my body? "Salvaging" implies the same and, moreover, a use-value to the owner. Is the life-extension of certain individuals then a public interest? "Affording" implies a critically vital level of such an interest—that is, of the loss or gain involved. And "society" itself—what is it? When does a need, an aim, an obligation become social? Let us reflect on some of these terms.

VI. What Society Can Afford

"Can society afford . . . ?" Afford what? To let people die intact, thereby withholding something from other people who desperately need

7*Proceedings*, pp. 50–51.

it, who in consequence will have to die too? These other, unfortunate people indeed cannot afford not to have a kidney, heart, or other organ of the dying patient, on which they depend for an extension of their lease on life; but does that give them a right to it? And does it oblige society to procure it for them? What is it that *society* can or cannot afford—leaving aside for the moment the question of what it has a *right* to? It surely can afford to lose members through death; more than that, it is built on the balance of death and birth decreed by the order of life. This is too general, of course, for our question, but perhaps it is well to remember. The specific question seems to be whether society can afford to let some people die whose death might be deferred by particular means if these were authorized by society. Again, if it is merely a question of what society can or cannot afford, rather than of what it ought or ought not to do, the answer must be: Of course, it can. If cancer, heart disease, and other organic, noncontagious ills, especially those tending to strike the old more than the young, continue to exact their toll at the normal rate of incidence (including the toll of private anguish and misery), society can go on flourishing in every way.

Here, by contrast, are some examples of what, in sober truth, society cannot afford. It cannot afford to let an epidemic rage unchecked; a persistent excess of deaths over births, but neither—we must add—too great an excess of births over deaths; too low an average life expectancy even if demographically balanced by fertility, but neither too great a longevity with the necessitated correlative dearth of youth in the social body; a debilitating state of general health; and things of this kind. These are plain cases where the whole condition of society is critically affected, and the public interest can make its imperative claims. The Black Death of the Middle Ages was a *public* calamity of the acute kind; the life-sapping ravages of endemic malaria or sleeping sickness in certain areas are a public calamity of the chronic kind. Such situations a society as a whole can truly not "afford," and they may call for extraordinary remedies, including, perhaps, the invasion of private sacrosanctities.

This is not entirely a matter of numbers and numerical ratios. Society, in a subtler sense, cannot "afford" a single miscarriage of justice, a single inequity in the dispensation of its laws, the violation of the rights of even the tiniest minority, because these undermine the moral basis on which society's existence rests. Nor can it, for a similar reason, afford the absence or atrophy in its midst of compassion and of the effort to alleviate suffering—be it widespread or rare—one form of which is the effort to conquer disease of any kind, whether "socially" significant (by reason of number) or not. And in short, society cannot afford the absence among its members of *virtue* with its readiness for sacrifice beyond defined duty. Since its presence—that is to say, that of personal idealism—is a matter of grace and not of decree, we have the paradox that society depends for its existence on intangibles of nothing less than a religious order, for which it can hope, but which it cannot enforce. All the more must it protect this most precious capital from abuse.

For what objectives connected with the medico-biological sphere should this reserve be drawn upon—for example, in the form of accepting, soliciting, perhaps even imposing the submission of human subjects to experimentation? We postulate that this must be not just a worthy cause, as any promotion of the health of anybody doubtlessly is, but a cause qualifying for transcendent social sanction. Here one thinks first of those cases critically affecting the whole condition, present and future, of the community we have illustrated. Something equivalent to what in the political sphere is called "clear and present danger" may be invoked and a state of emergency proclaimed, thereby suspending certain otherwise inviolable prohibitions and taboos. We may observe that averting a disaster always carries greater weight than promoting a good. Extraordinary danger excuses extraordinary means. This covers human experimentation, which we would like to count, as far as possible, among the extraordinary rather than the ordinary means of serving the common good under public auspices. Naturally, since foresight and responsibility for the future are of the essence of institutional society, averting disaster extends into long-term prevention, although the lesser urgency will warrant less sweeping licenses.

VII. Society and the Cause of Progress

Much weaker is the case where it is a matter not of saving but of improving society. Much of medical research falls into this category. As stated before, a permanent death rate from heart failure or cancer does not threaten society. So long as certain statistical ratios are maintained, the incidence of disease and of disease-induced mortality is not (in the strict sense) a "social" misfortune. I hasten to add that it is not therefore less of a human misfortune, and the call for relief issuing with silent eloquence from each victim and all potential victims is of no lesser dignity. But it is misleading to equate the fundamentally human response to it with what is owed to society: it is owed by man to man—and it is thereby owed by society to the individuals as soon as the adequate ministering to these concerns outgrows (as it progressively does) the scope of private spontaneity and is made a public mandate. It is thus that society assumes responsibility for medical care, research, old age, and innumerable other things not originally of the public realm (in the original "social contract"), and they become duties toward "society" (rather than directly toward one's fellow man) by the fact that they are socially operated.

Indeed, we expect from organized society no longer mere protection against harm and the securing of the conditions of our preservation, but active and constant improvement in all the domains of life: the waging of the battle against nature, the enhancement of the human estate—in short, the promotion of progress. This is an expansive goal, one far surpassing the disaster norm of our previous reflections. It lacks the urgency of the latter, but has the nobility of the free, forward thrust. It surely is worth sacrifices. It is not at all a question of what society can afford, but of what it is committed to, beyond all necessity, by our mandate. Its trusteeship has become an established, ongoing, institutionalized business of the body politic. As eager beneficiaries of its gains, we now owe to "society," as its chief agent, our individual contributions toward its *continued* pursuit. I emphasize "continued pursuit." Maintaining the existing level requires no more than the orthodox means of taxation and enforcement of professional standards that raise no problems. The more optional goal of pushing forward is also more exacting. We have this syndrome: Progress is by our choosing an acknowledged interest of society, in which we have a stake in various degrees; science is a necessary instrument of progress; research is a necessary instrument of science; and in medical science experimentation on human subjects is a necessary instrument of research. Therefore, human experimentation has come to be a societal interest.

The destination of research is essentially melioristic. It does not serve the preservation of the existing good from which I profit myself and to which I am obligated. Unless the present state is intolerable, the melioristic goal is in a sense gratuitous, and this not only from the vantage point of the present. Our descendants have a right to be left an unplundered planet; they do not have a right to new miracle cures. We have sinned against them, if by our doing we have destroyed their inheritance—which we are doing at full blast; we have not sinned against them, if by the time they come around arthritis has not yet been conquered (unless by sheer neglect). And generally, in the matter of progress, as humanity had no claim on a Newton, a Michelangelo, or a St. Francis to appear, and no right to the blessings of their unscheduled deeds, so progress, with all our methodical labor for it, cannot be budgeted in advance and its fruits received as a due. Its coming-about at all and its turning out for good (of which we can never be sure) must rather be regarded as something akin to grace.

VIII. The Melioristic Goal, Medical Research, and Individual Duty

Nowhere is the melioristic goal more inherent than in medicine. To the physician, it is not gratuitous. He is committed to curing and thus to improving the power to cure. Gratuitous we called it (outside disaster conditions) as a *social* goal, but noble at the same time. Both the nobility and the gratuitousness must influence the manner in which self-sacrifice for it is elicited, and even its free offer accepted. Freedom is certainly the first condition to be observed here. The surrender of one's body to medical experimentation is entirely outside the enforceable "social contract."

Or can it be construed to fall within its terms—namely, as repayment for benefits from past experimentation that I have enjoyed myself? But I am indebted for these benefits not to society, but to the past "martyrs," to whom society is indebted itself, and society has no right to call in my personal debt by way of adding new to its own. Moreover, gratitude is not an enforceable social obligation; it anyway does not mean that I must emulate the deed. Most of all, if it was wrong to exact such sacrifice in the first place, it does not become right to exact it again with the plea of the profit it has brought me. If, however, it was not exacted, but entirely free, as it ought to have been, then it should remain so, and its precedence must not be used as a social pressure on others for doing the same under the sign of duty.

Indeed, we must look outside the sphere of the social contract, outside the whole realm of public rights and duties, for the motivations and norms by which we can expect ever again the upwelling of a will to give what nobody—neither society, nor fellow man, nor posterity—is entitled to. There are such dimensions in man with trans-social wellsprings of conduct, and I have already pointed to the paradox, or mystery, that society cannot prosper without them, that it must draw on them, but cannot command them.

What about the moral law as such a transcendent motivation of conduct? It goes considerably beyond the public law of the social contract. The latter, we saw, is founded on the rule of enlightened self-interest: *Do ut des*—I give so that I be given to. The law of individual conscience asks more. Under the Golden Rule, for example, I am required to give as I wish to be given to under like circumstances, but not in order that I be given to and not in expectation of return. Reciprocity, essential to the social law, is not a condition of the moral law. One subtle "expectation" and "self-interest," but of the moral order itself, may even then be in my mind: I prefer the environment of a moral society and can expect to contribute to the general morality by my own example. But even if I should always be the dupe, the Golden Rule holds. (If the social law breaks faith with me, I am released from its claim.)

IX. Moral Law and Transmoral Dedication

Can I, then, be called upon to offer myself for medical experimentation in the name of the moral law? *Prima facie*, the Golden Rule seems to apply. I should wish, were I dying of a disease, that enough volunteers in the past had provided enough knowledge through the gift of their bodies that I could now be saved. I should wish, were I desperately in need of a transplant, that the dying patient next door had agreed to a definition of death by which his organs would become available to me in the freshest possible condition. I surely should also wish, were I drowning, that somebody would risk his life, even sacrifice his life, for mine.

But the last example reminds us that only the negative form of the Golden Rule ("Do not do unto others what you do not want done unto yourself") is fully prescriptive. The positive form ("Do unto others as you would wish them to do unto you"), in whose compass our issue falls, points into an infinite, open horizon where prescriptive force soon ceases. We may well say of somebody that he ought to have come to the succor of B, to have shared with him in his need, and the like. But we may not say that he ought to have given his life for him. To have done so would be praiseworthy; not to have done so is not blameworthy. It cannot be asked of him; if he fails to do so, he reneges on no duty. But *he* may say of himself, and only he, that he ought to have given his life. *This* "ought" is strictly between him and himself, or between him and God; no outside party—fellow man or society—can appropriate its voice. It can humbly receive the superogatory gifts from the free enactment of it.

We must, in other words, distinguish between moral obligation and the much larger sphere of moral value. (This, incidentally, shows up the error in the widely held view of value theory that the higher a value, the stronger its claim and the greater the duty to realize it. The highest are in a region beyond duty and claim.) The ethical dimension far exceeds that of the moral law and reaches into the sublime solitude of dedication and ultimate commitment, away from all reckoning and rule —in short, into the sphere of the *holy*. From there alone can the offer of self-sacrifice genuinely spring, and this source of it must be honored religiously. How? The first duty here falling on the research community, when it enlists and uses this source, is the safeguarding of true authenticity and spontaneity.

X. The "Conscription" of Consent

But here we must realize that the mere issuing of the appeal, the call-ing for volunteers, with the moral and social pressures it inevitably generates, amounts even under the most meticulous rules of consent to a sort of *conscripting*. And some soliciting is necessarily involved. This was in part meant by the earlier remark that in this area sin and guilt can perhaps not be wholly avoided. And this is why "consent," surely a non-negotiable minimum requirement, is not the full answer to the problem. Granting then that soliciting and therefore some degree of conscripting are part of the situation, who may conscript and who may be conscripted? Or less harshly expressed: Who should issue appeals and to whom?

The naturally qualified issuer of the appeal is the research scientist himself, collectively the main carrier of the impulse and the only one with the technical competence to judge. But his being very much an interested party (with vested interests, indeed, not purely in the public good, but in the scientific enterprise as such, in "his" project, and even in his career) makes him also suspect. The ineradicable dialectic of this situation—a delicate incompatibility problem—calls for particular con-trols by the research community and by public authority that we need not discuss. They can mitigate, but not eliminate the problem. We have to live with the ambiguity, the treacherous impurity of everything human.

XI. Self-Recruitment of the Scientific Community

To whom should the appeal be addressed? The natural issuer of the call is also the first natural addressee: the physician-researcher himself and the scientific confraternity at large. With such a coin-cidence—indeed, the noble tradition with which the whole business of human experimentation started—almost all of the associated legal, ethical, and metaphysical problems vanish. If it is full, autonomous identification of the subject with the purpose that is required for the dignifying of his serving as a subject—here it is; if strongest motiva-tion—here it is; if fullest understanding—here it is; if freest decision— here it is; if greatest integration with the person's total, chosen pursuit —here it is. With the fact of self-solicitation the issue of consent in all its insoluble equivocality is bypassed *per se*. Not even the condition that the particular purpose be truly important and the project reasonably promising, which must hold in any solicitation of others, need be satisfied here. By himself, the scientist is free to obey his obsession, to play his hunch, to wager on chance, to follow the lure of ambition. It is all part of the "divine madness" that somehow animates the ceaseless pressing against frontiers. For the rest of society, which has a deep-seated disposition to look with reverence and awe upon the guardians of the mysteries of life, the profession assumes with this proof of its devotion the role of a self-chosen, consecrated fraternity, not unlike the monastic orders of the past, and this would come nearest to the actual, religious origins of the art of healing.

It would be the ideal, but is not a real solution, to keep the issue of human experimentation within the research community itself. Neither in numbers nor in variety of material would its potential suffice for the many-pronged, systematic, continual attack on disease into which the lonely exploits of the early investigators have grown. Statistical requirements alone make their voracious demands; and were it not for what I have called the essentially "gratuitous" nature of the whole enterprise of progress, as against the mandatory respect for invasion-proof selfhood, the simplest answer would be to keep the whole population enrolled, and let the lot, or an equivalent of draft boards, decide which of each category will at any one time be called up for "service." It is not difficult to picture societies with whose philosophy this would be consonant. We are agreed that ours is not one such and should not become one. The specter of it is indeed among the threatening utopias on our own horizon from which we should recoil, and of whose advent by imperceptible steps we must beware. How then can our mandatory faith be honored when the recruitment for experimentation goes outside the scientific community, as it must in honoring another commitment of no mean dignity? We simply repeat the former question: To whom should the call be addressed?

XII. "Identification" as the Principle of Recruitment in General

If the properties we adduced as the particular qualifications of the members of the scientific fraternity itself are taken as general criteria of selection, then one should look for additional subjects where a maximum of identification, understanding, and spontaneity can be expected —that is, among the most highly motivated, the most highly educated, and the least "captive" members of the community. From this naturally scarce resource, a descending order of permissibility leads to greater abundance and ease of supply, whose use should become proportionately more hesitant as the exculpating criteria are relaxed. An inversion of normal "market" behavior is demanded here—namely, to accept the lowest quotation last (and excused only by the greatest pressure of need); to pay the highest price first.

The ruling principle in our considerations is that the "wrong" of reification can only be made "right" by such authentic identification with the cause that it is the subject's as well as the researcher's cause— whereby his role in its service is not just permitted by him, but *willed*. That sovereign will of his which embraces the end as his own restores his personhood to the otherwise depersonalizing context. To be valid it must be autonomous and informed. The latter condition can, outside the research community, only be fulfilled by degrees; but the higher the degree of the understanding regarding the purpose and the technique, the more valid becomes the endorsement of the will. A margin of mere trust inevitably remains. Ultimately, the appeal for volunteers should seek this free and generous endorsement, the appropriation of the re- search purpose into the person's own scheme of ends. Thus, the appeal is in truth addressed to the one, mysterious, and sacred source of any such generosity of the will—"devotion," whose forms and objects of commitment are various and may invest different motivations in different individuals. The following, for instance, may be responsive to the "call" we are discussing: compassion with human suffering, zeal for humanity, reverence for the Golden Rule, enthusiasm for progress, homage to the cause of knowledge, even longing for sacrificial justification (do not call that "masochism," please). On all these, I say, it is defensible and right to draw when the research objective is worthy enough; and it is a prime duty of the research community (especially in view of what we called the "margin of trust") to see that this sacred source is never abused for frivolous ends. For a less than adequate cause, not even the freest, un- solicited offer should be accepted.

XIII. The Rule of the "Descending Order"
and Its Counter-Utility Sense

We have laid down what must seem to be a forbidding rule to the number-hungry research industry. Having faith in the transcendent potential of man, I do not fear that the "source" will ever fail a society that does not destroy it—and only such a one is worthy of the blessings of progress. But "elitistic" the rule is (as is the enterprise of progress itself), and elites are by nature small. The combined attribute of motiva- tion and information, plus the absence of external pressures, tends to be socially so circumscribed that strict adherence to the rule might numerically starve the research process. This is why I spoke of a descending order of permissibility, which is itself permissive, but where the realization that it is a *descending* order is not without pragmatic import. Departing from the august norm, the appeal must needs shift from idealism to docility, from high-mindedness to compliance, from judgment to trust. Consent spreads over the whole spectrum. I will not go into the casuistics of this penumbral area. I merely indicate the principle of the order of preference: The poorer in knowledge, motivation, and freedom of decision (and that, alas, means the more readily available in terms of numbers and possible manipulation), the more sparingly and indeed reluctantly should the reservoir be used, and the more compelling must therefore become the countervailing justification.

Let us note that this is the opposite of a social utility standard, the reverse of the order by "availability and expendability": The most valuable and scarcest, the least expendable elements of the social organism, are to be the first candidates for risk and sacrifice. It is the standard of *noblesse oblige*; and with all its counter-utility and seeming "wastefulness," we feel a rightness about it and perhaps even a higher "utility," for the soul of the community lives by this spirit.[8] It is also the opposite of what the day-to-day interests of research clamor for, and for the scientific community to honor it will mean that it will have to fight a strong temptation to go by routine to the readiest sources of supply— the suggestible, the ignorant, the dependent, the "captive" in various senses.[9] I do not believe that heightened resistance here must cripple research, which cannot be permitted; but it may indeed slow it down by the smaller numbers fed into experimentation in consequence. This price —a possibly slower rate of progress—may have to be paid for the preservation of the most precious capital of higher communal life.

XIV. Experimentation on Patients

So far we have been speaking on the tacit assumption that the subjects of experimentation are recruited from among the healthy. To the question "Who is conscriptable?" the spontaneous answer is: least and last of all the sick—the most available of all as they are under treatment

---

[8]Socially, everyone is expendable relatively—that is, in different degrees; religiously, no one is expendable absolutely: the "image of God" is in all. If it can be enhanced, then not by anyone being expended, but by someone expending himself.

[9]This refers to captives of circumstance, not of justice. Prison inmates are, with respect to our problem, in a special class. If we hold to some idea of guilt, and to the supposition that our judicial system is not entirely at fault, they may be held to stand in a special debt to society, and their offer to serve—from whatever motive —may be accepted with a minimum of qualms as a means of reparation.

and observation anyway. That the afflicted should not be called upon to bear additional burden and risk, that they are society's special trust and the physician's trust in particular—these are elementary responses of our moral sense. Yet the very destination of medical research, the conquest of disease, requires at the crucial stage trial and verification on precisely the sufferers from the disease, and their total exemption would defeat the purpose itself. In acknowledging this inescapable necessity, we enter the most sensitive area of the whole complex, the one most keenly felt and most searchingly discussed by the practitioners themselves. No wonder, for it touches the heart of the doctor-patient relation, putting its most solemn obligations to the test. There is nothing new in what I have to say about the ethics of the doctor-patient relation, but for the purpose of confronting it with the issue of experimentation some of the oldest verities must be recalled.

A. THE FUNDAMENTAL PRIVILEGE OF THE SICK

In the course of treatment, the physician is obligated to the patient and to no one else. He is not the agent of society, nor of the interests of medical science, nor of the patient's family, nor of his co-sufferers, or future sufferers from the same disease. The patient alone counts when he is under the physician's care. By the simple law of bilateral contract (analogous, for example, to the relation of lawyer to client and its "conflict of interest" rule), the physician is bound not to let any other interest interfere with that of the patient in being cured. But, manifestly, more sublime norms than contractual ones are involved. We may speak of a sacred trust; strictly by its terms, the doctor is, as it were, alone with his patient and God.

There is one normal exception to this—that is, to the doctor's not being the agent of society vis-à-vis the patient, but the trustee of his interests alone: the quarantining of the contagious sick. This is plainly not for the patient's interest, but for that of others threatened by him. (In vaccination, we have a combination of both: protection of the individual and others.) But preventing the patient from causing harm to others is not the same as exploiting him for the advantage of others. And there is, of course, the abnormal exception of collective catastrophe, the analogue to a state of war. The physician who desperately battles a raging epidemic is under a unique dispensation that suspends in a non-specifiable way some of the strictures of normal practice, including possibly those against experimental liberties with his patients. No rules can be devised for the waiving of rules in extremities. And as with the famous shipwreck examples of ethical theory, the less said about it the better. But what is allowable there and may later be passed over in forgiving silence cannot serve as a precedent. We are concerned with non-extreme, non-emergency conditions where the voice of principle can be heard and claims can be adjudicated free from duress. We have conceded that there are such claims, and that if there is to be medical advance at all, not even the superlative privilege of the suffering and the sick can be kept wholly intact from the intrusion of its needs. About this least palatable, most disquieting part of our subject, I have to offer only groping, inconclusive remarks.

B. THE PRINCIPLE OF "IDENTIFICATION" APPLIED TO PATIENTS

On the whole, the same principles would seem to hold here as are found to hold with "normal subjects": motivation, identification, understanding on the part of the subject. But it is clear that these conditions are peculiarly difficult to satisfy with regard to a patient. His physical state, psychic preoccupation, dependent relation to the doctor, the submissive attitude induced by treatment—everything connected with his condition and situation makes the sick person inherently less of a sovereign person than the healthy one. Spontaneity of self-offering has almost to be ruled out; consent is marred by lower resistance or captive circumstance, and so on. In fact, all the factors that make the patient, as a category, particularly accessible and welcome for experimentation at the same time compromise the quality of the responding affirmation that must morally redeem the making use of them. This, in addition to the primacy of the physician's duty, puts a heightened onus on the physician-researcher to limit his undue power to the most important and defensible research objectives and, of course, to keep persuasion at a minimum.

Still, with all the disabilities noted, there is scope among patients for observing the rule of the "descending order of permissibility" that we have laid down for normal subjects, in vexing inversion of the utility order of quantitative abundance and qualitative "expendability." By the principle of this order, those patients who most identify with and are cognizant of the cause of research—members of the medical profession (who after all are sometimes patients themselves)—come first; the highly motivated and educated, also least dependent, among the lay patients come next; and so on down the line. An added consideration here is seriousness of condition, which again operates in inverse proportion. Here the profession must fight the tempting sophistry that the hopeless case is expendable (because in prospect already expended) and therefore especially usable; and generally the attitude that the poorer the chances of the patient the more justifiable his recruitment for experimentation (other than for his own benefit). The opposite is true.

C. NONDISCLOSURE AS A BORDERLINE CASE

Then there is the case where ignorance of the subject, sometimes even of the experimenter, is of the essence of the experiment (the "double blind"-control group-placebo syndrome). It is said to be a necessary element of the scientific process. Whatever may be said about its ethics in regard to normal subjects, especially volunteers, it is an outright betrayal of trust in regard to the patient who believes that he is receiving treatment. Only supreme importance of the objective can exonerate it, without making it less of a transgression. The patient is definitely wronged even when not harmed. And ethics apart, the practice of such deception holds the danger of undermining the faith in the bona fides of treatment, the beneficial intent of the physician—the very basis of the doctor-patient relationship. In every respect, it follows that concealed experiment on patients—that is, experiment under the guise of treatment—should be the rarest exception, at best, if it cannot be wholly avoided.

This has still the merit of a borderline problem. The same is not true of the other case of necessary ignorance of the subject—that of the unconscious patient. Drafting him for nontherapeutic experiments is simply and unqualifiedly impermissible; progress or not, he must never be used, on the inflexible principle that utter helplessness demands utter protection.

When preparing this paper, I filled pages with a casuistics of this harrowing field, but then scrapped most of it, realizing my dilettante status. The shadings are endless, and only the physician-researcher can discern them properly as the cases arise. Into his lap the decision is thrown. The philosophical rule, once it has admitted into itself the idea of a sliding scale, cannot really specify its own application. It can only impress on the practitioner a general maxim or attitude for the exercise of his judgment and conscience in the concrete occasions of his work. In our case, I am afraid, it means making life more difficult for him.

It will also be noted that, somewhat at variance with the emphasis in the literature, I have not dwelt on the element of "risk" and very little on that of "consent." Discussion of the first is beyond the layman's competence; the emphasis on the second has been lessened because of its equivocal character. It is a truism to say that one should strive to minimize the risk and to maximize the consent. The more demanding concept of "identification," which I have used, includes "consent" in its maximal or authentic form, and the assumption of risk is its privilege.

XV. No Experiments on Patients Unrelated to Their Own Disease

Although my ponderings have, on the whole, yielded points of view rather than definite prescriptions, premises rather than conclusions, they have led me to a few unequivocal yeses and noes. The first is the emphatic rule that patients should be experimented upon, if at all, *only* with reference to *their disease*. Never should there be added to the gratuitousness of the experiment as such the gratuitousness of service to an unrelated cause. This follows simply from what we have found to be the *only* excuse for infracting the special exemption of the sick at all—namely, that the scientific war on disease cannot accomplish its goal without drawing the sufferers from disease into the investigative process. If under this excuse they become subjects of experiment, they do so *because*, and only because, of *their* disease.

This is the fundamental and self-sufficient consideration. That the patient cannot possibly benefit from the unrelated experiment therapeutically, while he might from experiment related to his condition, is also true, but lies beyond the problem area of pure experiment. I am in any case discussing nontherapeutic experimentation only, where *ex hypothesi* the patient does not benefit. Experiment as part of therapy—that is, directed toward helping the subject himself—is a different matter altogether and raises its own problems, but hardly philosophical ones. As long as a doctor can say, even if only in his own thought: "There is no known cure for your condition (or: you have responded to none); but there is promise in a new treatment still under investigation, not quite tested yet as to effectiveness and safety; you will be taking a chance, but all things considered, I judge it in your best interest to let me try it on you"—as long as he can speak thus, he speaks as the patient's physician and may err, but does not transform the patient into a subject of experimentation. Introduction of an untried therapy into the treatment where the tried ones have failed is not "experimentation on the patient."

Generally, and almost needless to say, with all the rules of the book, there is something "experimental" (because tentative) about every individual treatment, beginning with the diagnosis itself; and he would be a poor doctor who would not learn from every case for the benefit of future cases, and a poor member of the profession who would not make any new insights gained from his treatments available to the profession at large. Thus, knowledge may be advanced in the treatment of any patient, and the interest of the medical art and sufferers from the same affliction as well as the patient himself may be served if something happens to be learned from his case. But this gain to knowledge and future therapy is incidental to the bona fide service to the present patient. He has the right to expect that the doctor does nothing to him just in order to learn.

In that case, the doctor's imaginary speech would run, for instance, like this: "There is nothing more I can do for you. But you can do something for me. Speaking no longer as your physician but on behalf of medical science, we could learn a great deal about future cases of this kind if you would permit me to perform certain experiments on you. It is understood that you yourself would not benefit from any knowledge we might gain; but future patients would." This statement would express the purely experimental situation, assumedly here with the subject's concurrence and with all cards on the table. In Alexander Bickel's words: "It is a different situation when the doctor is no longer trying to make [the patient] well, but is trying to find out how to make others well in the future.[10]

But even in the second case, that of the nontherapeutic experiment where the patient does not benefit, at least the patient's own disease is enlisted in the cause of fighting that disease, even if only in others. It is yet another thing to say or think: "Since you are here—in the hospital with its facilities—anyway, under our care and observation anyway, away from your job (or, perhaps, doomed) anyway, we wish to profit from your being available for some other research of great interest we are presently engaged in." From the standpoint of merely medical ethics, which has only to consider risk, consent, and the worth of the objective, there may be no cardinal difference between this case and the last one. I hope that the medical reader will not think I am making too fine a point when I say that from the standpoint of the subject and his dignity there is a cardinal difference that crosses the line between the permissible and the impermissible, and this by the same principle of "identification"

[10]*Proceedings*, p. 33. To spell out the difference between the two cases: In the first case, the patient himself is meant to be the beneficiary of the experiment, and directly so; the "subject" of the experiment is at the same time its object, its end. It is performed not for gaining knowledge, but for helping him—and helping him in the *act* of performing it, even if by its results it also contributes to a broader testing process currently under way. It is in fact part of the treatment itself and an "experiment" only in the loose sense of being untried and highly tentative. But whatever the degree of uncertainty, the motivating anticipation (the wager, if you like) is for success, and success here means the subject's own good. To a pure experiment, by contrast, undertaken to gain knowledge, the difference of success and failure is not germane, only that of conclusiveness and inconclusiveness. The "negative" result has as much to teach as the "positive." Also, the true experiment is an act distinct from the uses later made of the findings. And, most important, the subject experimented on is distinct from the eventual beneficiaries of those findings: He lets himself be used as a means toward an end external to himself (even if he should at some later time happen to be among the beneficiaries himself). With respect to his own present needs and his own good, the act is gratuitous.

I have been invoking all along. Whatever the rights and wrongs of any experimentation on any patient—in the one case, at least that residue of identification is left him that it is his own affliction by which he can contribute to the conquest of the affliction, his own kind of suffering which he helps to alleviate in others; and so in a sense it is his own cause. It is totally indefensible to rob the unfortunate of this intimacy with the purpose and make his misfortune a convenience for the furtherance of alien concerns. The observance of this rule is essential, I think, to at least attenuate the wrong that nontherapeutic experimenting on patients commits in any case.

XVI. On the Redefinition of Death

My other emphatic verdict concerns the question of the redefinition of death—that is, acknowledging "irreversible coma as a new definition for death."[11] I wish not to be misunderstood. As long as it is merely a question of when it is permitted to cease the artificial prolongation of certain functions (like heartbeat) traditionally regarded as signs of life, I do not see anything ominous in the notion of "brain death." Indeed, a new definition of death is not even necessary to legitimize the same result if one adopts the position of the Roman Catholic Church, which here at least is eminently reasonable—namely that "when deep unconsciousness is judged to be permanent, extraordinary means to maintain life are not obligatory. They can be terminated and the patient allowed to die."[12] Given a clearly defined negative condition of the brain, the physician is allowed to allow the patient to die his own death by *any* definition, which of itself will lead through the gamut of all possible definitions. But a disquietingly contradictory purpose is combined with this purpose in the quest for a new definition of death—that is, in the will to *advance* the moment of declaring him dead: Permission not to turn off the respirator, but, on the contrary, to keep it on and thereby maintain the body in a state of what would have been "life" by the older definition (but is only a "simulacrum" of life by the new)—so as to get at his organs and tissues under the ideal conditions of what would previously have been "vivisection."[13]

[11]"A Definition of Irreversible Coma," Report of the *Ad Hoc* Committee of the Harvard Medical School to Examine the Definition of Brain Death, *Journal of the American Medical Association* 205, no. 6 (August 5, 1968), pp. 337–40.

[12]As rendered by Dr. Beecher in *Proceedings*, p. 50.

[13]The Report of the *Ad Hoc* Committee no more than indicates this possibility with the second of the "two reasons why there is need for a definition"; "(2) Obsolete criteria for the definition of death can lead to controversy in obtaining organs for transplantation." The first reason is relief from the burden of indefinitely drawn out coma. The report wisely confines its recommendations on application to

Now this, whether done for research or transplant purposes, seems to me to overstep what the definition can warrant. Surely it is one thing when to cease delaying death, another when to start doing violence to the body; one thing when to desist from protracting the process of dying, another when to regard that process as complete and thereby the body as a cadaver free for inflicting on it what would be torture and death to any living body. For the first purpose, we need not know the exact borderline between life and death—we leave it to nature to cross it wherever it is, or to traverse the whole spectrum if there is not just one line. All we need to know is that coma is irreversible. For the second purpose we must know the borderline with absolute certainty; and to use any definition short of the maximal for perpetrating on a *possibly* penultimate state what only the ultimate state can permit is to arrogate a knowledge which, I think, we cannot possibly have. *Since we do not know the exact borderline between life and death*, nothing less than the maximum definition of death will do—brain death plus heart death plus any other indication that may be pertinent—before final violence is allowed to be done.

It would follow then, for this layman at least, that the use of the definition should itself be defined, and this in a restrictive sense. When only permanent coma can be gained with the artificial sustaining of functions, by all means turn off the respirator, the stimulator, any sustaining artifice, and let the patient die; but let him die all the way. Do not, instead, arrest the process and start using him as a mine while, with your own help and cunning, he is still kept this side of what may in truth be the final line. Who is to say that a shock, a final trauma, is not administered to a sensitivity diffusely situated elsewhere than in the brain and still vulnerable to suffering, a sensitivity that we ourselves have been keeping alive. No fiat of definition can settle this question.[14] But I wish to emphasize that the question of possible suffering (easily brushed aside by a sufficient show of reassuring expert consensus) is merely a subsidiary and not the real point of my argument; this, to reiterate, turns on the indeterminacy of the boundaries between *life and death*, not between sensitivity and insensitivity, and bids us to lean

---

what falls under this first reason—namely, turning off the respirator—and remains silent on the possible use of the definition under the second reason. But when "the patient is declared dead on the basis of these criteria," the road to the other use has theoretically been opened and will be taken (if I remember rightly, it has even been taken once, in a much debated case in England), unless it is blocked by a special barrier in good time. The above is my feeble attempt to help in doing so.

[14]Only a Cartesian view of the "animal machine," which I somehow see lingering here, could set the mind at rest, as in historical fact it did at its time in the matter of vivisection. But its truth is surely not established by definition.

toward a maximal rather than a minimal determination of death in an area of basic uncertainty.

There is also this to consider: The patient must be absolutely sure that his doctor does not become his executioner, and that no definition authorizes him ever to become one. His right to this certainty is absolute, and so is his right to his own body with all its organs. Absolute respect for these rights violates no one else's right, for no one has a right to another's body. Speaking in still another, religious vein: The expiring moments should be watched over with piety and be safe from exploitation.

I strongly feel, therefore, that it should be made quite clear that the proposed new definition of death is to authorize *only* the one and *not* the other of the two opposing things: only to break off a sustaining intervention and let things take their course, not to keep up the sustaining intervention for a final intervention of the most destructive kind.

XVII. Conclusion

There would now have to be said something about nonmedical experiments on human subjects, notably psychological and genetic, of which I have not lost sight. But I must leave this for another occasion. I wish only to say in conclusion that if some of the practical implications of my reasonings are felt to work out toward a slower rate of progress, this should not cause too great dismay. Let us not forget that progress is an optional goal, not an unconditional commitment, and that its tempo in particular, compulsive as it may become, has nothing sacred about it. Let us also remember that a slower progress in the conquest of disease would not threaten society, grievous as it is to those who have to deplore that their particular disease be not yet conquered, but that society would indeed be threatened by the erosion of those moral values whose loss, possibly caused by too ruthless a pursuit of scientific progress, would make its most dazzling triumphs not worth having. Let us finally remember that it cannot be the aim of progress to abolish the lot of mortality. Of some ill or other, each of us will die. Our mortal condition is úpon us with its harshness but also its wisdom—because without it there would not be the eternally renewed promise of the freshness, immediacy, and eagerness of youth; nor would there be for any of us the incentive to number our days and make them count. With all our striving to wrest from our mortality what we can, we should bear its burden with patience and dignity.

6.
Against the Stream:
Comments on the Definition
and Redefinition of Death

The by now famous "Report of the *Ad Hoc* Committee of the Harvard Medical School to Examine the Definition of Brain Death" advocates the adoption of "irreversible coma as a new definition of death."[1] The report leaves no doubt of the practical reasons "why there is need for a definition," naming these two: relief of patient, kin, and medical resources from the burdens of indefinitely prolonged coma; and removal of controversy on obtaining organs for transplantation. On both counts, the new definition is designed to give the physician the right to terminate the treatment of a condition which not only cannot be improved by such treatment, but whose mere prolongation by it is utterly meaningless to the patient himself. The last consideration, of course, is ultimately the only valid rationale for termination (and for termination only!) and must support all the others. It does so with regard to the reasons mentioned under the first head, for the relief of the patient means automatically also that of his family, doctor, nurses, apparatus, hospital space, and so on. But the other reason—freedom for organ use —has possible implications that are not equally covered by the primary rationale, which is the patient himself. For with this primary rationale (the senselessness of mere vegetative function) the Report has strictly

Written in 1970, this essay is a postscript to Essay 5. It has not been published previously.
[1]See Essay 5, note 11.

speaking defined not death, the ultimate state, itself, but a criterion for permitting it to take place unopposed—e.g., by turning off the respirator. The Report, however, purports by that criterion to have defined death itself, declaring it on its evidence as already given, not merely no longer to be opposed. But if "the patient is declared dead on the basis of these criteria," i.e., if the comatose individual is not a patient at all but a corpse, then the road to other uses of the definition, urged by the second reason, has been opened in principle and will be taken in practice, unless it is blocked in good time by a special barrier. What follows is meant to reinforce what I called "my feeble attempt" to help erect such a barrier on theoretical grounds.

My original comments of 1968 on the then newly proposed "redefinition of death" (p. 129–131 above) were marginal to the discussion of "experimentation on human subjects," which has to do with the living and not the dead. They have since, however, drawn fire from within the medical profession, and precisely in connection with the second of the reasons given by the Harvard Committee why a new definition is wanted, namely, the *transplant* interest, which my kind critics felt threatened by my layman's qualms and lack of understanding. Can I take this as corroborating my initial suspicion that this *interest*, in spite of its notably muted expression in the Committee Report, was and is the major motivation behind the definitional effort? I am confirmed in this suspicion when I hear Dr. Henry K. Beecher, author of the Committee's Report (and its Chairman), ask elsewhere: "Can society afford to discard the tissues and organs of the hopelessly unconscious patient when they could be used to restore the otherwise hopelessly ill, but still salvageable individual?"[2] In any case, the tenor and passion of the discussion which my initial polemic provoked from my medical friends left no doubt where the surgeon's interest in the definition lies. I contend that, pure as this interest, viz., to save other lives, is in itself, its intrusion into the *theoretical* attempt to define death makes the attempt impure; and the Harvard Committee should never have allowed itself to adulterate the purity of its scientific case by baiting it with the prospect of this *extraneous*—though extremely appealing—gain. But purity of theory is not my concern here. My concern is with certain practical consequences which under the urgings of that extraneous interest can be drawn from the definition and would enjoy its full sanction, once it has been officially accepted. Doctors would be less than human if certain formidable advantages of such possible consequences would not influence their judgment as to the theoretical adequacy of a definition

[2]See Essay 5, p. 114.

that yields them—just as I freely admit that my shudder at one aspect of those consequences, and at the danger of others equally sanctioned by that definition, keeps my theoretical skepticism in a state of extreme alertness.

Since the private exchanges referred to (which were conducted in the most amicable spirit of shared concern) somewhat sharpened my theoretical case and in addition brought out some of the apprehensions that haunt me in this matter—and which, I think, should be in everyone's mind before final approval of the new definition takes matters out of our hands—I base the remainder of this paper on a statement titled "Against the Stream" which I circulated among the members of the informal group in question.[3]

I had to answer three charges made à propos of the pertinent part of my *Daedalus* essay: that my reasoning regarding "cadaver donors" counteracts sincere life-saving efforts of physicians; that I counter precise scientific facts with vague philosophical considerations; and that I overlook the difference between death of "the organism as a whole" and death of "the whole organism," with the related difference between spontaneous and externally induced respiratory and other movements.

I plead, of course, guilty to the first charge for the case where the cadaver status of the donor is in question, which is precisely what my argument is about. The use of the term "cadaver donor" here simply begs the question, to which only the third charge (see below) addresses itself.

As to the charge of vagueness, it might just be possible that it vaguely reflects the fact that mine is an argument—a precise argument, I believe —*about* vagueness, viz., the vagueness of a condition. Giving intrinsic vagueness its due is not being vague. Aristotle observed that it is the mark of a well-educated man not to insist on greater precision in knowledge than the subject admits, e.g., the same in politics as in mathematics. Reality of certain kinds—of which the life-death spectrum is perhaps one—may be imprecise in itself, or the knowledge obtainable of it may be. To acknowledge such a state of affairs is more adequate to it than a precise definition, which does violence to it. I am challenging the undue precision of a definition and of its practical application to an imprecise field.

The third point—which was made by Dr. Otto Guttentag—is highly relevant and I will deal with it step by step.

a. The difference between "organism as a whole" and "whole organ-

[3]Of its members I name the renal surgeon Dr. Samuel Kountz, specializing in kidney transplantation, and Drs. Harrison Sadler and Otto Guttentag, all of the Medical Center of the University of California in San Francisco.

ism" which he has in mind is perhaps brought out more clearly if for "whole organism" we write "every and all parts of the organism." If this is the meaning, then I have been speaking throughout of "death of the organism as a whole," not of "death of the whole organism"; and any ambiguity in my formulations can be easily removed. Local subsystems—single cells or tissues—may well continue to function locally, i.e., to display biochemical activity for themselves (e.g., growth of hair and nails) for some time after death, without this affecting the definition of death by the larger criteria of the whole. But respiration and circulation do not fall into this class, since the effect of their functioning, though performed by subsystems, extends through the total system and insures the functional preservation of its other parts. Why else prolong them artificially in prospective "cadaveric" organ donors (e.g., "maintain renal circulation of cadaver kidneys in situ") except to keep those other parts "in good shape"—viz., alive—for eventual transplantation? The comprehensive system thus sustained is even capable of continued overall metabolism when intravenously fed, and then, presumably, of diverse other (e.g. glandular) functions as well—in fact, I suppose, of pretty much everything not involving neural control. There are stories of comatose patients lingering on for months with those aids; the metaphor of the "human vegetable" recurring in the debate (strangely enough, sometimes in support of redefining death—as if "vegetable" were not an instance of life!) say as much. In short, what is here kept going by various artifices must—with the caution due in this twilight zone—be equated with "the organism as a whole" named in the classical definition of death—much more so, at least, than with any mere, separable part of it.

b. Nor, to my knowledge, does that older definition specify that the functioning whose "irreversible cessation" constitutes death must be spontaneous and does not count for life when artificially induced and sustained (the implications for therapy would be devastating). Indeed, "irreversible" cessation can have a twofold reference: to the function itself or only to the spontaneity of it. A cessation can be irreversible with respect to spontaneity but still reversible with respect to the activity as such—in which case the reversing external agency must continuously substitute for the lost spontaneity. This is the case of the respiratory movements and heart contractions in the comatose. The distinction is not irrelevant, because if we could do for the disabled brain—let's say, the lower nerve centers only—what we can do for the heart and lungs, viz., *make* it work by the continuous input of some external agency (electrical, chemical, or whatever), we would surely do so and not be finicky about the resulting function lacking spontaneity: the functioning as such would matter. Respirator and stimulator could then be turned off, because the nerve center presiding over heart contractions (etc.) has again taken over and returned *them* to being "spontaneous"—just as systems presided over by circulation had enjoyed spontaneity of function when the circulation was only nonspontaneously active. The case is wholly hypothetical, but I doubt that a doctor would feel at liberty to pronounce the patient dead on the ground of the nonspontaneity at the cerebral source, when it can be *made* to function by an auxiliary device.

The purpose of the foregoing thought-experiment was to cast some doubt (a layman's, to be sure) on the seeming simplicity of the spontaneity criterion. With the stratification and interlocking of functions, it seems to me, organic spontaneity is distributed over many levels and loci—any superordinated level enabling its subordinates to be naturally spontaneous, be its own action natural or artificial.

c. The point with irreversible coma as defined by the Harvard group, of course, is precisely that it is a condition which precludes reactivation of any part of the brain in *every* sense. We then have an "organism as a whole" minus the brain, maintained in some partial state of life so long as the respirator and other artifices are at work. And here the question is not: has the patient died? but: how should he—still a patient —be dealt with? Now *this* question must be settled, surely not by a definition of death, but by a definition of man and of what life is human. That is to say, the question cannot be answered by decreeing that death has already occurred and the body is therefore in the domain of things; rather it is by holding, e.g., that it is humanly not justified—let alone, demanded—to artificially prolong the life of a brainless body. This is the answer I myself would advocate. On that philosophical ground, which few will contest, the physician can, indeed should, turn off the respirator and let the "definition of death" take care of itself by what then inevitably happens. (The later utilization of the corpse is a different matter I am not dealing with here, though it too resists the comfortable patness of merely utilitarian answers.) The decision to be made, I repeat, is an axiological one and not already made by clinical fact. It begins when the diagnosis of the condition has spoken: it is not diagnostic itself. Thus, as I have pointed out before, no redefinition of death is needed; only, perhaps, a redefinition of the physician's presumed duty to prolong life under all circumstances.

d. But, it might be asked, is not a definition of death made into law the simpler and more precise way than a definition of medical ethics (which is difficult to legislate) for sanctioning the same practical conclusion, while avoiding the twilight of value judgment and possible legal ambiguity? It would be, if it really sanctioned the same conclusion, and no more. But it sanctions indefinitely more: it opens the gate to a whole range of other possible conclusions, the extent of which cannot even be foreseen, but some of which are disquietingly close at hand. The point is, if the comatose patient is by definition dead, he is a patient no more but a corpse, with which can be done whatever law or custom or the deceased's will or next of kin permit and sundry interests urge doing with a corpse. This includes—why not?—the protracting of the in-between state, for which we must find a new name ("simulated life"?) since that of "life" has been preempted by the new definition of death, and extracting from it all the profit we can. There are many. So far the "redefiners" speak of no more than keeping the respirator going until the transplant organ is to be removed, then turning it off, then beginning to cut into the "cadaver," this being the end of it—which sounds innocent enough. But why must it be the end? Why turn the respirator off? Once we are assured that we are dealing with a cadaver, there are no logical reasons against (and strong pragmatic reasons for) going on with the artificial "animation" and keeping the "deceased's" body on call, as a bank for life-fresh organs, possibly also as a plant for manu-facturing hormones or other biochemical compounds in demand. I have no doubts that methods exist or can be perfected which allow the natural powers for the healing of surgical wounds by new tissue growth to stay "alive" in such a body. Tempting also is the idea of a self-replenishing blood bank. And that is not all. Let us not forget research. Why shouldn't the most wonderful surgical and grafting experiments be conducted on the complaisant subject-nonsubject, with no limits set to daring? Why not immunological explorations, infection with diseases old and new, trying out of drugs? We have the active cooperation of a functional organism declared to be dead: we have, that is, the advantages of the living donor without the disadvantages imposed by his rights and interests (for a corpse has none). What a boon for medical instruction, for anatomical and physiological demonstration and practicing on so much better material than the inert cadavers otherwise serving in the dissection room! What a chance for the apprentice to learn *in vivo*, as it were, how to amputate a leg, without his mistakes mattering! And so on, into the wide open field. After all, what is advocated is "the full utiliza-tion of modern means to maximize the value of cadaver organs." Well, this is it.

Come, come, the members of the profession will say, nobody is think-ing of this kind of thing. Perhaps not; but I have just shown that one *can* think of them. And the point is that the proposed definition of death has removed any reasons not to think of them and, once thought of, not to do them when found desirable (and the next of kin are agree-

able). We must remember that what the Harvard group offered was not
a definition of irreversible coma as a rationale for breaking off sustaining
action, but a definition of death by the criterion of irreversible coma as
a rationale for conceptually transposing the patient's body to the class
of dead things, *regardless* of whether sustaining action is kept up or
broken off. It would be hypocritical to deny that the redefinition amounts
to an antedating of the accomplished fact of death (compared to conventional signs that may outlast it); that it was motivated not by exclusive concern with the patient but with certain extraneous interests in
mind (organ donorship mostly named so far); and that the actual use of
the general license it grants is implicity anticipated. But no matter what
particular use is or is not anticipated at the moment, or even anathe-
matized—it would be naive to think that a line can be drawn anywhere
for such uses when strong enough interest urge them, seeing that the
definition (which is absolute, not graded) negates the very principle for
drawing a line. (Given the ingenuity of medical science, in which I have
great faith, I am convinced that the "simulated life" can eventually be
made to comprise practically every extraneural activity of the human
body; and I would not even bet on its never comprising *some* artificially
activated neural functions as well: which would be awkward for the
argument of nonsensitivity, but still under the roof of that of nonspontaneity.)

   e. Now my point is a very simple one. It is this. We do not know with
certainty the borderline between life and death, and a definition cannot
substitute for knowledge. Moreover, we have sufficient grounds for
suspecting that the artificially supported condition of the comatose patient may still be one of life, however reduced—i.e., for doubting that,
even with the brain function gone, he is completely dead. In this state
of marginal ignorance and doubt the only course to take is to lean over
backward toward the side of possible life. It follows that interventions as
I described should be regarded on a par with vivisection and on no
account be performed on a human body in that equivocal or threshold
condition. And the definition that allows them, by stamping as unequivocal what at best is equivocal, must be rejected. But mere rejection
in discourse is not enough. Given the pressure of the—very real and
very worthy—medical interests, it can be predicted that the permission
it implies in theory will be irresistible in practice, once the definition is
installed in official authority. Its becoming so installed must therefore
be resisted at all cost. It is the only thing that still can be resisted; by
the time the practical conclusions beckon, it will be too late. It is a clear
case of *principiis obsta*.

   The foregoing argumentation was strictly on the plane of common sense and ordinary logic. Let me add, somewhat conjecturally, two philosophical observations.

I see lurking behind the proposed definition of death, apart from its obvious pragmatic motivation, a curious revenant of the old soul-body dualism. Its new apparition is the dualism of brain and body. In a certain analogy to the former it holds that the true human person rests in (or is represented by) the brain, of which the rest of the body is a mere subservient tool. Thus, when the brain dies, it is as when the soul departed: what is left are "mortal remains." Now nobody will deny that the cerebral aspect is decisive for the human quality of the life of the organism that is man's. The position I advanced acknowledges just this by recommending that with the irrecoverable total loss of brain function one should not hold up the naturally ensuing death of the rest of the organism. But it is no less an exaggeration of the cerebral aspect as it was of the conscious soul, to deny the extracerebral body its essential share in the identity of the person. The body is as uniquely the body of this brain and no other, as the brain is uniquely the brain of this body and no other. What is under the brain's central control, the bodily total, is as individual, as much "myself," as singular to my identity (fingerprints!), as noninterchangeable, as the controlling (and reciprocally controlled) brain itself. My identity is the identity of the whole organism, even if the higher functions of personhood are seated in the brain. How else could a man love a woman and not merely her brains? How else could we lose ourselves in the aspect of a face? Be touched by the delicacy of a frame? It's this person's, and no one else's. Therefore, the body of the comatose, so long as—even with the help of art— it still breathes, pulses, and functions otherwise, must still be considered a residual continuance of the subject that loved and was loved, and as such is still entitled to some of the sacrosanctity accorded to such a subject by the laws of God and men. That sacrosanctity decrees that it must not be used as a mere means.

My second observation concerns the morality of our time, to which our "redefiners" pay homage with the best of intentions, which have their own subtle sophistry. I mean the prevailing attitude toward death, whose faintheartedness they indulge in a curious blend with the tough-mindedness of the scientist. The Catholic Church had the guts to say: under these circumstances let the patient die—speaking of the patient alone and not of outside interests (society's, medicine's, etc.). The cowardice of modern secular society which shrinks from death as an unmitigated evil needs the assurance (or fiction) that he is already dead when the decision is to be made. The responsibility of a value-laden decision is replaced by the mechanics of a value-free routine. Insofar

as the redefiners of death—by saying "he is already dead"—seek to allay
the scruples about turning the respirator off, they cater to this modern
cowardice which has forgotten that death has its own fitness and dignity,
and that a man has a right to be let die. Insofar as by saying so they
seek to provide an even better conscience about keeping the respirator
on and freely utilizing the body thus arrested on the threshold of life
and death, they serve the ruling pragmatism of our time which will let
no ancient fear and trembling interfere with the relentless expanding of
the realm of sheer thinghood and unrestricted utility. The "splendor
and misery" of our age dwells in that irresistible tide.

7.
Biological Engineering—
A Preview

In recent years the life sciences have been moving toward the point where the technological or engineering potentials inherent in the progress of all physical science are beginning to knock at the door of the biological realm and of human biology in particular. The practical possibilities offered by the new knowledge may prove as irresistible as have those in the older fields of technology, but this time we do well to consider the implications in advance so that for once we are not caught entirely unawares by our own powers as we allowed ourselves to be in all earlier cases. The biological control of man, especially genetic control, raises ethical questions of a wholly new kind for which neither previous praxis nor previous thought has prepared us. Since no less than the very nature and image of man are at issue, prudence becomes itself our first ethical duty, and hypothetical reasoning our first responsibility. To consider the consequences before taking action is no more than common prudence. In this case, wisdom bids us to go further and to examine the use of powers even before they are quite ready for use. One conceivable outcome of such an examination could be the counsel not to let those powers get ready in the first place, i.e., to stop certain lines of inquiry leading to them, considering the extreme seducibility of man by whatever power he has. And more than mere counsel could be indicated

Portions of this essay have been presented orally at the University of Chicago and elsewhere.

if in the nature of the case the readying of the powers in the course of inquiry involves already the very actions, in the form of "experiment," which the examination finds it necessary to interdict in the eventual use of those powers: if, in other words, the powers can be acquired only by their actual exercise on the true "material" itself. This exercise, moreover, must be on a trial-and-error basis: that is, only through necessarily faulty biological engineering could we perfect the theory for eventually faultless biological engineering—which alone might be enough to interdict the acquisition of the art even if its foreseen final performance were approved.

Interference with the freedom of research is a grave ethical matter by itself, yet it is like nothing against the gravity of the ethical issues posed by the eventual success of that research; and bringing up the possibility of a self-imposed halt in these preliminary remarks at all is just to suggest a measure of the perils which a biological engineering fully matured and enfranchised might visit upon man. Let us be at least forewarned. The utmost resources of our moral reason are called upon for dealing with this subject—alas, at a time when ethical theory is in greater disarray than ever before. Given this condition, and given the unprecedentedness of the matter itself and its still largely hypothetical status, my comments on its ethical aspects can only be tentative and humble. But humility is perhaps the one virtue now required as an antidote to the rampage of technological arrogance.

I. The General Nature
of Biological Engineering

First let us see in what sense one can speak of biological engineering in analogy to what is normally understood by "engineering." In its accepted sense it means the designing and constructing of complex material artifacts for human use. This includes the redesigning, for adaptation or improvement, of existing designs, i.e., the further development of what the engineering art has already created. The rationale, as stated, is always use for the benefit of some user, i.e., for a supposed human good, be that even the killing of some men by other men, or of many by few.

Up to the present, all technology has been concerned with lifeless materials (most typically metals), shaping them into nonhuman artifacts for human use. The division was clear: man was the subject, "nature" the object of technological mastery (which did not exclude that man became mediately the object of its application.) The advent of biological engineering signals a radical departure from this clear division, indeed a break of metaphysical importance: Man becomes the direct object as well as the subject of the engineering art. Other differences are concomitant with this most obvious one and greatly qualify the analogy with conventional engineering.

(1) First, the extent of "making" involved. In hardware or dead-matter engineering, construction and production goes all the way up from first elements to final product, putting it together completely from independent parts. Biological engineering proposes to work as a modifier on pregiven structures, whose very reality and type are the primary datum: they are neither invented nor produced *de novo*, but as found are made the object of inventive improvement.[1] Thus we have partial instead of total making, design alteration rather than designing, and the result is not completely an artifact but only with a tiny fraction of its make-up.

(2) This implies an important difference in "engineering" procedure. With hardware, the maker is the sole agent vis-à-vis the passive material. With organisms, the modifier is a co-agent with the self-acting material, viz., the given biological system, into whose self-activity he inserts the new fractional determinant, to be integrated into the totality of its autonomous determinants by their own working. The modifying effect is brought about by the self-moving entity itself; its autonomy is enlisted as the main agency. Thus we have determination by intervention only, not by building.

(3) This affects the important issue of predictability. In hardware engineering, the number of "unknowns" is practically nil, and the engineer can accurately predict the properties of his product. For the biological engineer, who has to take over, "sight-unseen," the untold complexity of the given determinants with their self-functioning dynamics, the number of unknowns in the design is immense. To them he must commit his contributory share in the totality of causes. Prediction of its fate is thus reduced to guessing, planning—to gambling. The intended redesigning or modification or improvement is in fact an *experiment*, and one with so long a run—at least in the genetic field—that its outcome (if identifiable at all) lies normally beyond the purview of the experimenter himself.

(4) This again completely changes the conventional relation between mere experiment and real action. In normal engineering (as in natural science), experiments are non-committal, performed with substitute models which can be altered or scrapped at will, tested and retested,

[1]The *de novo* design and fabrication of organisms is indeed not ruled out in theory, but at present not anticipated in practice. A first beginning would be a synthetic virus.

before a finally approved model reaches the production line: only then does commitment begin. No such substitution of the as-if for the serious is possible in biological, especially human, engineering: for valid experiment, it must operate on the original itself, the real thing in the fullest sense. And what here intervenes between initiation and conclusion of the experiment is the actual lives of individuals and even whole populations. This nullifies the whole distinction between mere experiment and definitive action. The comfortable separation of the two is gone, and with it the innocence of mere experiment. The experiment *is* the real deed, and the real deed is an experiment.

(5) Add to this the matter of reversibility versus irreversibility. Everything in mechanical construction is reversible. It is the peculiar property of the organic that its modifications are irreversible. This is too deep a subject to go into here. Be it just said that conventional engineering can always correct its mistakes; and not only in the planning and testing stages: even the finished products, automobiles for example, can be recalled to the factory for correction of faults. Not so in biological engineering. Its deeds are irrevocable. When its results show, it is too late to do anything about it. What is done is done. You cannot recall persons nor scrap populations. Indeed, what to do with the unavoidable mishaps of genetic interventions, with the failures, the freaks, the monstrosities— whether to introduce the term "discards" into the human equation, which the adoption of at least some contemplated forms of genetic engineering would compel us to do—these are ethical questions to be faced and answered before permitting even the first step in that fateful direction.

(6) The fact that biological engineering, as spoken about, means mostly genetic engineering, introduces another significant difference from dead-matter engineering. There is no analogy in machines to generation and heredity. From the maker's perspective this means the difference of indirect from direct causal relation to the final result. Production in biological engineering is indirect, through injecting the new determinant into the genetic sequence, where its effects will first show in the next generation and then self-propagate through the generations. "Making" here is launching, setting adrift in the stream of becoming which carries along the maker himself.

(7) Herewith arises the question of power, so intimately allied to that of technology. By the Baconian formula, science and technology increase man's power over nature. They also, of course, increase the powers of men over men, thus the subjection of men to the power of other men, not to speak of their joint subjection to the very wants and dependencies created by technology itself. But, collectively speaking, it

is reasonable to assert that the total or cumulative power of humankind has increased, most certainly in relation to extra-human nature.[2] Now man's impending control over his own evolution is hailed as the final triumph of this power—"nature" now significantly including man himself, reclaiming him as it were from his splendid isolation. But of whom is this a power over what and whom? Plainly, of the living over posterity; more correctly, of present men over future men, who are the defenseless objects of antecedent choices by the planners of today. The obverse of *their* power is the later servitude of the living to the dead. Agent power is here entirely unilateral and of the few, with no recourse to countervailing power open to its patients, for they are the results and by whatever they do will execute the law placed on their being by the power that ruled over their coming-to-be.[3] I have pointed out before that the power, once exercised, is out of the wielder's hand, dispatched into the play of life's vaster complexity which defies complete analysis and prediction: on that count the power, however fateful, is blind. But whether blind or seeing, fumbling or competent, it raises the question, unknown to dead-matter engineering, of what *right* anyone has to so predetermine future men; and, hypothetically granting the right, what *wisdom* he has that entitles him to exercise it. Two different rights are thus involved, the second—that of exercising an abstract right—predicated on the possession of wisdom as the necessary condition, which possession, however, may well result in dismissing the hypothesis of the first right.

(8) This brings me to the last point in this survey of the differences between conventional and biological engineering—that of *goals*. It is for their discrimination that we need wisdom in the first place. The goals of conventional technology, questionable as they often are, can at least always be defined, if not defended, in terms of utility. This still extends to biological engineering with reference to plants and animals. But utility means "for the use of man," and unless men themselves are conceived as being for the use of men, to be designed accordingly, the utilitarian rationale of all other technology fails us in the case of man's

[2]It must be admitted that "Man" with a capital M is a dubious abstract, and that it is a moot point whether individual men today have greater control over *their* environment (which in the main is the man-made world of technical civilization) than former men had over theirs; even more so, whether their control over themselves has increased or decreased; and, yet more, whether they—individually *or* collectively—are masters over the promptings, logic, and immanent dynamics of the technical juggernaut. Still, the above statement for the species as a whole remains defensible so long as the collective powers don't get out of hand and make their wielders their victims.

[3]This sums up the observations of C. S. Lewis in his excellent little book, *The Abolition of Man*, (New York: Macmillan, 1947) pp. 69–72.

engineering of himself. What then are *its* aims? Surely not to create man—he is already there. To create better men? But what is the standard of better? Better adapted men? But better adapted to what? Supermen? But how do we know what is "super"? We stumble into ultimate questions as soon as we propose to tamper with the making of man. They all converge into one: in what image?

We must now descend from generalities to particulars, and from the "what is it?" to the "how done?", i.e., to the different—available or anticipated—modes of execution, which also differ in their ends.

II. Presently Available Modes

The possible *goals* define the *kinds* of biological control that are being contemplated, and in this second section of my paper, as later in the third, I shall discuss the ethical aspects of certain kinds of control distinguished by their ends. It may well be the case that certain ends are first suggested by the mere becoming available of the means; even then, they can serve to categorize the adopted course of action. According to this criterion, which answers to the question *why* something is to be done and thereby determines *what* is to be done, we can distinguish between protective, melioristic, and creative biological control. "Control" is here the wider genus, of which "engineering," in the strong sense, is a particular kind (their being nonengineering types of control); and "protective," "melioristic," "creative" have usually the species for their object rather than the individual (though, of course, working through individuals). I will progress from weaker to stronger modes on a rising scale.

A. NEGATIVE OR PREVENTIVE EUGENICS

1. Controlled mating

First, then, about protective or preventive control, whose best-known form is negative eugenics, that is, a mating policy that prevents the transmission of pathogenic or otherwise deleterious genes by barring their carriers from procreation. The congenital diabetic, e.g., is to be barred or restrained from producing offspring. I am not here concerned with the means of restraint, which may go all the way from persuasion to sterilization, from voluntary to compulsory, and which raise their own problems. I confine my attention to the rationale, which is twofold: humanitarian and evolutionary. The humanitarian relates to the well-being of the potential offspring individually, and for their own sake as it were, trying to avoid future misery. No possible violation of the rights of such potential offspring is involved in desisting from producing it, since there is no right to existence for hypothetical individuals not yet conceived.[4] But though not the right *of* the merely imagined offspring, the right *to* offspring of the hindered progenitor is involved. He or she is asked to forgo it, and he can counter the appeal to his humanitarian responsibility, i.e., to his pity, with the claim that he, a sufferer from the disease himself, is the best judge on whether such a life is still worth living, and that he is prepared to take the risk (it is usually no more than that) on behalf of his offspring. There is merit to this at least in a number of cases—definitely where only one parent is afflicted, and arguably even where both are and the risk amounts to near-certainty. But the humanitarian appeal is strengthened, independently of the individual risk factor, by the evolutionary one, which argues that the *species* or population must be protected against the danger of deterioration of its gene pool through a progressive increase of deleterious factors—an increase threatened by the very protection which civilization affords to those factors otherwise held in check by natural selection. The diabetic can be told that he owes his very candidacy for procreation to the medical art which (through the provision of insulin) has kept him from perishing before reaching the proper age: as a *quid pro quo* he can be asked to sacrifice this one right in the interest of the species. This is ethically in order at the individual level. At the population level, negative eugenics is ostensibly modest, aiming at preservation rather than innovation, not presuming to improve on nature but wishing merely to redress its balance, disturbed by human intervention in the first place. This too seems to be in order, *if* the specter of a sickly and debilitated species otherwise to be expected from civilized conditions is true (which I cannot judge). Negative eugenics thus looks more like an extension of preventive medicine than a beginning of biological engineering.

Certain necessary caveats will qualify this all too unambiguous picture. Thus the remedial zeal can easily (in deciding what genes or gene packages warrant elimination) widen the concept "pathogenic" to include the "undesirable" in more arbitrary senses and then forfeit the sanction of nature which a mere compensating for the curtailment of natural selection can claim. The same goes for the temptation to extend the control from the manifest, i.e., dominant or double-dosed, presence of the offending gene, which represents only the tip of the iceberg, to

---

[4]This argument, of course, no longer applies to the device of feticide, i.e., abortion, which is always a violation of the most fundamental of all rights, the right to live.

the vastly greater number of recessive carriers. Genetic death decreed on them can no longer claim to be consonant with self-regulating evolutionary mechanics: it plainly runs counter to it and represents innovative manipulation, highly questionable biologically and indefensible ethically.[5] Sifting and restructuring the genetic pool is different from protecting and preserving it, and we have no self-evident warrant for the former. In fact, with this variant of negative eugenics, and in spite of its still negative mechanics of elimination, we pass already over to the much more critical case of positive or melioristic eugenics which wants to improve the species.

2. Fetal screening

Before turning to this, some consideration should be given to a variant of the preventive eugenics of mercy, namely that which operates not on potential but on incipient progeny *in utero*. Through the technique of amniocentesis (extraction of embryonic cells from the amniotic fluid) it has become possible to diagnose genetic diseases in the fetus at an early stage of its development. So far, only a small number of them can be thus detected, but this may grow with further refinement of cell diagnostics. The method, which involves puncturing of maternal tissues, entails some risk for mother and embryo: again, this may in time become acceptably small compared to the gravity of the suspicion which must be there in the first place from the parental record to suggest the intervention at all. We are here concerned with what then follows.[6] The purpose of the diagnosis, since in the present and forseeable future it cannot be curing, is to open a decision on whether to continue or discon-

---

[5]One can, of course, demand that identified recessive carriers avoid mating with corresponding carriers—or at least strongly advise them so. To advise *against* certain matches in consideration of the phenotypes likely to result from them is a legitimate role of the marriage counselor. But to try and sift out genes from the pool altogether is an entirely different matter.

[6]For a much fuller discussion of the ethics of prenatal screening than offered here see Paul Ramsey, "Screening: An Ethicist's View" in *Ethical Issues in Human Genetics*, ed. Bruce Hilton, Daniel Callahan, *et al.* (New York: Plenum Publishing Corporation), pp. 147–67, and Leon R. Kass, "Implications of Pre-Natal Diagnosis for the Human Right to Life," Presented at Airlie House on October 12, 1971 at a Conference on Ethical Issues in Genetic Counselling, sponsored by the National Institutes of Health and the Institute of Society, Ethics, and the Life Sciences.

Prenatal screening, of course, is not confined to amniocentesis. Somewhat later in pregnancy, nongenetic malformations can also be detected; or they may be predicted from maternal rubella, use of thalidomide, etc. Though the grounds for "weeding out" do not completely coincide in the genetic and the nongenetic cases, it is to be understood that the following discussion on the whole covers accidental and non-transmissible abnormality as well.

tinue pregnancy. The latter option is contingently affirmed with the diagnostic performance as such.[7] The issue before us thus falls into the general abortion issue, on which moral views and legal policy are very much in flux throughout the Western world, and whose ethics is here not our concern, since in general it is unrelated to eugenics or biological control. However, the genetic indication for terminating pregnancy introduces a special angle into the question, which we must probe.

The normal grounds, let us remember, for the progressive relaxing of former anathemas in this field were permissive in intent and centered on the mother-to-be: first (to construct a typical progression) danger to her life, then to her future health, then hardship of one kind or another —familial, social, psychological, etc.—finally her mere unwillingness to have a child at this time, were admitted to warrant abortion—always, to be sure, at *her* request, certainly with her consent.[8] The total permissiveness of the last step (already adopted in some legislations) is predicated on the philosophical and legal proposition that the fetus is part of the mother's body, and that a person has complete disposition over her body, thus also over her state of pregnancy as her purely private affair—the public interest in a decision to abort being confined to its *lege artis* execution (an inconsistency this, viz. an invasion of privacy itself, not

[7]At this point, both Ramsey and Kass give thought to certain moral side effects of genetic abortion not explored here. Thus Ramsey: "Intrauterine monitoring aims to prevent the birth of abnormal children. As screening becomes part of standard medical practice, the concept of 'normality' sufficient to make life worth living is bound to be 'upgraded', and the acceptance of 'abnormality' and care for abnormals is bound to be degraded in our society," with the final result "that abnormals must become outcasts in our society" (*op. cit.* p. 158f.); and Kass: "The practice of abortion of the genetically defective will no doubt affect our view of and behavior toward those abnormals who escape the net of detection and abortion . . . The parents of such children . . . may be disinclined to give [them] the kind of care they might have before the advent of amniocentesis and genetic abortion." These are chilling possibilities, especially in conjunction with the habit of killing engendered by the intendedly humanitarian practice as such. And here one is made to wonder what is morally more dangerous: indiscriminate killing because of unwillingness to bear (like God, "no respecter of persons"), or discriminate killing on fetal "merits" biologically and socially defined. (To me, the latter in its very rationality seems to hold graver dangers.) I avoid such issues by confining my considerations to a eugenics of *mercy*, where—as in euthanasia—the negative interest of the *patient*—here: the embryo—is paramount, which tends to move abortion criteria up the scale toward the extreme and somehow irresistible cases (e.g., Tay-Sachs disease). But I am aware that the *societal* interest will quickly take over from there and base its rules on considerations of "social costs", i.e., the anticipated burden of the abnormal to the normal; then, indeed, the floodgates are open to all the worrysome possibilities I have left aside.

[8]There is, of course, no uniformity in this, and it may happen under some legal system that the mother's contrary wish to have the child at all cost is overruled, especially if the cost be her life.

easily reconciled with the logic of the argument). Much could be said on principle about this position which is not our present business.[9] But whatever its merits, it is clear that it does not quite cover the termination of pregnancy on genetic grounds. There, in the first place, not the mother but the future child (and through it perhaps society) is the ruling consideration—precisely what was ruled out or overruled in all the permissive reasonings for legalized abortion. Secondly, and in consequence, the mother's wishes and even consent do strictly not count in the matter: it is extremely difficult, if not impossible, to reconcile recognition of the genetic consideration with the principle of purely maternal privacy of the whole affair. If the negative interest of the child-to-be, viz., to be spared existence, is acknowledged in the case of a sufficiently severe prognosis—not to speak of the interest of society—then it would seem unreasonable to simply defer to the mother's wishes or whims, e.g., her insistence on going through with the pregnancy, and reasonable that public authority institute itself, if need be against the mother, the guardian of fetal rights. But then, what goes for negative rights should also go for positive rights, and the champions of exclusive maternal authority in the abortion issue find themselves in an uncomfortable position. This is by the way.

What we have thus isolated from the general abortion syndrome— namely, the eugenics of mercy killing *in utero*: not mother-centered but child- or progeny-centered, and in idea not permissive but mandatory —poses its own problems within the field of "negative eugenics." To decide on incipient progeny is not the same as to decide on imagined progeny, with no rights yet but the progenitors' to be respected or violated; and killing what is already there is not as cloudless ethically as desisting from bringing it about in the first place. And here we enter a spectrum with no sharp definitions. Infanticide we reject; feticide, in spite of the lack of clear boundaries, our moral sense is willing to consider at sufficiently early stages. Then, if anything, the anticipation of grave deformity, genetic or accidental (e.g., the thalidomide babies), would seem the most defensible if not outright compelling ground, surely surpassing that of maternal disinclination. Even there (assuming prognostic certainty), the spectrum with its insuperable vagueness of shadings stays with us. What debility is sufficiently grave? Hopeless idiocy would hardly pose a problem (here the rationale would not even

[9]It is a bad position at least tactically in that it does identify itself unilaterally with one principle at all, instead of modestly acknowledging that here is a genuine conflict of first principles or rights between which some compromise must be found. The latter position is less assertive than the monolithic one, but safer from the obvious challenges to which this is exposed from opposing and no less valid principles.

be mercy but the prevention of the totally subhuman). But what about epilepsy? Condemnation based on its fetal recognition would have deprived mankind of a Dostoevsky.[10] No such hyperbolic compensation, of course, is needed to vindicate the worth of an existence. My two examples were chosen wide apart. Where on a scale between them should the pragmatic line between admission and condemnation fall? This is also the occasion, with respect to the whole subject of negative eugenics, to draw first attention to a point we shall meet with again, viz., the clustering of genes or gene properties, by which it can happen that the elimination of undesirable traits means also the elimination of desirable ones ("desirable" biologically or otherwise), and to observe that here the area of our ignorance is and always will be greater than that of our knowledge.

Of course, in a socio-legal situation where abortion is a generally free option *and*, in the given case, is readily considered by the pregnant woman anyway, *all* warnings of the kind that amniocentesis can provide will most naturally become a potent factor in tipping the scales; or, where the option is legally qualified, they or some of them may be among the selective criteria by which a request for abortion is granted. But outside of such conjunctions, and as possibly mandatory, it would seem on the whole that only in the strongest and best understood cases should the results of prenatal diagnosis be given *overruling* (as distinct from contributory) negative force:[11] in all others, the eugenic interest established for those that are yet to have their chance ought to be entrusted to the later, behavioral restraints on *their* procreation, which we have discussed, and which are the true province of negative eugenics.

B. POSITIVE OR MELIORISTIC EUGENICS

We now move on to positive or melioristic eugenics, the much more ambitious, bolder, therefore also more dangerous program—which, of course, comprises negative eugenics as an automatic byproduct of its larger schemes. Far from bent on preserving, it wants to improve the quality of the race and make it more perfect than nature has made it. In its more modest form, this may still be on the lines of given types

[10]Rightly so, replied to me a young geneticist in a memorable discussion of the American Association for the Advancement of Science some years ago. Mankind, she said, cannot afford that price for genius and should wait for a Dostoevsky without epilepsy. I cherish that episode for reasons of symbolic significance at which the reader can guess.
[11]Evidently this means, e.g., at the very least that amniocentesis yields a clear distinction between the affected and the heterozygous, i.e., between dominant and recessive presence of the disease factor. It should count for nothing unless dominance is beyond doubt.

or traits, which only are to be made more and more prevalent in the population. In its fanciful form, it may reach out for "creative" innovation, and in that case it passes beyond what is normally called "eugenics" into biological engineering proper. We comment first, very briefly, on the more conventional idea, which is unconventional enough in its methods.

A chief method of improving the race is seen in selective breeding, but this time with positive and not merely negative selection. Planned mating, based on genetic charts of the partners, family histories, etc., is to take the place of amateurish amatory choices. Untutored partners, meeting by chance in the first place, attract each other, fall in love with each other, choose or reject each other on the basis of their phenotypes. The marriage counselor of positive eugenics will replace this by a, possibly computerized, matching of genotypes, *insofar as known*. Since such knowledge is minimal and bound to remain so with regard to the majority of the population, the eugenic matchmaker's role will either be silly presumption (except in counseling *against* matches), or it must, as in cattle breeding, restrict candidacies to a chosen number of well-typed individuals. Let us assume that such typing is possible under optional conditions of information. This then leads to the institution of human studs, eugenically certified semen donors, eventually also ovum donors, with artificial insemination (and inovulation) replacing the sexual act—thus to a complete separation of love and sex from procreation, of marriage from parenthood, and so on. All this, mark you, not in order to avert a mortal danger to the race but to improve the race; not under the pressure of extreme emergency but from gratuitous choice. But *what* choice, concretely? Who is to judge the excellence of the specimens—of the semen and ovum donors, and by what standards? Let us remember that it is much easier to identify the undesirable than the desirable, the *malum* than the *bonum*. That diabetes, epilepsy, schizophrenia, hemophilia are undesirable, to afflicted and fellow men alike, is noncontroversial. But what is "better"—a cool head or a warm heart, high sensitivity or robustness, a placid or a rebellious temperament, and in what proportion of distribution rather than another: who is to determine that, and based on what knowledge? The pretense to such knowledge alone should be sufficient ground to disqualify the pretender. And whatever the standards of selection agreed or hit upon—is standardization as such desirable?

Discounting humanistic values, which are always debatable (and outside the scientists' domain), biologists are agreed on the plain biological value of the prolix manifoldness in the gene pool, with its vast reserve of presently "useless" traits the only safeguard of adaptability to novel conditions. Any standardization would restrict this shadow zone of indeterminacy by the hasty determinations of ephemeral preferences. To this technical, in itself "value-free," survival aspect take (to include the "debatable") the human poverty of breeding to types, which achieves its positive goal, as all selection does, via the exclusion of alternatives, viz., of indefinitely many in favor of the defined few. It was the biological *and* metaphysical strength of human evolution that it somehow avoided the shortrange advantages of specialization, the blind alley of so many evolutionary lines, successful no less than unsuccessful ones. That man is nonspecialized—the "unfixed animal," as Nietzsche said—constitutes an essential virtue of his being. Shortsightedness is the indelible signature of all conscious intervention in the unconscious processes of nature, and normally the risk price to be accepted, because intervene we must. In the incalculably long terms of human genetics, the shortsightedness would be raised to the nth power, but without the excuse of that must. Against this august argument of essence, it sounds almost trivial to add the point, touched upon before, that genetic traits come in packages, in which even the decidedly undesirable may be linked with the desirable (e.g., sickle-cell anemia with protection against malaria)—then, of course, also vice versa: the decidedly desirable with the undesirable —and that we simply *cannot* know what linkages we are affecting, what in effect we are jettisoning in adopting, and what adopting in jettisoning, when we single out "separate" traits for either condemnation or promotion. And, apart from such technicalities, can there be any forecast of how the selection will work out in the continued combinations of reproduction? Except for the most unequivocal objects of *negative* eugenics, surely in the dreamland of positive genetic perfectibility, we are *not* buying greater certainty with surrendering the unplanned for the planned.[12] Why then exchange the blissful blindness of personal mating choices for the doctored ignorance of arrogant art? Its only certainty is the impoverishment of the genetic stock, apart from the destruction of basic, not to say sacred, interpersonal values.

III. Futuristic Modes

A. CLONING

The two kinds of genetic control discussed so far, negative and positive eugenics, both based on selective breeding, suffer from the uncertainty

---

[12]The place for planning with regard to perfectibility, and thus for the shortsightedness clinging to all planning, is education. There we do impose our necessarily shortsighted image on the forming individual and commit blunders together with our good according to our lights of the hour: but there, in conditioning, we also impart, at least do not foreclose, the means for revision, and certainly leave the inherited nature what it is.

injected by the lottery of bisexual reproduction with its unpredictable chances of crossing-over and recombination—which guarantee that no two individuals are the same. This frustrating interference of nature and chance the planners can circumvent by the device of *cloning*. It is at once the most unorthodox device in its method and the most slavish in its goal.

1. What is cloning?

Cloning is a form of asexual reproduction, like that found in many plants side by side with the sexual mode and, unlike the latter, resulting in exact genetic replications of the parent organism. It rests on the ability of normal, diploid cells to germinate. On the whole, this alternative is closed to animals: all their orders above the lowest are confined to sexual reproduction through specialized germ cells (gametes), whose half-set of chromosomes requires complementation by a like half of the opposite sex in order to germinate toward a new individual. However, utilizing the fact that all other cells of the organism carry each a complete set of the chromosomes that define the genetic identity of the whole, a laboratory method has been devised to induce a suitably chosen body cell[13] to start the same process "on its own"—that is, since it contains all the genetic "information" which governed the growth of the original individual, to produce a "clone" of the parent organism. The method, which so far has succeeded with some amphibians (e.g., a frog), involves inserting the nucleus of the chosen body cell (intestinal in the known case) into an enucleated ovum of the kind, which then behaves as if fertilized. Actual adult individuals (also some monstrosities) have been thus generated. This promising beginning was, of course, facilitated by a sexual organization that lets spawned eggs be fertilized and develop outside the maternal body anyway. Internal fertilization and intra-uterine development present a more difficult proposition for the tech-

---

[13]It must be a nonspecialized cell, i.e., with none of the genetic potencies in its nucleus suppressed. So far, such cells can be obtained from embryonic tissue only. This, of course, is not good enough for the cloning ambitions we are going to discuss, and which require adult cell donors. Since it is unlikely that undifferentiated body cells, with "totipotent" nuclei, exist in human adults, a method must first be found to "despecialize" cells by agencies counteracting the suppressing agencies. This is theoretically possible since the "suppression" is thought not to alter the gene in question but merely to inhibit its action. It is thus a question of freeing the always intact chromosomal nucleus from secondary restraints. Our later discussion assumes—as did Joshua Lederberg and others—that this and other technical break-throughs will eventually be achieved. If the expectation turns out to be false, biologists and philosophers alike will have wasted their breath in debating the cloning proposition. But the biologist was the authority in estimating the probabilities, and the philosopher had to take his word for it. Even then, he may have discovered something in pondering the hypothetical possibility.

nique in its possible application to mammals. But with fertilization *in vitro* (even of the human ovum!) already a laboratory fact, and re-implantation into a host uterus (inovulation) a reasonable next prospect, the renucleated ("cloned") ovum would not fare differently from the fertilized one, and the way would be open for asexual reproduction in placental mammals, including man. The only left-over from bisexuality would consist in the double fact that the donor nucleus (male or female) needs for its proximate "host" a female ovum (minus its own nucleus), and this again for its host, during embryonic development, a functional kindred uterus—which means actual, full-term pregnancy of a female adult of the species. Whether and to what extent these limitations can eventually be overcome it is impossible at the moment to foretell. (Since unfertilized eggs are so much easier to come by, in numbers and other-wise, than pregnancy hosts, efforts will probably concentrate on extra-uterine embryo culture.) But mark the changed female role even in this "conservative" setting: the "mother," a mere incubator, contributes nothing of herself genetically—except if she happens to play host to a cloning nucleus taken from her own body;[14] the host ovum may or may not come from herself; the end product may or may not be the replica-tion of an individual known to her (a sharpening of what holds for artificial insemination). But while her role would still be vital at least instrumentally, that of the male would vanish to nothing, at least in this context: since fertilization—the one biological compulsion for the existence of males—is dispensed with, male representation can be dis-pensed with in a population wholly regenerated by cloning. Science fiction writers have here a field for amusing speculation.

2. Questions about cloning

The questions we have to ask have nothing to do with the conjec-tural extents of a practice which—if it comes to it at all—may never reach numerical values that are genetically significant for the population. The most important questions in its hypothetical use on man are those that apply to the single no less than to the multiplied case and must be answered before even the first is allowed to occur. They must, therefore, first of all be asked.

We ask three questions: *What* is brought about by cloning? *Why* is it supposedly to be brought about, i.e., what reasons are there for wishing it? *Ought* it to be brought about, i.e., is its very idea to be accepted or rejected?

---

[14]In which case she would be replicating "herself," but merely by the arbitrary coincidence of donor role and host role in one subject: the two are intrinsically unrelated, and the outcome would be the same with a different host.

a. *The physical outcome of cloning.* What is brought about by cloning? A genetic double of the donor, with the same degree of resemblance of phenotype as is known from identical twins. Clone and donor are indeed identical twins with a time lag: the non-contemporaneity will become a relevant facet in our later appraisal. With identical twins one can speak of mutual mirror images; the clone is unilaterally the copy of a preexisting individual. The time lag is indeterminate: since tissue cultures can be kept alive and growing indefinitely, the clone may be derived from a long dead donor (a new sense of individual immortality). By the same token, many clones may be derived, and may continue to be derived, from the same self-replenishing source, with a mediated twinhood among themselves, in principle not different from that with the original donor, but allowing for any relation of time lag, overlap, or simultaneity whatsoever. With the genetic potential presumably identical among the replicated genotypes, one pheno-actualization of that potential at least, and possibly more, is already on record before any clone begins his.

b. *Reasons for cloning.* The last statement provides the main answer to the question of *why* cloning should be done at all: a known individual life performance sufficiently outstanding in some desired respect to prompt the wish for more of its kind, and rare enough in its (presumed) genetic basis not to expect the desired frequency of it from the chances of ordinary or even selective interbreeding. Indeed, it is the "unique" in some sense which by cloning is to be saved from its uniqueness and secured in its repetition. This has obvious advantages in animal husbandry: the prize milch cow is much more certain to be reproduced by direct asexual replication than by the fortuitous detour of even the most careful mating, and moreover—because not requiring her own motherhood—with the option of incomparably greater numbers (any cow can be made the host bearer of another prize cow); and so for the exquisite race horse, and so on. Thus the perpetuation and multiplication of excellence (peak performance) would be a major reason for cloning. The multiplication of specimens would then also furnish the broadened numerical basis for renewed cross breeding, with the prospect of topping even the previous peak that has become a take-off plateau; and so forth, with appropriate switching between the two methods in an upward curve. In this way, cloning—in itself fixating evolutionary results—would become part of a progressive evolutionary drive. Another goal may be the utility value of uniformity as such; and also the well-balanced mean rather than the more vulnerable, onesided excellence may be made the selective criterion. All this concerns the utility-ruled sphere of animal husbandry, where the interests of the species itself are not consulted. Additional considerations (but ruling out none of the above) enter in the human sphere. I can do no better than reproduce here the "laundry list of possible applications [that] keeps growing, in anticipation of the perfected technology," which Dr. Leon Kass has compiled.

> (1) Replication of individuals of great genius or great beauty to improve the species or to make life more pleasant. (2) Replication of the healthy to bypass the risk of genetic disease contained in the lottery of sexual recombination. (3) Provision of large sets of genetically identical humans for scientific studies on the relative importance of nature and nuture for various aspects of human performance. (4) Provision of a child to an infertile couple. (5) Provision of a child with a genotype of one's own choosing—of someone famous, of a departed loved one, of one's spouse or oneself. (6) Control of the sex of future children; the sex of a cloned offspring is the same as that of the adult from whom the donor nucleus was taken. (7) Production of sets of identical persons to perform special occupations in peace and war (not excluding espionage). (8) Production of embryonic replicas of each person, to be frozen away until needed as a source of organs for transplantation to their genetically identical twin. (9) To beat the Russians and the Chinese, to prevent a cloning gap.[15]

The list is less facetious than it sounds; no wish is perverse enough (as, e.g., that for self-replication), or cynically utilitarian enough (as Number 7), or scientifically fanatic enough (as Number 3), that it might not, on the offer of its feasibility, find bidders and defenders among the children of Adam and Eve. On the whole, however, we may assume that the argument for excellence to be perpetuated and multiplied (i.e., Number 1 of the list) will hold sway in the human context and would, if the method ever graduated from the laboratory, confine its practice to the extraordinary. It is certainly the most exalted of the proposed aims and for that reason not only more seductive than any other, but also more apt to force philosophical comment to its radical declaration. We shall accordingly concentrate on this aspect.

    c. *Replication of excellence examined.* The argument of excellence, though naive, is not frivolous in that it enlists our reverence for greatness and pays tribute to it by wishing that more Mozarts, Ein-

---

[15]Leon R. Kass, "New Beginnings in Life," in *The New Genetics and the Future of Man*, ed. Michael P. Hamilton (Grand Rapids, Mich.: Eerdman's Publishing Company, 1972), pp. 14–63, at 44f. A revised version was published in the Winter 1972 issue of *The Public Interest* under the title "Making Babies—The New Biology and the 'Old' Morality," pp. 18–56 (the "laundry list" on page 41f.).

steins, and Schweitzers might adorn the human race.[16] It is naive in taking it for granted that more than one of each would really be to the good of mankind, let alone of the Mozarts and Einsteins of this world— generally in holding that, if a thing is good, more of it would be better.[17] It is also an unblushing consumer argument, not asking whether the genius, granted that he is a blessing to us, is not a curse to himself, often the unhappiest of men, and whether we have the right to condemn any- one deliberately to this terrible price of our enrichment. If, on the other hand, we let the candidate model himself decide about the worth- whileness of a *da capo* in his case, we may get a selection of the vain.[18] Also, of course, what really would happen with these would-be geniuses of the second and third try, once the star hour favoring the first—the unique constellation of subject and occasion—has passed, nobody can even remotely divine. (Let's find out, opposing counsel will say, at least the odds for superior performance are better than with all knowable alternatives to begin with.) Nor can we foresee how the presence of these precertified ones in their midst will affect their fellow men, includ- ing upcoming, *de novo* geniuses among them; even the bygone arche- type, once revered, might come to be resented for his greedy intrusion by proxy into the open business of the present.

But all this is speculative and largely extraneous to the one *ethical* issue we wish to raise, namely, what to *be* a clone would mean for the subject concerned; and here the case of the distinguished donor merely serves to bring into sharper light what would apply to all cases, i.e., to the cloning proposition as such. Here, also, we get not caught in con- jectural questions of quality, of dosing, of relative merits of selection, of benefits and costs to the rest of us—questions which only experience can settle, but can hope for the transempirical certainty which matters of essence sometimes grant: the single, unspecified case X will be as valid as any number of any specification can be.

---

[16]Nobody ever mentions Nietzsche in this connection, or Kafka, few even Bee- thoven or Michelangelo—a revealing symptom of the tacit eudaemonism of the whole dream: one wants his genius happy or at least serene; but most of all, edifying in his "contribution."

[17]The vision of a limitless supply from each master die, to cater to this general idea and any private request (the eventuality of commercial tissue banks and an open market for their wares is by no means unthinkable)—the vision thus of many such "identical" issues, of every age from childhood to decrepitude, simultaneously walking the earth and meeting their "own" past or future in the flesh, has an out- right ghostly quality about it.

[18]See Kass, *op. cit.*: "Indeed, should we not assert as a principle that any so- called great man who *did* consent to be cloned should on that basis be disqualified, as possessing too high an opinion of himself and of his genes? Can we stand an increase in arrogance?"

3. Existential critique

a. *Contemporaneity of identical twins.* The focal question of essence is that of unprejudiced selfhood, and it can be attacked from the situation of a twinhood that lacks contemporaneity. The situation of identical twins (or triplets, etc.) has its own problems, for which, as a rule, no human agency is responsible. This changes, of course, if it is induced by chemical or other prenatal means which are likely or even intended to cause an incipient embryo to split into multiple equivalents of itself. (This seems to happen now with a statistical frequency as a—still unintended—byproduct of certain fertility drugs and may soon be in our choice to cause deliberately.) Whatever objections of an existential nature can be raised against causing the situation knowingly—and condoning the risk is only a weaker form of doing so—one essential feature shared with the accidents of nature sets its results apart from those of cloning: the "multiplets" who have to face the reiteration of their genotype in one another are strictly contemporaneous, none has a head start, and none has to relive a previously completed life. It is irrelevant to what extent the genotype actually dominates individual history, and how far "identity" here goes in determining the final effect. What matters is that the sexually produced genotype is a novum in itself, unknown to all to begin with and still to reveal itself to owners and fellow men alike. Ignorance is here the precondition of freedom: the new throw of the dice has to discover itself in the guideless efforts of living its life for the first and only time, i.e., to *become* itself in meeting a world as unprepared for the newcomer as this is for himself. None of the siblings, though continually confronted with his likeness, suffers from the precedence of a firstcomer who has already demonstrated the potentials of his being (at least one set of them) and thereby preempted their authenticity for him. It may well be, as has been suggested, that he is still injured in a more transcendental (and on principle unverifiable) right, namely, that to the possession of a unique genotype shared with none. If there is such a right, then its denial would be a wrong already in the case of wilfully induced one-egg sibling sets, their genetic firstness and simultaneity notwithstanding, and *a fortiori* in the case of cloning.[19]

[19]The point has been raised tentatively by Leon Kass, who asks (*loc. cit.*) "Does it make sense to say that each person has a natural right not to be deliberately denied a unique genotype?" and finds parenthetically that, if this right exists, "then the deliberate production of identical human twins . . . must also be declared morally wrong." The main context of his question, however, is cloning. "Is one inherently injured by having been made the copy of another human being, independent of *which* human being? . . . Central to this matter is the idea of the dignity and worth of each human being," familiar to us from the Judaeo-Christian

b. *Uniqueness of genotype and uniqueness of being.* Much as I am in sympathy with the underlying idea, I will not make it my argument. For if there is a right to uniqueness, it is to uniqueness of being, of which uniqueness of genotype may or may not be a necessary condition: we just don't know. (I myself don't believe it is; in fact, the cloned double of another will on that very count be quite unique in his own, probably miserable, way!) Nor is uniqueness of genotype itself a verifiable fact—though normally of the highest statistical probability— and only its absence is known in the exceptional cases under discussion: but what bearing this absence as such (apart from its being known or believed) has on the objective chances of unique selfhood is hardly determinable. I suspect, the real object of the "right" in question is not genotypes at all. An objective, enabling ground of individual uniqueness is in truth a metaphysical, not a physical, postulate (its name was once "the soul") and as such is not only beyond finding out, but also transcendent to the whole question of rights, which it literally antecedes. But it is a different matter altogether that the existing subject, whatever his objective foundations, has an existential right to certain subjective terms of his being—and these are in question in our present probing. It was deliberate that we spoke of the *situation* of identical twins, not of the objective force of identical genotypes; and so we propose to treat of the *situation* of the human clone—an immanent matter of his experience and that of those around him: this makes for an existential, not a metaphysical, discourse, and one that can entirely waive the moot question of the extent of biological determinism.

c. *Non-contemporaneity and the right to ignorance.* Contrary to the equality of twins, the replication of a genotype creates inherently unequal conditions for the phenotypes concerned—and an inequality deadly for the clone. Here it is where our argument substitutes a manifest right to ignorance for any hidden right (which we need neither deny nor

---

tradition with its "notion of the special yet equal relationship of each person to the Creator" and beautifully illustrated by the Midrash: "For a man stamps many coins in one mold and they are all alike; but the King who is king over all kings . . . stamped every man in the mold of the first man, yet no one of them resembles his fellow." Kass' own conclusion is: "To answer the question posed above: We may *not* be entitled, in principle, to a unique genotype, but we *are* entitled not to have deliberately weakened the necessary supports for a worthy life. Genetic distinctiveness would seem to me to be one such support" ("New Beginnings in Life", pp. 46–47; the Judaeo-Christian reference and the Midrashic passage were omitted from the *Public Interest* version). With this cautious verdict one may well agree. My discussion in (b) seeks to make clear *why* a unique genotype, whether we are entitled to it or not, is not the real point at issue.

affirm) to a unique genotype.[20] The invocation of a right to ignorance is, I believe, new to ethical theory, which has consistently deplored lack of knowledge as a deficiency in the human condition and an obstacle on the path of virtue—surely as something to be remedied to the best of our possibility. Self-knowledge above all had from Delphic days been exalted as the mark of a higher life, of which there can be only too little, never too much. Yet knowledge of the future, especially one's own, has always been tacitly excepted and the attempt to gain it by whatever means (astrology is one) disparaged—as futile superstition by the enlightened, but as sin by theologians; and in the latter case with reasons that are also philosophically sound (and, interestingly, not committed on the question of determinism per se). But from thus disputing a right or permission to know, there is still a step to asserting a right not to know; and this step we must take in the face of an entirely novel, still hypothetical, contingency which indeed constitutes the first occasion ever for activating a right which had lain dormant and hidden for lack of a call for it.

The simple and unprecedented fact is that the clone knows (or believes to know) altogether too much about himself and is known (or is believed to be known) altogether too well to others. Both facts are paralyzing for the spontaneity of becoming himself, the second also for the genuineness of others' consorting with him. It is the known donor archetype that will dictate all expectations, predictions, hopes and fears, goal settings, comparisons, standards of success and failure, of fulfillment and disappointment, for all "in the know"—clone and witnesses alike; and this putative knowledge must stifle in the pre-charted subject all immediacy of the groping quest and eventual finding "himself" with which a toiling life surprises itself for good and for ill. It is all a matter much more of supposed than real knowledge, of opinion than truth. Note that it does not matter one jot whether the genotype is really, by its own force, a person's fate: it is *made* his fate by the very assumptions in cloning him, which by their imposition on all concerned become a force themselves. It does not matter whether replication of genotype really entails repetition of life performance: the donor has been chosen with some such idea, and that idea is tyrannical in effect. It does not matter what the real relation of "nature and nurture," of genetic premise and contingent environment is in forming a person and his possibilities:

[20]Kass, though not relinquishing genetic distinctiveness, takes in substance the same step when attending next to the "related problem" that the cloned individual "is saddled with a genotype that has already lived": there he touches on all the aspects—surprise, knowledge, ignorance, and freedom—I am now going to treat as the central issue.

their interplay has been falsified by both the subject and the environment having been "primed."[21] The trial of life has been cheated of its enticing (also frightening) openness; the past has been made to preempt the future as the spurious knowledge of it in the most intimate sphere, that of the question "who am I?", which must be a secret to the seeker after an answer and can find its answer only with the secret there as condition of the search—indeed as a condition of *becoming* what may *then be* the answer. The spurious manifestness at the beginning destroys that condition of all authentic growth. No matter whether the "knowledge" is true or false (there are reasons for saying that in essence it is false per se), it is pernicious to the task of selfhood: existentially significant is what the cloned individual *thinks*—is compelled to think—of himself, not what he "is" in the substance-sense of being. In brief, he is antecendently robbed of the *freedom* which only under the protection of ignorance can thrive; and to rob a human-to-be of that freedom deliberately is an inexpiable crime that must not be committed even once.

One may object that the clone need not know; but this will not wash, for the secret will out. As long as it is kept from him, it means the existence of others privy to it, who know "all about him"—an intolerable situation in itself and an unsafe one to boot; not to mention the existence of archives, data banks, etc., with their chronic proneness to "leaks." But apart from being thus the object of an illicit knowledge, equally degrading in the success and the failure of keeping it from him, the clone is bound to find out for himself. For the whole point of cloning him was the distinction of his "donor," established by outstanding feats and certified by fame: so that the day must come when the (presumably not stupid) copy makes the connection between himself and the publicly enshrined original. The choice between being told early or discovering later is one between two unacceptable alternatives. The only remedy against the certainty of the second would be random cloning from the anonymous and insignificant: but then, why cloning at all?

d. *Knowledge, ignorance, and freedom.*   We have dwelt on this, still wholly hypothetical, contingency of human cloning so extensively because its theoretical possibility has begun to fascinate biologists, which is in itself alarming; because it may be impending, and we should for once be forewarned; and because its discussion, profiting from the purity of an extreme case without analogy in the previous experience of mankind, breaks new ground in moral theory with a bearing, beyond the

---

[21]Kass: "For example, if a couple decided to clone a Rubinstein, is there any doubt that early in life young Arthur would be deposited at the piano and 'encouraged' to play?"

special case, on the whole issue of genetic engineering. Even with no agreement on the particular ethics of our deliberation, the simple principle of not experimenting on the unborn (making them means of our gaining knowledge) should interdict already the first try, even bar the "experiments" paving the way to it, for they would have to be performed on human "material" and thus already fall within the forbidden field. Those dazzled by the vision of a glorious specimen emerging from the try should also think of the inevitable failures—abnormal embryos to be discarded, or malformed beings to be guilty for—even if they lack the imagination to foresee the glorious specimen itself (perhaps most of all) become their accuser for abuse of power. But the major gain from our example for ethical theory I see in its demonstrating a *right to ignorance*, which rules the situation in even the technically flawless cases, where no mishap of any sort gives cause for more extraneous complaints. That there can be (and mostly is) too little knowledge has always been realized; that there can be too much of it stands suddenly before us in a blinding light. Obviously, two different kinds of ignorance and knowledge must be at issue. When discussing the responsibilities of technological power we have heretofore pleaded for the modesty of an ignorance conceded: tribute to a failing of ours, the doers; now we plead for the right, and its protection, to an ignorance needed: tribute to the possible freedom of others subject to our deed. In the one case, we may not know enough for doing something which only full knowledge could justify; in the other, we may know too much for doing anything with the guessing spontaneity of true deed. The ethical command here entering the enlarged stage of our powers is: never to violate the right to that ignorance which is a condition for the possibility of authentic action; or: *to respect the right of each human life to find its own way and be a surprise to itself*. How this plea for ignorance about one's presumptive being tallies with the old command of "Know thyself" is a question whose none-too-difficult answer would make it plain that the self-*discovery* enjoined in that command is precisely the process of generating one's self at once with coming to know it in the tests of life which the "knowledge" here repudiated would obstruct.

B. DNA ARCHITECTURE

1. No strict analogy to engineering in the preceding

So far, the analogies of genetic manipulation with real, classical engineering were weak. In strict formal analogy, biological engineering would be the designing and constructing of biological entities, i.e. living organisms, and/or the design-altering of existing types for the sake of improvement. Of these two modes, the first, radical one of really *de novo* design and fabrication of advanced organisms (by artificial chromosome building from molecular elements), even if feasible,[22] would be sheer waste in view of the enormous offer by nature of ready-made genetic material for practically infinite, supervening modification by art. "Re-designing" by intervention is thus the realistically elective engineering mode in the biological field, but this can go pretty far and approach closer analogies with true engineering, i.e., "making."

All the methods discussed so far were conservative in that they consisted in the controlled redistribution (by selective breeding, cloning, or what not) of *existing* genes in the population rather than the introduction of newly contrived genotypes into it. What is being "engineered" in these cases is the macro-design of the species or population without direct intervention in the micro-design of the species members, i.e., of individual genotypes. *Their* "manipulation" is entrusted to the indirect mechanism of the selection and elimination in its effect on future recombinations. In all these cases, therefore, engineering takes over the one agency of natural evolution, viz., selection, but not the other, viz., innovative variation. It could still be innovative enough by virtue of the statistically altered terms of recombination which the newly assorted gene pool provides. And it is clear that so long as the results of these recombinations are not predictable, at least statistically, the enterprise is one of gambling (at best influencing the odds) rather than designing —a procedure for which "engineering" might be too good a name.

2. The engineering potential of molecular biology

a. *The concept of genetic surgery.* The advent of molecular biology (genetics) has opened up new and more ambitious prospects, speculative at present, but sound enough theoretically to warrant hypothetical discussion. It is the possibility of direct intervention in genotypes by what is called, in anticipation, "genetic surgery" and would amount to taking over also the second, "mutational" agency of evolution: first the substitution of single genes (desirable for undesirable, pathogenic ones) in the chromosomal nucleus of gametes or zygotes, i.e., in the starting points of future individuals—the intent being corrective rather than innovative; but then also the adding to and reshuffling of the given DNA pattern—the rewriting as it were of its script, which a complete "cracking" of the genetic code together with micro-techniques still to be developed makes at least conceivable: ultimately, a kind of DNA archi-

---

[22]It is safe to say that such fabrication would never be feasible, since the complexity involved exceeds the capacity of any imaginable computer of terrestrial dimensions.

tecture. This would result in the production of new *types* of creatures, in the deliberate generation of freaks and, mediately, future lines of freaks; and when practiced on a human take-off basis, would depose the image of man as an object of ultimate respect and renounce allegiance to its integrity. It would be a metaphysical breach with the essence of man as well as the most reckless gamble in view of the utter unpredictability of the consequences—the blundering of a blind and arrogant demiurge at the delicate heart of creation.

Here at last, "engineering" comes into its own with one aspect of it that was lacking before: though still bound to pre-given structures for starting off, *invention* takes over from mere sifting, and with it arbitrariness of design at the service of arbitrary goals. What can these goals be? Apart from a *l'art pour l'art* playing with possibilities as such (which is not beyond the consuming curiosity and experimental passion of scientists), they must be ultimately utilitarian, i.e., a supposed utility value of the products for the collective business of the group. It cannot be the good of the future individuals themselves, because for novel kinds of creatures we cannot form an idea of their good. But we can estimate that the atrophy of certain faculties or properties, the hypertrophy of others, the addition of still others, will be useful for certain tasks of a technological world (space travel, for instance), for which man has not been properly constructed by nature. I will not go into the weird dreams to which some of the frontiersmen of molecular biology have given voice (some, to be fair, the voice of fear and warning). It is enough to note a few points of principle.

b. *Elements of a critique.*   First, the one saving grace of cloning: honoring the *species that is* in the touching, if childish, wish to repeat its highest displays of excellence, is denied to the goals we now consider. To them, on the contrary, Man as he happens to be is a mere fact of nature, no more sanctioned than other results of evolutionary accident, thus like all of them a no-man's land for growing freely eligible alternatives.[23] No conception of the transcendent worth of man and thus of any moral obligation flowing from it can survive this waiving of the inviolability of his generic image. Besides this instrinsic degradation, the very unity of the species would be broken up, and the meaning of the name "man," no longer unique, would become equivocal. What are

---

[23]Incidentally, the most effectual object of "creative" DNA surgery would be diploid cells for subsequent cloning, which would keep the result unadulterated by sexual combination. In such a synthesis of techniques, cloning—released from its saving grace—would cease to be an instrument of copying, and from the most slavish would turn into the most innovative form of biological engineering.

the freaks, what their rights, what their status in the fellowship of men? (The question could become reversed if *they* were ever to dictate the terms.) More down to earth is the consideration that the technique will bring forth, besides the freaks desired, undesired ones: the surely much more numerous mishaps of the method, which will routinely be disposed of; and even freaks at first desired may be proved undesirable by later experience—and why should *they* not then be disposed of? (What has been made with a purpose, can be scrapped when failing the purpose.) Once the utilitarian disposal habit is started, who is to say where and by what non-utilitarian principle it is to stop? What superior right can the natural product claim over the artificial one? Surely not that of mindless accident in its coming-to-be. By definition, none of the products of inventive, or "freakish," engineering will have been produced for its own sake; utility was the only rule of its conception. The expansion hence to the universal view that men are for the use of men, entirely appropriate to engineering products, will be irresistible and leave no one recognized as an end in himself. But if no member of the class, then why the class? The very being of mankind for its own sake looses its onto-logical ground. I am not overlooking that, besides the unabashed utility angle, the ghost of superman as an end in itself haunts some of the dreamers in this twlight zone of science; but this, unlike the hardnosed pragmatism of the former, is immature nonsense. For the image-makers would have to be asked for their credentials; and if they can demonstrate *knowledge* of what is above man (the only valid credential), then super-man is already there, and the species that brought him forth is thereby proved as biologically adequate; and if only pretended knowledge (as it is bound to be), then the pretenders are the last to be entrusted with the fate of man.

C. CONCLUDING APPEAL

We have been moving for some stretch now at the very boundaries of things human and of possible discourse about them. A spectral sense of unreality must have communicated itself to the reader, which I share. Yet he would be wrong to regard the discourse therefore as otiose. The danger is that we may be gliding into fateful beginnings unawares, innocently as it were by the thin end of the wedge, namely pure science. I have tried, in discussing these borderline cases, to suppress the meta-physical shudder I feel at the idea of man-made homunculus. To let it out now with an archaic word, the production of human freaks would be an abomination; let alone the unspeakable thought of human-animal hybrids which, quite consistently, has not failed to enter the list.

Steering clear of metaphysics and categories of the sacred, which this topic makes it not easy to do, I resort at the end, and with reference to the whole field of biological control, to the plainest of moral reflections: Deeds with no accountability are wrong when done to others. The moral dilemma in all human-biological manipulation, other than negative—and the greater, the more artificial the procedure and goal—is this: that the potential accusation of the offspring against his makers will find no respondent still answerable for the deed, and no possible redress. Here is a field for crimes with complete impunity to the perpetrator. This also should call forth the utmost scrupulousness and sensitivity in applying the rising powers of biological control on man. And though much more is involved, the simple ethics of the case are enough to rule out the direct tampering with human genotypes (which cannot be other than amateurish) from the very beginning of the road—that is, impalatable as it sounds to modern ears, at the fountainhead of experimental research.

8.
Contemporary Problems in Ethics from a Jewish Perspective

The crisis of modern man—at least one aspect of it—can be put in these terms. Reason triumphant through science has destroyed the faith in revelation, without, however, replacing revelation in the office of guiding our ultimate choices. Reason disqualified *itself* from that office, in which once it vied with religion, precisely when it installed itself, in the form of science, as sole authority in matters of truth. Its abdication in that native province is the corollary of its triumph in other spheres: its success there is predicated upon that redefinition of the possible objects and methods of knowledge that leaves whole ranges of other objects outside its domain. This situation is reflected in the failure of contemporary philosophy to offer an ethical theory, i.e., to validate ethical norms as part of our universe of knowledge.

How are we to explain this vacuum? What, with so different a past, has caused the great Nothing with which philosophy today responds to one of its oldest questions—the question of how we ought to live? Only the fact that philosophy, once the queen of the sciences, has become a camp follower of Science, made the situation possible; and contemporary religions (it would be too flattering to grace them with the name of theologies) are anxious not to fall too far behind among the stragglers. How this concerns ethics and its present condition has to be articulated.

Reprinted, with minor modifications, from the *Central Conference American Rabbis Journal*, January 1968.

Three interrelated determinants of modern thought have a share in the nihilistic situation, or less dramatically put, in the contemporary impasse of ethical theory—two of them theoretical and the third practical: the modern concept of nature, the modern concept of man, and the fact of modern technology supported by both. All three imply the negation of certain fundamental tenets of the philosophical as well as the religious tradition. Since we are here concerned with gaining a Jewish perspective on the situation, we shall note in particular the biblical propositions that are intrinsically disavowed in those three elements of the modern mind.

I

1. First, then, we have the modern, i.e. scientific, concept of *nature*, which by implication denies a number of things formerly held, and first of these is *creation*, that is, the first sentence of the Bible "In the beginning God created the heaven and the earth." To say of the world that it is created is to say that it is not its own ground but proceeds from a will and plan beyond itself—in whatever form one conceptualizes the dependence on such a transcendent "cause." In the view of modern science, by contrast, the world has "made" and is continuously making "itself." It is an ongoing process, activated by the forces at work within it, determined by the laws inherent in its matter, each state of it the effect of its own past and none the implementation of a plan or intended order. The world at every moment is the last word about itself and measured by nothing but itself.

2. By the same token, this scientific philosophy denies the further sentence "And God saw everything which He had made, and, behold, it was very good." Not that physics holds that the world is bad or evil, that is, in any sense the opposite of good: the world of modern physics is neither "good" nor "bad," it has no reference to either attribute, because it is *indifferent* to that very distinction. It is a world of fact alien to value. Thus such terms as "good" or "bad," "perfect" or "imperfect," "noble" or "base," do not apply to anything in or of nature. They are human measures entirely.

3. A third negation then follows. A nature pronounced "good" by its creator in turn proclaims the goodness of the maker and master. "The heavens tell the glory of God and the firmament proclaims His handiwork" (Psalm 19). That is to say, the glory of God, visible in His works, calls forth in man admiration and piety. The modern heavens no longer tell the glory of God. If anything, they proclaim their own mute, mindless, swirling immensity; and what they inspire is not admiration, but dizziness; not piety, but the rejoinder of analysis.

4. The disenchanted world is a purposeless world. The absence of values from nature means also the absence of goals or ends from it. We said that the noncreated world makes itself blindly and not according to any intention. We must now add that this renders the whole status of intentions and ends in the scheme of things problematical and leaves man as the sole repository of them. How is he qualified for this solitary role, for this ultimate monopoly on intention and goal?

II

With this question we turn to the second theme, from the modern doctrine of nature to the modern doctrine of man, where again we shall look for the negations of biblical views implied in the affirmations of modern theory. We easily discover such negations in the ideas of evolution, of history, and of psychology as they appear in the forms of Darwinism, historicism, and psychoanalysis—three representative aspects of the contemporary concept of man.

1. The cardinal biblical statement on the nature of man, let us remember, is contained in the second great pronouncement of the creation story after that of the creation of the universe—the statement, made with particular solemnity, that "God created man in his own image, in the image of God he created him." This sentence is the second cornerstone of Jewish doctrine, no less important than the first supplied by the all-inclusive, opening sentence of the Bible. And just as the first, concerning nature as a whole, is denied by the modern doctrine of nature, so the second, concerning man, is denied by the naturalistic doctrine of evolution as it applies to the human species.

In the Darwinian view, man bears no eternal "image" but is part of universal, and in particular of biological, "becoming." His "being" as it actually turned out is the unintended (and variable) product of unconcerned forces whose prolonged interplay with circumstances have "evolution" for their joint effect but nothing (not even evolution as such) for their aim. None of the forms arising in the process has any validity other than the factuality of its having "made the grade"; none is terminal either in meaning or in fact. Man, therefore, does not embody an abiding or transcendent "image" by which to mold himself. As the temporal (and possibly temporary) outcome of the chance transactions of the evolutionary mechanics, with the survival premium the only selective principle, his being is legitimized by no valid essence. He is an accident, sanctioned merely by success. Darwinism, in other words, offers an "image-less" image of man. But, it was the image-idea with its transcendent reference by whose logic it could be said "Be ye holy *for* I am holy, the Lord your God." The evolutionary imperative sounds distinctly different: Be successful in the struggle of life. And since biological success is, in Darwinian terms, defined by the mere rate of reproduction, one may say that all imperatives are reduced to "Be fruitful and multiply."

2. Evolution, however, only provides the natural backdrop for another and uniquely human dimension of becoming, *history*; and the modern concept of man is as much determined by historicism as by Darwinism. Here again it clashes with biblical lore. As Darwinism finds man to be a product of nature and its accidents, so historicism finds him to be the continuous product of his own history and its man-made creations, i.e., of the different and changing cultures, each of which generates and imposes its own *values*—as matters of fact, not of truth: as something whose force consists in the actual hold it has on those who happen to be born into the community in question, not in a claim to ideal validity which might be judged objectively. There *are* only matters of fact for the positivist creed of which historicism is one form. And, as facts are mutable, so are values; and as historical configurations of fact, i.e., cultures are many, so are value-systems, i.e., moralities. There is no appeal from the stream of fact to a court of truth.

This historical relativism-and-pluralism obviously negates the biblical tenet of *one* Torah, its transcendent authority, and its being knowable. "He has told you, O man, what is good": this means that there is one valid good for man, and that its knowledge is granted him—be it through revelation, be it through reason. This is now denied. Relativism—cultural, anthropological, historical—is the order of the day, ousting and replacing any absolutism of former times. Instead of the absolute, there is only the relative in ethics; instead of the universal, only the socially particular; instead of the objective, only the subjective; and instead of the unconditional, only the conditional, conventional, and convenient.

3. The finishing touch on all this is put by modern *psychology*—after evolutionism and historicism the third among the forces shaping the modern concept of man which we have chosen to consider. The psychological argument—because it seems to put the matter to the test of everyone's own verification—has proved to be the most effective way of cutting man down to size and stripping him in his own eyes of every vestige of metaphysical dignity. There has been underway in the West, at the latest since Nietzsche's depth-probing into the genealogy of morals, a persistent "unmasking" of man: the exposure of his "higher" aspects as some kind of sham, a "front" and roundabout way of gratification for the most elementary, essentially base drives, out of which the

complex, sophisticated psychic system of civilized man is ultimately constructed and by whose energies alone it is moved. The popular success of psychoanalysis, which gave this picture the trappings of a scientific theory, has established it as the most widely accepted view of man's psychical life and thus of the very essence of man. True or not, it has become the common currency of our everyday psychologizing: the higher in man is a disguised form of the lower.

This psychological doctrine denies the authenticity of the spirit, the transcendent accountability of the person. The moral imperative is not the voice of God or the Absolute, but of the superego which speaks with spurious authority—spurious because dissembling its own questionable origin—and this speaker can be put in his place by *reminding* him of his origin. Note here the reversed meaning which the "reminder of origin" takes on with the reversal of origin itself: it is now forever looked for in the depth, where formerly it was sought in the height. The reductionism, borrowed from natural science, that governs the theory of man, results in the final debunking of man, leaving him in the engulfing miserableness which Christian doctrine had attributed to him as a consequence of the Fall, but now no longer opposed by the "image" to which he might rise again.

Now the paradox of the modern condition is that this reduction of man's stature, the utter humbling of his metaphysical pride, goes hand in hand with his promotion to quasi-God-like privilege and power. The emphasis is on *power*. For it is not only that he now holds the monopoly on value in a world barren of values; that as the sole source of meaning he finds himself the sovereign author and judge of his own preferences with no heed to an eternal order: this would be a somewhat abstract privilege if he were still severely hemmed in by necessity. It is the tremendous *power* which modern *technology* puts into his hands to implement that license, a power therefore which has to be exercised in a vacuum of norms, that creates the main problem for contemporary ethics.

III

Herewith we come to the theme of technology which I had named, together with the theories of nature and man, as the third, and practical, determinant of the present situation. It will be my contention in what follows that the dialectical togetherness of these two facts—the profound demotion of man's metaphysical rank by modern science (both natural and human), and the extreme promotion of his power by modern technology (based on this self-same science)—constitutes the major ethical challenge of our day, and that Judaism cannot and need not be silent in the face of it.

Modern technology is distinguished from previous, often quite ingenious, technology by its scientific basis. It is a child of natural science: it is that science brought to bear on its object, indifferent nature, in terms of action. Science had made nature "fit," cognitively and emotionally, for the kind of treatment that was eventually applied to it. Under its gaze the nature of things, reduced to the aimlessness of their atoms and causes, was left with no dignity of its own. But that which commands no reverence can be commanded, and, released from cosmic sacrosanctity, all things are for unlimited use. If there is nothing terminal in nature, no formation in its productions that fulfills an originative intention, then anything can be *done* with nature without violating its integrity, for there *is* no integrity to be violated in a nature conceived in the terms of natural science alone—a nature neither created nor creative. If nature is mere object, in no sense subject, if it expresses no creative will, either of its own or of its cause, then man remains as the sole subject and the sole will. The world then, after first having become the object of man's knowledge, becomes the object of his will, and his knowledge is put at the service of his will; and the will is, of course, a will for power over things. That will, once the increased power has overtaken necessity, becomes sheer desire, of which there is no limit.

What is the moral significance of technological power? Let us first consider a psychological effect. The liberties which man can take with a nature made metaphysically neutral by science and no longer accorded an inherent integrity that must be respected as inviolable; the actual and ever increasing extent of the mastery exercised over it; the triumphal remaking and outwitting of creation by man according to his projects; the constant demonstration of what we can do plus the unlimited prospects of what we might yet do; and finally the utterly mystery-free, businesslike rationality of the methods employed—this whole power experience, certified by cumulative success, dissipates the last vestiges of that reverence for nature, that sense of dependence, awe, and piety, which it had inspired in man throughout the ages, and some of which could still survive the purely theoretical analysis of nature. Kant, sober Newtonian that he was, could still voice the profound admiration with which the starry sky above filled his heart, and could even place it alongside the admiration for the moral law within. "Which one did we put there?" asked the post-Sputnik boy when his father explained one of the constellations to him. Some ineffable quality has gone out of the shape of things when manipulation invades the very sphere which has always stood as a paradigm for what man cannot interfere with. "How is it

done? How could we do the same? How could we do it even better?"—
the mere question divests the nature of things of a sublimity which
might stay our hands.

If it is true that both religion and morality originally drew sustenance from a sense of piety which cosmic mystery and majesty instilled
in the soul—a sense of being excelled in the order of things by something not only physically beyond our reach but also in quality beyond
our virtue: if the wonder and humility before nature had something to
do with a readiness to pay homage also to norms issued in the name of
an eternal order—then there must be some moral implication in the loss
of this sense, in the nakedness of things without their noumenal cloak,
offered up for our conquering rape. If reverence or shame has any share
in the hold which moral laws may have on us, then the experience of
technological power, which expunges reverence and shame, cannot be
without consequences for our ethical condition.

IV

But, it may be objected, if *nature* has lost man's respect and ceased
to be an object of his reverence, one might expect his respect for himself to have risen in proportion. Man must have gained in metaphysical
status what nature has lost—even what God has lost: man has stepped
into His place as creator, the maker of new worlds, the sovereign re-
fashioner of things. And indeed, admiration for man's achievement after
his long ages of helplessness, and for the genius behind it, is profound
and surely not unjust. The collective self-congratulation in which it finds
voice sometimes takes the form of humanistic deification: the divine is in
man—witness what he can *do*. But there we come before the paradox
noted before, viz., that with his very triumph man himself has become
engulfed in the metaphysical devaluation which was the premise and the
consequence of that triumph. For he must see himself as part of that
nature which he has found to be manipulable and which he learns how
to manipulate more and more. We have seen before how through modern
science he lost the attribute of "image-of-God," as he is not only the
subject but also the object of his scientific knowledge—of physics,
chemistry, biology, psychology, etc. What we must see now is that he is
not merely the *theoretical* object of his knowledge and of the consequent
revision of the image he entertains of himself: he is also the object of
his own technological power. He can remake himself as he can nature.
Man today, or very soon, can make man "to specification"—today already through socio-political and psychological techniques, tomorrow

through biological engineering, eventually perhaps through the juggling of genes.

The last prospect is the most terrifying of all. Against this power of his own, man is as unprotected by an inviolable principle of ultimate, metaphysical integrity as external nature is in its subjection to his desires: those desires themselves he may now undertake to "program" in advance—according to what? According to his desires and expediencies, of course—those of the future according to those of the present. And while the conditioning by today's psychological techniques, odious as it may be, is still reversible, that by tomorrow's biological techniques would be irreversible. For the first time, man may be able to determine, not only *how* he is to *live*, but *what* in his constitution he is to *be*. The accident of his emergence from a blind but age-long dynamic of nature (if accident indeed it was) is to be compounded by what can only be termed accident of the second power: by man's now taking a hand in his further evolution *in the light of his ephemeral concepts*.

For let no one confound the presence of a plan with the absence of accident. Its execution may or may not be proof against the intervention of accident: its very conception, as to motives, end, and means, must in the nature of things human be thoroughly accidental. The more far-reaching the plan, the greater becomes the disproportion between the range of its effects and the chance nature of its origin. The most foolish, the most deluded, the most shortsighted enterprises—let alone the most wicked—have been carefully planned. The most "farsighted" plans—farsighted as to the distance of the intended goal—are children of the concepts of the day, of what at the moment is taken for knowledge and approved as desirable: approved so, we must add, by those who happen to be in control. Be their intentions ever so unblemished by self-interest (a most unlikely event), these intentions are still but an option of the shortsighted moment which is to be imposed on an indefinite future. Thus the slow-working accidents of nature, which by the very patience of their small increments, large numbers, and gradual decisions, may well cease to be "accident" in the outcome, are to be replaced by the fast-working accidents of man's hasty and biased decisions, not exposed to the long test of the ages. His uncertain ideas are to set the goals of generations, with a certainty borrowed from the presumptive certainty of the means. The latter presumption is doubtful enough, but this doubtfulness becomes secondary to the prime question that arises when man indeed undertakes to "make himself": *In what image* of his own devising shall he do so, even granted that he can be sure of the means? In fact, of course, he can be sure of neither, not of the end, nor of the means, once he enters the realm where he plays with the roots of life. Of one thing only he can be sure: of his *power* to move the foundations and to cause incalculable and irreversible consequences. Never was so much power coupled with so little guidance for its use. Yet there is a compulsion, once the power is there, to use it anyway.

V

Modern ethical theory, or philosophical ethics, has notoriously no answer to this quandary of contemporary man. Pragmatism, emotivism, linguistic analysis deal with the facts, meanings, and expressions of man's goal-setting, but not with the principles of it—denying, indeed, that there are such principles. And existentialism even holds that there ought not to be: Man, determining his essence by his free act of existence, must neither be bound nor helped by any once-for-all principles and rules. "At this point," as Brand Blanshard remarks, "the linguistic moralists of Britain make a curious rapprochement with the existentialists of the continent. The ultimate act of choice is, for both alike, an act of will responsible to nothing beyond itself."[1]

To me it is amazing that none of the contemporary schools in ethical theory comes to grips with the awesome problem posed by the combination of this anarchy of human choosing with the apocalyptic power of contemporary man—the combination of near-omnipotence with near-emptiness. The question must be asked: Can we afford the happy-go-lucky contingency of subjective ends and preferences when (to put it in Jewish language) the whole future of the divine creation, the very survival of the image of God have come to be placed in our fickle hands? Surely Judaism must take a stand here, and in taking it must not be afraid to challenge some of the cherished beliefs of modernity. So I will dare a few Jewish comments on the contemporary ethical predicament.

First a word about the alleged theoretical finality of modern immanence and the death of transcendence, or, the ultimate truth of reductionism. This is very much a matter of the "emperor's clothes" in reverse: "But he has nothing on!" exclaimed the child, and with this one flash of innocence dispelled the make-believe, and everybody saw that the emperor was naked. Something of this kind was the feat of the Enlightenment, and its was liberating. But when in the subsequent nihilistic stage—our own—the confirmed reductionist or cynic, no longer the open-eyed child but a dogmatist himself, triumphantly states, "there is nothing there!"—then, lo and behold, once said with the tautological

---

[1]*Reason and Goodness* (New York: Humanities Press, 1967), p. 254.

vigor of the positivist dogma behind it, namely that there *is* only that which science can verify, then, indeed, with eyes so conditioned, or through spectacles so tinted, we do see nothing but the nakedness we are meant to see. And there is nothing more to be seen—for certain things are of a kind that they are visible only to a certain kind of vision and, indeed, vanish from sight when looked at with eyes instructed otherwise. Thus, the bald assertion that the emperor has no clothes on may itself be the cause for the clothes not to be seen anymore; it may itself strip them off; but then its negative truth and our verification of it by our induced blindness are merely self-confirmatory and tautological.

This is the fate suffered by the biblical propositions that God created the heaven and the earth, that he saw that his creation was good, that he created man in his image, that it has been made known to man what is good, that the word is written in our heart. These propositions, i.e., what through the symbolism of their literal meaning they suggest about reality, are of course in no way "refuted" by anything science has found out about the world and ourselves. No discovery about the laws and functions of matter *logically* affects the possibility that these very laws and functions may subserve a spiritual, creative will. It is, however, the case, as in the reversed story of Christian Andersen, that the *psychological* atmosphere created by science and reinforced by technology is peculiarly unfavorable to the *visibility* of that transcendent dimension which the biblical propositions claim for the nature of things. Yet some equivalent of their meaning, however remote from the literalness of their statement, must be preserved if we are still to be Jews and, beyond that special concern of ours, if there is still to be an answer to the moral quest of man. Shall we plead for the protection of a sense of mystery? If nothing more, it will put some restraints on the headlong race of reason in the service of an emancipated, fallible will.

VI

Let us just realize how desperately needed in the field of action such biblical restraints have become by that very triumph of technology which in the field of thought has made us so particularly indisposed to recognize their authority. By the mere scale of its effects, modern technological power, to which almost anything has become feasible, forces upon us goals of a type that was formerly the preserve of utopias. To put it differently: technological power has turned what ought to be tentative, perhaps enlightening plays of speculative reason, into competing blueprints for projects, and in choosing between them we have to choose between extremes of remote effects. We live in the era of "enormous consequences" of human action (witness the bomb, but also the impending threat of biological engineering)—irreversible consequences that concern the total condition of nature on our globe and the very kind of creatures that shall or shall not populate it. The face or image of creation itself, including the image of man, is involved in the explosion of technological might. The older and comforting belief that human nature remains the same and that the image of God in it will assert itself against all defacements by man-made conditions, becomes untrue if we "engineer" this nature genetically and be the sorcerers (or sorcerer's apprentices) that make the future race of Golems.

In consequence of the inevitably "utopian" scale of modern technology, the salutary gap between everyday and ultimate issues, between occasions for prudence and common decency and occasions for illuminated wisdom is steadily closing. Living constantly now in the shadow of unwanted, automatic utopianism, we are constantly now confronted with issues that require ultimate wisdom—an impossible situation for man in general, because he does not possess that wisdom, and for contemporary man in particular, because he even denies the existence of its object: transcendent truth and absolute value, beyond the relativities of expediency and subjective preference. We need wisdom most when we believe in it least.

VII

It is not my purpose here to argue the "truth" of Judaism in general, or of those biblical propositions in particular which we found to be repudiated by modern beliefs. Rather I ask: *if* we are Jews—and a corresponding question Christians and Muslims must ask themselves—what counsel can we take from the perennial Jewish stance in the pressing dilemma of our time? The first such counsel, I believe, is one of modesty in estimating our own cleverness in relation to our forebears. It is the modern conviction, nourished by the unprecedented progress in our knowledge of things and our consequent power over things, that *we know better*, not only in this but *in every respect*, than all the ages before us. Yet nothing justifies the belief that science can teach us everything we need to know, nor the belief that what it does teach us makes us wiser than our ancestors were in discerning the proper ends of life and thus the proper *use* of the things we now so abundantly control. The arrogance with which the scientifically emboldened reason looks down on past ignorance and, thus blinded to past wisdom, assumes confident jurisdiction over the ultimate issues of our existence, is not only terrifying in its possible consequences, i.e., objectionable on grounds of prudence, but also impious as an attitude in lacking the humility that must balance any self-confidence of finite man. Such humility, or modesty, would be willing to lend an ear to what tradition has to say about the transempirical, nondemonstrable meaning of things. Attention to our tradition is a Jewish prescription, directing us, not only to the human wisdom we may pick up there, but also to the voice of revelation we may hear through it. At the least, the modesty of thus listening—a modesty amply justified by our helplessness before the fruits and uses of our acquired powers—may guard us from rashly dismissing the seemingly archaic biblical views as mere mythology that belongs to the infancy of man and has been outgrown by our maturity. The simple attentiveness of such a stance may help us realize that we are not completely our own masters, still less those of all posterity, but rather trustees of a heritage. If nothing else, the tempering of our presumed superiority by that injection of humility will make us cautious, and caution is the urgent need for the hour. It will make us go slow on discarding old taboos, on brushing aside in our projects the sacrosanctity of certain domains hitherto surrounded by a sense of mystery, awe, and shame.

VIII

The recovery of that sense, something more positive than the merely negative sense of caution which humility suggests, is the next step. Informed by the idea of creation, it will take the form of *reverence* for certain inviolable integrities sanctioned by that idea. The doctrine of creation teaches reverence toward nature and toward man, with highly topical, practical applications in both directions.

As to nature, it means especially living nature, and the reverence in question is reverence for life. Immediately we see the practical impact of a creationist view on the choices open to modern technology. God, in the Genesis story, set man over all the other creatures and empowered him to their sovereign use: but they are still his creatures, intended to be and to adorn his earth. Subjection, not biological impoverishment, was man's mandate. Nowhere does the Jewish idea of man's preeminence in the created scheme justify his heedless plundering of this planet. On the contrary, his rulership puts him in the position of a responsible caretaker, and doubly so today, when science and technology have really made him master over this globe, with powers to either uphold or undo the work of creation. While biblical piety saw nature's dependence on God's creative and sustaining will, we now also know its *vulnerability* to the interferences of our developed powers. This knowledge

should heighten our sense of responsibility. Exploit we must the resources of life, for this is the law of life itself and belongs to the order
of creation, but we ought to exploit with respect and piety. Care for the
integrity of creation should restrain our greed. Even if it means for-
going some abundance or convenience, we must not reduce the wealth
of kinds, must not create blanks in the great spectrum of life, nor need-
lessly extinguish any species. Even if it hurts the interest of the moment,
we must, for instance, stop the murder of the great whales.

I say this is a religious or ethical responsibility derived from the idea
of creation which sanctions the whole of nature with an intrinsic claim
to integrity. It is, of course, also plain utilitarian common sense, putting
the long-range advantage of our earthbound race before the short
calculations of present need, greed, or whim. But quite apart from these
parallel counsels of prudence (so easily buffeted by the winds of partisan
argument, and always conditional upon the conceptions of our advantage
and the cogency of our reasoning), it is something absolute, the respect
for the manifestation of life on this earth, which should oppose an unconditional "no" to the depletion of the six-day's plentitude—and also,
we might add, to its perversion by man-made genetic monstrosities.

IX

With even greater force than for nature does the idea of creation
inspire reverence for *man*, for he alone is said to be created "in the image
of God." The ethical implications of this mysterious concept are vast
and would deserve fuller elaboration, I will here just indicate a few.

Concerning the "shaping" of this image by man himself, the Jewish
posture should be, in the briefest formula: education—yes; genetic
manipulation—no. The first kind of shaping is our duty, and of necessity
mankind has been doing it, badly or well, since the beginnings of
civil society. We may grievously err in the ends and the means of education, but our mistakes can still be redeemed, if not by their victims
themselves, then by a coming generation: nothing has been irretrievably
prejudged, the potential of human freedom is left intact. At its best,
education fosters this very freedom; at worst, it does not preclude a new
beginning in which the struggling, true form of man may yet be
vindicated.

A different thing is the dream of some of our frontiersmen of science:
the genetic remaking of man in some image, or assortment of images,
of our own choosing, which in fact would be the scientist's according to
his lights. The potentially infinite, transcendent "image" would shrink
to charts of desired properties, selected by ideology (or will it be expediency? or fad?), turned into blueprints by computer-aided geneticists,

authorized by political power—at last inserted with fateful finality into the future evolution of the species by biological technology. From sperm- and ovary-banks there is only one step to synthetic gene-patterning, with a catalogue of samples to suit different tastes or needs.

Here again, quite apart from the terrible danger of error and short-sightedness inherent in our fallibility, quite apart, that is, from considerations of prudence—we simply must not try to fixate man in any image of our own definition and thereby cut off the as yet unrevealed promises of the image of God. We have not been authorized, so Jewish piety would say, to be makers of a new image, nor can we claim the wisdom and knowledge to arrogate that role. If there is any truth in man's being created in the image of God, then awe and reverence and, yes, utter fear, an ultimate metaphysical shudder, ought to prevent us from meddling with the profound secret of what is man.

Or, to take a less apocalyptic or fanciful and at the moment much more real example, Jewish morality should say: persuasion—yes; but not psychological manipulation such as brainwashing, subliminal conditioning, and what other techniques there are, be they practiced in Peking or New York. I need not elaborate. The reader can easily draw the connection from the idea of the image of God to the principle of respect for the person, his freedom, and his dignity. The protest should always be against turning men into things. My general point is that the idea of creation provides a ground for reverence, and that from this reverence there issue definite ethical precepts in the context of our present situation.

One may object that these precepts, as far as our examples show, are of the restraining or prohibiting kind only, telling us what not to do, but not what to do. True, but it is at least a beginning. Also, we may remember that even the Ten Commandments are mostly don't's and not do's. Moreover, the negative emphasis fits the modern situation, whose problem, as we have seen, is an excess of power to "do" and thus an excess of offers for doing. Overwhelmed by our own possibilities— an unprecedented situation this—we need first of all criteria for rejection. There is reasonable consensus on what decency, honesty, justice, charity *bid* us to do in given circumstances, but great confusion on what we are *permitted* to do of the many things that have become feasible to us, and some of which we must *not* do on any account.

X

Let me conclude with one last instance of such rejection, which may not fall on too willing ears among Jews, who notoriously value length of life. Contemporary biology holds out the promise of indefinite prolongation of individual life. This must seem glad tidings to those who, in accord with an ever sounded theme of mankind, consider mortality an evil, a curse, which may yet be lifted from us, at least be lessened by indefinite delay. But if we abolish death, we must abolish procreation as well, the birth of new life, for the latter is life's answer to the former; and so we would have a world of old age with no youth. But youth is our hope, the eternal promise of life's retaining its spontaneity. With their ever new beginning, with all their foolishness and fumbling, it is the young that ever renew and thus keep alive the sense of wonder, of relevance, of the unconditional, of ultimate commitment, which (let us be frank) goes to sleep in us as we grow older and tired. It is the young, not the old, that are ready to give their life, to die for a cause.

So let us be Jews also in this. With young life pressing after us, we can grow old and, sated with days, resign ourselves to death—giving youth and therewith life a new chance. In acknowledging his finitude under God, a Jew, if he still is a Jew, must be able to say with the Psalmist:

> We bring our years to an end as a tale that is told.
> The days of our years are threescore years and ten,
> Or even by reason of strength fourscore years . . . . .
> So teach us to number our days,
> That we may get us a heart of wisdom.

(Ps. 90:10–12)

PART TWO

ORGANISM,
MIND,
AND HISTORY

9.
Biological Foundations
of Individuality

I

In the philosophical tradition, the concept of the individual was for long governed by the concept of numerical singularity. The question was asked: what makes two things that are otherwise entirely the same, different in number? "Otherwise the same" meant: the same in kind; and since "kind" comprises whatever is predicable and thus common, the mere difference in number must mean a difference in something inexpressible. This inexpressible, it was held, is "matter," the unresolvable support for essence in the world of fact, ("Whatever is many in number, has matter," Arist., *Met.*, XII, 8.) Matter conjoined to form is that which makes a particular, beyond its general determinations, a particular; and thanks to the "division" of matter there exist many particulars of the same form: *Individuorum multitudo fit omnis per divisionem materiae* (Avicenna, *In Met.* XI, 1.). Matter, therefore, was regarded as the *principium individuationis*. But how can matter, the very indeterminate itself, the mere potential for form, be the principle of ultimate determination? To that, Thomas Aquinas gave the answer that it was not *materia prima*, indeterminate matter, but *materia signata*, matter prestructured "by quantity" along "certain dimensions," that affords individuation. Matter individuates form through its own *spatial*

Originally published in *International Philosophical Quarterly* 8 (June 1968).

determinations. In a sense, then, matter itself is individuated as a whole by quantitative structure (*quantitas dimensiva*), before it individuates any particular form.[1] This leads straight to the view (still held by Schopenhauer) that the principles of individuation are "space and time": the *hic et nunc*, the "here and now," determines each existence as individual. This amounts to saying that something formal and relational individuates form; and it clearly makes of individuality a matter of external reference only, a function of place in a neutral medium. A thing is individual, not in virtue of what it is, but in consequence of where and when it is.

We feel, however, that over and above external relations, individuality must have a hold in the entity itself to which it is attributed—that it is something internally owned by it and inseparable from its idea. That feeling finds its voice in another train of traditional thought about the individual which stresses the uniqueness of each thing as grounded in its essence rather than in the accident of its location or the constraint of its matter. Duns Scotus claims for each individual its own "form," even a "form of individuality" as a necessary constituent of concrete essence: *haecceitas* ("thisness") complements *quidditas* ("whatness"); *Socratitas* complements *humanitas*. Still a step further goes Leibniz when he completely individualizes "essence" as such: there *are* only individual essences, each the law of a unique career of being implicit in the monad that represents that one essence. The necessary difference in content of any two monads, which would otherwise be one—and it is in Leibniz' case a difference of *subjective* content—means the *essential* individuality of each, an individuality self-realizing in its total autonomous history, of which the essence is the generative law.[2]

We are dissatisfied with both these traditional accounts of individuality. One makes it too extraneous, relational and adventitious; the other too immanent, self-contained and absolute; and both make it a universal possession of all concrete entities, coexistensive with particular existence as such. On the whole, traditional theory views the individual from without, as an object of knowledge, noting the traits by which for the beholder its exceeds its general concept. In contradistinction I wish here to take a stand "within," asking what it is to *be* an individual—for the individual itself; and I shall try to expound a concept which makes in-

---

[1]*De ente et essentia*, c. 2; *Summa theol.* III, 77, 2.

[2]Strictly speaking, this individuality too is a function of the total universe: an individual cannot be reduplicated in the same universe, but it would be repeated in a recurrence of this universe, and must be repeated innumerable times in an eternal recurrence of all things (Nietzsche's "ewige Wiederkunft")—and in that sense the essence again becomes universal.

dividuality the prerogative of a specific mode of existence and therefore the peculiarity of beings endowed with that mode of existing. The criterion I propose in advance is this.

Only those entities are individuals whose being is their own doing (and thus, in a sense, their task): entities, in other words, that are delivered up to their being for their being, so that their being is committed to them, and they are committed to keeping up this being by ever renewed acts of it. Entities, therefore, which in their being are exposed to the alternative of not-being as potentially imminent, and achieve being in answer to this constant imminence; entities, therefore, that are temporal in their innermost nature, that have being only by everbecoming, with each moment posing a new issue in their history; whose *identity* over time is thus, not the inert one of a permanent substratum, but the self-created one of continuous performance; entities, finally, whose *difference* from the *other*, from the rest of things, is not adventitious and indifferent to them, but a dynamic attribute of their being, in that the tension of this difference is the very medium of each one's maintaining itself in its selfhood by standing off the other and communing with it at the same time.

Thus far the ontological conditions we lay down as requisite for individuality. Manifestly all these are descriptions "from within." But the internal features so described must, of course, first be approached by their signs in the "external" evidence, the purely physical record— which we are equipped to "read," i.e. to recognize *as* signs of individuality, by being individuals ourselves. And it must be shown that the being-structures thus revealed indeed represent the conditions of individuality as a distinct mode of being, not an indifferent attribute of all being. Should it be the case that, unbeknown to us, all real entities satisfy those conditions in some measure—a not inconceivable possibility —then all entities would have individuality to that extent. If, on the other hand, as might seem at first, only beings of the order of "person" fit them, then the range of individuality would be contracted to the human sphere. My contention will be that, on the evidence penetrable to us, the proposed conditions are exhibited by organisms and organisms only, but in some measure by *all* organisms: that they are integral to organic being as such; and that therefore the realm of individuality, in all its grades, is coextensive with the biological realm as a whole. The contention is, in brief, that individuality in any serious sense, and not the merely formal sense of numerical singularity, that is, individuality as a substantial quality, is an organic and only an organic phenomenon, and that for the organism it is an essential phenomenon. In what follows, I shall try to show how individuality is grounded in the mode of being of organism, and to exemplify how its more pronounced grades emerge as elaborations of the original groundwork offered by this mode on its primary level.

II

Let us approach the question of individuality from that of *identity*, and ask: in what manner does an entity possess identity? If we take the classical exemplar of ultimate individuality, the *atomon* of the ancient Atomists, we should there expect to find the rock-bottom of identity as such. But what does identity here mean? To put the question differently: If I equate the atom at moment *A* with the atom at moment *B*, what right do I have for that equation? On what basis does the claim of identity rest? Ontologically speaking, it rests on the presumed inertness or constancy of matter; epistemologically, on my confidence that on demand I can verify, by continuous observation, that the atom was "present" through all of the intermediate moments between *A* and *B*, and was missing from none.[3] In the ontological respect, then, the classical Atomist thinks of the unmediated, fixed, but also empty self-identity that is equivalent with immunity to time: with the fact, that is, that the final residue of all reduction exists in each of its bits "once for all," and that these bits are mutually external once for all. The single stubborn particle is then simply and inertly what it is, immediately identical with itself, without need to maintain that self-identity as an act of its existence. Its enduring is mere remaining, not re-assertion of being; and in remaining it is successively "identical" thanks to the homogeneous continuity of the dimensions—space and time—in which the sequence of "its" states takes place. On the same count it is identifiable for knowledge. It is now this one and not that one, because this is now here and that now there: it "remains" this, that is to say, is "the same" at a different (later) point of space-time, because from its present to its new position there leads the continuous sequence of all intermediate positions which, as it were, hand it on from one to the next without ever letting it outside their bond. Such sequence constitutes the "path" of the unit, and for the assigning of identity it is essential that this path has no gaps in fact, even if it has in observation: in principle at least, the spacetime continuity of the particle must be verifiable throughout. The *identity* of a particle in its temporal career is the *continuity* of its space-time path

---

[3]For the concept of time underlying this concept of identity, i.e., time as a dimension composed of mutually extraneous parts, see Principle XXI, Part I, of Descartes' *Principles of Philosophy*.

which we can plot. If there were gaps, if the path were in fact discontinuous, if there were "jumps" in the sequence of actuality, and this were even its normal form, then we should have no way of identifying succeeding "presences," no warrant even for applying the concept of identity at all—unless we endow the elemental with an "inwardness" which by a kind of memory bridges the discontinuity of actual presences. In that case, we have made atoms "historical." Or else, we may substitute for the continuity of individuals that of the probability-spread or the "field" in which such intermittent presences take place, thus saving some descriptive sense of "identity" on a more comprehensive plane. In that case, of course, we have again resorted to the space-time continuum as the logical determinant. The first course—the historicizing of simple entities and their nexus—was chosen by Whitehead, who significantly called his general theory of being a "philosophy of organism": it solves the problem of *physical* identity by extending to it a principle of *organic*, i.e. biological, identity. But short of such metaphysical conjecture, by the more orthodox terms of physical theory—whether they uphold the principle of "simple location" and permanent compact entities, or replace it by that of the "field" and of dynamic transactions—physical identity rests on the continuity of the *principia individuationis*, space and time, that is, on the determinable form of the common receptacle, and is thus a matter of *external reference*. It is here that the jejune equation of "individuality" with numerical singularity holds. Concerning the single element of endurance, e.g. the "corpuscle," the traceable steady presence in the continuum is the sole operational meaning of "identity," and the traced "path" is its complete verification; no obvious claim to an internal principle of identity, such as a historical inwardness, or an urge for "self"-perpetuation, issues from its manner of inert permanence. We may, of course, if we wish, read into the fact of its enduring a conative tenaciousness of existence, a hold on being ceaselessly reasserted, but, lacking any suggestion of a *threat* to its existence, we have no warrant for doing so.

The distributive identity, then, which accordingly is all that accrues to complex bodies, to aggregates, is represented by the "bundle" of individual "paths," running as it were in juxtaposition and presenting the same pattern, or continuous variations of it, in succeeding cross-sections of time—which they do as long as they run, more or less, "parallel." The identity of a material object is thus the collection of the identities of all its simultaneous member units while they travel together through space-time.

Wishing to ascertain, therefore, whether a body has stayed "the same" between two observations the physicist would ideally have to put identifying marks on all of its atoms and check on the later occasion whether is still consists of all the marked ones and of no others. Barring evidence to the contrary, this is taken for granted, and weighing the mass is deemed a sufficient control. The general assumption is that, left alone, and whatever the lapse of time, a substance will offer to repeated inspection the same inventory of parts. This is what is strictly meant by the sameness of the thing.

III

Let us now turn to the organic case. Suppose that from among a number of amoebae one has been "marked" for identification in subsequent inspections. And suppose that in addition all its atomic parts at the time too have been marked individually. Upon later inspection the organism, identified by its mark, is found to be still there, but—with the sum roughly unchanged—to consist only partly of marked and partly of unmarked elements; and upon still later inspection it will be found that, though the "collective" mark has stayed, none of the individual units has remained under the common label: that is, the assemblage, still bearing as a whole the original label, having the same form, and comprising the same quantity, now consists wholly of new members and has not one element in common with the object of the initial inspection. Which is true, the testimony of the "label" or the testimony of the "elements"? By the testimony of the elements, i.e. physically speaking, the object of the later inspection is a different entity altogether. Yet no biologist would take this evidence to mean that he is not dealing with the same organic individual. On the contrary, he would consider any other evidence incompatible with the sameness of a *living* entity *qua* living: with the same "inventory" of parts after a long enough interval, he would judge that the body in question has meanwhile (and very shortly after the first inspection) ceased to be alive and is in that decisive respect no longer "the same." In other words, the persistence of the collective "label" in defiance of the impersistence of the component ones is to him not a deception but the truth. And to him, as to any observer with a commonsense understanding of life, it is not a mere matter of choice, of point of view, or of convenience, whether or not to speak here of "the same." The sameness here in question, we feel, is possessed by the "individual" itself, not attributed to it *qua* object; it originates with its own activity of exchange, not with the categorizing of our mind or the crudity of our perception. In short, it is a real, not an ideal character of it. The testimony of the "label" is true precisely *in conjunction* with that of the "elements," for the latter testimony tells the *story* of the identity which the former proclaims. Thus we are faced with the ontological (not only epistemological) fact of an identity totally different from physical identity, yet grounded in transactions among substrates of physical identity. We must evaluate this highly intriguing fact of ontology.

There seems to obtain a rather paradoxical situation. On the one hand the living being *is* a composite of matter, and at any time its reality totally coincides with its contemporary stuff—that is, with one definite manifold of individual components. On the other hand, it is not identical with this or any such simultaneous total, and its reality is not bound to the assemblage making it up now, as this is forever vanishing downstream in the flow of exchange; in this respect it is different from its stuff and not the sum of it. We have thus the case of a substantial entity enjoying a sort of *freedom* with respect to its own substance, an independence from that same matter of which it nonetheless wholly consists. However, though independent of the sameness of this matter, it is dependent on the change of it, on its progressing permanently and sufficiently, and there is no freedom in this. Thus the exercise of the freedom which the living thing enjoys is rather a stern *necessity*. This necessity we call "need," which obtains only where existence is unassured and identity a continual task.

Again, we cannot solve the problem of identity by saying that the subject of life is identical with the *sum* of composite states through which it moves *in time*. For the single now-state in the sequence of states, the present about to make place for another present, cannot be considered a fraction of the one individual, so that its wholeness would result from the progressive addition of subsequent states to past ones: the individual is whole and its complete self in each of its successive "materializations," *so long as the succession goes on*. If a creature is killed midway in its normal lifespan, the whole has been killed and not half of it.

This deepens the paradox. The living individual exists at any one time in one simultaneous composition of stuff, but is not identical with it—because it is, while coinciding with it, already in the act of passing beyond it. It then exists, over the whole timespan of its life, in a succession of such material compositions through which it passes, but is not identical with the succession or its completed sum either—because it is whole in each of them. Its identity is thus neither the momentary one of its co-temporaneous space-parts—in that case it would have as many identities as successive moments, that is, none at all—nor is it the aggregate of its serial time-parts, that is, of all the successively co-temporaneous sets together—in that case it would always be only a fraction of itself. Being thus different from the sum of its own stuff, considered both in the single co-temporaneous sets and in their total time-series, what is it?

IV

It would be simple if we could say that the bearer of identity in this continual change is the "soul," posited as an entity apart. In that case, the bodily change would be to this persisting subject as a change of garment is to its wearer; and the image is completed by making the wearer also the wearer of the garment.[4] However, this would be to evade the problem by a metaphysical substitution. It amounts to saying that what is alive is not the body but something else: then the "living" body would be no better than a puppet. Yet the problem consists precisely in the manner of being of the organism itself, whether this in addition be the "garment" of something else or not. The activities it is engaged in are its own, or it is not alive. The identity we are investigating cannot be dissociated from it and assigned to another bearer. The separation of the "weaver" from the "woven," borrowed from the human handling of lifeless materials, in fact destroys the object of the inquiry. What other analogies of experience, then, might shed light on the puzzle of organic identity?

It is obvious that in some way we are dealing with the relation between matter and form. For at least one of the things which is preserved in the change of component elements, or one aspect of the sameness preserved in the change, is surely the "form" of the organic whole, and this in the sense not only of visual shape but of the whole structural and dynamical order of a manifold. A classic example of such preservation of identity through that of form is the famous Athenian state-ship which from time immemorial performed the annual voyage to the Delian sanctuary: repaired over and over again by the replacement of worn-out parts, it finally contained not one of its original planks, ropes, or sails, yet was still held to be the same venerable vessel of old. On what does the claim of identity here rest? First, of course, on the sameness of form. But this is not enough: an exact replica would be an individual of the same kind, but not the same individual. At the same time, it is too much, for even some changes of form, the addition or removal of a structure,

---

[4]Cf. Cebes' tentative argument in Plato's *Phaedo* 87d (trans. Jowett): "that every soul wears out many bodies, especially if a man lives many years. While he is alive the body delinquesces and decays, and the soul always weaves another garment and repairs the waste."

would leave a ship the same "individual." Besides the continued similarity of form, there must be a space-time continuity in its material representation, that is, in the existence of the physical compound that is its bearer: an unbroken sequence of physical presence such that it constitutes the history of one subject. Now, in view of the actual exchange of parts this can only mean that in each such change the bulk of the compound is inherited from the preceding stage; in other words, that the exchange is gradual and in small portions. In that case, we may consider the few new elements introduced on each occasion as being absorbed into the old identity and as henceforth being legitimate heirs to the history of the one original object. Accordingly, at the next overhaul they are counted already among the bulk whose preservation assures the identity of the whole in its wide margin over the new replacements; and so on. Thus it is similarity of form and unity of history that together constitute the sameness of the object in the face of total exchange of material and, as the case may be, of partial change of form.

How far does the analogy carry with regard to the problem of organic identity? All the observed features are exhibited in the history of the organism, too, but we immediately note some important differences. For one thing, in the ship the changes are effected from without, that is, by agents other than the entity itself: this is merely the passive object of them. In the organism the changes—waste no less than replacement— are effected from within: it is its own agent for change.

Secondly, the very necessity for replacement arises in the case of the ship by accident only: it can be more or less lucky on its voyages, and in shelter may not undergo any wear at all. In the organism, the need is as concurrent with the act of existing (because arising from it) as is its supply: its very being consists in the constantly self-renewing interplay of both. And whereas it would be considered a mark of excellence for the ship to withstand use without the need for repair, for the organism the mark of excellence is not immunity to wear, but efficiency of repair—nay, even the very variety and scope of the *needs* which are generated by its existing as such. For its existence *is* performance, whereas for the ship existence and performance are two different things.

But the decisive observation, of course, is that to the artefact the identity is *accorded*; and, insofar as this requires a continuity of memory and tradition in those who do accord it, the identity is the function of another identity, namely, that established in memory, individual and social. This originative identity of the cognitive subject is a prerequisite for the accorded identity of the object. But this original identity, being that of living beings, is just a case of what we are enquiring into, and if this is required for explaining the presumed analogue, then the analogy itself fails, and we are back at the question of organic identity itself. This we have acknowledged as owned by, not loaned to its subject.

Lastly, the observation on identity as "merely accorded" must be expanded into the observation that the extraneous *purposiveness* which insists on regarding the ship as still "the same" after all its repairs, is the same purposiveness that went into *making* the repairs, and making, first of all, the ship itself: in the active as well as in the cognitive respect the identity is the function of a *teleology* outside the object. It is this teleology of maker, user, and beholder to which the matter is accidental and the form essential. We cannot credit the ship itself with any such teleology: in Aristotelian terms, it is not an "entelechy." It is therefore also no true individual, and thus has, in fact, quite apart from the series of successive states, no unitary identity at any one time, but merely the collection of all the identities of its parts. Consequently, the question of "its" identity in change does not really arise.

V

Back then to the interrogation of organism. In the precarious metabolic continuity of the organic form, with its perpetual turnover of constituents, identity cannot derive from the substratum. Nor would the mere propagation of pattern through the sum of the transactions be enough to yield identity. For one thing, it may be nothing but the neutral outcome of the collective transactions. For another, pattern is a universal capable of occurring in any number of individual instances. Thus likeness (at its maximum, sameness) of form is different from identity of being; and the fact that the same form is continuously exhibited in a sequence of physical situations does not by itself make the serial presence that of an identical individual. Else a candle-flame, with the constancy of bounded form maintained through the measured consumption of fuel, which it successively incorporates and gives off, would be a case of individual identity. And we are intuitively certain that the flame is not an individual. Thus neither matter nor form nor even their conjunction—the *synholon* which in Aristotle defines individual substance—answers the question of identity in the case of the organism.

In order, therefore, to understand the individuality of the organism, we must go beyond the aspect of mere form: if, before, we noted the sameness of the form freely sustaining "itself" by the exchange of its matter, we have now to take seriously the reflexive pronoun "itself," that is, to locate the identity in something that exercises and enjoys this freedom—which abstract form as such cannot do. In short, the ontologi-

cal individual requires, behind the continuity of form, *internal* identity
as the subject of its existing *in actu*. Even "form" itself, i.e. the very
structure dynamically securing its own preservation—and with it the
whole fitness of organization to this effect, which formally is the vicious
circle of a fitness to preserve fitness—must be deemed to be in the
service of that self-related identity.

It is the aspect of "need" which gets us beyond the indifference of
the mere form-matter relation. We said before that the "freedom" which
the living, i.e. metabolizing, entity enjoys relative to matter is matched
by the necessity to exercise that freedom. This necessity is its need,
namely, the need for constant self-renewal, and thus need for the matter
required in that renewal, and thus need for "world."

Need, indigence, insufficiency is no less unique a distinction of life
than is its power, of which it is but the other side. This is where Leibniz'
monadology goes wrong, and also, as far as I can see, Whitehead's
concept of "actual entity," which has something monadically enclosed
too. I am not entirely sure of the latter, but Leibniz' monad, self-enclosed,
self-actualizing, invulnerable, certainly exemplifies the classical concept
of independent substance which, as the definition has it, "requires
nothing else in order to exist." But such self-sufficiency applies, if to
anything at all, to lifeless stuff. Of a particle of matter we may at least
imagine that it does not "need" anything outside itself to exist. It is
what it is, whether there are others around it or not. We can imagine
the rest of the world annihilated and would still have the same lone
atom; and the continuance of its existence is assumed to follow entirely
from the fact of its once being there. If surrounded by others, it will
interact with them: but its acting and suffering are accidents of which
the substance is the invariant subject. This independence, however, has
nothing to do with freedom; on the contrary, it excludes it. The existence
of the particle is given, not a task to be performed; thus it has necessity,
but no need. Its very autarky is a sign of the sheer necessity of its
being.[5]

Life's insufficiency, on the other hand, is both a sign and the very
measure of the freedom to which the organism is committed in relation
to its own concretion. Metabolism essentially includes these two sides,
which means that the liberty of life is itself its peculiar necessity. Its

[5]Cf. Karl Marx, *The Holy Family*: "The members of civil society are not *atoms*.
The *specific property* of the atom is that it has *no* properties and is therefore not
connected with beings outside it by any relations determined by its own *natural
necessity*. The atom *has no needs*, it is *self-sufficient*; the world outside it is absolute
vacuum, i.e., it is contentless, senseless, meaningless, just because the atom has *all
its fullness in itself*." From *The Economic and Philosophical Manuscripts of 1844*,
trans. M. Milligan (New York: International Publishers, 1964), p. 162.

being, suspended in possibility, is to be actualized by the *use* of the world. The power to use the world, this unique prerogative of life, has its precise reverse in the necessity of having to use it. For the organism, to exist, in fact, *is* to use and keep using "something else"—therefore to need it. The dependence here in force is the cost incurred by primeval substance in venturing upon the career of organic, that is, self-constituting, identity, in the place of merely inert persistence. Because of the metabolizing mode of this identity, need is of its very essence and it is thus with it from the beginning. But the very *means* evolved to serve this need, such as perception, locomotion, desire, add new kinds of need to the basic, metabolic one—and therewith new kinds of satisfaction. This dialectic too is of the essence of life. The spectrum of needs belonging to an organism is the measure of the degree of its freedom and individuality.

VI

What has just been outlined amounts to saying that the mere phenomenon of *metabolism*, often considered to be no more than the elementary level that underlies, and supplies energy for, the quite different higher functions of life (such as perception, locomotion, and desire), in fact contains in its own primary constitution the groundwork as it were of all those functions, which may or may not evolve on its basis. It presages them by enacting *within itself* the cardinal polarities which those functions will expand and span with their more determinate relationships: the *polarity of being and not-being, of self and world, of freedom and necessity.*

The introduction of the term "self," unavoidable in any description of the most elementary instance of life, indicates the emergence, with life as such, of internal identity—and hence, as one with that emergence, its self-isolation as well from all the rest of reality. Profound singleness and heterogeneity within a universe of homogeneously interrelated existence mark the selfhood of organism. An identity which from moment to moment reasserts itself, achieves itself, and defies the equalizing forces of physical sameness all around, is truly pitted against the rest of things. In the hazardous polarization thus ventured upon by emerging life, that which is not "itself" and borders on the realm of internal identity from without assumes at once for the living individual the character of absolute otherness. The challenge of "selfhood" qualifies everything beyond the boundaries of the organism as foreign and somehow opposite: as "world," within which, by which, and against which it is committed to maintain itself. Without this universal counterpart of "other," there would be no "self."

Now this polarity of self and world stands, for the self, under the sign of the polarity of being and not-being, that is, under the *alternative* of "to be or not to be" with which the organism is constitutionally faced. "To be" is its intrinsic goal. *Teleology* comes in where the continuous identity of being is not assured by mere inertial persistence of a substance, but is continually executed by something *done*, and by something which *has* to be done in order to stay on at all: it is a matter of to-be-or-not-to-be whether what is to be done *is* done. Now to an entity that carries on its existence by way of constant regenerative activity we impute *concern*. The minimum concern is to be, i.e. to carry on being— what Spinoza has called the *conatus* to stay in existence. But Spinoza, with the knowledge of his time, did not realize that the *conatus* to persevere in being can only operate as a movement that goes constantly *beyond* the given state of things. What, in its total effect, appears to be the maintaining of the given condition, is in fact achieved by way of a continuous moving beyond the given condition. There is an openness, a horizon, intrinsic to the very existence of the organic individual. Concerned with its being, engaged in the business of it, it must *for the sake* of this being let go of it as it is now so as to lay hold of it as it will be. Its continuation is always more than mere preservation. Organic individuality is achieved in the face of otherness, as its own ever challenged goal, and is thus teleological.

Teleology is the concomitant of want (or vice versa). The organism basically is "in want," therefore always does want something. The *animal* reflexion of this wanting is "desire." For what? In the classical scheme, desire is for the good, and the good is what completes or perfects a being. But can there be completion and perfection for a living being? It would mean cessation of want, therefore of the being itself, which *is* the dynamics of want and satisfaction. Thus the *telos* of the organic individual, the teleology of individuality as such, is the acting out of the very tension of the polarities that constitute its being, and thus the *process* of its existence as such.

These are some of the categories with which we can articulate an ontologically relevant concept of individuality. Their fuller concretion appears only in the *centralization* of *animal* individuality, which manifests itself in motility, perception and emotion. The remainder of this paper will deal with the first of these.

VII

To be functionally "centered" is an original trait of organism, exhibited already in the nuclear organization of the single cell. In the protozoa, the cell nucleus (itself an organized structure) performs controlling functions somewhat analogous to those of a nervous center in vastly more complex organizations. With the smallness and relative "simplicity" of the system, the control can for its communication dispense with special channels, such as ducts and nerves, and works (probably) by direct chemical diffusion. However "rudimentary" this is as a type of centralization, it is significant for the nature of life not only regarding the technique of its functioning, but as a morphological sign of its essential individuality.

It is an intriguing fact that early in the evolution toward metazoic life this degree of individuation is temporarily lost—to be recovered, on a higher level, only in subsequent steps, and in *animal* evolution only. The association of many cells in certain types of aggregates presents a situation in which the single cells have in part renounced their individualized existence in favor of the collective entity, but without the latter's superimposing a comparable individuality of its own that would structurally betray itself in comparable centralization. Thus the career of the multi-cellular organism, which in the event produced the highest type of individuation, started out with partial obliteration of that degree of individuality which had been achieved already in the original, protozoic units of life. This original individuality is not recovered throughout the *vegetable* kingdom, in spite of the high integration and functional differentiation exhibited by the higher plants: the most pronounced *morphological* individuality of a tree is not matched by an internal individuality, such as is evident in the centralization of even the solitary amoeba.

It is only in animal life that the aggregate regains on a higher level the individuality which had been surrendered by the component parts. Consequently, if we adopt the most *prima facie* and popular, but nonetheless pertinent, distinction between animal and plant, namely, that the one moves about while the other is rooted to its place, we have in this naive distinction indeed a symbol for all the subtler distinctions regarding sentience, centralization, individuality, and freedom, with which the philosophical analysis is concerned. The stationary plant could no more profit from centralization and individuality than the moving animal could be without them. We see accordingly that *centralization* is not the same as organic *unity* of the complex whole, nor always accompanying such unity, but is a new fact in the evolution of metazoic (multi-cellular) organisms, confined to animal life and coincident with the evolution of sentience and motility.

To establish the point for sentience, it suffices to spell out the truism that the function of a sense-organ is obviously not to enjoy its own sensitivity but to "report" to the common center of all sentience: it is not the eye that sees, for itself, but we see with our eyes. The seeing self is presupposed in the possession of such an organ as the eye, as the hearing self is in the possession of ears; and furthermore, the identity of the hearing-plus-seeing (etc.), in short, of the sensing individual, is implied in the possession of these several organs by one organism; and finally, the identity of the subject of sentience what that of motility is implied in the animal organization as such.

Animal *motility* even more forcefully than sentience demonstrates the fact of centralization, because there it means *control* of action; and motility links centralization to the most basic fact of animal nature, viz. the special form of its *metabolism*, in whose service motility stands. The animal mode of nutrition as determined by the absence of photosynthesis —the intake of solid food, instead of the mere osmotic absorption of dissolved nutriment by plants—involves an important modification in the dynamics of that inside-outside relation which is incumbent on all living things: it must interpose an auxiliary, "mechanical" stage before the direct, chemical stage of metabolic appropriation. This mechanical mediation, on which the intra-organic work of metabolism has been made entirely dependent, consists in the external activities of locomotion and manipulation, entrusted to distinct motor structures that serve no other organic purpose. Even on the protozoic level, where the basic metabolic condition of animality already obtains, flagella and cilia functionally prefigure the limbs of true, metazoic animals.[6]

---

[6]There is an even more primitive type of animal motility. In the amoeba, the least "mechanized" (i.e. structurally defined) of animal forms, it operates, without benefit of special motor equipment, on the protoplasmic level itself. The incidence of something external on the sensitive surface provokes a reaction, which may take the form of either withdrawal or advance, and whose execution eventually involves the whole cytoplasm of the individual. We may take it that in this case, as probably in all cases prior to the emergence of nervous apparatus, the "sensing" really consists *in* the reacting, or, that feeling and responsive motion are one and the same event. Such a complete fusion of stimulation and response, and therefore of whatever "sentience" and "motility" are present, is suggested by the unicellular situation as such; and in the amoeba in particular, where no specialized organs for either sensory or motor functions are present, the whole body-surface, if not the whole cytoplasm, seems equally disposed for both at any one point which the accident of external stimulus may single out. Temporary protoplasmic projections are called forth, the "pseudopodia," extruded with undefined, flowing shape from any part of the cell-body, to serve both locomotion and food capture. This "amoeboid" mode, considering its primitiveness and the undifferentiated plasticity upon which it rests, may well represent the oldest mode of animal motion.

But in all other classes of protozoa (excepting the secondary, parasitical forms) motility has already special structures at its command: flagella or cilia, i.e. permanent, whiplike or hairlike extensions of the protoplasm ("ectoplasm"), endowed with special contractility and used in energetic movement for locomotion and getting food. In some cases, the use is also tactile (as may be that of pseudopodia too). With these efficient organs, which on the unicellular level prefigure certain achievements of metazoic organization, the rate of movement—as seen, e.g., in the violent lashing of the flagellum—is considerably increased over the sluggish amoeboid mode. (Even

Limbs proper are complex structures for mechanical, i.e. neither metabolic nor sensory, commerce with the outside world, and their evolution means increasing mechanization in the macroconstitution of the organism itself. Multipartite, jointed limbs of skeleton-supported animals represent an advanced stage of the "mechanization" to which animal living is geared by its *mediate* mode of sustenance. A composite limb is a mechanical arrangement of connected, movable parts, each with a certain definition of its motions toward the combined functioning of the whole, but also—to meet the variable conditions of living and obviate the need for multiplication of structures—with degrees of freedom exceeding those that would generally be permitted in a machine. Such a system requires for its proper functioning a continual coordination of the part-functions, and moreover continual adjustment to the external conditions of its action. The elements of the mechanism are deprived of the status of independently sensitive and reactive bodyparts and are subjected to common control.

The element of control is decisive. Real motor activity means controlled motion, as distinct from the mere local stimulus-response functioning of lower orders. The control must be exercised from a level superior to or more comprehensive than that of the particular limb, so as to secure not only mutual correlation of its part-functions, but correlation also of its total function with that of the organism as a whole. Here we encounter the principle of sub- and super-ordination. In other words, controlled motion requires, in addition to the mechanical structure of the limb, a *nervous* system pervading the total manifold of the body. This is in itself an entirely new feature, and its presence must be postulated on the mere external evidence of articulate limbs. The nervous system, as a system of intercommunication distributed throughout the body, may then be said to constitute the "higher level" we have indicated, and in this role it provides a first answer to the question of who or

---

among the amoebae, the place of the shapeless pseudopodia is in some species taken by sets of temporary hairlike tentacles, moving in concert to row the body through the water.) Little is known of the mechanism of activation and control, which, e.g., in the case of the combined vibration of many cilia, involves definite coordination. Presumably, in the absence of nervous apparatus, the action is governed by local sensitivity, so that, even apart from tactile function, these "protolimbs" are carriers of enhanced motility and sensitivity at once. (However, certain flagellata seem to have some kind of central control of the motor apparatus in the so-called "kinetic" nucleus, a smaller companion of the principal nucleus.) And throughout the protozoic level, with some rare, possible exceptions such as light-sensitive pigment spots in some flagellata, feeling and acting must be assumed to reside in the same substratum and to constitute one indivisible fact. The separation of the two sides, i.e. the dissociation of moving and sensing, with neural mediation between them, comes about in the metazoic stage.

what is the source of the control: it would be the organism as a whole, functionally integrated by its nervous system. In this case, "higher" denotes "more comprehensive." But really efficient integration of motility requires more than mere mutual, as it were self-balancing, coordination among the parts of the body—thus more than mere distributive intercommunication: it requires a unifying center as the seat of control. With its presence, the question as to the source or agent of control is answered by reference to this center, while the nerves issuing from it are the channels of control, as also of the information necessary for control.

VIII

Now this fact of centralization, whose rise goes hand in hand with that of sentience and motility, and is really inseparable from it, raises the unity and individuality of the organism to an entirely new level. Almost everything said before about individuality and freedom in organic existence applies fully on this level only. Centralization is as essential to perception as it is to controlled motility. Specific sense-organs are as much evidence of it as are specialized motor-organs. Just as sentience and motility imply each other, so each and both together imply centralization: and the latter functions essentially in these two directions.

It is therefore entirely a matter of choice and not of intrinsic priority when in the remaining pages we continue with motility rather than perception. The advantage is merely that the former is more in the physical, public domain; and with the *embarras de richesse* of the subject we can afford to humor the scientific allergy against the domain of "subjectivity." On the same count we pass over the volitional character of animal motion, and generally its coupling with emotion.[7] Even without these aspects—which of course are indispensable in a full account of motility—it is obvious that animal motion is more than merely an intensified or magnified case of organic motion in general. We may note its difference from vegetative motion in these physical respects: in speed and spatial scale; in being occasional instead of continual; variable instead of predefined; reversible instead of irreversible.

As to the quickness and spatial scope of animal motion, this is not a mere matter of degree compared to the motions of plant life but represents a qualitatively new level of existence above the vegetative one.

[7]See H. Jonas, "To Move and to Feel," *The Phenomenon of Life: Toward a Philosophical Biology* (New York: Harper & Row, 1966), p. 99ff.

Its outward sweep first opens up that horizon of a world which is latent in the self-transcendence of life. The ability to respond quickly to changes and opportunities in the environment means an immense increase in the powers of life. But success in this respect cuts both ways: it launches the organism upon a mode of life in which it is irrevocably committed to quickness. With its very acquisition, the faculty turns from an unambiguous advantage into a matter of life and death and thus makes its privileged possessor critically dependent upon it. And this not only because its possession engenders specialization in such habits of life as make its exercise indispensable, but also because its widespread (namely, mutually stimulated) adoption by animal evolution all around creates an environment in which quickness is prevalent as the endownment of competitors, enemies and prey alike. This situation, taxing the adaptive quickness of all participants, puts a strain on life which earlier forms had been spared. Thus the speed of animal motion does not merely widen the external range of life: it alters the nature of the world itself over which this range extends, creating a new setting for life from without at the same time that it alters its mode from within.

The next obvious distinction of animal from vegetative motion is its variability and the revocable nature of the changes which it performs. A process of growth or formation runs, on the whole, on predetermined tracks, and its results are there to stay—to be added to, perhaps, but not to be reversed. Animal motion, on the contrary, consists in the operation of structures whose future condition is not prejudged by their acts: throughout the train of action and at the end of it the condition remains what it was at the start, viz., that of free motility. The motions of limbs are reversible, and the change which they bring about is not a new state of the animal but a new state in its relations to other things. It is an unaltered animal which proceeds from this to the next motion, and the limb resumes its proper function each time under identical structural conditions. In other words, the operation of a limb does not entail its own and thereby the agent's transformation in the process. This is equivalent to saying that a limb is a mechanical structure, and animal motion is outward motion, which as such changes only spatial relations and leaves the nature of the agent unaffected.

All this is profoundly different from vegetative motion of whatever kind, and this difference is of supreme importance for the kinds of identity which animals and plants respectively enjoy. It is unqualifiedly the same animal which now has one of its fore limbs stretched as that which before had it flexed: witness the unqualified ability to revert to the former position "at will." The blossoming tree is not so unqualifiedly "the same" as that which was bare in winter or budding in spring: it really has changed in its being, as shown by the inability to withdraw the blossoms again into the buds (etc.); and it will be different again when its leaves turn yellow.

Animal motility, peripheral and variable, admits of an identity in change such as is on principle closed to the vegetative level. The implications of this for the issue of "individuality" and "freedom" are manifold. We are content with the point made that greater *variability* goes with more *identity*. By its outward character, animal motion concerns the *relations* of the organism to the environment. On each occasion, a temporary relation, inherited from past movement, is altered by an unaltered agent in response to outside changes or inner demands; each time the actual movement is one from a number of possible ones; and the result is a new relation equally non-definitive and temporary. This, in conjunction with what has been stated about the rate of animal motion, lends to the animal "situation" an essential fluidity which strongly contrasts with the settled and unidirectional periodicity of plant life.[8]

[8]Phototropism in plants might seem to blur some of the distinctions just made. It is a motion in response to outside changes of a short-term nature; it is relatively fast and perceptible; and since it returns to the initial condition upon appropriate stimulation, it can even be called reversible. Yet the difference between this and animal motion holds. The turning of the leaves is, as to occurrence, rate, and rhythm, entirely governed from without; and it is only owing to the cyclical nature of the light-changes involved, that is, to the external agent, that the phototropical motion does "revert." It is not the motion in progress that has the capacity to reverse itself; there is but one direction open to it at any given phase. And its change of direction is as reactive as is the bare fact of a motion as such: neither is under the agent's control.

The same goes for the opening and closing of blossoms and even for the startling performance of certain insectivorous plants. There the outward likeness to the animal pattern is indeed strong. First, of course, the digestive use of food (i.e. of captured protein) as such, and in some cases also the mechanics of the capture. The suddenness and swiftness, e.g., with which the leaf-halves of the Venus Flytrap, upon stimulation of their sensitive hairs, fold together over the prey and interlock their toothed edges, look very much like a feat of goal-directed animal motility. Yet the "direction" here is not central but strictly in local response to local stimulation, with no central control involved. Also the return to the original condition, when digestion is finished and the flaps reopen, is not the true reversibility of muscular movement. The difference can most simply be brought out by asking: Can the plant close and open those leaves? The animal can close and open its jaws freely, whenever it feels like doing so—to chew, yawn, or merely to exercise the faculty—and can stop and reverse each movement while in progress. The leaves of the flytrap close or open as conditions determine, and each phase of motion is unidirectional when it occurs, with no accompanying alternative. In brief, it is not "the plant" that moves "its" leaves, as the animal moves *its* limbs: it is those leaves that by a predetermined mechanism react to determinate affections of their own condition.

IX

The centeredness of animal organization brings out the "indivisibility" which lies in the literal meaning of "individual." And it is the order of individuation that marks the ontological difference between animal and plant. The difference can be defined by the phenomenon of *distance* which the mediate mode of animal metabolism introduces into the relationship between organism and environment, as compared to the immediacy of plant metabolism (a relative "immediacy," to be sure, since metabolism as such is a mediating mode of continuous being.) The mediacy interposes distance between subject and object, need and satisfaction, action and goal, and these "gaps" opened in animal existence are spanned by perception, emotion, and movement. The spatial gap between subject and object, which is provisionally spanned by perception, is at the same time the temporary gap between need and satisfaction that is provisionally spanned by emotion (desire) and practically overcome by motion. All three modes express the mediacy of animal being, or the split between self and world—a qualitative widening of the split which metabolism opened first, and which is thus at the root of life. The lesser integration of the animal into its environment as compared to the plant, of which these modes of mediacy bear witness, is a measure of its greater individuality. To be an individual means not-to-be-integrated with the world, and the less so, the more it is an individual. Individuality implies discontinuity.

If there is a more-or-less in the conditions of individuality, as the last statements suggest, then individuality itself is something that can be present in greater or smaller measure. Since, obviously, such terms as mediacy, gap, distance do admit of a more-or-less, they adumbrate with their quantitative meaning a scale along which should be found different degrees of individuality. Needless to say, shifts on this scale represent qualitative differences of being.[9] For a fuller treatment I must refer the reader to what I have said elsewhere on the phenomenon of "mediacy and distance" as the mark of animality in distinction from plant life, and again of humanity in distinction from animal life.[10] But

---

[9]Whether the "scale" is nearly continuous, or rather articulated by major divisions, is a matter for more concrete determination. But at least within the division of animality, the scale certainly goes on with increasing values, determinable by the kinds of perception, motility, and neural centralization of the different taxonomic forms.

[10]*The Phenomenon of Life*, pp. 99–107; 183–87.

I may be permitted to conclude this paper with a passage borrowed from that earlier discourse.

The "selfhood" adumbrated in the original condition of organism on the unicellular level has from the beginning its counterpart in the otherness of the world. The further accentuation of this tension is nothing but the accentuation of life itself. Here lies the real advantage of developed animality: its mediacy of world-relation, by way of perception and action, is an increase of the mediacy which metabolizing existence involves as such. This increased mediacy buys greater scope, internal and external, at the price of greater hazard, internal and external. A more pronounced self is set over against a more pronounced world. The progressive neural centralization of the animal organism indicates that "self" for which the environment has become open space wherein the free-moving sentient has to meet the changing situations of life. In its greater exposure and the pitch of awareness that goes with it, its own possible annihilation becomes an object of dread just as its possible satisfactions are objects of desire. Its enjoyment has the suffering of frustration as its shadow side; its isolation is compensated by communication. The gain lies not on either side of the balance sheet but in the togetherness of both, i.e., in the enhancement of that selfhood with which "organism" originally dared indifferent nature. This is the biological meaning of individuality.

10.
Spinoza and the Theory
of Organism

I

Cartesian dualism landed speculation on the nature of life in an impasse: intelligible as, on principles of mechanics, the correlation of structure and function became within the *res extensa*, that of structure-plus-function with feeling or experience (modes of the *res cogitans*) was lost in the bifurcation, and thereby the fact of life itself became unintelligible at the same time that the explanation of its bodily performance seemed to be assured. The impasse became manifest in Occasionalism: its tour de force of an extraneous, divine "synchronization" of the outer and the inner world (the latter denied to animals) not only suffered from its extreme artificiality, the common failing of such *ad hoc* constructions, but even at so high a cost failed to accomplish its theoretical purpose by its own terms. For the animal machine, like any machine, raises beyond the question of the "how" that of the "what for" of its functioning—of the purpose for which it had thus been constructed by its maker.[1] Its performance, however devoid of immanent teleology, must serve an end,

[1]The concept of "machine," adopted for its strict confinement to efficient cause, is still a finalistic concept, even though the final cause is no longer internal to the entity, as a mode of its own operation, but external to it as antecedent design.

and that end must be someone's end. This end may (directly) be itself, as indeed Descartes had implied when declaring self-preservation to be the effect of the functioning of the organic automaton. In that case the existence as such of the machine would be its end—either terminally, or in turn to benefit something else. In the former case, the machine would have to be more than a machine, for a mere machine cannot enjoy its existence. But since, by the rigorous conception of the *res extensa*, it cannot be more than a machine, its function and/or existence must serve something other than itself. Automata in Descartes' time were mainly for entertainment (rather than work). But the *raison d'être* of the living kingdom could not well be seen in God's indulging his mechanical abilities or in the amusement of celestial spectators—especially since mere complexity of arrangement does not create new quality and thus add something to the unrelieved sameness of the simple substratum that might enrich the spectrum of being. For quality, beyond the primitive determinations of the extended per se, is the subjective creature of sensation, the confused representation of quantity in a mind; and thus organisms cannot harbor it because as mere machines they lack mentality, and pure spirits cannot because they lack sensuality, or the privilege of confusion and thereby of illusion with its possible enjoyment. And as to their intellectual enjoyment, even that, deprived of the thrill of discovery by the same token, would pale in the contemplation of what to sufficiently large intellects is nothing but the ever-repeated exemplification of the same few, elementary (and ultimately trivial) truths.

There remained, then, the time-honored—Stoic as well as Christian—idea that plants and animals are for the benefit of Man. Indeed, since the existence of a living world is the necessary condition for the existence of any of its members, the self-justifying nature of at least one such member (= species) would justify the existence of the whole. In Stoicism, Man provided this end by his possession of reason, which makes him the culmination of a terrestrial scale of being that is also self-justifying throughout all its grades (the end as the best of many that are good in degrees); in Christianity, by his possession of an immortal soul, which makes him the sole *imago Dei* in creation (the end as the sole issue at stake); and Cartesian dualism radicalized this latter position by making man even the sole possessor of inwardness or "soul" of *any* kind, thus the only one of whom "end" can meaningfully be predicated as he alone can entertain ends. All other life then, the product of physical necessity, can be considered his means.

However, this traditional idea, in its anthropocentric vanity never a good one even where it made sense, no longer made sense in the new dualistic and occasionalist setting. For man, the supposed beneficiary of living creation, i.e., of all the other organic mechanisms, was now himself an inexplicable, extraneous combination of mind and body—a combination with no intelligible relevance of the body for the existence and inner life of the mind (as also, of course, vice versa). Therefore, even if it was shown that the existence of the organic world was necessary for the existence of human bodies, as indeed it is, it could not be shown that the existence of this very body was necessary for the existence of "man" considered as the thinking ego. Furthermore, the very distinction of man's body within the animal kingdom, viz., to be at least partially an organ of mind—that distinction for the sake of which Descartes had been willing to brave the contortions of the pineal gland doctrine—was also nullified by the occasionalist fiction, in which the human body became no less completely an automaton than all other organisms. Thus the existence of the entire living kingdom became utterly unintelligible as to purpose and meaning as well as to origin and procreative cause. A vast scheme of delusory "as ifs" superseded all question of real issue in the working of things.

All this amounts to saying that the main fault, even absurdity, of the doctrine lay in denying organic reality its principal and most obvious characteristic, namely, that it exhibits in each individual instance a striving of its own for existence and fulfillment, or the fact of life's willing itself. In other words, the banishment of the old concept of appetition from the conceptual scheme of the new physics, joined to the rationalistic spiritualism of the new theory of consciousness, deprived the realm of life of its status in the scheme of things. Yet, since sheer unrelatedness never satisfies theory, and since the irrepressible evidence of every one of our psycho-physical acts obstinately contradicts the dualistic division, it was inevitable that attempts were made to overcome the rift.

For this there were in principle three ways open, each of which was in fact chosen at one time or another: to accord primacy alternatively to matter or to mind, or to transcend the alternative by a new concept of substance. The third choice was Spinoza's, in one of the boldest ventures in the history of metaphysics. Its important implications for a philosophy of the organism, only partially explicated by Spinoza himself, are seldom noticed.[2]

II

Let us briefly recall the general principle of Spinoza's system. Its basis is the concept of one absolute and infinite substance, transcending those

[2]Some excellent observations on the biological aspect of Spinoza's metaphysics, with special reference to modern developments in the physical and biological sciences, are found in Stuart Hampshire, *Spinoza* (Pelican Books, 1951), pp. 75–81.

specifications (viz., extension and thought) by which Descartes had distinguished between different kinds of substance. Besides difference of kind, the oneness of Substance also excludes plurality of number: the infinity, being non-partitive, leaves no room for the existence of finite substances. Thus whatever is finite is not a substance but a modification or affection of infinite substance—a "mode." This is to say that individual being is not self-subsistent but inheres in the self-subsistent as a passing determination thereof. On the other hand, the infinity of the one substance involves an infinite number of "attributes" expressing the nature of that substance—each adequately insofar as it is itself infinite and in this conforms to the infinity of substance (as, e.g., the infinity of spaces does for the attribute of extension), but inadequately, namely incompletely, insofar as it expresses it only under this form. The sum of the attributes is the essence of substance itself, thus each attribute is "part" of the essence (or, the essence in one aspect) and as such complementary with all the rest. The same can also be stated by saying that the attributes all together "constitute" the essence, not however additively, but as abstract moments that are only abstractly separable. Individual existents, then (the "modes" mentioned before), are variable determinations of substance *in terms* of its invariable attributes ("*this* particular cube, " "*this* particular thought"); and each individual affection of infinite substance as it occurs is exhibited, equally and equivalently, throughout all its attributes at once. Extension and Thought are two such attributes, the only ones of which *we* are cognizant. Thus, while the "modes" (affections) are what really happens to substance, the particular actualities of its existence, the "attributes"—e.g., extension and thought—are the universal forms in which such actualities manifest themselves and under which they can be conceived with equal truth by any finite mind that enjoys cognition of some of these forms. Since, in the human case, this is limited to the two indicated, our world consists in fact of body and mind, and nothing else.

The point for our context is that what to Descartes and to Cartesians like Geulincx were two separate and independent substances—as such requiring for their existence neither each other nor a ground common to both[3]—are to Spinoza merely different aspects of one and the same reality, no more separable from each other than from their common cause. And he stresses that this common cause—infinite substance or God—*is* as truly extension as it is thought, or, as truly corporeal as mental; but there is as little a substance "body" as there is a substance

---

[3]They do require the latter in the extraneous sense of first having had to be created and then continuously to be confirmed in existence by God; but the *creative* (as well as preserving) cause is not an immanent cause; and insofar as those things were created *as* substances, they were precisely created as self-subsistent, however revocable that subsistence may be.

"mind." Now since both these attributes express in each individual instance an identical fact, the whole problem of interaction, with which
Occasionalism had to wrestle, or of the interrelation generally between
the two realms, vanished. Each occurrence (mode) as viewed under the
attribute of extension is at the same time, and equivalently, an occurrence
viewed under the attribute of thought or consciousness, and vice versa.
The two are strictly complementary aspects of one and the same reality
which of necessity unfolds itself in all its attributes at once. It would
even be too disjunctive to say that each material event has its "counterpart" in a mental event, since what externally may be registered as a
parallelism of two different series of events is in truth, that is, in the
reality of God or nature, substantially identical. Thus the riddle created
by Cartesian dualism—of how an act of will can move a limb, since the
limb as part of the extended world can only be moved by another body's
imparting its antecedent motion to it—this riddle disappears. The act of
will and the movement of the body are one and the same event appearing
under different aspects, each of which represents in its own terms a complete expression of the concatenation of things in God, in the one eternal
cause.

III

Spinoza's central interest, it is true, was not a doctrine of organism,
but a metaphysical foundation for psychology and ethics; but incidentally
his metaphysical basis enabled him to account for features of organic
existence far beyond what Cartesian dualism and mechanism could accommodate. In the first place, Spinoza was no longer compelled to view
those complex material entities we call organisms as the products of
mechanical design. The idea of a purpose, in analogy to man-made
machines, was replaced by the eternal necessity of the self-explication of
the infinite nature of God, that is, of substance, that is, of reality. Therefore, what mattered in the understanding of an organism was no longer
its lesser or greater perfection as an independent piece of functioning
machinery, but its lesser or greater perfection as a finite "mode," measured by its power to exist and to interact (communicate) with the rest of
existence, or, to be a less or more self-determined part of the whole: on
whatever level of such perfection, it realizes one of the intrinsic possibilities of original substance in terms of matter and mind at once, and
thereby shares in the self-affirmation of Being as such. And the principle
of infinite reality, involving infinity of possible determination, would
account for the wealth and gradation of organic forms. The purpose,
then, is not ulterior and certainly does not lie in man, but lies entirely in

the infinite self-expression itself; and even this does, strictly speaking, not merit the term "purpose," since it is governed by the immanent necessity of the absolute cause.

Secondly, the very image of "machine" could be dropped. Here we must note one of the inherent limitations of that image, quite apart from the psychophysical question. The model—meant from the outset for animals and not for plants—provides: (a) for a connected *structure* of moving parts, such as levers, hinges, rods, wheels, tubes, valves; and (b) for the generation of *movement* from some source of power, such as the tension of a spring in a clock, or the heat of fire in a steam engine. Though the latter, or any combustion engine, was unknown to Descartes, he anticipated the model when he declared heat to be the moving force in the animal machine, and this heat to be generated by the "burning" of food. Thus the combustion theory of metabolism complements the machine theory of anatomical structure. But metabolism is more than a method of power-generation, or, food is more than fuel: in addition to, and more basic than, providing kinetic energy for the running of the machine (a case anyway not applying to plants), its role is to build up originally and replace continually the very parts of the machine. Metabolism thus is the constant becoming of the machine itself—and this becoming itself is a performance of the machine: but for such performance there is no analogue in the world of machines. In other words, once metabolism is understood as not only a device for energy-production, but as the continuous process of self-constitution of the very substance and form of the organism, the machine model breaks down. A better analogy would be that of a flame. As, in a burning candle, the permanence of the flame is a permanence, not of substance, but of process in which at each moment the "body" with its "structure" of inner and outer layers is reconstituted of materials different from the previous and following ones, so the living organism exists as a constant exchange of its own constituents, and has its permanence and identity only in the continuity of this process, not in any persistence of its material parts. This process indeed *is* its life, and in the last resort organic existence means, not to be a definite body composed of definite parts, but to be such a continuity of process with an identity sustained above and through the flux of components. Definiteness of arrangement (configuration) will then, jointly with continuity of process, provide the principle of identity which "substance" as such no longer provides.

On these lines indeed, Spinoza seeks to answer the problem of organic identity. Substance cannot by the terms of his ontology furnish such identity, because substance is not individual, and the organism is an individual. What is individual is a "mode," and so must be the organism as a species of individual. In fact, it is under the title of "individuality," i.e., in considering what makes an individual, and not under the title of "living things" in particular, that Spinoza treats the phenomenon of organism. Now *any* mode of universal substance, whether simple or complex, whether brief or enduring, is an individual (by definition, for to be a "mode" means just to be a distinct occurrence in the eternal self-unfolding of infinite being), and is this in all of the attributes if in any one of them. In that of extension this means to be a *body*, either simple or composite, *distinct* from other bodies. Since this distinctness cannot lie in its substance (by which on the contrary it is one with all), it must lie in its modal *determinations*, such as figure and motion, and in their interaction with other instances of determination in the same attribute. The continuity of determinateness throughout such interactions (a continuity, therefore, not excluding change) bespeaks the self-affirming "conatus" by which a mode tends to persevere in existence, and which is identical with its essence. Thus it is the *form* of determinateness, and the *conatus* evidenced by the survival of that form in a causal history, i.e., in *relation* to co-existing things, that defines an individual. All three— form, continuity, and relation—are integral to the concept of an individual and provide a clue to the meaning of its identity. The manner of "relation," i.e., of the causal communication with the environment in acting and suffering (affecting and being affected), depends on the given *form* of determination, i.e., on the kind of body involved: the affections of a simple body will simply reflect the joint impact of the environment, fusing the many influences into one, without discrimination of the various individual agents; whereas composite bodies of a certain kind, as we shall see, may embody the affections of the environment differentially in their condition and thus also act on the environment differentially. Here we note one divergence from the machine model, to be taken up later: the point of such compositeness, i.e., of degree of complexity, is not variety of mechanical performance by a self-contained automaton, but range and variety of reciprocal *communication* with things, or, the manner of being part of the whole while yet being something apart from the whole.

IV

However, the interactional aspect (the being part of a whole) is based on the formal nature of the individual; and as this may be composite, and is so in all cases of higher relatedness, we have first to consider the meaning of compositeness as such, or, the manner in which an individual itself can be a "whole" of its own parts, a "one" of many. This—as the parts of a composite are in turn individuals—is the same as asking how a plurality of individuals may be so united that all together form a larger (and higher-order) individual. Now any union of individuals must be in terms of interaction, i.e., of mutual determination; and if it is more than a haphazard collection, the order of grouping may engender an *order* of interaction such that the *total* of mutual determinations will be a *form of determinateness* itself. But form of determinateness, as we have seen, is precisely what defines "individual," as it constitutes the distinctness of a mode: and thus a body composed of many and diverse bodies (which again may be "composite to a high degree") may truly be an individual—if this total *form* of multiple inner relations maintains itself functionally in the interactions of the compound with the outside world, thereby testifying to a common conatus of the whole.

The possible advantage of such compositeness in terms of the external relations of an individual has been provisionally indicated and is not our concern at present. What matters now is the new possibility of "identity" opened up by the concept of individual here expounded. If it is the (spatial and dynamic) *pattern* of composition and function in which the individuality of a composite consists, then its identity is not bound to the identities of the simpler bodies of which it is composed; and the preservation of that identity through time rests with the preservation of the pattern rather than of the particular collection presently embodying it. The identity of a whole is thus compatible with a change of parts; and such a change may even be the very means by which the identity of certain individuals is sustained.

This train of thought obviously permits an understanding of organism quite different from the Cartesian one and, we think, more adequate to the facts; and this even in terms of "extension" alone, i.e., without the full benefits of the doctrine to be reaped from complementing the physical facts with those in the attribute of "thought." The main propositions touching upon the physical side of organism are found in Part II of the *Ethics*, entitled "Of the Nature and Origin of the Mind" and thus preeminently dealing with the mental side. However, from Proposition XI onward, Spinoza deals with the soul-body problem, and in that context makes certain statements concerning the type of body that corresponds to a soul or mind, and the type of identity that pertains to it. They are Lemmata 4–7 after Prop. XIII—as follows:

LEMMA IV.   If a certain number of bodies be separated from the body or individual which is composed of a number of bodies, and if their place be supplied by the same number of other bodies of the same nature, the individual will retain the nature it had before without any change of form.

DEMONSTRATION.   Bodies are not distinguished in respect of substance

(Lem. I);[4] but that which makes the form of an individual is the union of bodies (by the preceding definition).[5] This form, however (by hypothesis), is retained, although there may be a continuous change of the bodies. The individual, therefore, will retain its nature with regard both to substance and to mode, as before.—Q.E.D.

LEMMA V.   If the parts composing an individual become greater or less proportionately, so that they preserve towards one another the same kind of motion and rest, the individual will also retain the nature which it had before without any change of form.

LEMMA VI.   If any number of bodies composing an individual are compelled to divert into one direction the motion they previously had in another, but are nevertheless able to continue and reciprocally communicate their motions in the same manner as before, the individual will then retain its nature without any change of form.

LEMMA VII.   The individual thus composed will, moreover, retain its nature whether it move as a whole or be at rest, or whether it move in this or that direction, provided that each part retain its own motion and communicate it as before to the rest.

Lemma 4 refers to metabolism, 5 to growth, 6 to movement of limb, 7 to locomotion. There follows an important scholium to this whole series of lemmata.

SCHOL.   We thus see in what manner a composite individual can be affected in many ways and yet retain its nature. Up to this point we have conceived an individual to be composed merely of bodies which are distinguished from one another solely by motion and rest, speed and slowness, i.e., to be composed of the most simple bodies. If we now consider an individual of another kind, composed of many individuals of diverse natures, we shall discover that it may be affected in many other ways, its nature nevertheless being preserved. For since each of its parts is composed of a number of bodies, each part (by the preceding lemma), without any change of its nature, can move more slowly or quickly, and consequently can communicate its motion more quickly or more slowly to the rest. If we now imagine a third kind of individual composed of these of the second kind, we shall discover that it can be affected in many other ways without any change of form. Thus, if we advance *ad infinitum*, we may easily conceive the whole of nature to be one individual whose parts, i.e., all bodies, vary in infinite ways without any change of the whole individual.

[4]LEMMA I. Bodies are distinguished from one another in respect of motion and rest, quickness and slowness, and not in respect of substance.
[5]DEF. When a number of bodies of the same or of different magnitudes are pressed together by others, so that they lie one upon the other, or if they are in motion with the same or with different degrees of speed, so that they communicate their motion to one another in a certain fixed proportion—these bodies are said to be mutually united, and, taken altogether, they are said to compose one body or individual which is distinguished from other bodies by this union of bodies.

After this, a number of postulates deal with the human body in particular, of which we quote postulates 1, 3, 4, and 6.

POST. 1.   The human body is composed of a number of individual parts of diverse nature, each of which is composite to a high degree.

POST. 3.   The individual parts composing the human body, and consequently the human body itself, are affected by external bodies in many ways.

POST. 4.   The human body needs for its preservation many other bodies by which it is, as it were, continually regenerated.

POST. 6.   The human body can move and arrange external bodies in many ways.

V

If we ponder these statements in the total context of Spinoza's theory, we realize that, for the first time in modern speculation, an organic individual is viewed as a fact of wholeness rather than of mechanical interplay of parts. The essence of organic being is seen, not in the functioning of a machine as a closed system, but in the sustained sequence of states of a unified plurality, with only the form of its union enduring while the parts come and go. Substantial identity is thus replaced by formal identity, and the relation of parts to whole, so crucial for the nature of organism, is the converse of what it is in the mechanistic view. There, the finished product, the complete animal machine, is the sum of the component parts, and the most elementary of such parts, the simplest units of matter, are the ultimate and the only true subjects of individuality. Identity then, as identity of individual corporeal substances, comes down to the mere inert persistence of matter, and from this basic type of individuality and identity every other individuality and identity in the extended realm is derived. Conversely, identity in Spinoza's theory of individuality is the identity of a whole which is so little the mere sum of its parts that it remains the same even when the parts continually change. And since the individual is a *form of union*, there are qualitative grades of individuality, depending on the degree of differentiated order, and quantitative grades, depending on the numerical extent of inclusion (both scales, on the whole, tending to coincide)—so that the All forms a hierarchy of individualities, or wholes, of increasing inclusiveness culminating in the most inclusive one, the totality of nature as such. Within a certain range along this line are those grades of individuality, i.e., of complexity of organization, which we term "organic": but this is a matter of degree only, and on principle all nature is "alive." On whatever level of compositeness (but the more so, the higher the level), the various orders of individuality exist essentially in the succession of their states, i.e., in the continuous series of their changes, rather than in any momentary structure which a mechanical analysis into elements would reveal. The specifically "organic" bodies, then, are highly composite minor totalities of subordinate individuals which again are composed of lesser ones, and so on. In such a stratification, the variability of being which compositeness enjoys as such, is communicated upward cumulatively, and with each supervening level is raised to a higher power, so that the uppermost level representing the totality in question is the beneficiary of all its subordinate members.

Thus the concept of organism evolves organically, without a break, from the general ontology of individual existence. Of every such existence it is true to say that as a modal determination it represents just one phase in the eternal unfolding of infinite substance and is thus never a terminal product in which the creative activity would come to rest.[6] While a machine certainly is such a terminal product, the modal wholes, continuing their conative life in the shift of their own parts and in interchange with the larger whole, are productive as much as produced, or, as much "natura naturans" as "natura naturata."

VI

So far we have dealt with the phenomenon of life in the attribute of extension only, that is, with life as represented by organized bodies. If we now turn to the inward aspect, the progress of Spinoza's monism over Cartesian dualism becomes even more manifest. Extension as a whole, as we have seen, represents but one attribute by which the infinite essence of substance is of necessity expressed. It is equally expressed, with equal necessity and equal validity, by the attribute of thought. This means that to every *mode* of extension there corresponds a mode of "thought" which is only another aspect of the same underlying cause complementarily expressed in either way. Now since individuals are modes of the one substance, and in each such mode substance is affected throughout its attributes, it follows that *any* individual in the world of bodies (and not just a certain class of individuals) has its co-ordinate counterpart in an individual of thought. This principle discards two connected Cartesian ideas at once: that "life" is a fact of physics alone, and that "soul" is a fact of man alone: according to the first, life is a particular corporeal *behavior* following from a particular corporeal

---

[6]That activity, being that of substance as a whole, can of course in its universal movement overrule any individual conatus, and inevitably does so sooner or later.

structure which distinguishes a *class* of objects in nature, viz., the natural automata; according to the second, "soul," equated with consciousness of any kind, be it feeling, desiring, perceiving, thought (anima = mens = cogitatio), as such not required for physical function of any kind *and thus not for life*, is absent in animals and present in man, but is neither in *his* case a principle of "life," which remains a purely behavioristic phenomenon in all cases. To Spinoza, soul still is not a principle of life considered physically (as it was to Aristotle), but neither is life itself mere corporeal behavior. The concurrence of outwardness and inwardness is here no longer a unique arrangement in the case of man, nor even a distinctive mark of the whole class of things normally called "animate": as the essence of substance, that concurrence is the pervading trait of all existence. Yet the universality of the principle by no means obliterates those distinctions in nature by which we speak of animate as against inaminate things, of sentient as against merely vegetative organisms, and of conscious and reasoning man as against unreasoning animals. On the contrary, for the first time in modern theory, a speculative means is offered for relating the degree of organization of a body to the degree of awareness belonging to it.

Let us recall that dualism did not offer such a means, i.e., did not provide for an intelligible relation between the perfection of a physical organization and the *quality* of the life supported by it: all it provided for was the relation between organization and observable behavior. The wealth of gradation in the animal world between the most primitive (i.e., simple) and the most subtle (i.e., complex) structure could not be overlooked but had to remain meaningless. Since no other kind of soul but the rational was recognized, all the mechanical perfection displayed in animal organisms amounted just to a gigantic hoax, as no higher type of experient life corresponded to greater excellence of mechanical performance. Thus the very perfection in terms of external construction and function mocks all justification in terms of lives and purposes. Even in man, as noted before, there is no intelligible connection between the excellence of his body and the uniqueness of his mind, as these two are only extraneously joined together. On materialistic premises such a connection was plausible enough, since mind, if it is a function of the brain, must needs be determined in its quality by the quality of the brain. But this plausibility is paid for by too heavy a price in difficulties concerning the nature of mind itself. Spinoza's psychophysical parallelism offered an ingenious theory of connection between grade of organization and grade of mentality without violating the principle of non-interaction between the two sides. That such interaction cannot be is no less axiomatic to him than to the whole Cartesian school: "The body cannot determine the mind to thought, neither can the mind determine the body to motion nor rest, nor to anything else, if there be anything else" (*Ethics*, III, Prop. 2). The positive complement of this negative rule is thus stated for the corporeal side: "A body in motion or at rest must be determined to motion or rest by another body, which was also determined to motion or rest by another, and so on ad infinitum" (*ibid.*, Lem. 3 after Prop. 13). At least in this application to the physical realm, the ontological rigor of the rule admits no exception; and we may add that none of the leading thinkers of the period down to, and including, Kant ever challenged the validity of it. The reasons for thus ruling out of court the most insistent evidence of common experience—that fear or love or deliberation can determine action and thus be the cause of bodily motion—cannot be discussed here: we just note that they commanded overwhelming consensus. But if interaction is ruled out, the alternative need not be mutual independence or unrelatedness of the two sides. The Occasionalists, in their attempt to account for the prima facie facts of interconnection, acquiesced in a mere externality of correlation, which was no less miraculous a coincidence for the fact that God saw to its happening time and again. This unsatisfactory construction Spinoza replaced by an intrinsic belonging-together of mind and matter, which gave causal preference neither to matter, as materialism would have it, nor to mind, as idealism would have it, but instead rested their interrelation on the common ground of which they both were dependent aspects.

VII

Applying this formula to the doctrine of organism and the diversity of biological organization, of which man represents one, and perhaps the highest, degree, we have to ask more concretely in what the correlation of mental to physical modes consists. Spinoza answers that the "soul" is an individual mode of thought, that is, an "idea" in God, whose one and continuous object (*ideatum*) is an actually existing individual body. This "idea" of one determinate body, if it is as sustained as the existence of its object, must of course be a *series* of ideas, corresponding to, and concomitant with, the series of states in which the pertaining body exists; and it must at each moment be a *complex* idea, in accordance with the complexity of the body. What is represented in the idea is the total state of the body at each given instant. Now that state of the body is determined by two factors: (1) by what it is in itself, its own formal nature, that is, by the form or pattern of its composition; and (2) by its affection from outside, i.e., the influence of other bodies on its condition. Thus the state of a body represents at each moment itself *and* those bodies of the surrounding world which do affect it at the moment. And it does represent the latter insofar as they affect it, which they do again, not only in virtue of their own power or their own intrinsic nature, but also in virtue of the way in which the affected body can be affected: that is, its own organization determines the manner in which other things besides itself can be represented in its own state.

Now, clearly, degrees of organization can be understood precisely as degrees of the faculty of a body to be affected more or less variously, distinctly and thus adequately by other bodies individually (being in any case affected by them collectively). Thus a more differentiated, because more complex organization—for instance, of the sensory aparatus —would make for a more perfect, that is, more differential way in which the body receives the affections from other bodies. In brief, degree of organization may mean degree of discriminatory sensitivity–both understood in strictly physical terms (as, e.g., in a camera). Now, since the soul is nothing but the correlate "idea" of an actually existing body, the degree of distinctness, differentiation, and clarity enjoyed by this idea is exactly proportionate to the state of the body that is its sole object. Thus, although the immediate object of the soul is only the co-ordinate body, which is the same mode of substance in terms of extension that the soul is in terms of thought, yet through this body's being affected by other bodies and affected in different degrees of perfection according to its own organization (and to circumstances), the corresponding mental state will have mediate awareness of the world—as represented through affections of the body—in different degrees of obscurity and clarity, of limitedness and comprehensiveness. Therefore "soul" is granted to animals and plants on exactly the same principle as to man, yet not the same soul. The soul, being the equivalent of the body in a different attribute, or the expression of the same mode (determination) of substance of which the body is the expression in extenso, must be completely conformal to the kind of body whose soul it is, and there are as many kinds and degrees of soul as there are kinds and degrees of vital organization.[7] The two are in each case just two equivalent aspects of one and the same basic reality, which is neither matter nor mind, but is equally expressed by both.

The general principle is stated in the famous Prop. 7 of Part II, the *Magna Carta* of "psychophysical parallelism": "The order and connection of ideas is the same as the order and connection of things." With

[7]This, incidentally, is the first theory after Aristotle's to show why a human soul cannot be transposed into an animal or vegetable body, i.e., which excludes the *possibility* of metempsychosis. Leibniz's *Monadology*, while avoiding most of the pitfalls of Cartesian dualism, falls short of Spinoza on this point.

reference to the human mind, the doctrine is expressed in the following propositions of the same part:

PROP. XI.   The first thing which forms the actual being of the human mind is nothing else than the idea of an individual thing actually existing.

PROP. XII.   Whatever happens in the object of the idea constituting the human mind must be perceived by the human mind; or, in other words, an idea of that thing will necessarily exist in the human mind. That is to say, if the object of the idea constituting the human mind be a body, nothing can happen in that body which is not perceived by the mind.

PROP. XIII.   The object of the idea constituting the human mind is a body, or a certain mode of extension actually existing, and nothing else.

SCHOL.   Hence we see not only that the human mind is united to the body but also what is to be understood by the union of the mind and body. But no one can understand it adequately or distinctly without knowing adequately beforehand the nature of our body; for those things which we have proved hitherto are altogether general, nor do they refer more to man than to other individuals, all of which are animate, although in different degrees. For of everything there necessarily exists in God an idea of which He is the cause, in the same way as the idea of the human body exists in Him [which idea is the human mind]; and therefore, everything that we have said of the idea of the human body is necessarily true of the idea of any other thing [being the "mind" of that other thing]. We cannot, however, deny that ideas, like objects themselves, differ from one another, and that one is more excellent and contains more reality than another, just as the object of one idea is more excellent and contains more reality than another. Therefore, in order to determine the difference between the human mind and other minds and its superiority over them, we must first know, as we have said, the nature of its object, that is to say, the nature of the human body. . . . I will say generally that in proportion as one body is fitter than others to *do or suffer many things* [*severally*] *at once*, in the same proportion will its mind be fitter to perceive many things at once; and the more the actions of a body depend upon itself alone, and the less other bodies co-operate with it in action, the fitter will the mind of that body be for distinctly understanding. We can thus determine the superiority of one mind to another; we can also see the reason why we have only a very confused knowledge of our body. . . .

PROP. XIV.   The human mind is adapted to the perception of many things, and its aptitude increases in proportion to the number of ways in which its body can be disposed.

PROP. XV.   The idea which constitutes the formal being of the human mind is not simple, but is composed of a number of ideas. [This follows from the high degree of compositeness of the human body.]

PROP. XVI.   The idea of every way in which the human body is affected by external bodies must involve the nature of the human body and at the same time the nature of the external body.

DEM.   All ways in which any body is affected follow at the same time from the nature of the affected body and from the nature of the affecting body; therefore, the idea of these modifications necessarily involves the nature of each body; and therefore the idea of each way in which the human body is affected by an external body involves the nature of the human body and of the external body.

COROLLARY 1.   Hence it follows, in the first place, that the human mind perceives the nature of many bodies together with that of its own body.

COR. 2.   It follows, secondly, that the ideas of external bodies indicate the constitution of our own body rather than the nature of the external bodies.[8]

VIII

The conclusion from these general propositions, regarding the question whether animals have souls, that is to say, whether they feel, strive, perceive, even think in a way, is stated by Spinoza in no equivocal terms. Since mind is not a species of substance, defined by fixed attributes like reason and intellect, but itself a total attribute of infinite substance, and as such admits on principle of the same infinity of different modes as extension has in its own sphere, animals can obviously enjoy a degree of mind congruent with their bodies without any prejudice to the distinctive characteristics of the human mind, as congruent with its body. Thus we read in Part III:

PROP. LVII.   The affect of one individual differs from the corresponding affect of another as much as the essence of the one individual differs from that of the other.

SCHOL.   Hence it follows that the affects of animals which are called irrational (for after we have learnt the origin of the mind we can in no way doubt that brutes feel) differ from the affects of men as much as their respective natures differ from human nature. Both the man and the horse, for example, are swayed by lust to propagate, but the horse is swayed by equine lust and the man by a human one. The lusts and appetites of insects, fishes, and birds must vary in the same way; and so, although each individual lives contented with its own nature and delights in it, nevertheless the life with which it is contented and its joy are nothing else but the "idea" or soul of the individual [body] in question, and so the joy of one differs in character from the joy of the other as much as the essence of the one differs from the essence of the other. . . .

[8]The following quotation from *Ep. 66* may here be added as a succinct summary of Spinoza's doctrine of mind: "The essence of the mind consists in this alone that it is the idea of an actually existing body; and accordingly the mind's power to understand extends to those things only which this idea of the body contains in itself or which follow from it. But this idea of the body involves and expresses no other attributes of God but extension and thought. Hence I conclude that the human mind cannot apprehend any attribute of God save these two."

The last scholium, in conjunction with that to Prop. 13 of Part II, clearly establishes the principle of an infinite gradation of "animateness," co-extensive with the gradation of physical composition, for which the entirely simple is merely a limiting case: even this would not be devoid of a minimum of inwardness, since to its distinctness, such as it is, there must correspond the idea "of" it in God—and this is its "thought" or "soul." Note how in Spinoza's logic a *genitivus objectivus*—the idea of this body—turns into a *genitivus subjectivus*—this body's thought. On the lowest level, this "thought" will not be more than an infinitesimal feeling, but even this will be compounded of an active and a passive aspect: namely, on the one hand, self-affirmation, whose physical equivalent is the *vis inertiae* (both expressing the conatus for self-continuation), and on the other hand, experience of otherness, or, perception, whose physical equivalent is the subjection to outside forces (both expressing the integration into the sum of things). Each thing asserts itself, but all things around it assert themselves, and in the case of the very simple, low-grade individual (illustrated perhaps by the atom), completely at the mercy of external impingements, the compound assertion of all others in its dynamic condition all but submerges its self-assertion, so that the active aspect will be at a minimum; and correspondingly, the very experience of otherness (its "affects") will not rise beyond an indiscriminate fusion of mere passivity: its perception will be as indistinct as its selfhood. Only complex functional systems afford the inner *autonomy* that is required for greater power of self-determination, *together* with greater variety of inner states responding to the determinations which impinge on it from without. The mental equivalent of both is, on the active side, higher degree of consciousness with its affirmation and enjoyment of *self*, and, on the passive side, greater distinctness of perception with its understanding (and possible mastery) of *things*. The idea of *power* is fundamental in the evaluation of the corporeal as well as of the mental side and furnishes the standard of perfection: the power of the body to exist, persist, to do and suffer many things, to determine others and itself, is at the same time affirmation of that power by the mind which is the "idea" of that body.[9] And since degree of power is degree of *freedom*, it is true to say that higher organization of the body, and correspondingly greater complexity of its idea, mean greater freedom of the individual both in body and in mind.

[9]Compare Spinoza's restatement of his principle of the degrees of mental perfection as *related* to, though not *causally* dependent on, degrees of bodily perfection, in the Explanation at the end of Part III: "Since the essence of the mind consists in its affirmation of the actual existence of its body, and since we understand by perfection the essence itself of the thing, it follows that the mind passes to a greater or less perfection when it is able to affirm of its body, or some part of it, something which involves a greater or less reality than before."

The phrase "fitness to do or suffer many things" expresses Spinoza's insight into the essentially dual character of the organism: its *autonomy* for itself, and its *openness* for the world: spontaneity paired with receptivity. Their concurrent, indeed interdependent, increase is a seeming paradox, since openness in perception means exposure to affection, thus determination from without, contrary to the self-determination which autonomy of action would imply and all conatus must seek. Yet increase in *passive* power is asserted by Spinoza together with increase in active power to be the mark of higher fitness of an organism and thus of its perfection. Here is proof of his profundity. For this dialectic is precisely the nature of life in its basic organic sense. Its closure as a functional whole within the individual organism is, at the same time, correlative openness toward the world; its very separateness entails the faculty of communication; its segregation from the whole is the condition of its integration with the whole. The affectivity of all living things complements their spontaneity; and while it seems to indicate primarily the passive aspect of organic existence, it yet provides, in a subtle balance of freedom and necessity, the very means by which the organism carries on its vital commerce with the environment, that is, with the conditions of its continued existence. Only by being sensitive can life be active, only by being exposed can it be autonomous. And this in direct ratio: the more individuality is focused in a self, the wider is its periphery of communication with other things; the more isolated, the more related it is.

This dialectic of individual life in the world Spinoza has seen, and provided for in his system, as neither Descartes before him nor Leibniz after him did.

11.
Sight and Thought:
A Review of "Visual Thinking"

Book reviews are not ordinarily included in a collection of essays, which must justify its entries, *inter alia*, by their ability to stand on their own. In this instance, however, the book in question[1] offered me an opportunity to discuss certain matters of general philosophical interest that fall very much into the area of my previous work on perception and imagination[2] but on which there is no other treatment by me in print. The review can thus, despite its frequent references to Arnheim's book, be read as an independent study of the subject itself.

Visual thinking is, in the author's words, "an attempt to proceed from earlier studies of art to a broader concern with visual perception as a cognitive activity" (p. v). The key word is "cognitive." Instead of: What can we know about art? the question is: What can art teach us about knowing, indeed, contribute to knowing? Art, in this context, functions as an eminent instance of perception, concerning which the book advances a theoretical thesis and, implied in it, a practical plea. The thesis is that "only because perception gathers types of things, that is, concepts, can perceptual material be used for thought; and inversely, . . . unless the stuff of the senses remains present the mind has nothing to

Reprinted from the *Journal of Aesthetics and Art Criticism*, Fall 1971.
[1]Rudolf Arnheim, *Visual Thinking* (Berkeley, University of California Press, 1969).
[2]See *The Phenomenon of Life*, sixth and seventh essays.

think with" (p. 1; on page 153 we read instead "to think about"—a difference I shall comment on). The implied practical plea is for the cultivation of the senses, whose "widespread unemployment" in education, from elementary school to academic studies, harms the very end, namely, the development of reasoning, for which the sacrifice is made. The antidote is in the arts, "the most powerful means of strengthening the perceptual component without which productive thinking is impossible in any field" (p. 3).

This review is concerned with the theoretical argument, which I follow in some of its stages. The groundwork is laid in the two chapters (2, 3) on The Intelligence of Visual Perception, which are a classic in their kind. Arnheim sets out to establish "that the cognitive operations called thinking are not the privilege of mental processes above and beyond perception but essential ingredients of perception itself" (p. 13), or in brief, that "sensory responsiveness as such [is] intelligent" (p. 17); and he does establish it, incontrovertibly I believe, for visual perception, his chosen subject. Nobody can quarrel with this choice. I shall ask later how far its singleminded pursuit may have resulted in endowing its object with a cognitive self-sufficiency that ignores its debt to other senses (and the hands), as perhaps also, at the opposite end of the spectrum, the genuine excess of pure thought over every sensuous thought, including vision. None of this, however, affects the basic thesis that "visual perception is visual thinking" (p. 14), and even that "vision is the primary medium of thought" (p. 18) in some of the possible senses of "primary." Various forms of past dualism—metaphysical, epistemological, psychological—used to contrast what is here united: e.g., sense is passive, thinking is active. To show that seeing is thinking begins properly, therefore, with showing that it is active—as, e.g., in attention, selection, fixation, and discrimination of depth—all of which can be interpreted as forms of "intelligence." But Arnheim's main evidence, and his favorite theme throughout much of the book, is *shape:* the element of *abstraction* inherent in even its plainest visual apprehension leads straight to concept and thought—indeed, makes the perception of shape an act of thought from the outset.

In what sense can it be said that "shapes are concepts" (p. 27)? Arnheim's answer, drawing on Gestalt psychology, runs somewhat like this. Perception consists in fitting the stimulus material with templates of relatively simple shape. These he calls "visual concepts" or "visual categories." The shape patterns perceived in this fashion have *generality* in addition to simplicity. "Strictly speaking, no percept ever refers to a unique, individual shape but rather to the kind of pattern of which the percept consists." Perceiving shape is the grasping of generic structural features: "There is, therefore, no difference in principle between percept and concept, quite in keeping with the biological function of perception. In order to be useful, perception must instruct about kinds of thing; otherwise, organisms could not profit from experience" (pp. 27–29). Indeed, even the inbred, selective responses of animals to signals or "releasers" are "an early instance of abstraction," only that it is "performed by the species rather than the individual" (p. 23). In every case, the recognition of shape is holistic and intuitive, very different from how machines read shape.

Generalization and abstraction are those traits in the perception of shape that make it continuous with concept and thinking. Abstraction is the more comprehensive of the two: it does more than generate generality, though this it does before everything else. It operates, e.g., in what Arnheim calls "subtracting the context" (as in the figure-ground relation); or in "completing the incomplete" (where there is a partial overlap of shapes); or in the straightening out of perspectival distortion ("abstracting" the rectangle from the projected parallelogram); or in the synthesis of successive, one-sided aspects to the perception of an identical three-dimensional shape ("abstracting" from the particularity of the various projections of the solid so that they appear as lawful sequences of representational change). The last instance, much elaborated by Husserl and his phenomenological school under the somewhat different title of "intentionality," gives Arnheim occasion to observe that perceptual abstraction can differ from the kind described in traditional logic. For here it does not consist (as does the latter) in the extracting of common elements from the particular instances, but in perceiving the particulars as deformations of an underlying structure. This type of abstraction, Arnheim rightly stresses, is a cognitive performance of high complexity, enabling us to see the momentary as an integral part of a larger whole, which unfolds in a sequence. Spanning the temporal flux, visual abstraction thus extracts permanence from change. In describing these feats of sight, Arnheim wishes us to share his sense of wonder at what we do. "To distinguish an object from the afflictions of its appearances is an awe-inspiring cognitive accomplishment. . . . The labors of vision create the view of a world in which persistence and change act as eternal antagonists" (p. 52f).

Let me stop here for a moment. Those "afflictions of appearance" from which the object must be rescued are peculiar to optics, i.e., to the *projection of images* wholly detached from the distant object. Sound has few analogies to them, touch practically none. Vision alone has to contend with them. But can it contend with them alone? Is it the rescuer all by itself? In describing Matisse's *Tabac Royal* (p. 56), Arnheim says that it shows (*inter alia*) "a pear-shaped mandolin s.tting on a curved chair." (Arnheim is here concerned with the formal "assonance" of pear-shaped and curved; I am concerned with the visual information on things.) Indeed, we "see" the mandolin "sitting on . . .", just as in the next figure, the drawing of a Palladio façade (p. 57), we see the pediment resting on, or supported by, the columns. Or do we? Yes, if in the feat of vision we include its instruction from other sources; no, if we strictly stick to the ocular record. To sit on . . . is a fact of gravity, and of gravity we know through our body, yet through none of the special senses of which vision is the most rarefied. Our upright posture, maintained against the force of gravity, bearing down on the supporting ground, supplies an all-pervading, dynamic feature of our experienced actuality very different from the presentational delivery of the senses. This "knowledge" informs our seeing. In the up-and-down orientation of the visual field it does so in terms that are visual themselves, and this contribution is recognized by Arnheim (p. 71). But this is a purely dimensional or positional, not a dynamic or causal trait—and "sitting on" is more than being situated above. The weighing on the suppòrt, co-intended in the visual understanding, is not a visual datum itself. Also, the mandolin *can be lifted* from the chair: this, in a way, is "seen" together with its sitting on it. But the knowledge of this "it *can*" and of what lifting means comes from manual experience. That is, manipulative thinking must complement visual thinking, else the abstraction which vision enjoys turns from a strength to a weakness—which has notably happened in the history of epistemology with its domination by the model of sight. We must remember that sight is in its essence "superficial"; more than any other sense is it bound to the surface of things, less than any does its evidence betray of their inner nature or condition. It is the sense of "appearances" par excellence, richest in their display, richest also in deception.

The acquaintance with enduring bodies and stubborn substance stems from the commerce of action, from its experience of resistance, inertness, etc. It can be doubted whether without prior handling of actually rigid bodies the mere ocular presentation of a series of deformations would suffice to yield the abiding solid shape, which presupposes rigidity. Be that as it may, the geometrical solid is not yet the "solid" thing. Would I "see" *things* at all on visual evidence alone? It is true that the various one-sided aspects stand for, and visually concresce into, the complete solid shape; but this in turn stands for, but does not *visually* concresce into, something else. As I walk down the tree-lined street, the massiveness of the old elm which I approach means more than the geometrical volume conveyed by its visible (and visually completed) shape. It means also what would happen when I run into it, when the ax is applied to it, when the squirrel climbs it. The edges of the iron signpost next to it induce different expectations. Should it turn out to be a clever rubber imitation, I should be surprised but couldn't blame vision, which told me all it had to tell. Fortunately, we all have been toddlers, have tried to stand up, fingered things, bumped into things. Our scratches and bruises teach us what shapes and colors never can. Even pictorial understanding feeds on such teaching: the original of the spear in the hunter's hand on the cave wall had many times been thrust with all the force behind it into a real buffalo's side. This extends right into the esthetic effect of representational visual art: the wind-blown hair and billowing garments in Botticelli's *Birth of Venus*—surely not a mere informative (cognitive) part of the painting— summon our experienced feeling of the force of wind.

All this does indeed not prevent the final result, as it is gathered in vision, from being a genuine percept (and not a reasoning process); and Arnheim is right in stressing the "purely perceptual" nature of the "completion of the incomplete" in all these cases. My point is that it is not purely visual; that visual perception is saturated with experience of other sorts, and that the subtraction of the latter would leave vision cognitively barren in important respects. For what vision "abstracts" *from* is not only elements within the visual itself: even before doing so in its single acts, it has abstracted *per se* from the whole underground of straining, acting-suffering, incarnate life on which its freedom is perched, and its consequent account of things is likewise purged of the strains and stresses of their reality. This detachment of the becalmed image is the strength of vision and its weakness. Obviously, the cognitive value of abstractions is bound to their preserving the connection with what is abstracted from: the severing of that connection makes abstraction perilous. As this holds for higher conceptual thought with respect to vision, so it holds also for vision with respect to the lower body experiences on which vision is based in turn. Sensing of qualities and forms, abstractive indeed, occupies a middle ground in the scale from densest concreteness to rarest abstractness.[3]

These observations complement rather than detract from the truth of

---

[3]To remember this is of importance in contexts beyond those with which Arnheim deals. I refer to what Whitehead had to say about "causal efficacy" and "presentational immediacy" (vision being the latter's eminent paradigm) as the two basic modes of perception, and about the difficulties which the exclusive stress on the latter in Western theory since Greek times has created for epistemology and metaphysics. To retrieve the object "from the afflictions of its appearances" is not only an awe-inspiring accomplishment: it is an impossible one for vision alone, without help from below.

Arnheim's thesis that visual perception has in it—or, if you will, is in itself—thinking. A different matter altogether is the thesis to which the book moves hence: that all thinking is visual or sensuous. Here serious criticism must be voiced. Much as Arnheim is at home with vision and has illuminating things to say about it, when he leaves this familiar ground (not aware indeed that he does so) and deals with the higher reaches of thought and with such things as language, logic, proof, etc., he becomes a victim of his love and overplays his hand.

Arnheim's argument hinges on the concept of "images of thought" which he claims to be integral to thinking and which are somehow of the family of visual shapes. Does the mind always think "with" images? Or is there image-less thought? Such questions are of little profit so long as it is not clear whether "with" means "accompanied by" or "assisted by" or "by means of" or "about" images; and especially so long as (having disposed of the associative, allusive, and illustrative by-play of phantasms) one does not carefully distinguish between *representative* and purely *significative* function of whatever sensuous content (words included) may be present in conceptual thought. Only the first requires an isomorphic or in any sense "pictorial" relation to the object, while the second does in no sense whatever—which is exactly its strength, not its weakness. Arnheim never makes the distinction properly and consequently misses the whole point of semantic thought. Here he pays the penalty for not availing himself of Husserl's insights into the nature and working of intentionality. "If thinking takes place in the realm of images [which rather dogmatically he takes to be established by re-iteration], many of these images must be highly abstract since the mind operates often at high levels of abstraction" (p. 116): this is a non-sequitur, except if the images are supposed to *portray* the object of thought, in which case the conclusion stands that they must be highly abstract if the object is, but also reveals the premise as absurd.[4] In fact, "taking place in the realm of images" (more often Arnheim says "in the medium of") is so vague an image itself as to be almost worthless. Somewhat but not much more informative is the statement that "thinking, in order to have something to think *about*, must be *based on* images of the

---

[4]The quoted sentence embodies the syllogism: (major) All thinking is operation with images; (minor) Some thinking is highly abstract; (conclusion) Some images are highly abstract. Submerged in this are the corollary syllogisms: Concepts are images; images are sensuous; concepts are sensuous. And: Concepts portray objects; concepts are sensuous; objects are sensible. Taking then vision as the most perfect mode of sensuous perception, and certainly the most competent for images, the last conclusion amounts to saying: Thought deals with visible objects only = there are only visible objects = the invisible is unthinkable—a strange result after the Platonic beginnings of Western theory.

world in which we live" (p. 153, my italics), implying (a) that we always think, and only can think, about the world, the images of which are "the perceptual elements in thought," which in turn suggests (b) that the "basis" extends upward through thought, presumably as its persistent tool, perhaps also its persistent direct object. Even granting the metaphor of "being based on" as valid in some specifiable sense, it does by no means follow that what is so based, namely, human cognition, is "a unitary process, which leads without break from . . . sensory information to the most generic theoretical ideas" (ibid.). Plato's "divided line" should have cautioned Arnheim about the question of a "break."[5] In short, where Arnheim comes to grief is in his move from the sound proposition that "shapes are concepts" to the highly dubious one that concepts are shapes. I briefly and selectively offer my critical comments.

Arnheim's argument may be summarized thus (1) Pictorial representations are suitable instruments of abstract reasoning (p. 116). In a wider sense, they are its only instruments, for (2) concepts are a sort of pictorial representations, namely, perceptual images, structurally similar (isomorphic) to the objects; and thought operations are the handling of these images (p. 227). (3) Human thinking cannot go beyond the patterns supplied by the human senses: it takes place in the realm of the senses exclusively (p. 233); therefore, (4) sensuous thought imagery must embody all the aspects of a piece of reasoning, since "what is not given shape is not there and cannot be supplied from elsewhere" (p. 241); but fortunately, (5) "Man can confidently rely on the senses to supply him with perceptual equivalents of all theoretical notions because these notions derive from sensory experience in the first place" (p. 233). (6) The visual medium is superior to all others because it offers structural equivalents to all characteristics of objects, events, relations (p. 232). (7) Language, another perceptual medium, is vastly inferior to sight and the other primary sense-vehicles of thought in powers of isomorphic representation by reason of its structural poverty: it is overrated, not indispensable to thought, merely helpful by affixing handy tags to the images of thought.

One is at a loss where to start setting straight so much mischief committed by overzeal in a noble cause (which the cause of vision is). Let me start with the end, the preposterous notion of language and its relation to thought. Where did Arnheim get the idea that language

---

[5]So should, concerning the "unitary" nature of the process, Diotima's speech in the *Symposium* about the ascent from beautiful bodies to beautiful deeds, characters, thoughts to the thought of "beauty itself"—surely no mere progression from the less to the more generic. Such teachings, whether in the end accepted or not, are ignored at one's peril.

should answer to the requirements of "representation" and then be found wanting? Not wholly wanting, Arnheim thinks: the little of isomorphic correspondences it does yield is "exactly as pictorial in principle as is the fact that in a drawing two dogs can be shown as two separate line patterns" (p. 251). By saying "two dogs" instead of "dog dog" (please go on to thirty dogs!), Arnheim explodes his own myth of what language is about. Must one really state the banality that language signs and sign configurations do *not* in their own physical morphology, i.e., by shape analogy, *portray* their subject? nor *try* to? Nothing of projection or conformal mapping is involved in the semantic function. To deplore its lack there is no better than to deplore that nerves do not do the work of muscles. Strangely enough, Arnheim, preoccupied with shape, structure, and isomorphism, overlooks the one real "representational" element which *per accidens* is sometimes conjoined with the significative function of (natural) language—namely, the onomatopoetic, sensuously expressive quality of certain words. Eliot's "not with a bang but a whimper" not only signifies the difference by meanings but also portrays it by phonetic qualities: "bang" sounds like a bang, "whimper" like a whimper. Smooth, prickly, gurgle, glide, hit, stop, sob are other examples; and swift is a swift word, and slow a slow one. Poets avail themselves of these "expressive" opportunities of language, where offered. But this is an accidental property of words (compare German *Blitz* with English *lightning*); and it is confined to a special class of acoustically descriptive names (of probably imitative origin). The true work of language is made possible by emancipation from this sensual soil and from all imitative intent; just as in the evolution of ideographic script it was the overcoming of the pictorial likeness which freed the stylized residues for semantic functions. To describe this as a process of generalization and abstraction is misleading because it veils the decisive break that here intervenes—the breakthrough to a new dimension. Arnheim, a master of the word himself (thus happily his own living refutation) takes the poorest view of the verbal medium. Language, he says (in a section entitled Language Overrated), "serves as a mere auxiliary to the primary vehicles of thought [i.e., sense images], which are so immensely better equipped to represent relevant objects and relations by articulate shape" (pp. 243ff.). This statement, as do many others, completely misses the difference between representation and signification: language is *not* in competition with perception for the task of representation through likeness, but superimposes on it a realm of pure signification, non-pictorial, free from the bonds of likeness, and therefore the genuine vehicle for intellectual, suprasensible thought —the kind of thought Arnheim is engaged in when he ponders perception, cognition, abstraction, and thought. Alas, unfair to what he is actually doing (and often doing so well), his own account of language and thinking makes this truly creative feat of semantics shrink to the utility job of mere tagging. "The function of language is essentially conservative and stabilizing, and therefore it . . . tends . . . to make cognition static and immobile . . . since the verbal name is a fixed label" (p. 244): as if language were principally a collection of *names* (the dictionary or vocabulary view of language) slapped on classes of percepts, that is, of things already there and preclassified by perception itself; and speech were the retrieval of items from this storehouse for use as handy but bloodless, i.e., cognitively barren, substitutes for the really informative images. This might, with some straining, just cover the case of protocol sentences on perceptual states of affairs of the simplest sort, where indeed the direct seeing or vivid imagining of a black cat does better than the sentence "the cat is black." Even here, the tiny change to *"our* cat is black," by introducing the possessive relation, makes the information surpass the perceptual order, for ownership is invisible (even when both the owner and the owned are visible—which the last is often not, e.g., "copyrights," and the first sometimes not, e.g., "the state"). What does Arnheim make of so simple a statement as "You shouldn't have done this"? And what of the sentence I once heard, to my unforgettable delight, a four-year old girl just back from an errand to the grocer's address to her mother: "If you had given me a larger basket, I could have brought more things"? I still remember the dazzling light this shed for me on the human mind: its transcendence and freedom, distinct from animal mentality not by degrees but by a qualitative leap. Not the liveliest imagination of baskets, sizes, volume capacities, food bulks—surely perceptual items all of them—supplies the *logical* thought conveyed in the sentence *construction* with its "irreal-conditional" clause: about what the mother *could* have done but did *not* do, and what *would* have been the case if she had, but was *not* because she hadn't (not to speak of the co-expressed intimation of criticism—"You ought to have," ability—"I had the strength," and willingness—"I would have been only too glad"). There is by nature no perceptual representation for the *whole* of the complex statement—and a whole it is, namely, an intellectual or logical whole: there only is for some (not all) of its parts, which may one by one be mentally pictured in visual images as the whole is being entertained (for myself, I find that the certainty of their being "on call" is enough). The percepts are many, the statement is one. Handy tags? Fixed labels? Arnheim speaks always of names, never of grammar. The intellectual act begets inner, synthetic *unity*, articulated in the *form* of the hypothetical proposition, of which the

names are the matter: the percepts referred to or conjured up by them
are multiple, juxtaposed or alternating, and more often than not quite
fleeting. Intellect is the unifier on *this* level of cognition, no longer perception—the reverse of what Arnheim takes to be the relation of intellect
and sense.

So far my samples were at least statements *about* perceptual entities,
and to that extent (as far as the "name-tags" are concerned) agreeable
to Arnheim's contention that concepts are percepts or derived from percepts by abstraction and generalization, so that their ultimate referents
are always immediate percepts. It is on this assumption that Arnheim
can say simpliciter that "words point to percepts," this being their
"help" to thinking, which "operates in a more appropriate medium, such
as visual imagery" (pp. 231f). Now surely, many words do point to
percepts, namely, those naming perceptual things or states—saying
which is a truism. But what about the concept "truism"? What about
Validity, Proposition, Meaning, Contradiction, Proof? Or: Probability,
Possibility, Contingency, Necessity? And what about Law, Rights,
Duties, Interests, Claims? And, last but not least, Justice, Virtue, Merit,
Guilt, Crime, Moral Responsibility? Obviously these are "abstract
universals" in a sense entirely different from cat, black, mammal, verte-
brate, animal. About *them* was the higher discourse of mankind, not
about cats and dogs. It was the discovery of Socrates that such like
concepts, far from being derived from and summing up experiences,
make possible and govern the appropriate experiences—nay, even make
possible the very existence of their objects. I cannot adjudicate an inference as to its validity before I have the concept of validity—as a
norm to which inferences are subject, not a property abstracted from
them by generalization (even in that case, neither the objects nor the
property would be perceptual). I cannot ask whether an action is just
without knowing or having an idea of what justice is, and that knowledge or idea must precede the inspection of instances. Induction through
observation is useless here. I may never, as things human are, meet with
an instance of justice (some prophets of Israel saw only injustice about
them); I should not recognize it when I saw it. The concept, instead of
reporting the result of observations, says what actions *must* have in
common in order to qualify for the attribute. Socrates went further and
maintained that the concept must be a constituent of the action itself,
i.e., that not only its recognition but already its production depends on a
true concept of justice. In that case, the particular is truly the creature
of the known universal, which precedes, begets and invests it throughout. Even where not so enlightened by knowledge, there is the submerged universal in the intent—what Kant called "the maxim of the

will"—which infuses the visible act with its invisible moral quality and puts its appraisal on principle beyond the perception of sense. It is no denigration of vision to say that it is cognitively powerless here.

This is not the place to offer a doctrine of "concept," whose long labor from Socrates to Hegel should not have been so entirely forgotten over the just concern with the labor of vision—and whose incredible trivializing matches that of language. (Charity bids me to pass over such a *non-plus-ultra* of blundering as that on analytical judgments, p. 231.) Let us merely note from our random remarks that there are at least two kinds of abstract concepts: those where the concrete comes first and abstraction follows; and those where the concept comes first and the concrete instantiation follows—produced from the concept by human action and recognized through it by human judgment. Without the second class, there could be no legal discourse, *nor its very objects*: laws and contracts and rights and obligations. We could not speak of institutions and constitutions, of powers of government and civil liberties, of the public and private realm, of interests and conflicts between them and their order of priority—*nor would these things themselves exist.* For they, the very real objects of our political (etc.) thought and speech, are themselves only generated in speech and have their being in the universe constituted by it. Thus their names are surely no mere tags affixed to things existing independently and beforehand. Nor (need I say it?) does the fact that such objects cannot exist other than in and through the speech of men mean that they are mere words. They are not, even though the ordinances of recognized and of disputed authority, of legitimate and of usurped rule, may "look" exactly alike.

It is doubly puzzling that so sensitive an interpreter of the arts should have suppressed these basic truths as they pertain to his own trade. The whole iconography, e.g., of medieval painting and sculpture presupposes the spiritual teaching of the Christian faith. As those works in color and stone were inspired by them, so they can only be understood in the light of them. Arnheim is fond of saying that words and concepts "stand for" percepts. In the inner sanctum of his most cherished field he has the converse case of percepts standing for concepts, visible shape for invisible truth. Here, the "word" is first in the profoundest sense, and the images forever strive to make it become flesh.[6]

---

[6]Just in passing, lest it be thought that only with such invisible things as I selected can the *logos* be "a priori" (in the literal sense) to the *phainomena*, let me add for reflection such thoroughly physical objects of our environment as automobiles, dynamos, computers, i.e., products of advanced technology, where the concept (embodying transperceptual elements of theory with its linguistics) presided over the origination of the things, and their eventual "look" (on which the superficial "concept" fastens, once the products belong to the visible furniture of our

This, in conclusion, leads us back to Arnheim's proper theme, visual thinking, on which he has to say many enlightening things. Precisely for their sake, it is a pity that his underplaying of language and pure concept so often compels him to overtax vision with cognitive claims it must disappoint, thereby compromising otherwise sound observations. This is a gratuitous disservice to his good cause. Thus, the abstract drawings by students in Figures 18–44 do show that non-visual notions like past-present-future, youth, good and bad marriage, democracy—or the musings they evoke in the subject—can find "expression" of a kind in visual shapes (recognizable as such when accompanied by verbal explanations!), and the nature of such symbolizations is surely worth exploring; but by no means do they show "that pictorial representations are suitable instruments of abstract reasoning." All the reasoning has been done before the "depicting" of its results started. The artist has been "telling" himself, and we have to be told in turn. The visual translation is second to the thought that was to be translated, and it cannot even speak for itself.

Or again, the geometrical (visual) representation of the squaring of $a + b$ does indeed give a better intuition of the operation and the result, of the *why* of the equation $(a + b)^2 = a^2 + 2ab + b^2$, than the algebraic notation does (p. 221); but already for $(a + b)^3$ it is the more cumbersome method, more of a hindrance than a help, and for all higher powers it completely fails: so that the example, contrary to the intention, proves the superiority of the non-visual method over the visual in all but the simplest cases, which moreover appear in its light as mere specializations of more generic, formal truths.

Again, and finally, Indian geometry may offer some nice examples of directly beholding the truth of (simple enough) theorems by themselves, waiving the Euclidian idea of proof: even if these should include the Pythagorean theorem—so long as it has to tell us no more than what the "visual analysis" of its figure yields, the fact of incommensurables and therewith the concept of irrational numbers, which contradicts all visual expectations and standards, would escape us forever. Was it perversity on Plato's part that he made *this* the touchstone of understanding—not commensurability, which we can see, but incommensurability, which we can never see but, looking at the perceptible from beyond perception,

---

world) is a sheer accident of constructional choices and restraints. Does the word "computer" then point to a percept or a concept? To both, once computers are there. But someone may have a perfectly adequate concept of a computer, even of a particular logical type, without ever having seen one, indeed without yet imagining how its execution in actual hardware will "look"—which, of course, is what happened in historical fact. Even afterwards, the concept is not a distillate of percepts but their illumination by the understanding.

can *prove* of it in defiance of sense? That he considered ignorance in *this* "ludicrous and shameful," "more worthy of swine than men," a cause for him "to blush for our whole Hellenic world" (*Laws* VII, 819c–820c)? Or is it we in this twentieth century of ours who are amiss when we seek shelter from this ancient thunder in the comforts of the immediate "Behold!" (p. 223)?

The cause of vision does not need such weighting of the scales. The love due to it must itself be, first of all, seeing. I am grateful to Arnheim for all he sees of it and makes us see—and his gift is rich in the extreme—but at the same time I must deplore his lover's blindnesses. Is this the inevitable price of love, even to a thinker? Sense has been shortchanged in praise of thought by a long tradition stretching from Plato to Kant. Now we see thought shortchanged in praise of sense. Can we always have one truth only at the expense of another? Can there not be truth with justice?

12.

Change and Permanence:
On the Possibility of Understanding History

Achilles sulks in his tent, mourns for Patroclus, drags Hector's corpse around the funeral pyre, weeps at Priam's words. Do we understand this? Surely, we do, without being Achilles ourselves, ever having loved a Patroclus and dragged a Hector through the dust. Socrates passes a life in discourse, examines opinions, asks what virtue and knowledge are, makes himself the gadfly of Athens in obedience to the god's command, and dies for it. Do we understand this? Yes, we do, without ourselves being capable of such a life and such a death. A wandering preacher calls to two fishermen: Follow me, I shall make you fishers of men; and they leave their nets, never to return to them. Even this we understand, although the like of it has happened to none of us, and none of us is likely to follow such a call. Thus do we understand the never-experienced from the words of ancient writings. But do we understand it correctly? Do we understand it as meant by Homer himself and as understood by the listeners of his time? As Plato and the readers for whom he wrote understood the words of Socrates? As the Palestinian

This is the author's translation of his original German essay entitled "Wandel und Bestand: Vom Grunde der Verstehbarkeit des Geschichtlichen." The German version in abridged form served as the opening address of the Fifth International Congress of Classical Studies held in Bonn during September 1969. The complete German text was published in *Durchblicke. Martin Heidegger zum 80. Geburstag*, and separately as *Wandel und Bestand*, both by Vittorio Klostermann, Frankfurt a.M., 1970. The English version was first published in *Social Research* 38 (Fall 1971).

Jew of the first century understood the nearness of the kingdom of God
and the call to it? Here we hesitate with our answer. Even he who affirms
the possibility (and more than the possibility of adequate understanding
no reasonable man will affirm) must add that we can never be sure
whether the possibility is realized in a given case. Only the nay-sayer
can afford to be categorical when he asserts that we never understand
"correctly," as this is deemed impossible by the very nature of things
historical and the uniqueness of each. But let us bear in mind that the
same span of answers already bestrides the question of understanding
the present, even of understanding the next fellow man, and applies by
no means only to the historically distant. Of this we will hear later. As
regards historical understanding those most engaged in it and most
familiar with its toils will be the readiest to answer "yes and no" to the
question whether it can be attained. Such an answer is neither an
evasion nor a concession of defeat. It signals the presence of a problem
that needs pursuing. This we shall attempt to do.

I

Several logical alternatives confront each other in this field. The "yes"
to our question can secure its position best by making appeal to a permanent, invariant nature, an "essence," of man. Man *qua* man, so the
argument would go, is the same at all times: his hunger and thirst, his
love and hate, his hope and despair, his seeking and finding, his speaking and fabling, his deceiving and truth-telling—they are all familiar to
us since, by either experience or disposition, we have them in ourselves.
Everyone, according to this view, contains "humankind" in himself, and
thus nothing human is alien to him. Drawing on this fund of identical
humanity he can imaginatively reproduce in himself the experience of
the past, not excluding its enormities, or let the attuned chords of his
nature resonate to it. The intelligibility of history would thus be
grounded in the once-for-all given nature of man. To this theory of the
"ground" of understanding there corresponds a theory of understanding
itself, namely, that it is a knowing of like by like: that we know love by
love, and mortal strife by strife. A hermeneutical theory is thus found
to rely on an ontological one, i.e., on a general theory of human nature,
in this case on the theory which first of all asserts that man *has* "a
nature."

We know, however, that this older, humanistic-ontological position
is countered in our day by an opposite one, which denies that there is
such a thing as a definite and definable essence of man; which rather
holds that *what* "man" is at any time is the product of his own de facto

existing and of the choices made therein; and, further, that the scope of his existing, even the kind and content of the choices open to it are, in their turn, predetermined by the facticity of spatio-temporal place, by the circumstance and accident of the historical situation; and, finally, that each such situation is unique. In brief, the specifically modern—and like everything modern, highly suggestive—contention is that "man," far from being always the same, is each time different. Understanding, therefore, if from this standpoint considered possible at all, would consist in knowing, not like by like, but other by other. The very meaning of understanding would be to get beyond oneself and to the other, and not at all to recognize oneself and one's familiar possessions in every other instance of man. *How* such a disclosure of the "other" is possible, is a question by itself. The contention is that only to the extent that it *is* possible—a possibility inferred from its experienced, if as yet unexplained, fact—can there be historical understanding, and even understanding of anything human at all.

However, the proposition of the irreducible uniqueness of all experience and the ever-otherness of man in history can also lead to the radically skeptical conclusion that "true" historical understanding is a priori impossible; and that what we take for it is always a translation of the foreign signs into our own language—a necessarily falsifying translation, which creates the deceptive appearance of familiarity where in fact we only explicate ourselves and can recognize ourselves in the past because we have first projected ourselves into it. Surprisingly, therefore, we see the most skeptical and the most confident views meet from opposite ends in agreeing that all understanding is a "knowing of the like," with the difference that in the one case this means the possible truth, and in the other, the necessary error of historical understanding.

We thus have two opposite ontological doctrines about man and, corresponding to them, two alternative views of understanding—as being knowledge of like by like, or of other by other; and in addition, as a corollary of the ontological *homo mutabilis* thesis, a third hermeneutical view according to which there is nothing but would-be understanding, since understanding of the other qua other is impossible per se. Obviously, only the first of the two ontological alternatives adduces a *ground* for the intelligibility of the historical past. Abiding identity of the historical subject directly constitutes such a ground and makes understanding itself understandable enough. To be sure, even with that ground there would be no dearth of problems for historical understanding: obscurity and ambiguity of language in the original documentation, doubtfulness and scarcity of the extant tradition, and so on. But whatever the technical difficulties, on principle there is from this standpoint no riddle in historical understanding as such. The other standpoint, by contrast, denies this ground, even if not denying understanding itself. It may then either hold that understanding lacks a natural ground outside itself, i.e., that it is an underivable, primary phenomenon, or it bids us to seek for a ground other than identity of essence.

When we look at these various possibilities, we may well feel that both ontological alternatives—as is so often the case with formulated theories—are too onesided and, in their exclusiveness, wrong; but also, that there is something in either that must not be overlooked and can correct the other. It surely betrays little thoughtfulness to abandon lightly (or even triumphantly), under the pressure of recent existentialist counter-assertions, the most venerable and oldest idea of an essence and norm of man—be it in the classical form of the *animal rationale* or in the biblical of the *imago Dei*. It may also betray a wanting nearness to what is being abandoned here, and its significance is in many respects subjective rather than objective. That all who bear the form of man have something fundamental in common, without which we could not even speak of "man," nor of human history either—let alone of man's "historicity" and, perhaps, even of "his" radical mutability in history—this much should be evident. Even the negators of the "essence" draw on this community, for they predicate their negation, after all, not of an empty, arbitrary x, but of Man, as something attributable to him uniquely and in distinction from the animal, which is captive in each instance to its specific essence: this very negativity, thus, is claimed for man as an "essential" property. "Essentialism," indeed, is far less easily disposed of than a vulgar "existentialism" wishes us to believe. It would be rash, at least, to pronounce Plato dead in compliance with Nietzsche's decree.

Nevertheless, unlike Plato, we know too much of the depth of historical change in man to still believe in one determinate, univocally binding definition of man. Too powerful was Nietzsche's message of the "non-fixed animal" and the openness of becoming. Too great is our resistance to regarding what seems new in history as not really new, or as a mere by-play that leaves the core untouched. Moreover, there is no denying the poverty and even boredom of an understanding which forever finds in all its objects nothing more than what it already knows: for which all the wealth of history reduces itself to the endlessly repeating *da capo* of a fixed repertoire—not to speak of the injustice which lies in the measuring of everything different by the standard of the one, acknowledged essence, assigning each its grade according as it conforms to it. We who first in all history have drunk from the intoxicating cup of its knowledge no longer enjoy the innocence of the faith in time-exempt essence.

But as insufficient as the concept of knowing like by like is for a theory of understanding, as untenable, even absurd, would be its formula as a knowledge of the absolutely Other. Between absolutely "others" there can be no understanding. To be understandable, the other must partake in the generic premises of my own possibilities, which include those of my imagination and sympathy, without coinciding with their contingent reality. The other—it is a truism to say it—must be a human other, an other within the domain of man. Of this alone do we expect, even demand, that it be understandable. Even in consternation at the utterly strange, in the very perplexity before the starkly incomprehensible, we still hold to the postulate that this, being human, *must* be understandable. For a theory of interhuman understanding the choice is not between "congruence of like with like" and "leap to a totally other"; simply to substitute the latter for the—admittedly unsatisfactory—former would be an indefensible exaggeration and a play with the absolute paradox. Absolute paradoxes are suspect per se. We may already guess that in the question of understanding, as elsewhere, the truth may be "the same *and* the other"; and in history, repetition *and* innovation.

What about the third possibility, the skeptical variant of the ontology of man's radical mutability, according to which all so-called historical understanding is merely putative and of necessity never true? The assertion is safe from refutation, as are all such negative theses, since by the nature of the matter there cannot be *proof* for a single case of adequate understanding. But, again like all of its kind, the thesis is faulted by the absurdity of its consequences, which follow when it is taken in its extreme sense, that is, beyond that of warning us against the ever-present danger of self-deception, or reminding us that no historical understanding is ever complete: these are salutary truths. But radical historical skepticism is self-defeating. For it is easy to show (but need not be shown in detail here) that the alleged nonintelligibility of the historical past can be advocated only in conjunction with the nonintelligibility of the present as well, and that of whole cultures only with that of every individual—since the arguments from otherness and uniqueness urged for the first are equally valid for the second, that is, for all human existence in general. The thesis, therefore, amounts to saying that there is no understanding of the human other of any sort—historical or contemporary, collective or individual. That is to say, it leads straight into solipsism and its absurdity. Its spokesmen cannot even utter it meaningfully, except in soliloquy, since they cannot hope for its being understood. Strictly speaking, one need not reply to them.

Apart from this formal objection to which every radical skepticism is exposed, one could ask the spokesmen of historical agnosticism why they concern themselves with history at all, why they so much as take notice of it. The charge of boredom levied earlier becomes in their case heightened to that of complete uselessness. Essentialism—vulnerable to the first charge only when it takes a shallow view of "essence"—allows for cognitive communication with the past to be not only possible but also worthwhile: it is consistent with its terms that the past may have something to teach us about the essence and its breadth. For even if each individual has it in him complete, it is reasonable to suppose that only the least part of it is ever realized (and thereby made manifest) in anyone's own experience, and that most of it remains hidden as an unknown potential. Thus, even if historical understanding does no more than show me "my own" by means of the "like," something has been gained for its discovery which could not have been gained otherwise. By contrast, radical historicist skepticism cannot expect such a gain from the eternally misunderstood past and cannot justify its study in any way. If we can do no more than read ourselves into it, while its own being remains closed to us and merely serves as a pretext for displaying ourselves, then we ought to take a straighter, truer, more direct way to this, and to knowing what we are and have, than indulge our illusive reflection in the opaque surface of history. We ought to converse with ourselves alone (whatever such a pointlike "self" may mean). And so we have the paradox that the advocates of radical historicism must arrive at the position of complete a-historicism, at the notion of an existence devoid of a past and shrunk to a now. In short, radical historicism leads to the negation of history and historicity. Actually, there is no paradox in this. For history itself no less than historiography is possible only in conjunction with a transhistoric element. To deny the transhistorical is to deny the historical as well.

Let us add that there is of course not the shadow of a proof—nor can there be—that man has a limitless capacity for innovation. The assertion that he has, however prestigious its source, is strictly without foundation and ultimately frivolous. It is "metaphysics" in the bad sense of the word.

So much by way of survey of the several logical possibilities in the domain of our question. With all our critique of the three abstract positions it should not be forgotten that this critique applies in each case only to the extreme and exclusive form of the criticized position and rules out none of them completely, except as a pure alternative. Each has its justified aspect which is indispensable for the totality of the complex situation—even the third position which has been so severely criticized. The doctrine of the one, permanent human nature contains the truth that an inalienable kinship links the children of man across the farthest distances of history and the greatest diversities of culture; that this common ground supports and holds together and explains all the manifoldness which unpredictably comes forth from it; and that only with this as a basis is history possible at all, as well as the understanding of it. The doctrine of man's fundamental mutability and actual changing, and of the uniqueness of each product of change, contains the truth that the particularization of humanity in the different cultures, and again in the progress of each culture, and again in the individuals sharing it, produces genuine and unpredictable otherness; that consequently the "knowledge of the like" must transcend itself; and that—taking off from the basis of the like—an understanding of the widely-different is possible and must be striven for. *How* it is possible, is as yet an open question. Finally, the doctrine of the necessary failure of all understanding contains the truth that the interpreter indeed imports himself into the interpreted, inevitably alienating it from itself and assimilating it to his *own* being, and also, that every advance of understanding leaves an indelible remainder of the nonunderstood, which recedes before it into infinity.

II

After the critical discussion, let us try to take a few steps of our own toward explaining historical understanding—of which we assume the fact but wonder how it is possible. Such an attempt leads necessarily into the theory of understanding in general, whose mysteries are no less than those of historical understanding in particular. From the outset I disclaim any ambition to compete with the sophistication which for more than a century has been devoted to this subject, i.e., to the theory of hermeneutics, especially in Germany. I take comfort from the reflection that after so much subtlety, a restatement of certain elementary facts may not be wholly useless.

Let us begin with the question known under the title "knowledge of other minds"—the question, that is, of how we can know of foreign consciousness, of any inwardness besides our own. How, in other words, can we reach over from the insularity of our private subject sphere to the equally insular one of another, assuming that it exists? And here, right at the outset, I wish to reverse the usual and so deceptively plausible opinion by answering: *not* by analogical inference, overt or covert, from myself to others; not by transference and projection, as the post-Cartesian doctrine of consciousness made it almost de rigueur to hold; rather, if there be a *prius* and *posterius* here, the genetic sequence is the reverse. Neither the knowledge of other minds, nor even the knowledge of mind as such, originates from the inspection of our own. On the contrary, already the knowledge of our own mind, even our having one in the first place, is a function of acquaintance with other minds. Knowledge of inwardness as such, whether one's own or that of others, is based on communication with a whole human environment which determines, certainly codetermines decisively, even what will be found in eventual introspection. Since we begin life as infants (a fact philosophers so easily forget), coming into a world already peopled with adults, the particular "I" to-be is at first far more the receiver than the giver in this communication. In the course of it, the rudimentary inwardness that is to be "I" evolves by gradually beholding from the address, utterance, and conduct of others what inward possibilities there are, and making them its own. We learn from others what we ourselves can be, can will, and can feel. Thus we must be able to understand others before we understand ourselves, in order for us to become persons who may eventually understand themselves—for there to *be* anything in us to understand. An understanding of the inwardness of others, in advance of and beyond what "introspection" could have found in one's own inwardness, is a precondition for the very emergence of such an inwardness.

The proposition that introspection, or self-experience, is our only or main or primary source for knowledge of inwardness leads to absurd conclusions. It would make of all our knowledge of other subjects a matter of analogical transference from what is already present in ourselves. Apart from the impossible setting this creates for the problem of learning, it would condemn to futility the best part of literature. As I could not possibly have Aeschylus, Shakespeare, and Goethe in myself beforehand, their labors would have been in vain; and superfluous if I had.

To approach the question on a much more primitive and preverbal plane: How do I know that a smile is a smile? that a face turned toward me means "someone looking at me"? that a facial expression is an *expression*? On the theory of introspection and analogical inference ("projection"), the three-month-old infant who seeks the eyes of his mother, or responds to her smile, would have had to perform an incredible series of mental operations in the past in order to do so—operations that would have to include: recognition of his own face in the mirror, discrimination of its expressions, their correlation with concurrent feelings, and the later memory use of these observations in interpreting the similar appearances on other faces. The construction need only be stated to obviate refutation. Against all such tortured theories stands the simple, if mysterious, truth that a smile is in essence something coming to me from without, and its genuine locus, first and always, is another face.

Once we are grown up, it is true, we do make use of self-knowledge and analogy in understanding and judging others. To the extent that our adultness entails unwillingness or incapacity to learn further, we may, to our own impoverishment, come to receive the testimony of the inwardness of others solely through the filter of our ready-made own. It can then tell us only what we already know, i.e., it fails to be really testimony of *other* inwardness, and knowledge is replaced by "projection." No one is entirely free from this kind of procedure, but we should judge that one confined to it would make neither a good psychologist nor a good companion. At least in the process of reaching this finished state of adulthood, one has to take other, more "open-minded" ways of perceiving inwardness in its expressions, especially the verbal ones, for otherwise we could never have become adult and possessed of the inwardness on which we then can draw.

If the original understanding is not an inferential one, on what then is it based? It is part of the intuitive beholding of life by life and thus begins with the accomplishments of animal perception, which is attuned to the accomplishments of animal expression. The recognition of other life is a fundamental feature of the outside relation integral to the animal organism. Among the objects of perception, neutrally classed as "things," living things *as living* are paramount. Their perception involves emotional discrimination—as prey, foe, fellow member of the species, sexual partner, as familiar or unfamiliar, noteworthy or negligible, harmless, threatening, or undetermined—and is thus anything but neutral. It includes an instinctive familiarity—sometimes in the mode of felt unfamiliarity—with the living behavior to which response is to be made. The basis of this familiarity is the community of animal nature, and in the case of intra-specific relations, the community of the species. A creature recognizes greed or aggression when it meets it in a fellow creature's eyes (or in posture, sound, and smell), and this far beyond its own kind.

It recognizes because something offers itself for recognition. The receptive feat of perception is matched, and made possible, by the spontaneous feat of expression. The latter may well be the primary phenomenon. *Animal life is expressive*, even eager for expression. It displays itself; it has its sign codes, its language; it communicates itself. Whole rituals of posture and gesture and expressive movement serve the role of signals before the action or take its place, making the action itself unnecessary, if warning was to be conveyed. Such spontaneous but strictly fixed symbolism counts on its being understood; untaught, animals do understand the mimics of aggression, anger, and sexual courtship.

It would be foolish to except man from all this. The cat looks up at my eyes, she seeks my glance, she wants something from me. Nobody has taught her that these are the body parts with which I notice her, and in which my noticing or not-noticing becomes visible to her. She "knows": she can reach me that way. And I, too, do not need information from physiology and neurology in order to feel here a gaze on me and to read the entreaty in it; intuitive physiognomics is at work. We look at each other, and something passes between us without which there could be no higher understanding, however far it surpasses this elemental stratum. Animals also know how to distinguish between play and earnest among themselves—such animals, that is, who are able to play, namely animals with brood rearing, especially mammals with their sheltered childhood, who are still free from the grim pressure of animal needs but enjoy already the powers of movement. This is why dolphins play, even when adult, but sharks do not. And we humans, mammals with the longest childhood who carry the paradisic freedom of play over into responsible adulthood, we understand the play of animals.

In man, it is true, this whole natural groundwork is overlaid with system upon system of invented, constructed, and freely manipulated expressions and symbols, culminating in speech and imagery, which open up entirely new dimensions of understanding and misunderstanding, openness and concealment, truth and falsehood. Of this, I will speak later. But the overwhelming role of these artifacts must not make us forget the role which the natural community of the species, i.e., the shared organic basis, plays in the understanding of man by man. In this respect most certainly, but not in it alone, there is indeed a "recognition of like by like." Empedocles was right in saying that we behold love by love, hate by hate. That this is not the whole truth does not make it untrue. We would not perceive fear in others were we not familiar with its stirrings in ourselves; we would not understand the statement "I am hungry" without our own past experience of hunger. Yet, although in the latter case actual self-experience must, and assuredly does, precede the understanding of the phenomenon in others (for what animal organism is spared that feeling?), this is not a universal condition where *human* understanding is concerned. There, the recognition of like by like is not bound to the use of analogy. To "know love by love" is not to infer, from my own experience of the feeling of love, what is probably going on in someone else. I may first be awakened by *Romeo and Juliet* to the potentialities of love, by the tale of Thermopylae to the beauty of sacrificial heroism. This is itself an experience, showing me undreamt-of possibilities of my own soul—or rather, of "the soul"—possibilities that may or may not become actualities of my own experience. *This experience of the potential, mediated by symbols, is precisely what is meant by "understanding."* The never-yet-heard *combination* of familiar meanings in the words of a communication begets *new* meaning in the recipient, and this opens the door to new inward realms of life. What was thus for the first time disclosed in the otherness of the paradigm may then be added to by what it has set in motion in ourselves.

The knowledge of other minds thus rests on the ground of the common humanity of men—in such a manner, however, that this common ground is effective, not by supplying parallels between what *is there* in the self and the other, but by allowing the voice of the other to call on the possibilities that lie latent in the soul of man or can be elicited from his nature. We understand through our possibilities, not necessarily through actual precedents in our own experience. In other words, we understand and answer with our possible being far more than with our actual one. All the better if sometimes we can also answer with the memory of self-experienced actuality, although this in turn has its obvious dangers. The well-known "I know exactly what you mean, for wasn't I myself once in such and such a situation" may help the understanding to its truth, but may also indicate the point where it shuts itself off against the other. Our "possibility," however, playing on the scale of a few generic constants that are predefined by our constitution (such as desire, fear, love, hate—but also reason and belief), is unforeseeable and becomes revealed, in unending novelty, only through the calls made upon it—mostly in the mutuality of communication which holds the real surprises concerning what is mind or soul.

On man's nature being "possibility" rather than determinate fact depends our empathic understanding of even those experiences of other souls—actual or fictitious—which we may never be able to duplicate in ourselves. This is to say that the very use of *language* for the generation of psychological novelty—an actual enlargement of the soul's estate—depends on this transcending trait of our nature by which we are always indefinably more than our present being. For it is language which must conjure up the hitherto unimagined. Without this conjuring power of words, there would be no poetry, nor history either, apart from the bare chronicling of events. The problem of "other minds" is thus closely bound up with the philosophy of language, which cannot do without a theory of imagination. It is by the same token closely bound up with the philosophy of art. Socrates' theory of "recollection," in which the idea of "possibility" is adumbrated, is with all its mythological pitfalls more adequate to the facts of the "dialogue" between minds than is the modern theory of analogical inference and projection.

III

So far I have dealt with understanding in general. What is the peculiarity of historical understanding? How does it differ from present understanding in which we are incessantly engaged? Many answers suggest themselves. There is the distance of the past as such and the vast gap of difference that separates it from us: circumstances and people have become other; ideas, customs, language, and associations of meanings have changed; so have social structure and institutions; even some feelings and passions are no longer the same. Then there is the fragmentary, selective condition of the testimony that has come down to us, pre-filtered first by the selection of the memorable on the part of the historical subjects themselves, then filtered once more through the accidents and mishaps of its physical survival. The always-deficient evidence thrusts on the interpreter the risk of tentative reconstruction, which is the more hazardous the more alien the life that here expresses and hides itself. Furthermore, contemporary understanding is continuous and obligatory, while historical understanding is occasional and optional. We could prolong the list.

All this is correct, but not decisive. On the contemporary plane, too, there are chasms of strangeness and difference which stand in the way of understanding, and much apparent familiarity which may lead it astray. Already the transition from one social class to another has its pitfalls, not to speak of the crossing of national, ethnic, and linguistic borders. And what shall we say of the generation gap, this most peculiar of all contemporary relationships, a veritable seedbed of misunderstanding? I am not sure that I understand my children, but I am convinced that they don't understand me. Or could I be mistaken there too? Do they perhaps understand me better than I might like? Later observers may be able to judge. This would be a case, and not the only one, where the distance of the past has the advantage over the all-too-engaged proximity of the present. One advantage, however, the present has always over the past: it enjoys unrestricted plenitude of evidence which can be multiplied ad libitum for any subject (the problem being that of abundance rather than scarcity), whereas paucity or strictly-drawn limits reign over the evidence of the past. Does perhaps the whole difference come down to this? To a matter of more or less? Namely, more remoteness and otherness for the past, more ambiguity and obscurity of its expression, less material to deal with? A quantitative difference in all these respects? Is, then, the problem of historical understanding perhaps merely a magnified form of the problems of understanding in general?

I do not think so. There remains a qualitative difference which looks inconsiderable but seems decisive to me. It does not consist in the time distance as such, but is given with it: *Present understanding has the aid of speech and counterspeech, historical understanding has only the one-sided speech of the past.* Misunderstanding of one's contemporary can be corrected by the misunderstood himself; I can question him and he can reply, and we both are members of a larger, inclusive fellowship of communication, of the general universe of speech that has nurtured us and goes on feeding us and continuously proffers us the keys for our reciprocal exchanges. The past, on the contrary, has spoken its word and cannot add to it. It comes to us, and we cannot return questions to its source. We must make of it what we can. And "what we can" may be more than is good. As the past cannot come to the aid of our interpretation, neither can it defend itself against it. Its defenselessness, however, obligates us doubly. Precisely because it is delivered into our hands, the residual speech of the past is entrusted to our most faithful care. In dealing with the historical subject, therefore, it is doubly improper to abuse the immunity of our freedom for the indulging of ingenuity, the thrill of originality, and the vanity of self-mirroring. The contemporary subject can retaliate for the sins of our license and rap our misunderstanding painfully over the knuckles. In the case of the historical subject we have nothing worse to fear than the contradiction of our academic colleagues—and with that one can live perfectly well. Sometimes, it is true, "history" itself can have its revenge on us through the surprise discovery of a new source that explodes our most beautiful hypothesis (as it may also surprisingly confirm it). But this does not change the basic fact that the past has spoken its word for all time and cannot be approached for any self-explanation.

It is, therefore, the absolutely monological character of the historical communication which creates the peculiar situation of historical understanding. In this respect, the understanding of history is on a par with the understanding of a work of art. In the work of art too—be it of word, sound, or shape—we stand opposite a self-enclosed, definitive entity which can tell us nothing about itself beyond what it already is. With its finished creation and dismissal into the world, it has assumed that silent infinity of a passive potential for interpretation and reiterated experience which it shares with the past. Its pronouncement, like the latter's, is onesided, monologic, and exposed to every appropriation. It could even

be said, in a sense, that the work of art instantly assumes the quality of
the past and thereby of eternal present. Tolstoi's *War and Peace* became
a historical fact at the moment of its appearance. Indeed, contrary to
what we might think, it is not the case that Tolstoi, Kafka, or Flaubert,
because they are nearer to us in time, are more easily and surely understood by us than Shakespeare, Dante, Aristophanes. This has nothing to
do with the question whether or not we feel more at home with the
later than the earlier. In principle, i.e., apart from technical questions,
such as availability of the semantic associations, we are in the same
position toward all of them, the living and the dead. It might be objected
that we can, after all, question the living author and let him explain
himself. Heaven keep us from trying. Nothing, neither experience nor
good sense, supports the view that the author is his own best interpreter.
Even if he has a great deal to say about his intention, in the last resort it
matters little what he had in mind: only what he said matters. The
"accursed ipsissimosity" of which Nietzsche asked "who has never once
been tired to death of it?" can well be that of the artist too. In any event,
he soon falls silent, and only the monologue of his work remains. Because of the analogy that here obtains, historical testimony and work of
art (both can coincide in the same object) are similarly entrusted to us—
albeit with the difference that in regard to the historical testimony our
understanding, qua historical, is committed to a goal of correctness and
truth, and therewith to a method of critical verification, which have no
place in the understanding of art.

   The strictly monological quality of the past does not, indeed, change
the nature of understanding as such, but it sharpens the question concerning the ground of its possibility. For the confidence in a shared
sameness is more heavily drawn upon where we cannot check back with
the originator of the message; and the time dimension adds the problem
of "permanence and change" to what was merely the atemporal problem
of "the like and the other" for simultaneous understanding. With the
expanding time horizon (as with the similar expansion of the geographic
horizon) the question concerning an "essence" of man, which is inseparable from the question of interhuman understanding as such, turns into
the slightly different question of what things we can count on in man
at all times and in all places. Only a philosophical anthropology could
answer such a question, and this is not the place for it. In order to make
any headway at all within the more limited frame of this paper, let us
invert the question, and instead of interrogating the elusive "essence"
about what according to it we *should* always expect to find, let us rather
ask ourselves what in actual fact, and without giving ourselves account
of it, we always *have* already understood implicitly in all our encounters
with history and prehistory.

IV

It is well to start with the biological dimension which we tacitly presuppose as a matter of course; although subhistoric itself, it pervades
everything historical and cannot be left out of our account. The reader
may therefore forgive the banality of the following enumeration of what
he beforehand and implicitly always knows. We always know, whatever
relics of past humanity we happen upon, that those who left them behind were organic beings who had to eat, took pleasure in eating, and
suffered from hunger. When we read in Homer that the Achaeans raised
their hands to the tastily prepared meal, we feel our own mouths water:
angels would have difficulties of empathy here. We know of human
want and mortality. We know of the earliest men that they, like us,
were subject to the alternation of waking and sleep, that to the weary
sleep was necessary and sweet, and that it was visited by dreams. Only
a Cartesian fool would consider this unimportant. We know about the
duality of the sexes—about the lust and pain of love, the mystery of
generation and birth, the suckling and rearing of the young; and we
know that this leads to the formation of families and kinships, to provident care, delimitation toward the outside, orders of authority and
reverence within, to bonds of loyalty and faith, but also to deadly strife.
We know about youth and old age, sickness and death. We know further
that the makers of the extant monuments, down to the simplest tool,
were erect creatures relying on eye and hand. We share with them the
pride, the intimacy, and the shame of the upright body. When we read
in the Bible that in a bloodbath all were slain "who piss on the wall,"
we understand immediately that all the males are meant, and also, why
only they are slain. We understand still more, namely why a description
of this type has been chosen from among so many possible ones: it is the
language of warriors, and we know to this day the speech habits of the
army camp, the soldiers' liking for coarsely sexual speech. (Well may
we regret that golden and silver Latinity prevented Roman historians
from telling us more about the language of the legionnaires. I for one
should like to know how Marius, who had risen from the ranks, really
addressed his men.)

Let us here break off the consideration of biological matters. Already
their survey did not keep in the bounds of mere animal nature. How
could it, seeing that it concerned humans? Passing from the body to the
products of man, what knowledge guides us there? How, for instance, do
we know that any buried objects we turn up are the works of man? We
know it because, long before there are the great dwellings of the gods

and the lettered stones, we find these three: tool, image, and tomb. It would indeed require a full-fledged philosophical anthropology to show why these—each in itself and all combined—are characteristic of man.[1] We must confine ourselves to a few remarks. The *tool* (any utensil, including weapon and vessel) tells us that here a being, compelled by his needs to deal with matter, serves these needs in artificially mediated ways originating from invention and open to improvement by further invention. The *image* tells us that here a being, using tools on matter for an immaterial end, represents to himself the contents of his perception, plays with their variations and augments them by new shapes—thus generating another object-world of representation beyond the physical objects of his need and its direct satisfaction. The *tomb* tells us that here a being, subject to mortality, meditates on life and death, defies appearance and elevates his thought to the invisible—putting tool and image to the service of such thought. These are basic forms in which man, in uniquely human fashion, answers and transcends what is an unconditional given for man and animal alike. With the tool he surpasses physical necessity through invention; with the image, passive perception through representation and imagination; with the tomb, inescapable death through faith and piety. All three, in their transcending function, are divergent modes of a freedom shared by us with the bygone makers of those artifacts and all who came between them and us; so shared, they can serve as universal "coordinates" of understanding valid for the whole course of human history. We may not always know the purpose of a particular tool, but we do know that it had one, that it was conceived in terms of the means-end, cause-effect relation, and was produced according to that conception: in the continuation of such causal thought lie technology and physics. We may not always recognize the meaning of an image, but we do know that it is an image, that it was meant to represent something, and that in such representation it let reality reappear in a heightened and validated form: in the continuance of such representation lies art. We may not know the particular ideas of a funeral cult (and may find them very strange if we knew them), but we do know that ideas were here at work—the bare fact of the tomb and the ritual tells it—and that in these ideas the riddle of existence and of what is beyond appearance was pondered on: in the continuation of such pondering lies metaphysics. Physics, Art, and Metaphysics, primevally foreshadowed by tool, image, and tomb, are here named less for the eventual products known by these names, which may

---

[1]Regarding the "image," I have once tried to show it in a special study, "Image-making and the Freedom of Man," *The Phenomenon of Life* (New York: Harper & Row, 1966), pp. 157–75.

or may not emerge in the contingencies of history, than for their indicating original dimensions of man's relation to the world, each with its own horizon of possibility. Such original dimensions of man's being must then also define dimensions of understanding him throughout his history —that is, they provide categories (or, as we expressed it before, coordinates) of historical interpretation.

Possibility, of course, does not assure actuality. Accordingly, our trinity of horizons should not be taken to imply that all of their primeval signs must be met with in all human groups at all times. Their presence is conclusive indeed, jointly and even singly, but not equally so their absence. Tools, for obvious reasons, are almost certain to be missing nowhere. But image and tomb, both more of a luxury in man's struggle with natural necessity, may for various reasons here and there fail to appear. The faculty for them must nonetheless be counted as integral to the fullness of being man, and no "culture" is entirely without either of them. If it should be true that ours is presently in the process of banishing metaphysics from the household of our mind, we should be the poorer for the loss of this dimension of our being. We should not cease to be men; but we should cease to be able to understand past history— if what has been pronounced dead (and has surely been stifled) had really died in us. I tend to believe that this is impossible.

Again we break off here. In our survey of that which always is "understood in advance" wherever we deal with remnants of the human past, we mentioned, first, the facts of man's corporeality as exemplified by nutritive need, sex, upright posture, and the dominance of hands and eyes. Then, in the works of his hands, we discerned the artificer, the image maker, and the brooder over mysteries. Much could be added here, considering, for example, *what* we find depicted in the images, especially in the most eminent of them all—that of man himself in his grace, majesty, or grimace. However, it is time that we name at last what was left unnamed in all those traits but was presupposed in each: language. Without it, none of the other phenomena could be; for each, it was tacitly assumed. This is true already of the organic-biological sphere. The human meal (though not the defecation) is social, as already was the procuring of it—the hunt, the gathering, and so on. Entirely wordless, love between the sexes would not be human. Rearing of the young means for man essentially teaching them how to speak—by speaking to them. Kinship and authority relations are defined and transmitted through speech. Even our dreams are permeated with words. How much more do words dominate in the life areas indicated by the tool, the image, and the tomb—in planning, work, remembrance, and veneration. And how completely speech-dependent are the worlds of politics and law, and most of all, the relations with the invisible, which nowhere gains form but in words. Man, then, is first and foremost a creature of speech —productive of speech and the product of it. And this one fact we know a priori: wherever and in whatever remote antiquity, historic or prehistoric, men existed—they have talked with one another. The philosophy of language must stand in the center of every philosophical anthropology. But even without it we know that it is of the essence of language to be intelligible across any distance of time and to be translatable into one's own however different in form and character—if only *what* is spoken about is otherwise within our grasp. This it is, in general, thanks to our being fellow men to the speakers of all ages; and in particular, thanks to our knowledge of things, which in part we must acquire through historical investigation itself.

Through surviving words indeed we know most—and the most important things—of past humanity. Buildings, implements, and images lend greater concreteness to this knowledge. But the words tell more than the stones, though they are sometimes given the lie by them. The word is also, together with the art styles, the eminently "historical" above the substructure of the ever-repeated themes of the species. Through the agency of the word history produces itself; in its medium, it expresses itself; with its record, historical understanding has to deal first and last. Its paradox is that this most "general" and shareable of all the properties of man, indeed the very repository of generality, is precisely the medium of the most particular: what is the fundament of sameness for everything human is at the same time the instrument and vessel of infinite otherness. The fact of language belongs to the timeless essence of man; what it speaks about and how, becomes the child of time and place and belongs eminently to history, wherever man enters into history.

V

Only now, so late in our discussion, can we turn to the theme which is the special concern of philologians, the "lovers of words," and the proper object of a theory of hermeneutics: the understanding of past verbal utterance, which under the circumstances means the interpretation of texts. I will not be so presumptuous as to try to discuss, or even merely to list, the many problems that here rise up and are familiar to the workers in the field. I am content to return once more to the theme of the unilateral character of historical information and what it means for the problem of understanding compared to the reciprocity of contemporary communication. This theme comes now into its own. For it is in speech, of course, that the difference of monologue and dialogue has its proper place. Images, edifices and utensils are "monological" by nature. Not so the word.

First to be noted is the difference of the written from the spoken word. Speech, notwithstanding the objectivity of its vocabulary and grammar, is first of all a speaker's personal and physical utterance which comes to the hearer borne along on the modulations of voice, accompanied by the play of features and gestures, and with the full background of the concrete situation. Writing is mediate, denatured speech which denies to the reader all the sensuous helps of the original expression and the shared occasion of utterance. But of the past, all we have is writings: we can only read and never hear it. Soundfilms and the like may change this for ourselves as objects of future retrospection. It is interesting to speculate on the effect this may have on the accuracy of a future understanding of our time. In any case, it will leave the monologue situation unchanged: never can posterity enter into the relation of speech and counterspeech with the past.

On the other hand, we must not forget that even contemporary understanding—certainly an understanding of "the present" in any broader sense—is overwhelmingly obtained by reading. Book-people that we are (a fact of history itself), we are incessantly open to the many-voiced monologue of contemporary literature, of which we can't even always say that it is readily open to us. It is true that for us this monologue is embedded in the matrix of contemporary talk, not excluding the chatter, in which we are partners, and whose associations are in varying degrees presupposed in contemporary writing—whilst we never were privileged to converse in ancient Hellas or Rome, in Persepolis, Thebes, or Jerusalem. However, that aid of participant idiomatic familiarity, which already deserts us in the presence of true linguistic creativeness, is in any case shortlived, and the more important creations of literature prove by their enduring that they can do without it. The word has the power to conjure up, together with its direct tale, the total ambience from which it came forth. Moreover, the literary word, unless it be intentionally committed to the colloquial "now," stands far more in a formal tradition with its own canons of validity than in the everyday speech-world of the moment. The most recent state of our own literature—something exceptional, if not unique—makes this easy to forget. But at least the classical philologian need not be reminded that the artificiality of scriptural statement engendered from the outset (as oral transmission in meter had done before) a separate, formalized language which, at the price of a further remove from immediacy, freed the communication from close dependence on the changing speech habits of place and time.

Understanding history, to be sure, is not the same as understanding art (although historical documents can be works of art, and vice versa), but it shares with it the unilateral relation to the dormant, monological "word." It is up to the reader to awaken it to new life, and he does so in the act of understanding. The poet who entrusts the sound to the mute letter counts on the reader's ability to become a speaker himself and to recreate the music of the words for his own hearing. This "score-like" character of any work of writing, which demands active reproduction every time and offers the coded instruction for it (as a play's script does to the actor), obtains also with regard to the historical source, the "text." The media of this reproduction are sympathy, imagination and—in dealing with theoretical texts preeminently—reason. If we take the last for granted in its changeless universality, we are left with *empathic imagination* as the mysterious power operating in historical understanding, as it does in interhuman understanding generally. We have attempted before to explain this power by the existential category of "possibility" with which we can respond to the appeal of "other" reality. Reaching beyond my actual experience—though nourished by it—my possibility extends into that which has never been a part of my experience but, as human, is in the general range of man; and what it lets me thus experience indirectly, by participation in the symbolically revealed reality of the other, enlarges my capacity for future, direct experience of my own. One precondition, of course, must here be satisfied: the sophistication of mind and external circumstances with which the interpreter is furnished by his own culture must not fall far short of that represented by the object of his interpretation; just as in the matter of translation, which plays so important a role in this context, the translator's language must be nearly the equal in differentiation to that of the original. However, since we believe ourselves on the peak of history, we assume for ourselves that condition as given in relation to every existence, past or present. We are expert in playing on the latent rainbow-scale of our being, readier to assimilate alien stimuli, and less bound to a single formula of feeling, than any civilization before us. It is not wholly unnecessary to add that when we undertake to interpret the voices of the past, we must do so with our humanity fully informed and alerted to its highest perceptiveness, and not with any theory of scientific psychology, however well accredited. The theory (e.g., psychoanalysis) "knows" everything in advance—the very negation of the category of possibility —and the terrible boredom of eternal repetition yawns at us from the sum of transient toil.

It also bears explicit saying that what sympathy and imagination elicit in us in response to the past is not the original experiences and feelings themselves—who could endure them all?—but their vicarious realization in the safe, yet not unfeeling, zone of representation. It is a "knowing" of the most peculiar kind, hovering between the abstract and the concrete, between thought and experience, which resembles nothing else— except the vicarious co-experience with the work of art, with which the the vicarious experience of history has this in common, that the induced feeling is not a reprise from the storehouse of our memory, but a generative responding of the imagination to the summons from without. The condition of the spectator of a tragedy and that of the reader of a historical source are not in principle different. I wish neither to deny nor to belittle the mystery that here still remains.

Only this we know: the self-transcending feat of understanding takes place on the base and within the bounds of that abiding common humanity which is somehow always at our call, and of which I have attempted to delineate some features earlier in these reflections. This bottom ground we still share with the most alien of other civilizations. But the manifoldness that arises up from this ground is not deducible from it and is generally unforeseeable. The "ground" does not determine, it merely enables things to arise. The closer human things stay to this elementary (but not for that, meager) level, the simpler is the task of understanding them—although we sophisticates may well need an effort even to recapture this simplicity. The extrahistorical element in history is thus what is most accessible to the historical understanding, available as it is in its sameness to all of us at all times; and it is the premise for everything else. But then, proliferating around this persistent core, come the mutations of historical man in their endless, never-recurring diversity; it is for their sake, for all the nuances they display, that we study history (as distinct from anthropology)—and not to meet old acquaintances. And here *language* is the vehicle of historicity par excellence: above the permanent substratum it creates and sustains *a temporal ground of its own, not common to mankind as is the first, but particular to each concrescence of it in time.* This bottom layer of language on the one hand, and its upper reaches on the other—the base and the summit —are of all phenomena the most genuinely historical, and the most difficult of access: on the one hand, the almost secret, primordial words or coded insights, in which a particular culture from the outset articulates its posture toward the world, its basic grasp of reality that preconditions all the rest—what we may call the animating spirit of a universe of speech which opens up, and at the same time delimits, its possible range of truth; and, on the other hand, the peaks of poetry and speculation, in which this primordial life of the words comes to its highest (but still deceptive) lucidity of symbolic and conceptual expression. Everything in between—the narrative and the descriptive, the political and the legal, wisdom proverb and morality tale, the coarse and the refined, eulogy and mockery, entertainment and instruction, and, of course, everything directly historiographic—is "easily" understood, if only philology has done its job well, and if we do not always think only of ourselves. But what *dike* and *moira*, what *arete*, *logos*, *ousia* really meant and mean, or, for that matter *atman* and *tao*—whether we ever have understood this completely, this we can never know.

But what does "completely" here mean? Did the contemporaries understand it completely? Has it ever been fully understood? Only the shallow is given to complete understanding. The deepest sayings of the thinkers were probably from the beginning veiled in a darkness of meaning whose beckoning infinity could only be gradually disclosed and never exhausted. Between misunderstanding and complete understanding there stretches here an infinite scale.

VI

The mention of *atman* and *tao* side by side with *ousia* prompts a last consideration. It is often said that it is one's "own" history, baring the roots of one's tradition, which is the genuine object of historical scholarship, and which also alone promises real success to the endeavor of understanding. Behind this saying is the idea of an enlarged autobiography, as it were, which we owe ourselves for many reasons, ranging from plain curiosity to the concern with better understanding ourselves. And it is true that here lies our first interest, our first duty, and also our first reward. Without Homer, Plato, the Bible, etc., we should not be the people that we are. Even the unread Homer, Plato, Isaiah can determine us, for they have entered into the anonymous background that has formed us and lives on in our speech. Better, of course, is Plato read than unread to enlighten us on the antecedents and constituents of our being (I am not speaking now of his philosophical validity); and a picture of Plato faithful to historical truth is better than a picture distorted by tradition or retouched by ourselves. Here we experience the joy of recognition, of a return to the origins, of salvaging what was buried under the rubble of time, of the renewal and deepening of our being. Only thus can we pierce through its invisible sedimentation, only thus can we really make what we possess our own. Of this, Goethe speaks in these famous lines:

> Wer nicht von dreitausend Jahren
> Sich weiss Rechenschaft zu geben,

Bleib' im Dunkeln unerfahren,
Mag von Tag zu leben.[2]

In giving account to ourselves, we are in our own company. Is this the limit of the interest and the understanding?

The unread Descartes determines us, whether we want it or not. The Upanishads unread cannot determine us. But perhaps they ought to? Then we ought to read them, precisely so that they can determine us. Alien tradition can be understood too, even though it takes greater effort. It is sometimes denied that we ever can properly understand the East Asian mind, or the East Asian ours. But what is meant by this is probably only that the East Asian's understanding of things Western is different from our own, and our understanding of things Eastern different from his. Some experiences with Indian and Chinese students of European philosophy tend to confirm this to me. But to understand differently is not necessarily to understand wrongly. Also, perhaps, the effort was just not great enough.

But why should the effort be made? First of all, because no significant voice in the orchestra of man should be missed. And, second, it could be that our Western inheritance is not entirely free of the need for some corrective or complement. We should not rule out that there might be something for us to learn elsewhere. Nietzsche, it is true, in "The Use and Abuse of History," warned that too much of such alien knowledge would make us unsure of ourselves. But this is perhaps just what we need. One unsettling profit we may derive from encounters with the non-Western mind could be, for example, its calling in question our very bias for history as such—the Western belief in its being integral to the nature of man. I conclude with a few remarks on this theme.

Our conviction of the essential historicity of man is itself a product of history. This makes it self-limiting rather than self-proving. At the moment when we are about to destroy the last remnants of a-historical existence left on earth, by forcing its sharers into history, we do well to remind ourselves that history is not the last word of humanness. The proclamation of change as man's genuine condition expresses a Faustian decision rather than an ontological truth.[3] To our vision, it has the full force of factual evidence on its side. Yet it is a prejudice, current only with us, that not to advance must mean to retrogress, and standstill equals decline. This is true only where progress reigns—thus true for us. But it is written nowhere that progress must reign. If it should happen

[2]He who cannot give account to himself of three thousand years—may he stay in darkness, inexperienced; may he live from day to day.
[3]Goethe, Faust I: "Nur wer sich wandelt, bleibt mit mir werwandt."

—as is not inconceivable—that its movement at last terminates in a new state of no-history (or, which comes to the same, in a rate of change slowed to imperceptibility), and the convulsions of history that brought us thither only survive in the minds of men as mythical memories, we should still be men. Those who rejoice in history may deplore such a prospect; those who suffer from history may welcome it; both will most likely regard it as a chimera. But no matter what our preference is, nothing justifies the dogmatic belief that man must always have history in order to be man. It is certain only that he must have had history first if ever he should attain a state where he needs it no more.

Our insatiable curiosity for history is perhaps nothing more than a sublime play. Possibly it is not true that we must know our whole antecedent history, and in addition that of all the other parts of mankind, in order to understand ourselves. Or, if this is true, then it is perhaps not true that we must understand ourselves in *this* sense in order to be true men. For this, the knowledge of the timeless may be more important than the understanding of the temporal, and to see himself in the light of the one may profit man more than to intepret himself by the data of the other. Who knows? But we, who have surrendered ourselves to history, and accordingly are under her whip as never men before—we have no choice. As long as we are caught in this current of perpetual event and becoming, we must, on pain of drifting blindly in it, endeavor to understand history—our own and that of all mankind. Else we have no right to our own—a right problematical enough as it is.

PART THREE

RELIGIOUS THOUGHT
OF THE
FIRST CHRISTIAN CENTURIES

13.
The Gnostic Syndrome:
Typology of its Thought,
Imagination, and Mood

Delimiting a phenomenon that exists as a manifold of diverse individuals involves the well-known circle of using the presumed unity of the many for the designation of a common name, and then using the meaning of that name to define the unity of the manifold—and hence to decide over the inclusion or exclusion of individuals. It is the paradox of, first, the evidence prescribing to us—persuasively; and, then, our concept prescribing to the evidence—normatively. In our case, this means that we must have some historical delimitation first so as to arrive at a typological one, and again the typological so as to re-assess the historical one. I shall not dwell here on the methodological problems of this hermeneutical circle—from felt unity to postulated principle of unity, and back to critically re-assigned unity: it is, with all its pitfalls, the necessity and creative risk of historical understanding, confronted as it is with the endless shadings and interpenetrations of historic phenomena. (The situation is different in other logical spheres which either permit the free fiat of definition, or offer such clearcut divisions that questions of delimitations are marginal.) Nor shall I defend here the employment, along the circle, of the "ideal type" construct which the

Originally presented at the International Colloquium on the Origins of Gnosticism at Messina in April 1966. Published with the title "Delimitation of the Gnostic Phenomenon—Typological and Historical" in *The Origins of Gnosticism*, ed. Ugo Bianchi (Leiden: E. J. Brill, 1967).

historian, at least for heuristic purposes, cannot do without. Waiving these preliminaries, I will, at this stage of cooperative international scholarship, simply assume a measure of consensus on the existence of such an entity as the gnostic phenomenon, on the spatiotemporal area in which it is located, on the body of evidence by which it is represented, and on the presence of certain pervading features which at least constitute a prima facie case for a unity of essence. On the other hand, we must be prepared to find this essence to consist in a spectrum rather than in one uniform hue, or perhaps in a nucleus surrounded by a less definite halo; and some of these shadings may well have genetic implications. Even so, phenomenology takes pride of place over genealogy, and since the historical locus is provisionally agreed upon, however subject to refinement, I begin with, and shall dwell mainly on, the typological task.

A natural starting point is the term 'gnosis' itself. Its verbal meaning, 'knowledge', is in our context specified as secret, revealed, and saving knowledge. This is to say that it is of mysteries, that it is not come by in a natural manner, and that its possession decisively alters the condition of the knower. In addition, however, it is specified by a particular *theoretical content*, the object-world of this knowledge, and this object-world significantly includes the role of knowledge itself within its scheme: The "what" of the knowledge contains the explanation of its own origin, communication, and promised effect. Indeed, the system of *universal being* which gnosis on its theoretical side expounds, is centered around the concept of gnosis itself and has thereby in its very constitution a reference to its becoming known by the individual knower. This broad metaphysical, theologico-cosmological underpinning of the saving power of 'knowledge', signalized by the appearance of the term on both the subject and object side of the system, is the first distinctive feature of gnostic speculation.

What system of reality, then, is it that thus provides for its knowledge as an intrinsic theme of itself? With this question we are inquiring into the objective content of the gnosis.

It is, first of all, a *transcendental genesis*, narrating the spiritual history of creation as a history of the upper worlds, i.e., ultimately of the Deity itself: beginning with the first beginnings, it unfolds the inner-divine drama in whose course the lower world originates.

There is, secondly, the outcome of this transcendental genesis: the existing system of the universe as a power structure which determines the actual condition of man. The emphasis here is on its stratification along a vertical axis, on the antithesis of the heights and the depths, on the distance between the terrestrial and the divine world, and the plurality of worlds in between.

The third theme, prepared by the first two and implicit in their logic, is man—his nature, and his place in both that past history and this present system: his origin 'beyond' in connection with the precosmic divine drama; his composite and sunken condition here; his true destination.

Finally, the doctrine of salvation, individual and universal: the last things answering to the first, the reversal of the fall, the return of all things to God.

Now, these themes, formally classifiable as theology, cosmology, anthropology, and eschatology, are as such shared by Gnosticism with other religious systems. What makes them uniquely gnostic in the cases where we feel moved to classify them as such?

One factor, already named, is the peculiar status of knowledge in everyone of the stages through which the metaphysical argument moves. A loss of knowledge is suffered by divinity in the primordial drama that affects part of it and modifies the condition of the whole. A lack of knowledge is at work in the arrogance and delusion of demiurgical creation and is permanently embodied in the resulting world. A want of knowledge, inflicted by the world and actively maintained by its powers, characterizes man's innerwordly existence; and a restoration of knowledge is the vehicle of salvation. Since each of these conditions follows from the preceding one, the whole can be considered as one grand *movement* of 'knowledge', in its positive and its privative moods, from the beginning of things to their end. This progressive movement constitutes the *time* axis of the gnostic world, as the vertical order of aeons and spheres constitutes its space axis. Time, in other words, is actuated by the onward thrust of a mental life: and in this thoroughly *dynamic* character which makes every episode productive of the next, and all of them phases of one total evolution, we must see another distinctive feature of Gnosticism. It is a metaphysic of pure movement and event, the most determinedly "historical" conception of universal being prior to Hegel (with whom it also shares the axiom—implicit in the ontological status of knowledge—that "substance is subject").

The dynamism is visible already in the doctrine of divinity itself which, from the repose of eternal preëxistence, is stirred into what becomes the "inward" history of creation, unfolding in a series of spiritual states of the Absolute whose primarily subjective, mental qualities become objectified, or hypostatized, in external realities—such that their succession marks the gradual progressus of the hierarchy of worlds out of the original deity. Thus, the history of creation—a history of the divine self—is *emanationist*; and, as the movement is inevitably downward, it is a history of "devolution". What is lower is later: this ontological axiom, so contrary to Hegel and any modern evolutionism,

Gnosticism shares with all the "vertical" schemes of later antiquity—with what has sometimes been called the "Alexandrian" scheme of speculation which, on the philosophical side, culminated in Plotinus. It must be noted, however, that gnostic emanationism, unlike the harmonistic one of the Neoplatonists, has a catastrophic character. The form of its progress is *crisis*, and there occur failure and miscarriage. A disturbance in the heights starts off the downward motion which continues as a drama of fall and alienation. The corporeal world is the terminal product of this epic of decline.

The pathomorphic form of gnostic emanationism directly implies another trait: its irresolubly *mythological* character. For tragedy and drama, crisis and fall, require concrete and personal agents, individual divinities—in short, mythical figures, however symbolically they may be conceived. The Plotinian descensus of Being, in some respects an analogy to the gnostic one, proceeds through the autonomous movement of impersonal concept, by an inner necessity that is its own justification. The gnostic descensus cannot do without the contingency of subjective affect and will. (This, of course, is among the major reproaches leveled by Plotinus himself against the Gnostics.) The mythological—and thus nonphilosophical—form belongs to the nature of Gnosticism: a difference not of form only but of substance. We shall see later that the mythology itself is of a peculiar type within its own genus.

The purpose of the first, precosmic and cosmogonic stage of the myth (and to have a definite purpose is characteristic of gnostic myth) is to derive from beginnings that may themselves be monistic, a dualistic result, viz., the given state of things, represented by the world and reflected in man.

It is therefore only at the cosmic stage of the universal history, and thus in gnostic cosmology, i.e., in the view of the lower universe as established by those antecedents, that dualism comes to its unequivocal expression, while it may be equivocal in the original stages of the metaphysical genealogy. Whatever the beginning, whether one, two, or three 'roots', the crisis history of original being issues into a divided state of things. With the 'cosmos', reality is clearly polarized; the towering, many-storied structure of the spheres and aeons images the width of the rift between the poles, its very multiplicity serves to express the separative power of the antidivine and thus, for the earthbound view, the remoteness from God. To 'this world', as the nethermost boundary of being, there applies the verdict of cosmic pessimism. Pronounced by man, it means that the divided state is at the same time a mixed state of things in which he himself is profoundly displaced.

With *dualism* we have touched upon a central theme in the symphony of Gnosticism. Its doctrinal elaboration is multiform and, as indicated,

admits of subtle combinations with a unitarian first principle, but it is
omnipresent in all Gnosticism as, first and foremost, a radical mood that
dominates the gnostic attitude and unites its widely diversified expressions. The dualism is between man and world, and again between the
world and God. In either case, it is a dualism of antithetical, not complementary terms, and it is basically one: that of man and world mirrors
on the plane of experience the primordial one of God and world and is
in gnostic theory deduced from it. The interpreter may hold conversely
that the transcendent doctrine of a world-*God* opposition sprang from
the immanent experience of a disunion of *man* and world, i.e., that it
reflects a human condition of alienation. In this sense, one may regard
dualism as an invariant, *existential* "first principle" of Gnosticism, as
distinct from a variable, *speculative* first principle employed in its
representation.

In the three-term configuration, man and God belong in essence
together over against the world, but are in fact separated by the world
which is the alienating, divisive agency in the gnostic view. The object
of gnostic speculation, then, is to derive these basic and experienced
polarities—the primary datum of gnostic existence—by way of genetic
myths from things that are first in theory; but also, through such genealogy and beyond mere theory, to point the way to their eventual
resolution. The myth, a conscious symbolical construction, is thus predictive by being genetic, eschatological by being explanatory, and it
takes itself to be instrumental in the salvation which its doctrine projects.
This predetermined purpose of gnostic myth dictates its conception and
actual course.

In the light of the purpose so defined, let us review once more the
successive stages of the myth and look for further revealing aspects in
their typology. The typical gnostic myth, as we have seen, starts with a
doctrine of divine transcendence in its original purity; it then traces the
genesis of the world from some primordial disruption of this blessed state,
a loss of divine integrity which leads to the emergence of lower powers
who become the makers and rulers of this world; then, as a crucial
episode in the drama, the myth recounts the creation and early fate of
man, in whom the further conflict becomes centered; the final theme, in
fact the implied theme throughout, is man's salvation, which is more
than man's as it involves the overcoming and eventual dissolving of the
cosmic system and is thus the instrument of reïntegration for the impaired godhead itself, or, the self-saving of God.

This typified abstract of gnostic myth offers the terms for our further
attention: divine transcendence, lower powers, man, salvation. Let us
briefly review them.

The transcendence of the supreme deity is stressed to the utmost degree in all gnostic theology. Topologically, he is transmundane, dwelling in his own realm entirely outside the physical universe, at immeasurable distance from man's terrestrial abode; ontologically, he is acosmic, even anticosmic: to 'this world' and whatever belongs to it he is the essentially 'other' and 'alien' (Marcion), the 'alien Life' (Mandaeans), also called the 'depth' or 'abyss' (Valentinians), even the 'not-being' (Basilides); epistemologically, because of this transcendence and otherness of his being, and since nature neither reveals nor even indicates him, he is naturally unknown (*naturaliter ignotus*), ineffable, defying predication, surpassing comprehension, and strictly unknowable. Some positive attributes and metaphors do apply to him: Light, Life, Spirit, Father, the Good—but not Creator, Ruler, Judge. Significantly, in some systems, one of his secret names is 'Man'. Mainly, the discourse about him must move in negations, and historically Gnosticism is one of the fountainheads of negative theology.

However, the Absolute is not alone, but is surrounded by an aura of eternal, graded expressions of his infinitude, partial aspects of his perfection, hypostatized into quasi-personal beings with highly abstract names and all together forming the hierarchy of the divine realm (the Pleroma). The progressus, or emanation, of this inner manifold from the primal ground, a kind of self-differentiation of the Absolute, is sometimes described in terms of subtle, spiritual dialectics, more often in rather naturalistic, e.g., sexual, terms. Among the tenuously mythological entities which thus arise, some more concrete ones stand out with definite roles in the further evolution of the transcendental drama: 'Man' as an eternal, precosmic principle (sometimes even identified with the First Being himself); 'Sophia', usually the 'youngest' of the Aeons; and 'Christ' or some similar restoring and saving agency. An extensive Pleroma speculation of this kind is the mark of advanced systems, but some degree of manifold on the upper reaches of being is requisite for all gnostic metaphysics as it provides the condition for divine passibility and failure on which the movement into creation and alienation depends. The paradoxical combination of extreme transcendence with partial fallibility is one of the characteristics of gnostic theology and explains its readiness, or rather its need, to make use of the forms of polytheistic myth in the service of a preponderantly monotheistic conception.

The downward movement that breaches the self-containment of the divine world may be occasioned by the action of dark forces from without (implying a preëxistent dualism) or, more typically, by an internal crisis and transgression in the divine realm itself (thus providing the cause for an evolving dualism). Protagonist of the fall is female Sophia or male Anthropos: either can personify the affected part of divinity and thus become chief *dramatis persona*. On the whole, the Sophia line seems the more richly developed. What matters is that the descensus set in motion by either agency must run its course even while the upper powers try to reverse it; and the counter-play of these two trends throughout the further process, making for a prolonged sequence of moves and countermoves, constitutes a main theme of gnostic narrative. In its imaginative elaboration, we observe a vivid sense for the use of stratagems on both sides: there is an element of cunning and outsmarting even in the strategy of salvation. With this trait again, Gnosticism stays unblushingly in the tradition of pagan polytheism, which blends curiously with the Jewish-Christian conception of divine sublimity.

Passing to the lower powers (whatever their origin), their eminent personification is the *Demiurge*. This figure of an imperfect, blind, or evil creator is a gnostic symbol of the first order. In his general conception he reflects the gnostic contempt for the world; in his concrete description he often is a clearly recognizable caricature of the Old Testament God: of this we shall have to say something later. Pride, ignorance, and malevolence of the Creator are recurring themes in gnostic tales, as are his humbling and outwitting by the higher powers bent on thwarting his designs. However, over the whole range of gnostic mythologizing, his image varies, and there are milder versions in which he is more misguided than evil, thus open to correction and remorse, even to final redemption. But he is always *a problematical and never a venerable* figure. His place may be taken by a plurality of powers (e.g., the collective 'Seven'); but the complete absence of any such symbol for an inferior or degraded cause of the world, or of its particular order, or of its matter, would make one greatly hesitate to accept a doctrine as gnostic.

The Valentinian version, the subtlest of all, depicts the Demiurge as trying vainly to imitate the perfect order of the Pleroma with his physical one, and its eternity with the counterfeit substitute of time—thus adding to the parody of the Biblical creator that of the Platonic demiurge.

With the term "imitation" we have touched on another significant gnostic theme. It occurs first (somewhat faintly) in the cosmic planning at large, but its chief place is in the creation of man. The copying of ideal archetypes by the demiurge was a Platonic teaching, and like the whole doctrine of 'forms' it meant to confer upon the 'copy' a measure of validity together with its necessary imperfection: its likeness, "as far as possible", to the original is its share in perfection and justifies its being. In Gnosticism, on the contrary, the motif is turned into that of illicit imitation (counterfeiting) which is at once presumptuous and bungling. Homage is turned into opprobrium. Thus when the archons say "Come, let us make a man after the image we have seen", Biblical and Platonic lore are perverted at the same time, and the resulting *imago Dei*-character of created man, far from being a straight metaphysical honor, assumes a dubious, if not outright sinister, meaning. The motive for the archontic resolve is either simple envy and ambition, or the more calculating one of entrapping divine substance in their lower world by the lure of a seemingly congenial receptacle that will become its most secure bond. At any rate, the final composition of man, though in the main an archontic product, includes a 'spiritual' element from beyond.

This presence of transcendent spirit in psychophysical man, variously explained in gnostic speculation (either as a success of the nether powers, or a ruse of the upper ones), but always in itself a paradoxical, "unnatural" fact, becomes henceforth the fulcrum of the soteriological drama. The spirit's innerworldly existence is as such a state of exile, the result of primeval divine tragedy, and the immersion in soul and body is the terminal form of that exile—but at the same time the chance for its retrieval. For the archons, on the other hand, the inclusion of this transmundane element is vital to their system: hence they must resist at all cost its extrication from cosmic captivity which the upper powers seek for the regaining of divine wholeness.

Some important points here entailed should be made explicit. One is the identity, or consubstantiality, of man's innermost self with the supreme and transmundane God, himself often called 'Man': utter metaphysical elevation coincides, in the acosmic essence of man, with utter cosmic alienation. Another point is the conception of the created world as a power system directed at the enslavement of this transmundane self: everything from the grand cosmic design down to man's psychophysical constitution serves this fearful purpose—such is the uniquely gnostic *Weltanschauung*. A third point is that the chief means of that enslavement is 'ignorance' actively inflicted and maintained, i.e., the alienation of the self from itself as its prevailing "natural" condition; and the fourth point, consequently, is that the chief means of extrication, the counteraction to the power of the world, is the communication of knowledge.

With the last point we have returned to our first theme, that of 'knowledge', now considered in its soteriological aspect, and thus in its bearing on the fortunes of mankind. The soteriological function of knowledge, which is rooted in the general ontology of the system, leads —in continuation of transcendent prehistory—to a conception of *human history* as the growing ingression of knowledge in the generations of man, and this requires *revelation* as a necessary vehicle of its progress. The need for revelation is inherent in the paralyzed innercosmic condition of the captive spirit, and its occurrence alters that condition in its decisive respect, that of 'ignorance'. Ignorance, to the Gnostics, is not a neutral state, nor simply a privation, the mere absence of knowledge, but a positive affect of the spirit, a force of its own, operative in the very terms of man's existence and preventing his discovering the truth for himself, even his realizing his state of ignorance as such. I need only mention the whole image-cycle of sleep, drunkenness, self-forgetfulness of the soul. Divine revelation, then, or the 'call', breaking through this power of ignorance, is itself already part of salvation. Beginning with Adam, thwarted time and again by the resistance of the worldly powers, it continues in a series of messengers through the course of history to a final consummation. Gnosticism indeed conceived of one pervading pattern and meaning of world history, with a definite goal and a particular mode of progress. Contrary to Jewish apocalyptics, kingdoms and nations have no place in it, only souls. Yet the stake is all mankind, and beyond mankind the total order of things, even the relief of suffering deity. The 'knowing ones', to be sure, are always a minority, but the scope of the process is truly ecumenical in space and time.

But note that mankind is not responsible for its plight and for the necessity of divine intervention. There is no fall or original sin of Adam: where he is the first recipient of revelation (as is often the case), he is this not as transgressor but as victim—directly of archontic oppression, and ultimately of the primordial fall to which the world's existence and his own are due. Insofar as guilt is involved, it is not his but that of the Aeons who caused the disruption of the higher order; it is not human but divine, arising before, and not in creation. This difference from the Jewish and Christian position goes to the heart of the gnostic phenomenon. Among other things, it made Gnosticism unable to assimilate any serious meaning of the incarnation and the cross.

And the content of the saving knowledge? Fundamentally it is nothing else but the transcendent history itself, because this either displays or implies all the enlightening truth that the world withholds and salvation requires: "the knowledge who we were, what we have become; where we were, wherein we have been thrown; whereto we speed, wherefrom we are redeemed; what is birth, and what rebirth" (Exc. Theod. 78:2). Gnostic myth is always, and essentially, the argument for the importance of its own communication, and also an account of its supranatural source. By virtue of both, revealed content and revelatory source, it claims saving power for itself *qua known*: it *is*, in short, the *gnosis*.

However, although this knowledge of truth is as such held to be liberating as it restores the awakened spirit to its native powers, it usually also includes a body of more practical—we might say, technical—information, an instruction on what to do: the 'knowledge of the way', i.e., of the sacraments to be performed now, of the 'names' to be employed later when the ascending spirit meets the powers after leaving the body at death, and whatever ritual or ethical preparation may assure this future passage. The Naassene psalm even defines 'gnosis' in this instrumental sense, pure and simple, as 'the secrets of the way'. This is an adequate definition only when the 'secrets' are understood to epitomize the theoretical totality of the system as well, as indeed they do: the ascent doctrine in its details, wherever such are given, spells out once more the topography and theological meaning of the gnostic universe, as the itinerary and adventures of the soul on this occasion lead through the complete order in reversal of the primordial fall.

At this point we break off the typified abstract of gnostic thought, incomplete as it necessarily is. Yet something, we feel, is missing which not even the most complete morphology of objective content can catch and which yet belongs to the typology of the gnostic phenomenon. I am thinking of such situationally determined things as the mood or tone of gnostic statement; the style of gnostic mythologizing as distinct from the content thereof; and the relation to other positions insofar as such relation is not an extraneous consideration but an element in the intrinsic meaning of the gnostic position itself. Let me make a few remarks on these points.

The gnostic mood, apart from the deadly earnest befitting a doctrine of salvation, has an element of rebellion and protest about it. Its rejection of the world, far from the serenity or resignation of other nonworldly creeds, is of peculiar, sometimes vituperative violence, and we generally note a tendency to extremism, to excess in fantasy and feeling. We suspect that the dislocated metaphysical situation of which gnostic myth tells had its counterpart in a dislocated real situation: that the crisis-form of its symbolism reflects a historical crisis of man himself. Such a crisis, to be sure, shows in other phenomena of the period as well, Jewish, Christian, and pagan, many of which betray a deeply agitated state of mind, a great tension of the soul, a disposition toward radicalism, hyperbolic expectations, and total solutions. But the gnostic temper is of all the least restrained by the power of traditions, which is rather treats with peculiar *impietas* in the cavalier use it makes of them: this lack of piety, so curiously blended with avid interest in ancient lore, must be counted among the physiognomic traits of Gnosticism. I refer to what I wrote many years ago about the revolutionary and angry element in Gnosticism.[1] A subtraction of this element, though it might leave conceptual doctrine unaffected, would not leave the gnostic essence what it

---

[1]*Gnosis und spätantiker Geist*, I (1934; 3rd ed. 1964), pp. 214–51.

is: historical or ethnological parallels to particular gnostic concepts, lacking that element, are to that extent less compelling than the mere propositional likeness might suggest.

On the other hand, against this immoderate emotionalism, we must observe the non-naïveté of gnostic myth: with all its crudities it is a work of sophistication, consciously constructed to convey a message, even to present an argument, and deliberately made up of the pirated elements of earlier myth. It is, in short, secondary and derivative mythology, its artificiality somehow belonging to its character. Some speculative intention, explanatory or other, is intrinsic already in primary myth, where the mythical language is the natural and only medium of thought as well as of its expression: already Aristotle remarked that mythology is the first form of theory, a precursor of philosophy. But original myth had no choice in the matter, thought and its mode of expression being then inseparably one, with no alternative of independent abstraction open to it. Also, imagination there originally determines the concatenation of thought (the "reasoning") rather than that prior thought would enlist imagination in its service. In the gnostic case, on the other hand, one has the feeling that myth is a chosen style of speculation, vying with—perhaps even reactive to—that of philosophy, which is in the field as another possible choice: both philosophy *and* earlier, naïve myth are presupposed as ready-made materials. As a result, in using the latter to *express* its own, preconceived *idea,* gnostic myth is often contrivedly allegorical rather than authentically "symbolical" (in the primary, nondeliberate sense of symbol). Hence the easy shifting of images for the same motif, the many variations on a common theme. Genuinely original as this gnostic theme itself is, with its disturbing interpretation of a disturbed reality, there is something unmistakably "second-hand" about the means of its representation. But then again, there is great ingenuity in adapting the borrowed detail to the grand gnostic design which in all the extravagance of embroidery is never lost sight of. All this is possible only in a historically "late", distinctly literate, and thoroughly syncretistic situation, which thus belongs to the phenomenology of Gnosticism, over and above its doxography. This situation includes the freefloating availability of traditions that are no longer binding, but pregnant with redefinable meaning; and those who availed themselves of them in the gnostic manner were "intellectuals" (half-educated, perhaps) who knew what they were about.

From this free and on the whole dispassionate, if high-handed, use of tradition we must distinguish the heavily polemical and at the same time most extensive use made of Jewish material. Its outstanding example, of course, is the degradation of the Old Testament God to the inferior, obtuse, and repulsive Demiurge, or the distribution of his names among the even lower archons—a truly unique demotion in the history of religions, and performed with considerable venom and obvious relish. This downgrading is matched by the upgrading of whatever came to hand for this purpose in the Biblical tale—notably the serpent which, as the first bringer of 'knowledge' in defiance of the creator, turns from seducer to a revered symbol of the acosmic, spiritual power that works for the awakening of its captive kin in the world. The continuation of the revelatory line thus started may include such Biblically rejected figures as Cain, Esau, and others, who as bearers of the pneumatic heritage down the ages form a secret lineage of gnosis and are therefore persecuted by the world-God, whereas his favorites, Abel, Jacob, etc., represent the unenlightened majority. The same value-reversal is practiced with regard to the Law, the prophets, the status of the chosen people—all along the line, one might say, with a very few exceptions, such as the misty figure of Seth. No tolerant eclecticism here.

What we are to make of this remarkable mixture of intimacy and antipathy, from which only a few gnostic voices are free, has become a major issue in the determination of the nature and origin of the whole movement. If it means inner-Jewish origin, as many nowadays hold, it implies a major revolt within Judaism. This cannot be ruled out a priori, but it lacks support in independent evidence and, to my mind, also psychological verisimilitude—considering the antagonism to the Jewish people as a whole, a kind of metaphysical antisemitism, which precisely the sources most lavish in the use of Jewish motifs (at the same time the most archaic ones) evince. Safer is the statement that Gnosticism originated in *close vicinity* and in partial reaction to Judaism. This is in accord not only with the evidence (the new sources strongly reinforce the impression of ambivalent proximity to Judaism) but also with general historical circumstances: the Jewish presence in the contemporary world was ubiquitous and powerful, its "fringes" were everywhere, its claims exorbitant; it was the only religion with an extensive, codified literature, parts of which were well known, and with continuing literary activity—indeed the only religious force in the cultural space worth taking issue with. Surely no new religious movement in the Semitic world could ignore this towering and unique fact. Also the this-worldly spirit of the Hebrew religion made it the natural target of gnostic dislike; the anti-Judaism is one form of expression of the anti-cosmic spirit as such, i.e., of the gnostic revolt against the world and its gods.[2]

[2]Incidentally, the Jewish information of most Gnostics seems not to extend beyond the book of Genesis, usually not even beyond the Flood. This would be what interested outsiders, or half-converts, would read or hear of first. Jews there

It was inevitable that in our quest for a gnostic typology we passed from definable doctrine to the less definable but nonetheless obtrusive matters of mood, style, and attitudinal relation to other thought. These involve in one way or another the factual situation in which gnostic thought was born and carried on—in other words: its unique historical *locus* which, it turns out, injects itself into the typology itself. Typological delimitation, though it may set out as a mere synthesis of thought content (of objective theory), would miss its own goal in complete abstraction from the historical reference. It is the irreducible situational factor which makes Gnosticism the essentially *dialectical* phenomenon that it is, and which qualifies all comparison with "doxographically" similar mythologumena and theologumena from other spaces and times.[3] The situation is that of the hellenistic-oriental world of the first Christian centuries: can one imagine the phenomenon anywhere else? Classical, fifth century A.D. Orphicism, e.g., certainly anticipates important facets of Gnosticism, perhaps bequeathed them to it, but it lacks, among other things, the *temper* and the comprehensiveness of cosmic derogation (projected in the figure of the Demiurge) which Gnosticism breathes. Who can doubt that it is in part the freshness of rediscovery, and the ruthlessness of deployment, of such milder antecedents that give Gnosticism its individuality?

As to the much debated question of "pre-Christian Gnosticism"— undecidable on the present evidence—I personally consider its importance overrated. What matters is that Gnosticism is roughly contemporaneous with the infancy of Christianity (certainly not later, witness Simon Magus; possibly earlier); that it is different and independent from it, but with natural points of contact, answering to the same human situation; and that from the start there was vigorous interpenetration of the two which provoked the well-known reactions in the Church.

Needless to say, our typology is an ideal construct and covers a whole spectrum of possible choices for the gnostic mind. Not all of its differentiae are found in all instances of the genus. How many and what combinations of them *must* be found to class the instance within the genus, must be determined from case to case, and often more "by ear", musically as it were, than by abstract rule. The schema I have here drawn is, I believe, represented in fair completeness and unambiguity by

---

certainly were amongst the Gnostics. The author of the Book of Baruch most probably was one: significantly, he counts Moses (and 'the prophets') among the historic messengers of truth, contrary to most systems, which exclude Moses from their prophetology.

[3]These, of course, will still be valuable. Professor Ugo Bianchi's extremely interesting ethnological findings come under this head.

most of the "heresies" from Simon Magus to Mani, as also by the Mandaeans. But there are borderline cases where the record is ambiguous and classification can become controversial. To name an outstanding example: Marcion has no 'transcendental genesis', no divine, precosmic drama, no mythology of the upper worlds, no speculation in general, no consubstantiality of soul and God—and not even the concept of a saving gnosis (he is a *pistikos*, not a *gnostikos*). The last fact alone would seem to put him squarely outside the gnostic sphere, considering the central role we ourselves accorded this element in its definition. Yet I would claim him for Gnosticism, "in spirit" if not "in letter": his contraposition, in its uncompromising vigor, of the unknown, otherwordly Father and the contemptible Creator, and the rebelliously ascetic refusal to comply with a wholly ungodly nature, are *in this milieu* of so unmistakeably gnostic vintage that we must regard him as a product of the gnostic spirit, its classic expression even in what he accepts, though completely sovereign in what he ignores of it, more determined than any of them to be a Christian of the Book: a gnostic maverick, if you wish.

Similar flexibility should be applied to other marginal cases, such as the Hermetic literature where, e.g., the polemical venom is absent and the dualism, even in the dualistic parts, is toned down, but where a sufficiently significant cluster of ideas (Anthropos, gnosis, ascent doctrine) argues for admittance into the fold. On the other hand, I do not think that any of the Qumran texts, even with what there is of dualism in them, qualifies for inclusion in the gnostic category.

This must suffice for the typological abstract I had in mind. All I wish to say in conclusion is that, once we move beyond the "hard core" of gnostic thinkers and into the region of the half-tones which surrounds all historic phenomena (in our case extending into parts of the New Testament), everything is up to such impalpable things as morphological sensitivity, empathy, and what I have before referred to, with great liberty, as a musical ear.

14.

The 'Hymn of the Pearl': Case Study of a Symbol, and the Claims for a Jewish Origin of Gnosticism

This is a polemic. The exploration of Gnosticism happily still offers the invigorating opportunity for those dramatic clashes of main interpretation which in more settled fields of historical inquiry have yielded to the paler and sometimes tedious wrangle about finer points. And although Professor G. Quispel's paper on "Gnosticism and the New Testament" to which mine responds is not before the reader here,[1] the points of method and principle I address myself to sufficiently transcend the particulars of the dispute to permit my side of the argument to be read by itself as exemplifying a certain conception of these matters in general. My argument consists of two parts. Part I is devoted to a refutation of Professor Quispel's views on the Hymn of the Pearl[2] and is also meant to serve as a methodological preface to the much larger theme of Part II, which deals with the alleged Jewish origins of Gnosticism.

Originally presented at the 100th meeting of the Society of Biblical Literature, December 1964. Published with the title "Response to G. Quispel's 'Gnosticism and the New Testament'" in *The Bible in Modern Scholarship*, ed. J. Philip Hyatt (Nashville, Tenn.: Abingdon Press, 1965).

[1]It appears, with R. McL. Wilson's and my responses, in *The Bible in Modern Scholarship*.

[2]The text, with commentary, of the Hymn of the Pearl can be found in my *The Gnostic Religion* (Boston: Beacon Press, 1963), pp. 112–29.

I

Quispel holds that the Hymn of the Pearl in the apocryphal Acts of Thomas is (a) not gnostic at all, (b) orthodox Christian tinged with Judaistic colors, and (c) based upon the parable of the pearl in Matt. 13:45-46, which reads: "Again, the kingdom of heaven is like a merchant in search of fine pearls, who, on finding one pearl of great value, went and sold all that he had and bought it." Of this, Quispel says, The Hymn is "a poetical amplification and illustration." Maybe it is, but then we must ask: what kind of amplification? What does it do with the given? Merely expand, or also add to it? Merely add, or also modify it? Merely modify, or perhaps entirely remake it? Each of these contingencies is a possibility. For it hardly needs saying that we have to distinguish between the constancy of a symbolical term (image) and the variability of meanings which it may be used to express. The meaning must in each case be determined from the context in which it figures; and if we should find the same symbolical term, such as the "pearl," serving two significantly different meaning contexts, then we must turn our attention to those contexts and ask how *they* stand to each other, e.g., whether one is an outgrowth of the other, or both are variations of one generic theme, or whether they are substantially heterogeneous. And when found to be heterogeneous, then we may sometimes, from an immanent comparison of two such contexts, form a judgment as to which is the more natural habitat of the simile in question: where it seems more genuine, more at home, in more adequate and congenial surroundings, allowing it as it were to spread its wings and unfold its full implications; or, seen from the standpoint of the whole: where the imagery in question is crucial and where perhaps a mere casual choice; where integral to the total meaning and where easily interchangeable with other similes. And this we must try to determine by pure morphological comparison of the two contexts, irrespective (within reason) of the chronological accidents of surviving testimony: so that it *can* happen that the earlier witness, e.g., that of the Gospel, turns out to represent a more derivative and attenuated use of the simile in question than a later representation we happen to possess. At least this is what the less compelling version *might* indicate: an atrophied version; though it may as well indicate the subsequent intervention of a new force which from such scanty cues freely and arbitrarily created the different, compelling version. In either case, this latter would represent a genuine conception of its own; and, in the matter under review, this may turn out to be what is commonly called a gnostic version.

With these considerations in mind, let me confront the Hymn of the Pearl first, not with the older source, the Gospel, but with one slightly later than itself, viz., the allegory of the pearl in the Manichaean *Kephalaia*. There[3] the simile is spelled out to the last dot on the i's, for Mani was anything if not explicit; and in the bright light of his didactic explicitness one realizes that in the Hymn the symbolism of the pearl itself, though vital to the story, is rather presupposed than really developed: but presupposed it is with its full connotations. This the later source makes clear, not the earlier, however much the historian would prefer it the other way around.

I summarize the extensive Manichaean allegory ("On the Holy Church") thus: the raindrop falls from on high into the sea; down there, in an oyster shell, it forms into a pearl; divers descend into the deep and bring up this pearl; the divers hand it on to the merchants; the merchants give it to the kings. Thus far the metaphor. Then comes the explanation, a kind of allegorical dictionary, symbol by symbol, as follows: the *raindrop* is "the spoil that was carried off [in the beginning, namely], the living Soul" (i.e., that part of the god Man which was lost to the powers of darkness in the primordial battle and swallowed up by them—the one "soul" now dispersed in the world); the *oyster shell* is "the flesh of mankind in which the soul is gathered and laid up" as pearl (the pearl, therefore, is the specifically human, redeemable form in which the incarnated soul exists in the world); the *divers* are "the apostles of God" (such as Mani himself), sent down for the pearl; the *merchants* are "the luminaries of the heavens" (i.e., mainly sun and moon, which in the Manichaean myth are conveyors of souls from this to the other world and thus a link in the chain of salvation); lastly, the *kings and nobles* to whom the pearl is finally transmitted, are "the Aeons of the Greatness" (i.e., the world of light from which the pearl came and to which it is now restored).

Thus far the Manichaean exposition, to which I may just add the key for one more term of the symbolic code: the *"sea"*—quite fittingly the element in which pearls are found, but having, besides, its own fixed code-meaning as the *world of matter and darkness* into which the divine has sunk. So well-attested is this symbol of the Sea or the Waters throughout gnostic literature that I can spare myself examples.[4] But I mention it here to throw light on the otherwise gratuitous addition, in the Hymn, of the "sea" as abode of the pearl to "Egypt," itself a wide-

---

[3]A. Böhlig and H. J. Polotsky (ed. and tr.), *Kephalaia*, Kap. LXXXIII, Stuttgart, 1940, p. 204.

[4]Cf. *The Gnostic Religion*, pp. 117–18, and the references under "Wasser" in the Index to *Gnosis und spätantiker Geist* I, 3rd ed., Göttingen, 1964, p. 444.

spread gnostic symbol for the world of matter: landlocked as the Prince's itinerary seems to be, the "sea" was called for by gnostic usage, by the authentic associations of the pearl image, and also as the only dwelling place for the fearful serpent who guards the pearl, the great dragon of primordial chaos which from times immemorial has been associated with the waters of the deep and the world-girdling ocean (no relation of the small, intellectual serpent of the paradise story). But why this grim guard over the pearl, the fierce resistance to letting it go? The whole Manichaean myth is an answer to this question, but so again are many gnostic myths long before Mani, once the equation of the pearl with the fallen and engulfed portion of divinity, i.e. with the totality of our spiritual selves, is recognized: the presence of this alien element is vital to the cause of the archons—if not to their own survival, at least to that of their work. As a Mandaen text puts it: "The treasurers of this world assembled and said 'Who has carried away the pearl which illumined the perishable house? In the house which it left the walls cracked and collapsed.' "[5]

Finally, lest it be objected that all this came after the Hymn, I add one piece of earlier evidence. The Naassenes as quoted by Hippolytus speak of the "live" elements in the universe—"words and minds and men"— as "the pearls that are the progeny of the Formless one cast[6] into the formation" (Refut. V 8, 32).[7]

---

[5]Left Ginza III 8: Mark Lidzbarski, Ginza. Der Schatz oder das Grosse Buch der Mandäer, Göttingen, 1925, p. 517. For the more extreme view, held also by Mani, that the very life of the archons, not only the continuance of their creation, depends on the retention of this element, see the gnostic teaching recorded by Epiphanius, Panar. 40, 2: "They say that the Soul is the food of the archons and powers without which they cannot live, because she is the dew from above and gives them strength." We see how consistent the imagery is: the "dew from above" is the "dew of light" which according to the Ophites fell from the overflow of the (female) "Holy Spirit" into the waters below, whence it assumed a body, and which to extract again from the nether powers is the saving work of the Christ (Irenaeus, adv. haer. I 30): here we have the "raindrop" of the (later) Manichaean pearl-allegorism still really "falling" in a movement of its own, as behooves the image, while the adaptation to the Manichaean myth of the primordial war had to make it, somewhat incongruously, a victim of violence—"the spoil carried off in the beginning": Mani, or his disciple, here as elsewhere slightly recasts an earlier gnostic imagery. But as the "hurling" of the pearls in the Naassene example shows (cf. next footnote), the violent picture alternated, already before Mani, with that of "sinking."

[6] ἐρριμένους from ῥίπτω: flung, hurled—a rather violent term, recalling the που ἐνεβλήθημεν of the Valentinian formula in Exc. Theod. 78, 2 "whereinto we have been thrown." Cf. also Hibil's lament "How long shall I pour living water . . . into the muddy water? . . . how long shall I abandon pearls to the perishable . . . ? When will at last this world come to an end?" (M. Lidzbarski [ed. & tr.], Das Johannesbuch der Mandäer, Giessen, 1915, p. 197).

[7]This is offered as the exegesis of an apocryphal logion, viz., "If you ate dead things and yet made (of them) live things, what might you not make once you eat live things?" which is also found in the Gospel of Thomas, but there in a stunted

"Formation" ($\pi\lambda\acute{a}\sigma\mu a$, as in the Gospel of Truth) denotes the material creation; the Unformed ($\dot{a}\chi a\rho a\kappa\tau\acute{\eta}\rho\iota\sigma\tau o\varsigma$) is the highest deity, First Man, whose lowered image, second Adam, subjected to shape ($\kappa\epsilon\chi a\rho a\kappa\tau\eta\rho\iota\sigma\mu\acute{\epsilon}\nu o\varsigma$) and enclosed in the earthly formation ($\pi\lambda\acute{a}\sigma\mu a\ \chi\omega\ddot{\iota}\kappa\acute{o}\nu$), is "the God that inhabits the flood" (Ps. 29:10), immersed in the "many waters" of "much-divided mortal becoming," from which his voice cries up to the Unformed one, his unfallen original, Primal Man (Hippol. V 8, 14 f.). This, in the final analysis, is the "pearl cast into the formation"—*one* pearl in essence, as the god sunken in the waters is one according to the theological myth.

Here, then, is one coherent "meaning context" for the pearl symbol and thus one candidate for the office of key to the Hymn. Let's call it "context A." Our next step must be to determine the meaning context of the NT parable, which Quispel claims to be the key, and our next then to determine which of the two (if they are two) better fits and unlocks the story of the Hymn.

Now the parable of the pearl in Matt. 13:45 is one in a long string of parables about the kingdom of heaven: the sown field, the mustard grain, the leaven, the treasure, the pearl. Directly preceding it is that which likens the kingdom to "a treasure hidden in a field which a man found and covered up; then in his joy he goes and sells all that he has and buys that field." The pearl parable, apart from omitting "field" and "hidden," makes the following variations in the metaphor; "merchant" for man, "searching" for (perhaps) accidental finding, "pearl" for treasure unspecified. Is the last switch significant? Hardly, for the merchant is said to search for "fine pearls" (in the plural), obviously signifying precious objects as such, and then to find one object more precious than all the rest: no associations peculiar to "pearl," as distinct from "treasure" in general, are called into play. Nor is there a suggestion that the pearl is where it should not be, that it got there by some inimical fate and must be rescued hence and restored to its right place and owners; nor that the merchant was *sent* for that or any purpose affecting the pearl's condition: his own salvation is the issue. And so "the one

---

and unintelligible form, to wit "In the days when you ate dead things you made them alive. When you are in the Light, what will you do?" (82, 19–22). Clearly in this rendering the logion, so perfectly clear in the Naassene rendering, is ruined: the parallelism is destroyed, the contrapuntal argument has vanished. The saying has literally become pointless, since its point consisted in the double use of the idea of "eating," and that idea has now been dropped from the second half of the statement. I mention this merely in passing as an instance of the very doubtful value which the *Gospel of Thomas*, as presently extant, has as a source for apocryphal logia: it strengthens the suspicion one has in many other instances where we have no second tradition to compare with, viz., that their mysterious obscurity is due not to profundity of meaning but to plain, dumb textual corruption.

pearl" just stands (as does the "treasure") for the surpassing *value* of that which the finder will own when he is wise enough to acquire it: a place in kingdom come—a good bargain for the price of all the treasures of the world.

This, then, is the meaning context for the pearl simile in the parable—let's call it "context B." And now we can ask and answer a number of plain questions.

(1) Are contexts A and B significantly different? They surely are. One is the context of the messianic kingdom to come, the other that of the lost and retrieved portion of God.

(2) To which of the two is the Hymn closer? Surely to context A, that represented by the Manichaean, Mandaean, and Naassene examples where the symbolism of the pearl is so richly unfolded and so fully utilized: all that the Hymn story has in excess of the Gospel parable (the prince being sent, the pearl's location far from the heavenly land, down in the sea, in alien custody, jealously guarded by hostile powers, difficult to rescue and finally to bring home, etc.) are without exception covered by the other context.

(3) This context A, which step by step fits the narrative of the Hymn —is it, or is it not, gnostic? It surely is, by a convention of speech I see no reason to subvert; but by whatever name we choose to call it, ortho-dox-Christian it is certainly not. Incidentally, it is with respect to this kind of context that competent Iranologists claim an Iranian background, or at least a contributory Iranian influence,[8] and I do not see good rea-sons for non-Iranologists (be it Scholem or Quispel or myself) to dismiss that claim lightly and summarily—as little, I hasten to add, as I would advocate at other points a like dismissal of expert Judaistic claims. Both, of course, and others perhaps as well, are mutually compatible when properly understood, especially in the case of Judaism which was itself so wide open to Iranian influences and may often have been the channel for their transmission. What we must beware of in these championships of causes is the fallacy of exclusiveness, the lure of fashion, and the hasty identification of any one with "the origin" of Gnosticism. This applies also to the present Judaistic mood of which I have to say something in the second part of this paper. But let me first finish our exercise in the model example, the pearl symbol, because it so well illustrates points of method vital in the study of Gnosticism.

(4) The next question would concern the genetic relationship between the two contexts: can one be considered a derivate from the other by way of immanent development? Here I can only, once more, record my con-viction that they are really heterogeneous, of different pedigrees, each an

[8]A small point: the opponent of Iranian background must explain the partiality for Parthia shown in the Hymn.

original conception of its own and neither reducible to the other in point of genesis as well as meaning.

(5) But this still leaves room for the question of whether the *pearl simile* (given the well-known mobility of coined symbols) might not have migrated from one context to the other, granted the prior existence of the contexts themselves; and if so, which side would more probably be the borrower in such a transfer. Now if we compare the full-fledged and vital role of the pearl simile in the gnostic context[9] with its limited and casual role in the Gospel context,[10] then, much rather than see in the former an outgrowth from that slender and differently pointed cue, we might see in the latter a faint and vestigial echo of the former, i.e., of a fuller symbolism already abroad at the time: in which case we must also allow the meaning context which alone gives it full scope—the gnostic context—a contemporary existence with the logion. I say, not that I do assume this, but that I find it easier to assume than a certain alternative. Easier still (too easy perhaps to the taste of some) it is to accept a mere coincidence of metaphor, seeing that the pearl *is* after all a thing of prized value and beauty and might just on that account (the only one utilized in the parable) have been picked by Jesus, without prompting from a symbolic tradition. Most difficult I find it to imagine the process suggested by Quispel whereby in effect the parable in Matthew would become the source not only for the Hymn in the Acta Thomae but for the whole spread of symbolical language centered around the pearl through Naassene, Mandaean, Manichaean literature—surely an overload of consequences for a modest impromptu not even especially emphasized in its original company. Not that such a process is *per se* impossible *as a feat of exegesis*: the Gnostics amply demonstrate what they can do in this respect. But Quispel was not thinking of such fanciful exegesis, but of orthodox amplification and illustration—which simply will not do.[11] And that other kind, the exegetical alchemy which *might* have transmuted the pearl of the parable into the extensive sym-

[9]Let us recall what, in addition to the mere preciousness of a gem, qualified the pearl in particular to become the symbol of the lost divine soul in the gnostic scheme: the purity of its white lustre in contrast to the darkness of its natural surroundings; the coarseness of its animal shell; its immersion in the waters of the deep; the dangers of bringing it up. And, indeed, whenever "pearl" is used as simile for the "soul," it is with the connotation of the lost pearl.

[10]Which makes use of just one, and for that matter the most interchangeable aspect of the pearl: its preciousness (and perhaps smallness?), which other gems supply just as well.

[11]Unfortunately for his thesis, not even the fanciful exegesis, when we do find it practiced in support of the gnostic pearl symbol, happens to turn to *this* logion: the Naassenes (Hippol. V 8, 33) quote Matt. 7:6 "do not throw the pearls before the swine" in connection with "the pearls of the Unformed one flung into the formation." Generally, the "lost sheep" serves the Gnostics as scriptural reference for the lost portion of divinity.

bolism of our texts? (We have no evidence that it did, but it admittedly might.) Well, this once again would *presuppose* the meaning context which could inspire and guide such a transmutation, supplying the intention in whose service its ingenuity would be employed—the gnostic context, in short. And once we grant this as a living force, we might even credit it, *horrible dictu*, with the invention of some of its own symbols.

The point of this discussion is still the same I tried to make long ago in my first study of Gnosticism: that it is the meaning context, taken in its wholeness and integrity, which matters, and not the traffic in single symbols, figures, and names. With this I leave the pearl and for the remainder of this paper briefly comment on the Judaic theme, on whose much larger terrain some findings of the limited case study may prove pertinent.

II

Let me first mark the area of agreement. On one point there can surely be no quarrel: the Gnostics, as a matter of plain fact, made liberal use of Jewish material; they must therefore have been acquainted with it; and in some cases this knowledge and use extends to Jewish mystical thought currents that ran alongside the more official and better known mainstream of biblical and rabbinic and even apocalyptic Judaism. This last point has been effectively established by G. Scholem. But even without this valuable addition to what had been known or mainly considered before, the abundance of OT exegesis alone is evidence of a proximity, even a fascination with Jewish themes, that could not be, and in fact never was, overlooked. Thus I am not sure whose "idle talk" about Gnosticism having "nothing in common with Judaism" Quispel deems to have been stopped "once for all" by the results of Scholem's investigations. I personally can only voice agreement when Quispel speaks of certain things in Gnosticism being "*derived* from a Jewish 'milieu,'" of its "owing not a little to Judaism," even of "a strong *influence* of Jewish conceptions," etc. (my italics). And, of course, I wholeheartedly agree with his "on the other hand"—*my* original thesis, after all: that Gnosticism is a religion of its own,[12] dominated by the idea of a tragic split within the Deity and the concept of the fallen God (which he rightly terms "the real issue of Gnostic theology"), and his underscoring of how

---

[12]Precisely this, and what follows, was the view I expounded as early as 1934 in *Gnosis und spätantiker Geist*, vol. I, as a novel conception against the prevailing *syncretistic* views of Gnosticism. It is gratifying to find this once heretical view now become so general that it can be voiced from a platform shared with me without there seeming a need any longer to connect it explicitly with its early champion.

far the Gnostics have removed themselves, with this dualism of theirs, with the consubstantiality of God and man, etc., from what he terms the Jewish origins and what I would less committingly term the Jewish antecedents. So far, so good. My difficulty begins with relating, in Quispel's presentation, these two sets of statements, the "on the one hand" and the "on the other hand"; or, what amounts to the same, my difficulty is with the essential vagueness and ambiguity of the terms "derived from," "influenced by," "transition from A to B," which figure in the first set of statements. And here would apply much of what I have said in the first part of this paper apropos of "amplification," "meaning contexts," and the transfer of symbols from one to the other. Let me illustrate this on one point in the present larger issue.

Quispel has said that the Apocryphon of John, an archaic document compared with the more sophisticated Valentinian gnosis, shows "a strong influence of Jewish conceptions." And so it does, as in the following example: Ialdabaoth the creator, after expelling Adam and Eve from paradise into black darkness because they had acquired knowledge of their higher origin in defiance of his command, became inflamed with lust for the virgin Eve, raped her, and begot with her two sons: Jahve the bear-faced, and Elohim the cat-faced, among men called Cain and Abel to this day. Elohim the "just" he set over fire and wind, Jahve the "unjust" over water and earth: together they rule over the tomb, i.e., the body. This, as a piece of OT exegesis, is strong meat, but no more than a fair sample of the kind of use the Gnostics—and the more so the more familiar they show themselves with Jewish sources—habitually make of the Jewish material they incorporate into their speculation; or, to use Quispel's words: of what happened in the transition from Judaism to Gnosticism. And what is the spirit of this use? Why, it is the spirit of vilification, of parody and caricature, of conscious perversion of meaning, wholesale reversal of value-signs, savage degrading of the sacred—of gleefully shocking blasphemy. It is as if the Gnostics had been speaking thus to the Jews: You say your God is the creator of heaven and earth? He is—and so yours is an inferior and obtuse god. He proclaimed himself the highest and only god? Proof of his presumption and ignorance. He made man in a likeness? A sly and blundering imitation of the envied, dimly perceived superior Godhead. He forbade the fruit of the tree? Sure, to keep man in darkness about his true being. He later issued the law? The better to secure his stranglehold over him. He rules the universe? Look at cosmic Fate, the *heimarmene* of the planets, and you know what to think of this sinister tyranny. He chose you for his people? By becoming it, you have cast your lot with unenlightenment. And so it goes on and on.

Is this merely exuberant license, pleasure in the novel and bizarre? No, it is the exercise of a determined and in itself thoroughly consistent tendency. Does its exercise merely add a flourish, an interesting gloss, to the original? No, it is a total turning upside down. And its result—is it marginal or central to Gnosticism itself? It is its heart and soul, without which it would be a limp and flabby body, a motley of mythologumena and theologumena not worth the study we spend on it. I add: it is also its pepper and salt without which it would be a stale and insipid dish; but this is a matter of personal taste.

In short, and with the oversimplification excused by extreme shortness, the nature of the relation of Gnosticism to Judaism—in itself an undeniable fact—is defined by the *anti-Jewish animus* with which it is saturated. "The greatest case of metaphysical anti-Semitism!" exclaimed Scholem once when we talked about these matters soon after the appearance of my first *Gnosis* volume; that was in the thirties (and in Jerusalem) when one was very much alive to this aspect of things. Professor Wilson too, in his beautifully judicious chapter on Judaism and Gnosticism,[13] repeatedly uses the term "anti-Semitism" in that context (minus the "metaphysical"—a reflection perhaps of the national difference in philosophical backgrounds between the two gentlemen). Not once did this term, or any reference to the phenomenon it names, appear in Quispel's story today.

So far I have not said or implied that the anti-Jewish animus *constitutes* the essence of Gnosticism, nor even that it was its originating cause: I have merely said that it is of the essence of Gnosticism, in a confrontation with Judaism, to react with that violent and insulting hostility; and it seems that such confrontations took place very early, perhaps even right from the beginnings of the movement. But perhaps the matter does go farther than that, and we have to consider the following scale of hypotheses, each more specific than the preceding one:

1. (As stated before:) Gnosticism as an evolving state of mind *reacted* against Judaism when and where it encountered it.

2. Gnosticism *originated* out of a reaction (that is, *as* a reaction) to Judaism.

3. It was so originated *by Jews*.

Hypothesis 1 is uncontroversial: the massive evidence of anti-Jewish use of Jewish material leaves no doubt of the reaction as such. And needless to say, an anti-relation *is* a relation, and hate involves, and in turn can induce, its own familiarity, even intimacy with the object of it.

Hypothesis 2: that this reaction is itself the generative cause, at least the midwife, of Gnosticism—who knows? The record does not preclude

[13]R. McL. Wilson, *The Gnostic Problem*. London, 1958, ch. VII.

it, and the ubiquity and force of Judaism at the time give it a certain plausibility. One may feel, as I do, that it takes too narrow a view of Gnosticism and of its basis in the contemporary world; also, by making it merely reactive, it is an inadequate view of its autonomy as a spiritual cause. And, like all negative genealogy, it leaves us with the question of the positive ground from which the reaction was determined: at least the "gnostic disposition" so to react, so to feel provoked by Judaism, must be presupposed. In that sense, the hypothesis begs the question. We are caught here in the fine question of whether a No produces a Yes, or presupposes one. Possibly both. Anyway, in some such polemical sense, Judaism may have been a focal fact in the genesis of Gnosticism. One observation which might be construed in this sense, but which should give pause to the proponents of Jewish origins, is that the more archaic the source, the more vehement the anti-Judaism. The comparatively conciliatory, mitigating views of a Valentinus are clearly second thoughts, and not the first thoughts. Whatever this observation, which I cannot enlarge upon here, may signify otherwise, it throws an interesting light on the next question.

So, then, the third hypothesis, somehow at the back of the mind of those who advocate the Jewish origins of Gnosticism: Was that reaction perhaps begotten, incubated, and brought forth in the midst of Judaism itself—by Jews? Who would say that this is impossible? We have learned that almost nothing is impossible in human psychology, not even anti-Semitism among Jews. And what an exciting, nay soul-shaking spectacle that would be: the greatest iconoclasm before modernity erupting in Judaism—Jews themselves turning against their holiest, tearing it down, trampling it into the dust, revelling in its utter humiliation, proclaiming the complete devaluation of all traditional values—Nietzsche, Sartre, Saint Genet rolled into one: how fascinating, how modern! Of all the many genealogies of Gnosticism tried out so far, this would surely be the most interesting. But before we surrender to the lure of mere possibility, we ask for evidence. Of what could it consist in the given state of our historical testimony? I can think of two tests, not indeed supplying proof (which would be asking too much), but either of them at least *indicative* one way or the other.

The first test is applied by asking: Are there *Hebrew* writings of that period which are Gnostic in the sense here specified? Now if Scholem's book,[14] which I read very differently from the way Quispel seems to read it, has demonstrated one thing to me, it is that there are not. And here I trust my friend Scholem: if he, with his avid appetite for the unorthodox

---

[14]Gershom G. Scholem, *Jewish Gnosticism, Merkabah Mysticism, and Talmudic Tradition* (New York: The Jewish Theological Seminary of America, 1960).

and aberrant, his exquisite nose for the scent of it, and his unique knowledge of the field, has failed to bring up from this hunting trip even one example of that kind of "unorthodoxy," I am satisfied that it wasn't there. Scholem himself is at pains to differentiate between "Jewish Gnosticism . . . which was striving . . . hard to maintain a strictly monotheistic character" (p. 42), and "Gnostics" pure and simple or "antinomian Gnostics" who "frequently borrowed such material and deliberately changed it" (p. 72), "used and turned [it] upside down" (p. 73); he, too, speaks of "parody"[15] and, rather disarmingly, of a "deterioration" which Jewish esoteric teaching suffered at the hands of its Gnostic appropriators who "put it into false context" (p. 34). Never is there a suggestion that those who did this were Jews, and it is only unfortunate that he insists on calling those to whom it was done, the Jewish mystics, also "Gnostics." But he leaves no doubt about *their* essential "orthodoxy," even if not in the rabbinic sense. And Quispel follows him when he says, "This Gnosis (sc. of esoteric Pharisaism) is completely Jewish-orthodox"; and yet he goes on to say that it "eventually *led to* the origin of Gnosticism, *properly speaking*, at the *fringe* of Judaism." (my italics) Led to . . .: here we see the semantic disservice which Scholem did to clarity when he called his Palestinian Hekhaloth mysticism a "Gnosis." An innocent enough label in its literal meaning, it encourages the view of a smooth "transition" instead of a decisive break, a mere mutation in the same genus. And what real process is designated by "eventually leading to"? How impersonal and abstract! Almost like a gnostic emergence of aeons from aeons. But Jewish-orthodox "Gnosis" of itself just cannot lead to something basically different from itself. *Somebody* must have taken it and *made* it into something new, *turned* it upside down. *Who* did so? Gnostics ("properly speaking") to be sure. Who were they? Perhaps Jews? This is a concrete and straightforward question of "Whodunit." In the spirit of generosity after the holocaust, our (the Jews') credit for creativity has been vastly extended; and Jewish vanity, which of course is not lacking, might be pleased to welcome into the record even the disreputable, which in the present climate (with all the alienation going around) enjoys its own paradoxical prestige.

However, since we have drawn a blank on the first and more ambitious test, viz., the existence of "properly" gnostic Jewish (i.e., Hebrew) writings, let us try the second, more modest test of asking: Are there at least any Jewish *names* among the many recorded names of gnostic authors and teachers? It is a rather simple-minded question, I admit, but the older I get, the more I favor simple-minded questions. I need

---

[15]In this case "calculated to put the prophet Elija to shame" (p. 73).

not tell this audience that in all the patristic lists there are none, with one interesting half-exception: Simon the Magician from Samaria, a Hebrew name indeed and, as it happens, the earliest of them all. Small wonder that he looms large in the argument for the Jewish origins of Gnosticism. But quite apart from his obtrusive paganism (evident in the Helena-Selene worship) which almost obliterates his residual Judaism, we must not forget that he was the member of a very specially placed community, a group discriminated against, rejected, despised. Here we have a palpable motive for a response of *ressentiment*, aggression and spite; and here for once we can connect a definite meaning with the much-invoked, hazy term "fringes (or, outskirts) of Judaism," "at" which, we are told, Gnosticism originated, a term that usually prompts me to ask: inside or outside the line? The Samaritans were partly in and partly out, and some of them apparently very far out. This is a rich field for non-sequiturs. Quispel takes the fact of Simon's teaching the fall of Wisdom and thus a split in the Deity to mean "that already at a very early date there existed among Samaritans (heterodox Jews) the concept of a double Wisdom." Unless this is a tautology, merely saying that if Simon, a Samaritan, taught so and so, there was at least one Samaritan who taught so and so, if it is to mean that Simon's teaching what he taught testifies to a Samaritan development, then it is a non-sequitur. For Simon might have been the first, he might have been unique, he might— *sit venia verbo*—have been original. But the non-sequitur is compounded (in reversed chronology) by Scholem when, after classing the Samaritans (mainly on Simon's account) as "heretical Judaism," he argues: "Once we admit that such a development could take place within the Samaritan variant of Judaism, the possibility of analogous developments within the main branch of Pharisaic or Hasidic Judaism must equally be admitted."[16] Not at all! Samaritans had reasons for kicking against official Judaism, for an antagonistic posture, which those in the main branch had not. No bonds of loyalty bound them; at least they were much weakened in their case. It is these particular circumstances of an alienated group driven into opposition which for me have always lent great credibility to the tradition on Simon Magus, at a time when it was much more the fashion to mythify the whole outrageous figure including his lovely whore. He indeed is the first individual Gnostic our records permit us to discern. But we should surely hesitate on that account to place—in a throwback to Irenaeus—the burden of having started the mighty gnostic tide on the frail shoulders of the very localized Samaritan group. They do not measure up to such an influential role in the world of their time. Much rather should we say that they, or some of them,

16*Op. cit.*, p. 4.

generally ready for heterodoxy, were especially receptive for the anti-
Jewish animus, or the anti-Jewish possibilities, of the incipient Gnostic
flood.

All this is not to deny that Judaism was a powerful factor in the formation, perhaps even in the nativity of Gnosticism. In a sufficiently loose
and non-committal sense of "fringe" one may safely say (but it says
little) that it did originate "at the fringes" of Judaism. I prefer to say:
in a zone of proximity and exposure to Judaism, where the Jewish share
—besides the contribution of much transmissible material—was in essence *catalytic* and *provoking*. To the breathtaking possibility of its
even being positive begetter of the essence, I keep an open mind but
will not lower my price. A Gnosticism without a fallen god, without
benighted creator and sinister creation, without alien soul, cosmic captivity and acosmic salvation, without the self-redeeming of the Deity—
in short: a gnosis without divine tragedy will not meet specifications.
For those are the things we have to account for when truly asking for
the origins of Gnosticism. A gnosis merely of the heavenly palaces, of
the mystical ascent, the ecstatic vision of the Throne, of the awesome
secrets of the divine majesty—in short: a *monotheistic* gnosis of the
mysterium numinosum et tremendum, important as it is in its own right,
is a different matter altogether. I would be thrilled to the bone if the
first could be shown to have been engendered within Judaism. It would
add the last touch to the kind of violent and defiant impulse I see at
work behind Gnosticism; and its revolutionary aspect, which I have
emphasized from the first, would be enhanced beyond my wildest imagination. So far there is not a shred of evidence that this is what happened.
Yet this, and only this, is to me the really relevant and challenging sense
of the phrase: Jewish origin of Gnosticism. All the other senses, conducive as they may be to particular lines of scholarly research, are apt
to obscure the decisive issue at stake.

15.
Myth and Mysticism:
A Study of Objectification
and Interiorization in Religious Thought

The title of this paper suggests a certain duality: that of an objective representation of reality on the one hand, and of a subjective realization of stages of being on the other. In the history of religion the objective representation is typically in the form of myth, and it generally precedes the mystical stage, which may appear as an internalized version of the same motif. Yet the term *objectification* used in our title suggests also that the original myth—or, more generally, the objective speculation—may itself presuppose a subjective condition which is symbolically represented by the objective hypostases of the theoretical doctrine. Indeed, the very fact of a structural similarity between certain speculative systems of thought and certain immanent programs of psychic discipline emerging within one and the same historical ambience suggests, even given a time lag between the two, that both spring from a common root of a more basic condition—a way of man's being in the world which either successively or simultaneously manifests itself in these different directions. In this sense one may regard the myth as a projection of an existential reality which seeks its own truth in a total view of things and may even at first satisfy its primary aspiration in such objective-symbolic representations. The time lag I just mentioned makes

Originally presented at the convention of the American Academy of Religion in Dallas, Texas, during October 1968. Reprinted from the *Journal of Religion* 44 (October 1969) by permission of the University of Chicago Press.

it probable that such a representation in transcendent terms (that is to say, the externalization of an inner principle and thereby in a way its disguise) is the naturally prior stage, and that the reappropriation of this content of the mythological "alienation" into the autonomous possibilities of the self is the later stage. In that case, the originative subjectivity which was operative in the production of the grand mythology or metaphysical speculation in the first place would then, by this detour, and only by means of such a detour, come to itself and to the direct realization of its secret primary intention. This is the general hypothesis by which I try to understand at least the sequence of phenomena in that area of myth formation and the emergence of mystical schedules with which I am most familiar, namely, in the period of late antiquity.

I

A good point to begin with is the doctrine of the soul's ascent through the spheres after its separation from the body, a doctrine which we find abroad with a wealth of mythological detail throughout that era, and especially in many gnostic systems where it is embedded in a wider, speculative framework that is itself dominated by the theme of a *descensus* and *ascensus* of Being writ large. A less mythological, in a way "rationalized" version of the theme can be discerned in Origen's grand theory of the spiritual upward movement of successive worlds in reparation of an original Fall, and a still more intellectualized, completely "ontological" version in Plotinus's metaphysics of the timelessly self-generating stairway of being.

The celestial journey of the returning soul[1] is one of the most constant common features in otherwise widely divergent gnostic systems, and its significance for the gnostic mind is enhanced by the fact that it represents a belief not only important in gnostic theory and expectation, and expressive of the conception of man's relation to the world, but of immediate practical relevance to the gnostic believer, since the meaning of *gnosis* is to prepare for this final event, and all of its ethical, ritual, and technical instruction is meant to secure its successful completion. Now, historically, according to my hypothesis, there is an even more far-reaching aspect to the ascent doctrines than their literal meaning. This is the fact that in a later stage of "gnostic" development (though no longer passing under the name of Gnosticism) the external topology of the ascent through the spheres, with the successive divesting of the soul of its worldly envelopments and the regaining of its original acosmic

---

[1]See H. Jonas, *The Gnostic Religion* (Boston: Beacon Press, 1963), pp. 165–67, part of which is reproduced or summarized in this and the next two paragraphs.

nature, reappears "internalized" in the shape of a psychological technique of inner transformations by which the self, while still in the body, might attain the absolute as an immanent, if temporary, condition. An ascending scale of mental states replaces the stations of the mythical itinerary; the dynamics of progressive spiritual self-transformation replaces the spatial thrust through the heavenly spheres. Thus could transcendence itself be turned into immanence, the whole process become spiritualized and put within the power and the orbit of the subject. With this transposition of a mythological scheme into the inwardness of the person, with the translation of its objective stages into subjective phases of self-performable experience whose culmination has the form of *ecstasis* or mystic union, gnostic myth passes into mysticism (Neoplatonic and monastic); and in this new medium it lives on long after the disappearance of the original mythological beliefs. As I suggested, this can be viewed as the recovery of the original essence from its embodiment in the mythological objectivation.

Just a few words about the mythological, "objectified" form of the ascent doctrine must here suffice. In the *Poimandres*, the first treatise of the *Corpus Hermeticum*, the upward journey of the soul after death is described as a series of progressive subtractions in sphere after sphere which finally leave the "naked" true self, an instance of Primal Man as he was before his cosmic fall, free to enter the divine realm and to become one again with God. In the language of other systems, the sum of the foreign accretions so discarded is nothing less than the whole *psyche*, the cosmic integument of the *pneuma*, which thus is set free again. Imagery and terminology vary; in any case, the topological ascent is at the same time a qualitative process, that of putting off the worldly nature.

Now, it is noteworthy that in certain *cults* the ultimate process was anticipated by ritual enactments which, in the way of sacraments, were to effect the transformation provisionally or symbolically already in this life and guarantee its definitive consummation in the next. Thus the mysteries of Mithras had for their initiates the ceremonial of passing through seven gates arranged on ascending steps representing the seven spheres;[2] in those of Isis we find a successive putting on and off of seven garments or animal disguises. The result achieved by the whole protracted and sometimes harrowing ritual was called rebirth (*palingenesia*): the initiate himself was supposed to have been reborn as a god. The terminology of "rebirth," "reformation" (*metamorphosis*), "transfiguration," was coined in the context of these rituals as part of the language of the mystery cults. But the borderline between mere sacra-

---

[2]The *klimax heptapylos;* see Origen, *Contra Celsum* 6. 22.

ment, understood as a symbolic substitute and advance guaranty, on the one hand, and some actual experiential verification of the real thing on the other, was necessarily fluid. In the order of the cult itself, or in private and spiritualized substitutions for it inspired by its general model, the "celestial journey" might become an actual visionary experience attainable in the brief ecstatic state. The so-called Mithras Liturgy gives a circumstantial description of such an experience, preceded by instructions on how to prepare for and induce the visionary state.

What happens here to an eschatological scheme is that the *eschaton* is taken into the range of the subject's own faculties of self-modification and becomes a supreme possibility of existence itself. Accordingly, the transcendent stations of the "ascent" turn into stages of an intra-psychic progress toward this utter possibility of selfhood; we may speak of a "psychologization" of the ascent. To repeat: an originally "existential" concern, first objectified in the representational mythical projection that confronts the subject as a theoretical truth, is returned as a practical possibility to its origin, existence itself.

Not every myth, of course, lends itself to such an inward replication, but only an "eschatological" or "salvational" myth of the kind that flourished in the Hellenistic-Near Eastern world of the early Christian era. Already in that myth the whole landscape of being was mapped with a view to a future condition of "worldlessness" of the generic soul that is split up into individual souls, a condition involving their return to an original state; and salvation was seen to consist in this condition. The saved residue is the nonmundane, original core of what at present exists in the lessened, mundane condition of "soul." Obviously this can serve, if so used, as the mythological prototype of an existential possibility: the substantive, external entities of the myth symbolically point to a possible inner process of the self's eliminating the relations to the world and reductively moving toward the limit of an acosmic experience. Yet the nexus here suggested must not be taken as necessarily that of a conscious application of symbolic myth to the inner life. Conceptual, mystical philosophy and gnostic myth need not know of each other: they may hang together by a common cause, and there may even, as here suggested, be a "natural" sequence of *prius* and *posterius* between them, without the later being derived from the earlier. Rather, they are analogical formations sprung from the same source in a certain temporal order.

II

The ascent myth is just one particularly obvious example of objective doctrine to which later mystical praxis offers an internal analogue. We could also refer to the emanation schema, with the world as the last stage of a universal descent, which, too, can be translated into a directional movement and sequence of mental states. It even is in that respect—that is, in mystical "applicability," or rather "convertibility" —superior to the astrological myth of the soul's descent and ascent. The emanation systems let the "soul" (*psyche*) come forth as a particular "degeneration" of the one primordial being at the appropriate point of its metaphysical "history"—a history whose total sense is decline and devolution. Contrary to the separate myth of the planetary soul, which could be extraneously grafted onto diverse mythologies, this is a speculative thought integral to the whole system.

The difference is not unimportant in our context. In the astrological myth the *psyche* is added to the *pneuma* from without, the lower to the higher "soul," as an alien element contributed by the existing cosmic powers; the *psyche* is an "envelopment" of the *pneuma*, a kind of spiritual "body" of the absolute spirit, etc. Accordingly, "salvation" must here be represented as a rending and casting off of this "soul" raiment, as a release of the pneumatic spark from the psychic fetter, and the like. The other, speculative type of derivation offers a different set of symbols: here the sinking, primordial *pneuma* itself becomes "psyche"—*by* its sinking. That is, *psyche* is nothing but a particular sunken condition, a specific stage in the metaphysical destiny of the original *pneuma*, namely, a form of alienation from itself. Or, seen from the *psyche*, the *pneuma* is the original, only temporarily impaired condition of itself, and the salvation is accordingly its retransformation to the former, a *restitutio in integrum* in a reverse process of metamorphoses.

This is not only the theoretically higher form of representation (because deliberately speculative instead of naïvely mythological) but also the form more significant for the development of a mystical principle. The superiority in this respect of the emanationist metaphysics is briefly indicated by these two distinguishing traits: (1) the unity of the principle from which the whole ontological process autonomously develops in the gnostic sense, all the way to the opposite of its beginning —whereby the myth acquires philosophical rank; (2) the consequence that therefore the reascent no longer has to deal with external obstructive forces, like the archons of the spheres, from whom passage must be obtained, but with a process of spiritual transformation not involving the interplay with independent mythical powers or conditions—whereby the translation to internal mysticism becomes more directly possible.

What matters in both and all variants is the typical directional "movement" of the eschatological myth. To repeat: I do not try to *derive* the mystical ascent from the mythological ascent doctrine nor from the emanationist version of mythology, but I say that the later, mystical way *corresponds* in mental immanence to the representational transcendence of the myth—and that both are rooted in a common existential ground.

III

I now have to say something about the role which the mystery cults, themselves endowed with a traditional myth but primarily interested in ritual performance, played in the development in question. In the later mystery religions ecstasy seems to have had a place within the sacramental context. Generally we have to realize that everywhere in this area the "sacramental," already in the ritual means employed, stayed closer to the emotional character of ancient arousal cults than did the purified sacrament mystique of the Christian church, which claimed to effect the "union" with the deity in the idea rather than in actual, as it were sensuous, experience. Precisely this actual—which means in practice, more or less orgiastic—experience was at least more openly suggested as a possible aim in the mystery cults of Hellenistic and Roman times, so far as we can reconstruct them; and in this aspect, which they owed to oriental influence, they certainly went far beyond the indigenous, old-Hellenic mysteries of the Eleusinian type.

In a certain sense, the mysteries generally were the cradle of the idea of "perfection," which hence was repeatedly, in antiquity, transferred into ethics and right into the contemplative ideal of philosophy (or, at the least, lent its language to them—cf. the description of the "erotic mysteries" at the climax of Plato's *Symposium*). One need only consider the terminology: the whole sequence of initiations and instructions was called *teletai*; the initiated, *tetelesmenos* (the perfected one); the highest grade of the ascending series, *telea mysteria* (also *epoptica*—see below); and the aim of it all, *teleiosis*—perfection or consummation. "Perfection" is the formal concept; in content, it is the union of man with God, his becoming God himself (*apotheosis*). The various images in which this in turn was depicted can still best be learned from A. Dieterich's chapter on "The Liturgical Images of the Mithras Mystery,"[3] which rises to a grand theory of the image repertory of mystical thought. The series of typical images by which the cultic union with the deity ("the sole and highest goal of all mysteries and all mysticism")[4] was represented, comprises the following: incorporation—the eating of the god; sexual or love union with the deity; begetting by the deity—rebirth

[3] A. Dieterich, *Eine Mithrasliturgie* (Leipzig, 1903), pp. 92–212.
[4] Ibid., p. 209.

as his child; celestial journey of the soul to god; and illumination by, and beholding of, the divine light, the blissful contemplation of which concludes the series as its most sublime form. In the sequence and inter-penetration of these images Dieterich detects something of a "law of religious thought which is valid in all mysticism of all religions."[5] To these forms of representation correspond cultic forms of securing and effecting the one goal—that is, the sacraments: ritual symbols of the union and of the way thereto, generally forming a scale of actions with imputed instrumental power but comprising more than that in their ecstatic forms, especially in that of ultimate vision. These are no longer merely symbolic-sacramental, but at the same time immediate fulfillment —no longer means only, but also in themselves actualization of the end. In connection with *teleisthai* (= to be initiated and perfected), it is well to remember the pregnant connotation which the term had by its verbal proximity to *teleutan* (= dying). For the mystery piety this was pro-foundly significant: rebirth requires a prior dying of the old man. And we find it directly spelled out that "as the word is like unto the word, so is the thing like unto the thing, namely dying and being perfected."[6]

Now, it is important for the eventual transposition of the mythological and ritual scheme into personal mysticism that the concepts of the *perfectus* (*teleios*) and of being perfected (*teleiousthai*), stemming from this context of hieratic formulas and enduringly wedded to its structure, implied from the outset the idea of a definite "way" (of perfection) and accordingly the idea of a definite "beginning" and "end," such as were physically prefigured in the performance of the mystery. Likewise, the idea of "transformation" (*metamorphosis*) was, at least since the Hel-lenistic era, lastingly bequeathed to the concept of "perfection" from this cultic origin. These formal elements could then also, after the dis-sociation from the cultic source (i.e., with the interiorization or ethical transference of the process), continue to determine personal *praxis* as a general schema.

Such a transition was facilitated by the later (postclassical) evolution of the mystery religions themselves, in which the initiate (*mystes*), from being a spectator, turns more and more into a subject of the action (*dromenon*) that reinacts the legend of the god and is now related to the initiate himself. Fate and triumph of the deity, mostly centered around the theme of death and resurrection—these he now experiences himself as actor on the stage, moving through the stations of the concluding cult action in magic identification with the god; the latter's resurrection as

---

[5]Ibid., p. 211.
[6]Themistius, in Stobaeus, *Florilegium* (Hense) 4. 1089, quoted by Dieterich, pp. 163–64.

celebrated in the mystery is the initiate's own rebirth as a god, his palingenesis.

Within the cultic framework the final act of apotheosis always retains the meaning of objective sacrament; but insofar as the cult itself allows it to assume, in its subjective aspect, the form of ecstatic union and transfiguration, which is its own evidence, two important developments are opened up: (1) Ecstasy, instead of merely certifying that apotheosis has taken place, can in its own right and experiential quality be taken to represent perfection itself (a natural enough claim for a culminating experience)—and in the light of a metaphysics for which perfection must lie in an "acosmic" state, this claim confers a certain meaning on the ecstatic condition which a suitable interpretation can indeed extract from its immanent evidence, namely, that the ecstatic condition is the experience of worldlessness achieved. The more or less "gnosticized" dogmatics of a mystery cult will more or less decidedly award this meaning to ecstasy. Therewith it is elevated to a genuine anticipation of the transmundane goal of the mysteries, in which otherwise even "deification" (apotheosis) is merely a voucher for a future release from the world. (2) At the same time, a new dynamic nexus is created between this now immanent *goal*, that can thus be set as a practical task, and the traditionally ascetic or cathartic *preparations* which the initiate must undergo in the preceding grades—namely, a means-ends nexus whose efficacy no longer depends on the sacramental (symbolic or magic) meaning of the various steps but rather on their intrinsic conditioning power, which can be elaborated into an autonomous system of self-transformation. "Purification" (*catharsis*) and "seeing" (*epopteia*) are, as Dieterich observed,[7] official steps of any initiation in antiquity. But it makes a difference whether the nexus between these two steps is an external one, mediated by the order of a ritual—that is, by reference to a believed-in, efficient agency outside the person—or whether it follows internally, as it were causally, from their own lived content. The latter will be the case the more the "seeing" becomes itself an inner, mental event, and as accordingly the preceding "sanctifications" and ascetic preparations of all kinds exchange their ritualistic for a more directly personal function in the life of the self. Both of these developments portend a significant emancipation of this functional complex from the objective-sacramental validation—its advance toward a self-validating status even when still contained within the framework of the cult.

However, one must not overlook the limitation which the mystery idea as such, so long as it was kept up, imposed on this development. By

---

[7]Dieterich, p. 210.

its terms, the palingenesis is not a typical experience which can become the norm for piety, but an initiatory experience happening only once and having its main significance in the persisting sacral quality which it confers upon the person. Thus, apart from this event of initiation, the mystery initiates (*mystai*) were by no means "mystics." The *telos*, contained within the cult, does not yet pervade existence as a whole and draw toward itself all of its practical, emotional, and even conceptual self-determination. This it can only do with the detachment from the cultic domain.

Among the forms of spiritualization which thus took off from the cult or mediated its transposition into free existence, Reitzenstein has in particular noted[8] the replacement of the act by the word, that is, of the physical *dromenon* by the revelatory writing (*logos teleios*) which, with its instruction of the solitary reader, promotes the interiorization of the complete action context. A good example of this is the Hermetic treatise on *palingenesia* (*Corp. Herm.* 13). For all such spiritualizations the system of a graded scale of mysteries, where the successive initiations represented steps on the way to *apotheosis*, had prepared the cultic prototype of a teleological organization of life which still survived in the language—now metaphorical—of later noncultic mysticism. Its terms have been converted into the new currency of inwardness. The place of the purifying rites as also of the trials and tribulations of the initiation ceremony, generally the place of the whole system of consecrations, is finally taken by a corresponding system of planned, individual asceticism which evolves its own ascending scale by the intrinsic logic of spiritual efficacy. Thus opens the dimension for a new, mystical concept of virtue and perfection.

A word of warning may not be amiss here. The typical mystery experience must be imagined as a not too spiritual one, in many cases even as quite a sensual one. I am thinking not only of the sexual forms of ecstasy but also of the role of illusionistic light effects, music, intoxication, drugs, and dance. I mentioned the breakthrough of primitive orgiastics which we witness in the midst of the sophisticated Greco-Roman culture. Ecstasy is a broad concept, comprising the crude as well as the refined: what is common is the breaking down and temporary cancelling of timebound, world-committed being—in its very extremism a potentially, if crudely, "eschatological" moment. My general contention is that the cult system of the mysteries, by involving the participants in its performances, was one of the ways in which the latent practical content of eschatological, and especially gnostic, myth could

---

[8]R. Reitzenstein, *Die hellenistischen Mysterienreligionen*, 3rd.ed. (Leipzig, 1927), p. 242ff.

become free, that is, transposed into human action. Through the cultic conjunction of *mythos* and *praxis* the transcendent finds a way to become immanent before the mind discovers the way for itself.

IV

The premise, of course, is that the archaic, official myth of a cult had first itself undergone a sweeping reinterpretation of its meaning which made it suitable for such a role. Allegory was the ready means, and the general direction was determined by the "transcendental" spirit of the age. Some such evolution must have occurred—we cannot tell precisely when—on the long road of the mysteries from originally chthonic cults to instruments of otherworldly aspiration. By the terms of truly gnostic myth, let us remember, the world takes the place of Hades and worldly existence that of death: it is then not too hyperbolic to say that now the cosmos as a whole becomes that cave wherein once, as the abode of the chthonic powers, the nocturnal celebration was performed; and life in this world as a whole, lived by gnostic norms, becomes the continuous, no longer sacramental, mystery action which leads out of the death of this darkness in stages of transformations and perfections. To the rising tide of this novel contemporary vision, the mystery communities themselves adapted their older myth.

A well-attested example is the myth of Attis, originally a nature myth like all the myths of vegetation deities to whom the mysteries were at first devoted. Its very different, later meaning can be found in the Naassene treatise,[9] in Porphyry,[10] Sallustius,[11] and the emperor Julianus.[12] Briefly, Attis, who turns away from the great Mother and toward the nymph, is equated with the Primal Man who falls from the height into the depth of matter (Naassenes), or with "the Demiurge of the things that become and pass away" (Sallustius, from whom the further quotations are taken as well). The cave into which he descends is the lower world; the water nymph with whom he cohabits there is the goddess of becoming, "for everything becoming flows." His union with her is cosmogonic as well as anthropogonic, accounting for the double nature of man. His castration is the staying of the downward movement of creation and his separation from it; his return to the Mother is the reunion with the divine world. All this the initiates relate to themselves. "This happened at no time, but always is." We too, so they say, fell from heaven and cohabit with the nymph, and "wishing to imitate the

---

[9]Hippolytus *Refut.* 5. 7 ff.
[10]Porphyrius *De antro nympharum.*
[11]Sallustius *De diis et mundo,* ch. 4.
[12]Julianus *Oratio* 5.

universe we celebrate the mystery in this order." The whole ancient ritual with its fasting, tree felling (for "castration"), milk feeding, etc., is then taken to be the symbolic and efficacious enactment by the devotees, for their own persons, of the allegorically reinterpreted divine story of emasculation, rebirth, and reunion: the old, starkly naturalistic myth, via its exegetic sublimation to an eschatology of the spiritual universe, is turned into a paradigm for the self-enactment of individual salvation. Concerning the practical aspect and its eventual detachment from the cultic framework, we have it expressly from Hippolytus (*Refut.* 5.9.10–11) that the castration motif of the original sexual nature myth was transformed into the idea of a gnostic-enkratic asceticism as a way of life: "They comport themselves like castrates without being castrates."

The Attis myth is the best-attested case of such a spiritualization of an archaic cult myth, which accordingly changed the meaning of the mystery itself. Similar exegetic developments can be partly discerned, partly surmised, in all of the mystery religions of later paganism. And the "gnostic" reinterpretation of the myth was a decisive step on the way from mystery to mysticism.

V

The mystery cults were one historic vehicle for the conversion of objective myth into subjective mysticism. They were hardly the pace-makers of the grand process in which the dialectic of objectification and interiorization played itself out. While the mysteries more or less success-fully, but always secondarily, adapted their archaic, crude mythology to the new spirituality, this spirituality evolved its own, independent ex-pression in the freely constructed systems of the gnostic, patristic, and Neoplatonic speculation. Although widely different in their theoretical type, ranging from the frankly mythological of the Gnostics to the rigorously conceptual of Plotinus, they have this in common that they all view the totality of being in terms of a double movement of spiritual fall and rise, descent from and ascent to an absolute spiritual source, with the downward movement coming first and explaining the given state of things, the upward movement reversing it and pointing ahead to an ultimate goal: the great chain of being, "vertical" in its order, is essentially a mental genealogy of alienation and reintegration. Ob-viously, the dynamism of these systems, objective as they were in their conception, is *ab initio* closer to possible "subjectivization" and mystical transposition than were the massive externalities of archaic myth. Indeed, one may well ask whether they and others of their kind, as, for example, those of Dionysius Areopagita and the Kabbala, were not in the first place inspired by a mystical rather than "theoretical" interest.

Or, to go still a step further, were they perhaps outright "objectifica-
tions" of mystical experiences—their projections, as it were, onto a
representational screen? Are they therefore to be read as coded con-
fessions rather than manifest thought systems? Behind such questions
looms a very general one of philosophic importance: What in the nature
of these things (or in their typical course) comes first—experience or
thought, feeling or concept, subjective practice or objective theory?
Does actual life express itself (and therefore also disguise itself) in ideas
of the mind, or do ideas of the mind, generated in speculative reasoning
or imagining, prepare for and make possible modes of living and feeling?

One must resist the first impulse to assign necessary priority to an
immediacy of life vis-à-vis the reflection of thought, to the concrete
vis-à-vis the abstract. There is an important sense in which theory, or a
system of beliefs about the objective nature of things, mediates the very
possibility of types and structures of experience which the subject would
not look for otherwise. Indeed, the readiness for certain experiences may
be the direct corollary of holding certain views, the propositions of
doctrine breeding dispositions of the person; and there is nothing absurd
in holding that the strength of a theory may even produce its correlative
inner evidence. These considerations are of special pertinence to the
historical relationship between objective dogmatics and subjective mysticism. As a case in point, I will make a few remarks on the speculative
system of Origen, propounded in *De principiis*, which regarding its
form of theory stands somewhere between gnostic mythology and
Plotinian metaphysics, and about whose relation to personal mysticism
there can be two different views.

One is exemplified by what Walter Völker[13] says apropos of Origen's
teaching on the *apokatastasis* of all things, the final consummation
toward which the spiritual creation moves through an indefinite succession of worlds with ascending grades of perfection, that is, in a gradual
restoration of its initial state before the Fall. In that far-off end, equal
to the beginning, all spirits, not excluding those that are Satan and his
hosts in the present order, "will form [again] a unity, and the hypostases
and numbers (i.e., plurality) will vanish together with the bodies. And
spiritual knowledge will be followed by the annihilation of the worlds
and the discarding of the bodies and the abolishing of the names
(etc.)."[14] In this doctrine of the *apokatastasis* Völker wants to see the
"expression of a feeling which directly stems from the experience of

---

[13]W. Völker, *Das Vollkommenheitsideal des Origenes* (Tübingen, 1931).

[14]Origen's teaching according to Anathema 14 of the Council of Constantinople
A.D. 543, which probably quoted from *De principiis* 3. 6, 4. See *Origen's 'On First
Principles,'* trans. G. W. Butterworth (New York: Harper & Row [Harper Torch-
books], 1966), p. 250, n. 3.

the *unio mystica* and strives to explicate that experience."[15] Everywhere in the system he sees "metaphysical projections of inner experiences," and so he takes what he calls "the purely metaphysical conception" as an intellectualized foreground datum from which to infer back to the secret experiences which it expresses and hides at the same time.

The opposite view, to which I tend, is that Origen's system, strictly speculative and neither mystical nor even mystically inspired, was yet by the very nature of its *objective* content capable of being given a mystical-subjective turn—if the mystic to do so came along. And he did: one and a half centuries after Origen, Euagrius Ponticus, the father and earliest theoretician of monastic mysticism, did perform the mystical conversion of Origen's eschatological speculation. In Euagrius's articulation of the inner life, in his instructions for the spiritual ascent, all of the metaphysical terms of Origen are indeed converted into mystical ones, and his metaphysical system is thereby converted into a mystical canon. For this it was first necessary to make the movement of the metaphysical stages neutral with respect to world time, so as to make them purely a function of "inner time," which in principle is at the disposal of each subject at all times. Then the objective hierarchy of being has become transformable into spiritual self-movement, and its paradigmatic articulation can act as a phenomenology (more than a mere allegory) of the order of inner ascent. This ascent has thereby gained an operable canon for itself.

The consideration of this case can protect us against anachronistic judgments, because (a) it shows in a historical example how Origenism turned mystical really looks, and (b) it teaches us something about temporal sequence: the metaphysical conception, the unfolding of the principle in terms of universal being—in brief, the objectivation— precedes; and the mystical transformation into an organon for immanent actualization follows at quite an interval; and it was reached via the prior objectivation. Origen's ascent of the souls in future aeons indeed provides the *idea* of an inner progress. I emphasize *idea*: the theory is the anticipation, not the projection, of experience, making it possible, not resulting from it—an inversion of the relationship as psychologism is fond of seeing it. Here, as often, objective thought is the condition of possible experience.

In a different sense I too consider the speculative system a "projection": not, however, of experiences actually made, but of a total attitude toward being, whose theoretical explication is its own urgent concern. The explicit theory, then, has indeed issued from an existential stance—I call this the primal "objectivation," by which I mean some-

[15]Völker, p. 134.

thing with transcendental validity. It furnishes the horizon for its evidential experiences and specifies them in advance. It inspires the search for them, fosters them, and legitimates them. Without an antecedent dogmatics there would be no valid mysticism. And mysticism, let it be noted, wants to be "valid," namely, more than a revel of feeling. The true mystic wants to put himself into possession of absolute reality, which already is and about which doctrine tells him. So it was, at least, with the mysticism of late antiquity which still stood in continuity with the intellectual and ontological speculation of the Greek past. Having an objective theory, the mystic goes beyond theory; he wants experience of and identity with the object; and he wants to be able to claim such identity. Thus, in order that certain experiences may become possible and even conceivable as valid anticipations of an eschatological future, or as actualizations of metaphysical stages of being, speculation must have set the framework, the way, and the goal—long before the subjectivity has learned to walk the way.

16.
Origen's Metaphysics of Free Will, Fall, and Salvation: A 'Divine Comedy' of the Universe

When Dante painted his majestic panorama of human destiny, he titled it a "Comedy," to which posterity added the adjective "Divine." The combined name, whether by accident or design, suggests several things. One is that the offered spectacle, in spite of its innumerable cast, forms one action, a drama with one pervading plot; another, that—unlike a tragedy, which ends in disaster—the action, through all its anxious parts, moves to a serene ending; yet another, that the drama, though focused in man, is more than human, that in fact it is God's great play in interaction with man, and that in it the divine cause is at stake. Looking then at the stage on which the drama is enacted, we note that it is not a one-storied plane, but consists of levels rising upon levels —hell, earth, and heaven—through which the action moves down and up as does the journey of Dante himself. The stage, in other words, is the universe in its ascending spiritual order.

The idea of such a cosmic-spiritual drama dates back to the beginning of the Christian era. During its first centuries there burst forth, inspired partly by the Christian message, partly by the general metaphysical climate of the age, a surprising efflorescence of bold, visionary; and speculative constructions of the total scheme of things, many of them Christian at least in name, others pagan, all of them reaching for an ultimate truth by which man could understand his own condition and

Reprinted from the *Journal of the Universalist Historical Society* 8 (1969–70).

goal. The many gnostic schools of the second century, with their ever shifting versions of the cosmic drama of salvation which they offered as saving "knowledge" (and which were almost immediately rejected by the then emerging official Church), were followed in the third century by the more rigorously constructed systems of Mani's mythology and Plotinus' philosophy—the latter belonging to this stream of speculation by its broader terms, in spite of Plotinus' resolute stand against its prevalent, nonphilosophical forms.

Among these early system builders in the grand style was Origen (185?–254?), the first systematic theologian of the Christian church. Following upon the Gnostics of the second century, and slightly preceding Plotinus (204?–270?) and Mani (216?–275?), he was a defender of orthodoxy, and by rational temperament as well as ecclesiastic discipline in no way inclined toward the heretical fancies of the gnostic kind. Yet when it came to his own attempt at integrating scriptural revelation with independent reason and intuition into a coherent and persuasive whole that meant to embrace the totality of things, all his care could not prevent him from producing a system which the later Church found it necessary to condemn as heresy. In consequence, the one work out of his vast literary output in which he presented this attempt—his only systematic writing,[1] the remarkable *De principiis* (*On First Things*, or *On Principles*), written between 220 and 230—suffered the fate of so many heretical writings. The Greek original was effectively destroyed and no copy survived. We possess, however, a Latin translation made in 398 by a defender of Origen, Rufinus, who saved the work for posterity at the price which defensiveness is willing to pay: his apologetic solicitude led the translator to blunt, and sometimes omit, the more daring and offensive points—which to us, of course, are the most interesting. The situation is somewhat remedied by the surviving of a countertranslation done in 401 by Jerome, who was hostile and therefore accurate.[2] In addition, a number of quotations from the Greek original are found in various Greek Christian authors. Lastly we have, also in Greek, the "anathemas" decreed by several Church councils on Origen which routinely summarize, or quote verbatim, the errors they condemn[3]—in some cases incidentally confirming the accuracy of Jerome's rendering. Using all these scattered sources, the German scholar P. Koetschau offered a brilliant reconstruction of *De principiis* in his edition

---

[1]Origen's other writings are exegetic, homiletic, and polemical.

[2]Jerome's translation as a whole is lost, but we have his *Letter to Avitus* (a bishop) with a large selection (almost 50) of just such passages from his translation which rectify that by Rufinus and show up the heresies of Origen.

[3]Most important are the 15 Anathemas of the Second Council of Constantinople in 553.

of 1913 which has become authoritative.[4] Koetschau's text was translated into English by G. W. Butterworth in 1963, and this translation is cited throughout.[5] What follows is a commentated account of Origen's system as it can be extracted from the surviving *De principiis*.[6]

1. *The divine One and the Trinity*

At the summit and source of the scale of being stands the divine One which is Unity absolute, devoid of all diversity in its own being. Considered purely by himself, the godhead is "one," "simple," "unity," "oneness";[7] he is "mind, or even beyond mind and being,"[8] "unmoved,"[9] and—at least for human thought—"incomprehensible."[10] He, the Father, alone is "uncreated"[11] (which makes "creatures" even of the two other persons of the trinity). But he never is purely by himself. As the primordial mind, he is at the same time "the fount from which originates all intellectual existence or mind," "the first principle of all things"; and in this creative, or procreative, role he is likened—by a simile widely used in the speculation of that age—to the light as related to the "brightness" (*splendor*) of the "rays" issuing from it. (Bu. p. 10). This clearly lends an aspect of natural necessity to the divine creativity—whose creation therefore, at least in its original form, must be "eternal creation" —as distinct from the biblical simile of the free *fiat* by a purposeful maker and shaper of things which issues in a temporally unique act. True to

[4]*Die griechischen christlichen Schriftsteller der ersten drei Jahrhunderte. Origenes Werke V, De principiis*, ed. Paul Koetschau (Leipzig, 1913).
[5]*Origen's 'On First Principles': Being Koetschau's Text of De Principiis*, trans. G.W. Butterworth, 1963; SPCK, (London: reprinted 1966 as a Harper Torchbook, with an introduction by H. de Lubac). This translation will be referred to hereafter as Bu.
[6]The general pattern of speculation into which Origen falls is discussed in section I of the following essay. For Origen in particular we have only to add the peculiar sharpening of the problem which *creation* posed to the theoretical type as such: If it precluded the simple biblical answer that God had just willed the world as his own free choice, then even a thinker committed to uphold (against the Gnostics) the creatorship of God, as a loyal Christian like Origen had to do, could not but think that He had exercised this creatorship under some sort of duress—not an easy proposition for a monotheist to accommodate. We shall see how Origen solved this difficulty.
[7]Bu. p. 10: "a simple intellectual existence, admitting in himself of no addition whatever, so that he cannot be believed to have in himself a more or less, but is Unity, or if I may say so Oneness throughout."
[8]Origen, *Contra Celsum* VII, 38; Bu. *loc. cit.*: "that simple and wholly mental existence."
[9]*Contra Celsum* VI, 64.
[10]Bu. p. 9: "incomprehensible and immeasurable."
[11]Bu. p. 19, n. 3: "nothing is uncreated except God the Father only"; p. 31: "everything whatever except the Father and God of the universe is created."

his principle, Origen derives already the Trinity from this creativity of the Father by whose effulgence it is generated and sustained, as an aura is generated and sustained by a source of light. His immediate *splendor* is the Son;[12] and again radiating from this first brightness and mediated by it, the Holy Spirit subsists as God's brightness at a second remove. Both hypostases are thus "creations,"[13] but from eternity,[14] as the light simile implies: eternal radiances of the eternal light. More significant than the dogmatically touchy point of createdness within the Trinity is the "subordinationism" which the light simile imports into the internal relations of the Trinity, establishing a clearly vertical, linear, descending order of divine natures, which accords well with the vertical structure of all reality. This latter is a pervading trait of the whole type of speculation to which that of Origen belongs—indeed its deductive and ordering principle. I cannot dwell here on the violently disputed particulars of this trinitarian doctrine, whose subordinationism loomed large in Origen's later condemnation.[15] At any rate, the second and third hypostases "succeed" the first in this order of dependence and perfection, and with them indeed already begins the descending series of creation. Their main ontological difference from all subsequent beings is that "only in this Trinity does goodness reside essentially (*substantialiter*): all others possess it as an accident, liable to be lost" (Bu. p. 53). Right after them,

[12]Bu. p. 20: "The only-begotten Son is the brightness of this light, proceeding from God without separation, as brightness from light, and lightening the whole creation."

[13]Bu. p. 31, n. 4: "he called the Holy Spirit a created being, as well as the Son, and included them in the number of the other created beings" (quoted from Justinian, *Ep. ad Mennam*).

[14]Bu. p. 26: "the Son's existence springs from the Father himself, yet not in time."

[15]A few quotations from *De principiis* may illustrate the more "objectionable" aspects of the doctrine. "Just as [the Son] is the image of the invisible God . . . so he is the image of the goodness, and yet not, as the Father is, good without qualification" (Bu. p. 27, cf. also n. 3: "a kind of breath and image of goodness, . . . [but not] good absolutely"). "The God and Father . . . is superior to every being that exists . . . ; the Son, being less than the Father, is superior to rational creatures alone . . . ; the Holy Spirit is still less and dwells with the saints alone (etc.)" (p. 33f, cf. also p. 33, n. 6). More vulnerable to attack in the rising christological disputes were the following statements: "The Son, who is the image of the invisible Father, is not the truth when compared with the Father; but in relation to us, who are unable to receive the truth of God almighty, he is a shadow and semblance of the truth" (p. 20, n. 1); and, perhaps most provocative: "God the Father is light incomprehensible. In comparison with the Father, Christ is a very small brightness, though to us by reason of our weakness he seems to be a great one"; "Again, as much as Paul or Peter differ from the Saviour, so much is the Saviour less than the Father" (p. 20, n. 5—quoting from Jerome). However, with respect to the last two quotations it should be pointed out that for Origen the incarnated "Christ" or "Saviour" is not quite identical with the "Son", the second person of the Trinity— see below.

yet still within the sphere of eternal creations, begins the realm of mutability.

2. *The eternally created minds*

"Before the ages," we are told (Bu. p. 67), God had surrounded himself with a world of pure minds,[16] in whose production the creativity inherent in the divine nature had, of necessity as it were, realized and also satisfied itself. As far as God's own initiative is concerned, this was what he wanted to produce. Everything else proceeds, in good gnostic manner, from the extradivine initiative of these created spirits, viz, from their acts of selfhood. It is at this point that Origen's speculation par excellence sets in, well summarized in the anathemas of the Constantinople Council of 553. In their original state, "all rational beings existed as minds bodiless and immaterial without any number or name, so that they all formed a unity by reason of the identity of their essence and power and activity and by their union with and knowledge of God the Word" (Bu. p. 125). Origen repeatedly stresses the point of the primordial equality, in nature and condition, of all created minds. Since, so he argues, God "had no other reason for creating them except himself . . . in whom there was neither variety nor change nor lack of power . . . he created them all equal and alike, for the simple reason that there was in him no cause that could give rise to variety and diversity" (Bu. p. 134). Origen, incidentally, considered their number as limited, for theological reasons interesting in themselves but of no concern to us here.[17]

3. *The beginning of movement; the fall of the spirits*

"How then did the spirits begin to move?" Into this realm of blessed tranquility, nondifferentiation and continuous enjoyment of God, "movement" entered through the *freedom of the will* with which the minds were naturally endowed; and movement could only be away from God. Origen is tantalizingly sparing in his indication of motive at this critical point. "They were seized with surfeit of the divine love and contemplation and turned toward the worse" (Bu. p. 125). He also speaks of a "cooling" of the ardor of love, "in consequence of which the minds

---

[16]"Minds" they are mostly called in their pure state, "rational natures" in all their states, including the fallen ones. However, the terminology is not entirely consistent.

[17]The reasoning is connected with the intriguing doctrine of God's own finiteness, cf. Bu. p. 129 and 323.

were called 'souls' " (Bu. p. 126)—a play on the etymological connection
between *psyche* = soul and *psychros* = cold, by which Origen could
enlist the testimony of his native language in support of his conceiving
the human soul as a deteriorated, lessened, cooled-off condition of
original mind or spirit.[18] The physical metaphor is, of course, no explanation and in fact goes none too well with the dominant theme of free
will. Of genuine psychological motives of the fall, "surfeit" (satiety,
weariness) and "negligence" (carelessness) are the only ones I find named
in *De principiis*. Elsewhere[19] Origen calls "pride" or "arrogance" the
cardinal sin which also caused Satan's fall, whose example started the
general "moving" down.[20] We have to deal with the theme of Satan
later, noting here only that he is not an evil principle but merely a fallen
angel. Given the initial equality of all rational creation combined with
the absolute freedom of will, there had to be one who, in the exercise
of that freedom, was first to turn away from God and in its continued
exercise moved farthest, i.e., "fell" deepest. To him, then, attaches the
name "Satan"—for so long as he occupies that place and role in the
hierarchy of beings: rehabilitation is open to him as to any other spirit;
and indeed in another world cycle another may take his place. It is the
place and the role that is denoted by the name, not a unique figure once
for all committed to that role. There is no eternal principle of evil opposing the goodness of God.

4. *Differentiation through the fall*

The "movement" away from the union with God, once initiated by the
original sin—that movement most commonly called the "fall"—is more
descriptively spoken of as a "decline by degrees," a "gradual sinking,"
a "gliding downward," and a progressive "emptying" (Bu. pp. 39–41).
The decisive fact is that the process is not uniform but varies with the
individual spirits,[21] carrying them to varying distances from the source.
According to the condition of their will, i.e., in proportion to the magnitude of their impulse towards the worse (Bu. p. 125), which differs in
them because of their freedom of choice, some come to a halt in their

[18]Bu. p. 123ff. Cf. of several statements: "We must see whether perchance, as we
said was made clear by its very name, the *psyche* was so called from its having
cooled from the fervour of the righteous and from its participation in the divine fire,
and yet has not lost the power of restoring itself to that condition of fervour in
which it was at the beginning." Cf. also p. 124.

[19]*Ezek. Homil.* IX, 2.

[20]Bu. p. 67, also Origen, *In Joh.* 32, 18.

[21]Bu. p. 77: "the variety and diversity of the motions and declensions of those
who fell away from the original unity and harmony in which they were at first
created by God"; cf. p. 240, n. 6.

descent sooner, some later, and some reach the utmost distance from God. Thus originate the different orders, the various ranks of being (Bu. pp. 67–68)—some become "Cherubim," others "Rulers," "Lordships" and "Powers," others archangels and angels, and those most sinful become "daemons," i.e., contrary powers (Bu. p. 126). This is how the hierarchy of beings came about. From the original unity of minds, diversity arises through defection and results in a difference of grades and places, of which even the highest still represent a diminution of their first estate. The highest is defined not as of those that acted best but as of those that sinned least. Only through guilt does multiplicity arise—and in further consequence: the manifoldness of the world. "This was the cause of the diversity among rational creatures, a cause that takes its origin not from the will or judgement of the Creator, but from the decision of the creature's own freedom. . . . And these were also the reasons which gave rise to the diversity of the world" (Bu. p. 134).

Now this idea: that diversity as such, subjects being of this kind or that, is a faulty condition, a defect brought about by themselves in the first place, and remains a function of their own will throughout their career; and the complementary idea: that the deed of differentiation can be undone, and that its undoing is the final goal—this is the central principle of Origen's system.

5. Creation of the world in response and in correspondence to the fall

How then does the fall of the spirits lead to the genesis of the world? Origen was orthodox enough to exclude any answer which would not make God himself the creator of the world. He could not, e.g., make the world the unauthorized work of some of the fallen powers, as many Gnostics did. But neither could he make it God's entirely free choice, seeing that God of himself would never have chosen diversity, let alone materiality. Indeed, by the immanent logic of Origen's principle, everything proceeds according to the self-motion of the spirits: in proportion to their individual downward momentum, to the natural gravity as it were of their different volitional dispositions, the plentitude of minds distributes *itself* along a vertical scale of being. "By their own causation" (or "fault": *aitia*), says Origen, but then adds that "on the basis of this fault, a divine judgement commensurate with the better or worse movements of each" assigns to each "according to merit" his rank in a world order now to be established (Bu. pp. 53–54).

Thus the creation of a world is the answer of divine justice (and, as we shall see, wisdom) to what the spirits have already done with themselves. It consolidates the results of their own motion. To this end God created *matter*, which the fallen minds need for their existence and their atonement. "In proportion to their particular sins they were enveloped in bodies as a punishment" (Bu. p. 126), bodies "either finer in substance or grosser," "ethereal, aerial, or fleshy" (Bu. pp. 40–41, 125–26), the degree of their materiality determined by the moral status of the bearer; and to each type of bodies, of course, God coordinates the appropriate physical environment. The result is a stratified scale of environments, whose totality is nothing other than the visible universe. With its creation, then, God objectified the spiritual rank order which the bodiless minds had set up among themselves, and provided the system of appropriate bodies and places for the further working out of their destiny: an instrument of his justice and providence alike.

But it is to be kept in mind that this creation had its origin not in the free will or plan of the creator, but was forced upon him by the fall of the spirits in general and by the diversity of their movement in particular. This willfull movement of the spirits is the true cause of the world, of its existence as well as of its structure. "Now since the world is so very manifold and comprises so great a diversity of rational beings, what else can we assign as the cause of its existence except the diversity in the fall of those who decline from unity in dissimilar ways?" (Bu. pp. 76–77). God by his creative intervention only gives visible and tangible subsistence to, and thereby pronounces sentence on, what has been committed in the intelligible realm—conferring on it a relative definiteness in the shape of a "world," viz., for the aeon in question. Especially the idea that the "diversity" of creation, which is at odds with the unity of the divine essence, derives from the self-made diversity of the aboriginal minds, and that its order only mirrors the gradation which their fall has instituted among them, is stressed again and again.

Even the celestial spheres are subject to this interpretation: "The sun, the moon, and the stars themselves belonged to the same unity of rational beings and have become what they now are through a declension towards the worse" (Bu. p. 126). "Just as we men for certain sins have been enveloped in these bodies of ours which are gross and heavy, so the lights of heaven have been given [their] bodies . . ." (Bu. pp. 62–63); they are "the souls of creatures once rational and incorporeal, but now 'subject to vanity', that is, to fiery bodies, which we in our crude ignorance call the lights of the world" (Bu. p. 62, n. 8; see also p. 127). One must know something of the high metaphysical honor in which the stars were held in pagan-classical thought, to appreciate this turn of speculation.[22]

---

[22]Origen's doctrine of the createdness of matter warrants special attention. He was conscious of departing with it from previous philosophy: "In regard then to this Matter, which is so great and wonderful as to be sufficient for all the bodies in the

Anyway, the structure of the visible world, certainly its vertical order, although mediated by the divine creator and his measure of justice, is in the last resort the expression of the outcome of a spiritual movement away from God. In this way Origen ingeniously combines the gnostic axiom that the world is the product of a fall with the biblical requirement that God himself is the creator of the world. The means of combination is the concept of justice, which in Origen is conjoined with that of providence and education—all three answering to the concept of free will that operates in the precosmic minds. Decisive are the two axioms: diversity as such is defection from sameness and unity; and its cause is a certain willful use of liberty.

6. *Free will as the principle of cosmic evolution*

This self-same liberty, viz, the unqualified capacity for good and evil that inheres and indelibly persists in all rational natures, and thus their never lost capacity for rising and falling, for ascent and descent, is the vehicle of the whole further world-process. It is indeed of so absolute a kind that it extends beyond the history of the given world, giving rise to ever new ones after it. There is no indifference in the movements of rational natures: "The will's freedom always moves in the direction either of good or of evil, nor can the rational sense, that is the mind or soul, ever exist without some movement either good or evil" (Bu. p. 228). Ultimately, "good" and "evil" are for Origen the only primary categories of mental action—a thoroughly different picture from that drawn by ancient philosophy with its main stress on the polarity of ignorance and knowledge. This means moreover, in virtue of the absolute position of the spiritual agencies in the ontological scheme, that *all* movement in all of reality takes place solely in acts of moral decision and their answer by divine justice.

The gnostic speculation that flourished before Origen had interpreted

---

world, which God willed to exist . . . I cannot understand how so many distinguished men have supposed it to be uncreated, that is, not made by God himself the creator . . ." (Bu. p. 79). Its createdness is matched by its transitoriness, i.e., its gradual sublimation and annihilation in step with the reëlevation and final return of the minds: "It must needs be that the nature of bodies is not primary, but that it was created at intervals on account of certain falls that happened to rational beings who came tó need bodies; and again that when their restoration is perfectly accomplished these bodies are dissolved into nothing, so that this is forever happening" (Bu. p. 325; see also n. 1, Jerome's somewhat fuller rendering of Origen's argument). Matter is at bottom a secondary phenomenon, a function of spiritual states. Origen's predecessors in this interpretation of matter were the Valentinian gnostics; cf. E. de Faye, "De l'influence du Gnosticisme sur Origène" (*Revue de l'histoire des religions*, 1923), "[la matière] est une sorte de condensation de la faute primordiale" (p. 201); ". . . la cristallisation de la faute dans le domaine visible" (p. 206).

the fall and rise underlying the cosmic drama in terms of the loss and recovery of *knowledge*, in this respect staying closer to the classical tradition. In its place Origen puts corruption and correction of the will, and the responsibility of each subject for its place in the cosmic scale. Secondarily, it is true, the fallen orders are, for Origen too, as many limitations of knowledge, and the rise to a higher order brings with it also a rise in knowledge. But the rise is not achieved through knowledge: it is sanctity of the will that leads to the higher order and thereby also to the knowledge coordinate with it.

7. Concerning Satan

Let us now turn to the teaching on Satan. "Among all rational creatures there is none which is not capable of both good and evil," says Origen (Bu. p. 69), and always in this context he adds sooner or later "not even the devil" (e.g., Bu. p. 44, p. 70). The teaching on Satan is the true touchstone of the radicalism of the dogma. As said before, he belonged to the same unity of minds as all "rational creatures." But he and a host of kindred minds "of their own fault departing from holiness precipitated into such a pitch of negligence as to be changed into opposing powers."[23] It is easily the greatest triumph of the absoluteness of the will that it can lead to the extreme opposite of its original quality, while yet retaining its essential nature, viz., the freedom for good and evil—and therefore the freedom to restore itself to the original state. Thus Satan and those of his party can rise again to the highest level, and indeed the ultimate consummation expressly includes the "restoration of the devil," who will be redeemed, not destroyed, and will enter as a complete equal (even with Christ!) into the restored unity of minds.[24]

By the same token, however, there can be defection from any other level of the spiritual order, all of which share this mobility of the will, and any of which may fall down to this nethermost limit, "the contrary powers": even "an archangel may become a devil as on the other hand

[23]Bu. p. 51, n. 1; cf. p. 70: "the devil was not created as such, but fell to this state as a result of his own wickedness." Origen holds it absurd to believe that the opposing powers "have not departed from the good of their own free will . . . but have possessed this determination from the beginning . . . not as a result of perversity of will but from the necessity of their creation", which is to "ascribe the cause of their wickedness, as something unavoidable, to their creator" (Bu. pp. 46–47).

[24]Bu. p. 251, n. 1; cf. p. 57, n. 1: "After many ages and the one restoration of all things Gabriel will be in the same state as the devil, Paul as Caiaphas, and virgins as prostitutes."

the devil may turn again into an angel" (Bu. p. 53, n. 3). All these movements proceed from free will, and the station in the hierarchy is assigned "according to merit." The station of Satan and his angels may thus be occupied by others in succeeding worlds. Whoever commits the extreme of evil in one, will be *diabolus* in the next period. But what holds for Satan holds for all—and this leads us to two main propositions of the system: the consubstantiality of all rational natures; and closely connected therewith: the unlimited metamorphosis of the "minds."

8. *Consubstantiality and commutability of all minds*

"All rational natures, that is, the Father, the Son, and the Holy Spirit, all angels, authorities, dominions and other powers, and even man himself in virtue of his soul's dignity, are of one substance" (Bu. p. 236, n. 1). "Of one nature, but of different wills," he asserts elsewhere with respect to angel, soul and daemon.[25] The extreme importance of this doctrine is evident. It leads directly to the further one "that any rational creature can change into any other" (Bu. p. 56, n. 4). And on this ontological foundation: sameness of substance and limitless mutability of volitional function, rests the pivotal doctrine of the cycle of beings, which is at the same time a cycle of worlds. Let us hear Origen himself on this at some length:

> Every rational creature can, in the process of passing from one order to another, travel through each order to all the rest, and from all to each, while undergoing the various movements of progress or the reverse in accordance with its own actions and endeavors and with the use of its power of free will. (Bu. p. 57).
>
> The daemons themselves and the rulers of the darkness in any world or worlds, if they desire to turn to better things, become men and so revert to their original condition, in order that being disciplined by the punishments and torments which they endure for a long or short period while in the bodies of men, they may in time reach the exalted rank of angels. It follows logically from this that any rational creature can develop out of any other, not once or suddenly but over and over again; that we may become angels or, if we live carelessly, daemons; and on the other hand daemons if they desire to possess virtue may attain the dignity of angels. (Bu. p. 56, n. 4)
>
> The soul-like condition [i.e., ours] comes from the angelic and archangelic condition, and the daemonic and human from the soul-like; and conversely from the human come angels and daemons, and each order of the heavenly powers is made up either wholly from those below or from those above, or else both from those above and those below. (Bu. p. 126: V; also VIa)

[25]Koetschau, *De Principiis*, p. 96, from Jerome, *Ep. ad Avit.* 4.

And this happens all the time, in an eternal up- and downward flow: "There always happens fall and reversal and new fall of the heavenly minds."[26]

9. World cycles

What does "always" mean here? Does it mean, in linear infinity? And generally, in what temporal form does the change occur on each occasion? Here we must record the doctrine of the cycle of worlds. Many worlds follow one another.[27] Within each, the grade of a rational subject is fixed. The change of roles occurs only with the change of scene, i.e., with the creation of another world after one is ended; then each mind will be reclassified according to his merit in the world just past.[28] The interval thus is each time a judgment, the "last judgment" of the respective world.[29] The judgment, however, consists really in the autonomy of the trend of "motion" which the spirits have adopted before: they seize their new station in pursuance of this trend, that is, they avail themselves of the change of scene accordingly and therewith have determined themselves for the newly beginning world (Bu. p. 65). This takes place at each "consummation of the world," and it is indeed "because of the variety of motions that a variety of worlds is created" (Bu. p. 241, n. 6).

For the individual then, the particular change may work in either direction, his new classification may be upward or downward. The total sense of the movement, however, thanks to the divine strategy of salvation, tends upward; in the succession of worlds there is a progressive reapproximation to the primal state; matter, e.g., becomes ever finer, lighter, less material as it were; ever more of the fallen minds find through penitence and purification their way back, until finally, at the end of such a world cycle of indeterminate number,[30] a great "Last

[26]Koetschau, p. CXXIV, from Maximus Confessor.
[27]Bu. p. 126: "It is probable that different worlds have existed and will exist, some in the past and some in the future"; p. 241, n. 6: "These different movements [i.e., of the rational natures] result in the creation of different worlds, and after this world in which we live there will arise another world quite unlike it."
[28]Bu. p. 56, n. 2: "appointed to different tasks in the single worlds according to their varying degrees of merit." I do not think that any of Origen's statements on this subject should be construed as referring to transmigration and reincarnation of souls *within* the history of a world.
[29]Of such a "small" consummation of the world, an "end" among many within one cycle, speaks e.g. the Jerome fragment in Bu. p. 65.
[30]Bu. p. 88: "What may be the number or measure of these worlds I confess I do not know; but I would willingly learn, if any man can show me."

Judgment"[31] brings about the complete annihilation of matter and the equalization of all differences, thus restoring the perfect unity of the beginning, "where all are one and diversity will be no more" (Bu. p. 250).[32] "Gabriel will be the same as Satan, Paul as Caiaphas, virgins as prostitutes" (Bu. p. 57, n. 1). The end has reverted to the beginning, beginning and end are the same.[33]

This is the consummation. And yet not the end. For in virtue of the unconditionally valid principle of free will, a new falling-away from unity will set in at some time,[34] matter will have to be created again, a world to be established, and the whole process starts once more[35]—with an indeterminable horizon. Because the end is equal to the beginning and has restored the conditions from which aeons ago the movement began, it becomes by the same logic a real beginning again.[36] We must, therefore, distinguish between two orders of magnitude in the "plurality of worlds": a smaller one, already consisting of an indefinite number of succeeding worlds which, however, form a connected whole of salvation history and eventually close, across any multitude of numbers, to the finite form of a circle; and a second order of magnitude, consisting of ever new of such closed world cycles, whose open sequence, linear, without a discernible terminus[37] and without relation of its members among themselves, loses itself in a mist of infinities into which no glance of speculation had ever ventured before.[38] Origen even debated with himself the possibility of an identical replication of a single world in these

[31] This is, for instance, the "judgment to come" of which Anathema XI of the Second Council of Constantinople treats: Bu. p. 246, n. 4.

[32] The full doctrine of consummation is given in Anathemas XII-XV (see section 13 at the end of this essay).

[33] Bu. p. 250, n. 3, Anathema XV: "so that the beginning is the same as the end, and the end is the measure of the beginning." Formulated as a general proposition: "For the end is always like the beginning; as therefore there is one end of all things, so we must understand that there is one beginning of all things (etc.)" (Bu. p. 53).

[34] "After the end of all things there occurs again outflow and downfall" (Koetschau, p. CXXXIV, from Maximus Confessor).

[35] Bu. p. 249, n. 1: "Nor can we doubt that after certain periods of time matter will exist again and bodies will be created and a world of diversity constructed in conformity with the varying wills of rational creatures, who *after* becoming perfect in blessedness at the end of all things (!) have gradually fallen [again] to lower levels and have admitted evil (etc.)."

[36] Bu. p. 246, n. 4: "a fresh beginning arises out of the end."

[37] Only to this *open* series, I think, can the expression apply, "in the infinite and unceasing ages during which the soul remains in existence" (Bu. p. 208, n. 5), or the "innumerable worlds" in p. 83, n. 1.

[38] Whether this in fact represents a serious belief of Origen and not merely a "hypothetical inference" from the system, is in dispute among Origen scholars—cf. W. Völker, *Das Vollkommenheitsideal bei Origenes*, p. 29, n. 2.

boundless permutations;[39] but unlike the stoics (and Nietzsche), he denied such a possibility, let alone an eternal recurrence of all things, as incompatible with the freedom of will (Bu. pp. 87–88).

10. Man's position between angels and daemons

From this vertiginous vision we turn once more to the smaller scenario of our world. Three major orders of rational beings were created commensurate with the "movements" of the aboriginal minds: angels, daemons, and between the two, men (Bu. pp. 71–72). Graded into ranks again are the angels among themselves, and likewise the daemons, who form a kind of hierarchy in reverse with its own manifold classes. All this is strictly commensurate with past merit: "Though it is not our business to know or to inquire what the actual deeds were through which they earned their entrance into a particular order," it is enough for us to be certain of God's justice in these dispensations, since "there is no respect of persons with God" (*loc. cit.*). There lastly are inborn differences, advantages and disadvantages, among men: these too are the consequence of a transcendent preexistence of the same soul in one life or more (human, daemonic, and angelic)—generally of "certain older causes" (Bu. pp. 240–41). A whole bundle of difficulties lurking in the problem of freedom and fate, of the antinomy of justice, predestination and grace—in short, of theodicy (Rom. 9:14 "Is there injustice on God's part? By no means!"), is deftly disposed of by this facile means.[40]

Few other teachings of Origen were as violently attacked by the orthodox as this doctrine of the preexistence of the human soul. It should be noted, however, that this is not a doctrine of *metempsychosis* in the Pythagorean manner. According to the general principle of the system, as we have seen, the new existence thus determined by former merit and guilt is situated "in another aeon,"[41] that is, separated from its antecedent by a cosmic change of scene. We do not hear of transmigration within one and the same world.

[39]Bu. p. 83, n. 1: "He is in doubt," reports Jerome, "whether there will ever be a world similar in every respect to another world (etc.)" or whether it is certain that this will never happen. Naturally the question could be asked, if at all, only in regard to the "great" series: in the smaller cycle the divine economy of salvation precludes *per se* such a repetition.

[40]For his favorite "demonstration" case Origen takes the problem of Jacob and Esau to which already Paul referred in Rom. 9: the one beloved, the other hated by God "before they were born and had done anything"—"in this life of course," Origen adds, and argues that divine election follows "merits in some previous life" (Bu. p. 135). The same argument is developed at length in the chapter on Free Will (Book III, Chap. I), where the Jacob-Esau theme is discussed in sections 22–3 (p. 204ff).

[41]Bu. p. 206; Jerome translates, *in alio saeculo.* Cf. n. 27, above.

The major aspect of Origen's doctrine of man is that he represents a middle order and thus a point of passage from and to the adjacent orders on either side—for reascending daemons on the one hand, who have earned the reward of becoming men, so that as such they may qualify anew for angelic rank (Bu. p. 56, esp. n. 4), and for falling celestials on the other hand, who hence may either turn upward again or continue down into the daemonic realm. Thus there exists a vertically connected chain of "rational natures" which also constitutes the order of ascent and descent for any of its members: only from step to step can movement proceed along this chain. Some centuries later, when the Origenist heresy had long been suppressed, Dionysius "the Areopagite" under Neoplatonic influence once more imported the doctrine of the chain of spirits into the Church. So firmly was the idea as such rooted in the thought typology of the epoch that it had a certain inevitability. In the later form, however, the chain is an "erotic chain," a vertical order of love, not as with Origen a chain of justice, linked by punishment and reward.

The middle position of man is especially characterized by its being the plane of the "soul." We have mentioned before the genealogical relation of "soul" (*psyche*) to "spirit" or "mind" as expressed in the pun of minds having "cooled" into souls: the soul is conceived as a derivative and transitory condition of something higher, destined to overcome itself again and having the moral capacity to do so. "When the mind declined from its original condition and dignity it became or was termed a 'soul,' and if ever it is restored and corrected it returns to the condition of being a mind."[42] So much does "soul" signify a state and not a substance that it can be treated like a term capable of comparative degrees: Origen speaks of mind in its downward course "turning into soul to a greater or lesser degree" (Bu. p. 127). But as a rule the term just refers to *our* place in the spectrum—it is the *human* soul, associated with the body of flesh, which is preeminently meant when Origen speaks of "soul." Of it he says that it morally occupies a middle ground between good and evil, between spirit and flesh.[43]

What matters most in the metaphysical theory of the soul's descent is the soteriological implication. By making of soul in general a passing, inauthentic metamorphosis of original mind, it makes the existent individual soul look to its own future abolition as the crowning eschato-

---

[42]Bu. p. 125; cf. p. 127, from Jerome: "Mind when it fell was made soul and soul in its turn when furnished with virtues will again become mind."

[43]Bu. p. 128: "a kind of medium between the weak flesh and the willing spirit"; cf. Origen, *In Joh.* XXXII, 18: "the soul is something median and receptive of either virtue or vice" (Bu. p. 233, n. 1).

logical possibility of its career. "The soul when saved remains a soul no longer."[44] However, this median position of man in the scale of being does not make him the center of the cosmic drama and the main object of divine concern. The coherent chain of spirits precludes the privileged position of any one link, all of which are the objects of God's justice and providence, as his aim is the restoration of the whole. We shall presently see that even the mission of Christ is not exhausted in the salvation of man.

11. *The graded structure of the universe*

The three main orders of spirits are matched by the tripartite structure of the universe—heaven, earth, and underworld (Bu. p. 303f). But, as the hierarchy of beings is articulated into many more ranks within both the angelic and daemonic orders, so the terms "heaven" and "underworld," apart from their absolute meaning, also have a relative use. Each plane is in one sense "underworld" for the next higher (even the visible sky for the "higher heaven") and in another sense "heaven" for the next lower (e.g., earth in relation to the underworld). This extends to the concept of death: as for us Hades is the place of the dead who died as sinners, so is our earth for the denizens of the higher world, "who die, so to speak, from their ministry in the heavenly Jerusalem . . . to occupy different positions on earth in proportion to their merits" (Bu. p. 303, n. 3, from Jerome). The same relation is repeated higher up and lower down—how many times, we are not told, as the number of cosmic tiers is not specified. To die above is to be born below, in the case of fault, or the reverse, in the case of merit. We see already how, with reference to the concept of salvation, the human-terrestrial scene and consequently the deed of redemption that happened down here lose all uniqueness: indeed, the doctrine of the strata of the universe is followed by the highly heretical doctrine of correspondingly many "passions"; diverse "gospels", locally, temporally, and qualitatively different redemptions (see below).

Those higher births of the soul—generally, its successive ascension through the succession of worlds—is accompanied by its parallel progress in knowledge. The spheres of the created universe are actually schools of instruction for the soul and thus stages of the "gnosis". Thus the self-improvement of the state of will, whose merit makes the soul rise in the orders of being, goes hand in hand with an ever brighter

---

[44]Bu. p. 122. Origen continues, ". . . as there was a time when that which has been lost was not lost, and there will be a time when it will not be lost, so there also was a time when the soul was not a soul and there will be a time when it will not be a soul."

illumination of knowledge which grows in each heaven until the primeval unity with God is restored, which is a condition as much of contemplation as of love.

12. *The divine economy of salvation: Origen's Christology*

How then does the saving dispensation of God work? Already his retributive justice is salutory by effecting atonement and inducing reflection. In addition, each level down to the angels, apart from being a punishment or reward to its occupants, has been instituted by God as an "office" or "ministry" with the task of helping the next lower level. This is the element of "providence" supplementing that of "justice" in the divine dispensation. In Origen's view it must cooperate with the free will of its objects.

And what about Christ? This at last is the place to relate Origen's peculiar Christology which lies almost entirely outside the trinitarian doctrine, is only by a slender thread connected with it, and has not failed to give strongest offense. Anathemas VIa-IX of the Constantinople Council of 543 are devoted to it.[45] The main point of the doctrine is that "Christ" is not the Logos, i.e. the second person of the Trinity, but what Origen describes thus: "Out of all the original unity of rational beings one mind [at the time of the general fall] remained steadfast in the divine love and contemplation, and he, *having become* Christ and king of all rational beings, created all bodily nature (etc.)" (Bu. p. 126). "Christ" is thus entirely of the equal-created class of all rational beings, by nature one of them, and is called "mind" in the emphatic sense only because he alone preserved this original ontological status unimpaired while the others forfeited theirs through the fall. Considering now that, in virtue of the unconditional principle of free will, it neither was predictable which of the equally endowed minds would remain faithful on that occasion, nor is it predictable which will remain so in coming and ever new beginnings—it appears that Christ is no less an exchangeable figure than Satan: he is Christ because he is the non-fallen mind of that world cycle. He too, therefore, exemplifies the general axiom of the equality of all rational natures combined with limitless mutability of the will—that axiom which admits no unique individual figures, thus no real proper names, into the system but knows only role and rank designations.

To continue with the Christology: Through the steadfastly maintained knowledge of the *Monas* (God the "One") this mind was made Christ

[45]Anathema VIa: see Bu. p. 126; VII: Bu. p. 320, n. 1; VIII and IX: see Koetschau, p. 142. Cf. also Bu. p. 110ff.

(IX); in particular he has before all ages been so intimately united with God the Word, i.e., the second person of the Trinity (VII) that "by a misuse of language" this too is called "Christ" whereas "genuinely" the name pertains to the mind thus clinging to him (VIII). Now, this mind "because he pitied the various falls that had happened to those who originally belonged to the same unity, and wished to restore them, went through all modes of being and was invested with different kinds of bodies and took different names, becoming all things to all, being changed into an angel among angels, into a power among powers, and into other ranks or species of rational beings according to the necessities of each particular case, and then at last shared in flesh and blood like us and became a man among men."[46] Of such a role the divine Logos, as part of the Trinity, was incapable because of his immutability.

Since the Christ in his saving mission has to deal with many different ranks of beings that stand in need of salvation, he may have to be crucified again, e.g., in the heavenly spheres for the salvation of the daemons situated there; and generally he must often suffer in coming aeons, "in order that the inhabitants of all places may be saved by his passion" (Bu. p. 310, and n. 3). Accordingly there will also be different "gospels": as, e.g., our gospel has fulfilled and replaced our law, so may later the heavenly law be fulfilled by the truth of a corresponding gospel, which "in comparison with ours which is temporal" would have to be called (with Rev. 14:6) the "eternal gospel" (Bu. p. 309, n. 7). Freed from the exegetical language, this means that it will be as superior to our gospel as the rank of being to which it is addressed is to ours.

Generally speaking, the function of Christ is to help fallen minds, by his instruction and example, to find their way back. The doctrine of his suffering many times in many different spheres and forms means that the uniqueness of his one appearance, on which the message of the New Testament grounds itself, somehow dissolves into the universality of a process in which "Christ" is a function rather than a unique event. There is a kinship here to certain gnostic teachings of a Messenger that goes through the world process as the bearer of Gnosis in many shapes and forms. Even the suffering of Christ is not the profound and central mystery that it is in the orthodox creed, but is rather one of the devices by which the divine pedagogy works and by which spiritis are won back. It is a help to, but not an indispensable condition for, salvation. The true vehicle of salvation is the operation of freedom in the self-determination of spiritual wills, be it the wills of humans, daemons, or angels. The disposition of a given world, the experiences made in it, the punishments and rewards meted out, and the ministry of Christ, or of the many Christs that appear to the different orders of being—they all

[46]Anathema VII: Bu. p. 320, n. 1; ibid.: "he emptied himself to the level of man."

are helps, but what ultimately actuates the drama of being, the motive power in the whole movement, are the decisions of individual wills at individual moments; and ultimately Christ can do no more than appeal to the will.[47]

Lastly, in view of all these premises, it is not surprising to hear that even the kingdom of Christ will come to an end: "one day he will lose his kingship",[48] since it is just the aim of his mission that in the end, when all beings are again equal to each other as they were in the beginning, even the devil "will be restored to his ancient rank . . . and Jesus will then together with the devil be reigned over by God" (Bu. p. 251, n. 1).

13. The consummation as the beginning restored

Herewith we come to Origen's doctrine of consummation which, in spite of the abstract perspective of unending repetitions that opens behind it, represents the internal closure of the system. Formally the consummation is a *restitutio in integrum*, a restoration to the first condition. It comes about as the final result of a progressive purification of the "rational beings." Through the succession of worlds, God's activity cooperating with the individual wills amounts to "pulling them, by his proffered hand as it were, towards the pristine state." And so, this is the description of the ultimate perfection: "The heavenly powers and all men and the devil and the spiritual hosts of wickedness are as unchangeably united to the Word of God as the mind itself which is called Christ and which was in the form of God and emptied itself; and there will be an end to the kingdom of Christ (XII). All rational beings will form one unity, hypostases and numbers alike being destroyed; and the knowledge of rational truth will be accompanied by a dissolution of the worlds, an abandonment of bodies and an abolition of names; and there will be an indentity of the knowledge as well as of the hypostases; and in the state of restoration only the bare minds will exist (XIV). The life of the spirits (minds) will be the same as it formerly was, when they had not yet descended or fallen, so that the beginning is the same as the end, and the end is the measure of the beginning (XV)."[49]

---

[47]Origen's Christology doubly avoids the bothersome Christian problem of what happens to all the generations that preceded the coming of Christ: for one thing, the "rational natures" are eternal and so no one is in danger of missing a unique coming; for another, there are many such comings and to rational natures of all grades.

[48]Koetschau p. 290, from Jerome, *Ep.* 96, and Bu. p. 250, n. 3.

[49]The four last anathemas of the Second Council of Constantinople: Bu. p. 250, n. 3. Anathema XIII is similar to XII and is therefore omitted here.

17.
The Soul in Gnosticism and Plotinus

First in St. Paul and later in Gnostic writings we meet the tripartition hylic (or sarkic)-psychic-pneumatic. It may refer either to the individual, denoting components of his being, or to mankind, denoting a grouping of types. In either case, *psyche* occupies a middle position between a higher and a lower state. (The tripartition as such is reminiscent of Plato's tripartite soul, but should not be confounded with it.) It goes without saying that 'soul' is superior to 'matter' or 'flesh', but this is hardly elaborated: what is emphasized is its being inferior to 'spirit' (*pneuma*), whose equivalent in more Hellenic versions of the doctrine is 'mind' (νους). In the contraposition to this higher principle, the word *psyche* and its derivative *psychicos* assume a certain derogatory sense. The theory behind it is furnished by the speculative systems of second century gnosis, especially of the Valentinian type, where 'Soul' writ large represents a fallen condition of original 'Mind' in the universal descent of Being. In the transcendental history of this descent, the origination of *psyche*, as a stage thereof, is often connected with the problematical figure of Sophia; and it is in particular identified with the ontological level of the Demiurge, whose inferior nature is telling evidence of its imperfection. *Psyche* is thus, apart from its anthropological aspect, a

Originally presented at the International Colloquium on Neoplatonism held at Royaumont during June 1969, and published in *Le Néoplatonisme* (Paris: Editions du Centre National de la Recherche Scientifique, 1971).

cosmogonic and cosmological principle, and it is this *qua modus deficiens* of absolute Being. A similar genealogy and status of 'soul' are met with in astrological and Hermetic teachings and in Origen. In all of them, 'soul' is derivative and not aboriginal in its nature; and derivative in a pejorative sense. This must therefore be regarded as a fairly pervasive teaching of the era. We are justified to speak of a Gnostic re-evaluation, i.e., a downgrading, of 'soul'.

I

In the Plotinian context we propose to deal mainly with the theory of 'Soul' as a universal hypostasis, that is, as a stage in the transcendental evolution of being. This calls for a characteristic of the general pattern of speculation into which this doctrine falls, and whose compelling intel-lectual force in those times reached beyond the boundaries of particular philosophies and creeds. Indeed, it is this pattern which Plotinus shared with the same Gnostics he opposed, and the very proximity in basic conception explains the strength of feeling which his polemic displays: it is the protest against a caricature of his own cause. Since this common ground, claimed by me, is the major premise on which my case for bring-ing Plotinus into the company of *Gnosis und spätantiker Geist* rests, I may be forgiven if I dwell on this theme at some length.

What must first be emphasized is that the thinkers of this group—such diverse men as Valentinus and Ptolemaeus, the anonymous authors of the *Poimandres* and the *Apocryphon of John*, Origen, Plotinus, and Mani—definitely wanted to offer speculative *systems*. The meaning of 'system' here requires explanation. What is aimed at throughout is a deductive whole where everything hangs together and one chain of reasoning or imagining leads from first principles to last consequences. Now, the very idea of such a system was rooted in an axiomatic convic-tion of the time, namely, that there is a *chain of being*, which the chain of reasoning does no more than reproduce. There can be a system of thought because being itself forms a system; and as the order of being, so is the order of demonstration: the "first" in theory is also the first in reality, the actual beginning of things.

Next to be noted is the directional sense of the deductive context: the "great chain of being" is *vertical*, and suspended from the highest point. The first is the highest, the last is the lowest. Nothing is more a priori certain to the thinkers of that era than this, nothing more self-evident to their inner eye—and nothing more in conflict with our way of think-ing, which traces the order of causes from the bottom up and bases the higher on the lower. As seen by them, the system of reality forms a hierarchy, an order of rank defined by the more and less of perfection, divinity, and goodness. Its grades are a diminishing extension from above, not a structure reared from and supported by the ground.

But the hierarchy, it must then be noted, is not static: the vertical order of things means necessarily the *descent* of all things, in that order, from a highest source down—and this involves the idea of one definite, linear *movement* of becoming by which everything in the hierarchy of being is produced. Again there is unanimity on this point (and sharp conflict with our conceptions): all creation is downward, and its course leads further and further away from the perfection of the source.

But this again is not the whole story. The complete movement of being was conceived as twofold and unfolding in a definite two-beat rhythm: first the downward movement to utter distance and otherness, to an extreme of alienation from the divine source—then a reversal of direction, an upward movement with the goal of return and reunion. The rise to higher levels of being is not creative but "decreative," an undoing of what has been done in the creative descent. The total account of being is thus a story of fall and redemption. Ascent matches descent, but is second to it; and indeed the theme of descent and re-ascent, of decline and restoration, dominates the whole family of systems we are referring to.

A final trait worthy of note is the universal tendency in that metaphysical climate to identify perfection with unity, and plurality with deficiency—from which it followed that the general nature of the fall was loss of unity and movement into diversity, and the correlative rise must mean unification. Such were some of the presuppositions common to the great variety of speculations of which that of Plotinus was one.

If, then, reality is such that everything derives from one first beginning and is to be explained in terms of that derivation, any "rational" demonstration of the manifold of reality must follow the order of origination, i.e., it must follow the transcendental movement of reality itself and move along that vertical axis from the heights to the depths and back from the depths to the heights along which reality has graded itself in consequence of its inner history. We do well to remind ourselves how different this approach is from our way of looking at things. None of these explanatory constructions took interest in the "horizontal" map of reality, in the *coordinated* manifold of things, their spread and interrelation on one and the same plane of being—which is what *we* are interested in and attend to in description and explanation. What fascinated those thinkers was the "vertical" order alone: the invisible hierarchy, not the visible breadth, of things. For them all reality was defined by this ordinate, and all theory concerned the secret dynamics of its generation. As the record of such a generation, the vertical axis of being, nothwithstanding its spatial connotations, is primarily a time axis whose progression as it were deposits the spatial stratification of the universe as a by-product along its course. 'Time' in this sense, as the dimension of process and change, is the paramount dimension of reality. But it is a curious, metaphysical 'time' of causal *prius* and *posterius* which could easily be transformed—from the mythological conception of events preceding those of the world and continued by the latter on the same plane of succession—into the philosophical conception of a timeless movement *behind*, and coextensive with, our world on a different plane. Even in the latter case, which Plotinus represents in its purity, an aspect of dynamics or inner event adheres to the sequence of ontological derivation. And in all cases there obtains the reverse sense of causation to that in the modern, evolutionary and historical view of things: insofar as we still speak at all of a higher and lower (as with "higher" forms of life), we see the higher evolve from the lower and almost a priori expect the highest to be the latest. In the theoretical scheme which in the gnostic-neoplatonic epoch had almost evidential force, the highest came first, and what is latest is the lowest.

Let us note, lastly, the *problem* with which every thinker committed to this general scheme had to cope: the problem of extreme polarization between the two ends of the scale of being. The distance between the here and the divine beyond had widened immeasurably, transcendence had been pushed to its utmost limit. The divine reality was beyond question; what called for special explanation was the fact that there is a world at all, which conflicts with the nature of divinity as such. Not only had the gulf to be bridged by intermediate stages (in whose invention gnostic fantasy excelled), but the cardinal question posed itself: How can something so low, so questionable and mixed as our world is, and as human existence in it is, have sprung from a source so pure, so perfect, so free of all admixture and ambiguity? What could have led from the perfection of absolute, eternal, spiritual being to the imperfection of temporal, material, terrestrial being? What accounts for the paradox of such a rift between the divine and the nondivine? The task of speculation was to furnish answers, or rather one comprehensive answer, to these questions. It was a premise in the very posing of the question that the pure state of the beginning, complete and satisfied in itself, had no motive to compromise its perfection by adding to itself a world. This strongly held premise precluded the simple biblical answer of a free *fiat* by God who willed the world as his own affirmative choice, but also the Platonic answer of a non-envious demiurge who, being good, communicates goodness to the receptacle as far as is possible. In whatever form, the demiurgical principle must be seen in a problematical light and its activity as a fall from perfection.

II

Within this generally shared scheme, speculation determined the origin and nature of the Soul. Let us consider here mainly Soul with a capital "S", i.e., the universal level in the scale of being from which all individual souls are derived. Among the Gnostics, it is the Valentinians who are most articulate about it. "Perfect redemption," so they said, "consists in the knowledge itself of the ineffable Greatness. For, since it was from Ignorance that Deficiency and Passion came into being, it is through Knowledge that the whole system which originated from the Ignorance is dissolved again. Therefore, knowledge is the redemption of the inner man; and it is not corporeal, for the body is corruptible; nor is it psychical, for *even the soul is a product of Deficiency* and like a lodging to the spirit. Spiritual must therefore also be the nature of redemption . . ." (Iren. I, 21, 4).

How is Soul a product of "Deficiency"? The tale is told at length in the precosmic story of the Sophia, the youngest of the Aeons in the divine Pleroma, who falls into ignorance and passion—initiated by some form of overreaching herself and overstepping her bounds. The successive stages of her fall and partial rehabilitation beget substantive hypostases that reflect the mental condition of each stage. Even matter is thus derived from the emotions of the Sophia. Soul originates from her repentance and "turning back" toward the source of life. The term is *epistrophe*: from this "all the Soul of the world and of the Demiurge took its origin." The Demiurge is the offspring of the fallen, lower Sophia, shaped out of the psychical substance which had emanated from her, and he becomes "father and king of all things psychical and material."

The ontological relation of Sophia and Demiurge is best expressed in the statement that "the Sophia is called *pneuma*, the Demiurge, *soul*" (Hippol. VI, 34, 1). Knowing something of the character of the gnostic Demiurge, one cannot be in doubt about the ambiguous nature of this principle behind him, viz. 'Soul'—a sunken form of 'Spirit'. His product then, the cosmos, necessarily reflects the deficiency from which it takes its origin. In this whole class of transcendental descent theories, *psyche* either is, or has an essential relation to, the principle of cosmic being—so that the cosmos as such is the prime and eminent product of that metaphysical stage of defection on which original Being became 'psychic'—i.e., on which it deteriorated to the psychic mode. The individual souls of all creatures, including man, are further derivatives of this all-soul.

III

Another example of gnostic soul speculation is found in the *Peri Archon* of Origen. He, of course, was an opponent of the Gnostics; but this prevented him no more than it did Plotinus from sharing major conceptions with them. Origen is an eminent representative of the general type of system which we have delineated. As an orthodox Christian, he could not admit a world soul, nor a creation of the universe by any other than the highest God himself. Yet with these constraints he managed to combine distinctly gnostic traits in the doctrine of both the soul and the world. The place of the gnostic Pleroma is taken by the world of pre-existent *minds* (νοῦς-νόες) surrounding the Godhead as his eternal creation. They are without difference among themselves, and united with God in contemplation and love. "Movement" entered this tranquil realm through their freedom of will—and movement could only be away from God, i.e., from unity with him and identity with one another to the diversity of individual self-determination. The "movement," in other words, is necessarily a fall; and it is in this fall that the "minds" turn into "souls" (ψυχη-ψυχαι). Origen in this context is fond of playing on the etymological connection between *psyche* and *psychros* in support of his conceiving the human soul as a deteriorated, diminished, "cooled-off" condition of original mind or spirit. "The *psyche*," he says, "was so called from its having cooled from the fervour of the righteous and from its participation in the divine fire, and yet has not lost the power of restoring itself to that condition of fervour in which it was at the beginning" (Bu. p. 125).[1] Soul, thus, is conceived as a derivative and transitory condition of something higher, destined to overcome itself again and having the moral capacity to do so. "When the mind declined from its original condition and dignity it became . . . a 'soul', and if ever it is restored and corrected it returns to . . . being a mind." (*loc. cit.*). So much does 'soul' signify a state and not a substance that it can be treated like a term capable of comparative degrees: Origen speaks of mind in its downward course "turning into soul to a greater or lesser degree" (Bu. p. 127). But as a rule the term just refers to *our* place in the spectrum—it is the *human* soul, associated with the body of flesh, which is pre-eminently meant when Origen speaks of 'soul'. Of it he

---

[1] All references are to the Butterworth translation, *On First Principles* (New York: Harper & Row, 1966).

says that it morally occupies a middle ground between good and evil, between spirit and flesh. The soteriological implication is that "the soul when saved remains a soul no longer" (Bu. p. 122).

Although 'soul' to Origen is individual, and he has no room for a universal soul, yet the cosmological significance of the level of being which soul represents is not absent. In his system too it is the fall of the spirits that leads to the genesis of the world. As an orthodox Christian, Origen was bound to regard God himself as the creator of the world: he could not, as so many gnostics did, make it the unauthorized work of some of the fallen powers. But neither did he make it God's entirely free choice, seeing that God himself would never have chosen diversity, let alone materiality. Diversity originated in the fall of the minds. The creation of a world is the answer of divine justice to what the spirits have already done with themselves. "On the basis of their fault," God assigns to each his rank and place in a physical order "commensurate with the better or worse movements of each" (Bu. pp. 53–54). To this end God created matter, consolidating by its order the results of the spiritual motions.

Thus the creation of the world had its origin not in the free will or plan of the creator, but was forced upon him by the fall of the spirits in general and by the diversity of their movement in particular. The willful movement of the spirits is the true cause of the world, of its existence as well as of its structure. "Now since the world is so very manifold and comprises so great a diversity of rational beings, what else can we assign as the cause of its existence except the diversity in the fall of those who decline from unity in dissimilar ways?" (Bu. pp. 76–77). In this way Origen ingeniously combines the gnostic axiom that the world is the product of a fall with the biblical requirement that God himself is the creator of the world.

                                    IV

Let us begin the account on Plotinus with the famous opening of Enn. V, 1, even though the language refers to the individual souls rather than 'Soul' as the third principal hypostasis. "What was it that made the souls forget their Father God and, although parts from There and wholly of that world, made them ignorant of themselves and Him? The origin of evil to them was the boldness (*tolma*) and the [entering into] becoming (*genesis*) and the first otherness and the will to belong to themselves. Rejoicing in their self-determination (*autexousion*), once they had come forth, they made ample use of moving on their own, taking the contrary road [i.e. away from God] and defecting to such extremes of distance that they lost knowledge of their origin from There." We note in particular the terms boldness (or audacity), self-determination, and enjoyment of separate selfhood. This is said of particular souls, presumably already existing before they began to fall, which fairly agrees with certain Orphic and Platonic ideas, as also with Origen. But the true teaching of Plotinus is that 'Soul' as such resulted from a primordial 'fall' which occurred in the inner evolution of Being writ-large. For this teaching we turn to chapter 11 of Enn. III, 7, which treats of the origin of time.

"We now must raise ourselves [in thought] again to that state we found to hold for eternity—that unmoved, wholly simultaneous, actually infinite Life [of the νοῦς], undeviating throughout, standing still in the One and directed towards the One. Time was not yet there, or was not for those intelligible beings. We now will bring it forth with the notion and the nature of the 'later' [i.e., we shall theoretically reproduce its arising]. Since those [intelligible beings] repose in themselves, how did time first fall forth [out of eternity]? On this question one cannot appeal to the Muses for information, because they did not yet exist. But perhaps . . . one can ask generated time itself how it is after it has stepped forth and come to be. Then one might speak of it somewhat as follows. As it were, 'before'—prior to having engendered this [intratemporal] 'before' and become needful of the 'after'—it reposed with and in Being and was not yet time, but was itself at rest in that Being. But there was there a nature which was forward (*polypragmon*) and wished to own and rule itself and had chosen to strive for more than it had present to it. Thus it started to move, and along with it also moved time, and the movement was towards the ever-still-coming and later, towards the not self-same but ever and again other—and once having travelled some distance of the way we have brought forth time as a copy of eternity. For, there was in the Soul an unquiet power, which always wished to transfer what it beheld There [i.e. in the intelligible world] into another medium, unwilling to let the assembled total be present to her. Just as from the quiescent seed the substantial form (*logos*) unfolds itself and takes passage through a supposed many, hiding the [simultaneous] manifold by dividing it up, and in exchange for its inner One spends the One outside itself and goes forth into weaker extension–thus also the Soul: when she made the sensible world in imitation of the intelligible and imparted to it a motion different from the intelligible but conforming to it and striving to be its likeness–she *first of all temporalized herself*, generating time as a substitute for eternity; *then* she made also the generated cosmos subject to time, placing it as a whole in time and encompassing all its processes within time. Since the cosmos moves in the Soul—for nothing other than the Soul is the place of this sensible universe—it must move also in the time of the Soul. As the Soul imparts her activity in portions—one succeeding another and again succeeded by a different one—she generated succession as such along with her being active; and at one with the discursive thought (*dianoia*), which is [each time] different from the preceding one, there [each time] came forth [in the creation also] what had not been before, since also its thought had not yet been actualized [in the Soul] and her present life is unlike that which went before . . . It was thus the distension of life which occupied time, and the perpetual advance of the life occupies ever new time, and the life already passed occupies past time. Therefore one can frame this definition: Time is the life of the Soul consisting in a movement that passes over from life-state to life-state . . . In this manner [alone] can she imitate the presently whole and assembled infinite [of the intelligible world], if she is willing to maintain herself in being by constant acquisition [of being]."

This is a mixture of ontology and drama, i.e. myth. The ontology articulates *what* time is in counterpoint to eternity; the myth relates *how* time seceded from eternity. In doing so, the myth tells of forwardness and unrest, of an unquiet force, of unwillingness or inability to remain in concentrated wholeness, of a power that is thus at the same time an impotence, of a desire to be selfsubsistent and separate. Just as in Origen, 'movement' is the beginning of a deterioration, and turning away from unity marks the beginning of movement. In both cases the motive force is *self-will*. We see that at this critical point—when the question is: why there should be this lower world at all outside the Intelligible—Plotinus cannot make do without the same language of apostasy and fall for which he takes the Gnostics so severely to task. In resorting to it he defies his own systematic intentions and all categories of derivation legitimized by the system. The straightforward, unequivocal principle of the power of plenitude and its necessary outward action, by which the system normally explains, in level after level, the coming forth of the many from the One, no longer suffices him when it comes to the Soul and the downward evolution it promotes. Regarding the origination of time in particular, we note the decisive and already linguistically striking expression that the Soul, in its willful turning away from pure being, "first temporalized herself": I know of no previous witness for the transitive verb *chronoō*; it is unique in Plotinus himself and probably coined by him to express a novel thought. Neither do I know of an after-history of the word. The coinage and its reflexive use bring out the difference from the Platonic model in the *Timaeus*. There, time is created; here, it is undergone by that which is going to create, as a self-alteration of its own being and a condition of its becoming creative. There, its creation is by rational intent and as part of the creative design; and its combination with the nonrational givenness of space (the receptacle) enables the latter to participate in the rationality of being by ordered motion: here, in Plotinus, time itself is of irrational origin, a product of the audacity of a restless, centrifugal principle, which loses by its self-temporalization; and only by its own dynamics of dispersion into *partes extra partes* does the temporality of the cause lead to the further externality of space (which did not preexist) and of body. Accordingly, in Plato the conspicuous trait of temporal movement is the repetition of the eternally same, in Plotinus—the progress to the always other.

This is only the beginning of an exposition of Plotinus' doctrine of the soul. Strictly, we have followed the descensus no further down than to the level of discursive thought, which, by contrast to the *homou panta*, the simultaneous intuition of the *Nous*, makes temporality necessary for its piecemeal apprehension of the intelligibles. Its successiveness signifies a weakness of the thinking subject, but also a presumption on its part. In a further progression to a lower reflection of Soul, accompanied by a further weakening of the power of beholding, even discursive thought no longer suffices, and its contents have to be set outside and particularized in space and matter. This nether reflection of the upper Soul is called *physis*, and her busy production is nothing but an inferior substitute for failing contemplation—evidence of the impotence to behold directly. This idea is propounded in Enn. III, 8, *On Nature and Contemplation and the One*, which the discerning Porphyry justly put after the treatise on *Eternity and Time* from which I have quoted.

However, we must leave matters here. I wish to conclude with a general observation on the structure of the Plotinian system which will bring us back to the gnostic comparison. According to Plotinus, each hypostasis exists, and is what it is, in virtue of relating itself *to* the next higher *from* which it stems: its relation to it is not just its being descended from it, but also its turning back toward it. The turning back or upward (*epistrophe*) belongs as much to the subsisting of the hypostasis as does its egressus downward (*proodos*): precisely this double movement is the complete act of its foundation. Generally, relation to—, direction toward—(*einai pros*—), is the form of being of every hypostasis besides the first, the One (which has no *pros ti* whatsoever in its nature). As direction to the originating "higher," this relation is at the same time the sustaining condition of its being. Now, it is peculiar to the hypostasis 'Soul'—and a peculiarity not derivable from the general principle of the metaphysics–that, in addition, it is *also* directed toward that which is "lower" than itself. The peculiarity is compounded in the *human* soul by the fact that in its case the direction to the Higher is a task and an optional goal rather than a preassured condition of its being: this is *au fond* irreconcilable with the rigorously understood, speculative principle of the system, congenial as it is to its ethical spirit. Here is one of those fissures in the system in which the theoretical violence of the Plotinian synthesis betrays itself. The theory of the Soul, as the one truly problematical magnitude in the system, brings its un-reconciled contradiction to light. A stylistic sign of it is that in describing the egressus of the Soul from the *Nous*, Plotinus, as we saw, feels con-strained to depart from his otherwise strictly dialectical style of deducing the steps in the general descensus of Being and resorts to psychological (even emotional) terms such as *tolma*, et al., to provide the "motivation" for this particular step. The language turns from philosophical to mythological and, with all his distaste for gnostic "tragedy-mongering," comes dangerously close to gnostic mythologizing.

18.
The Abyss of the Will:
Philosophical Meditation on the
Seventh Chapter of Paul's Epistle to the Romans

In 1930 I dedicated my first publication, *Augustin und das paulinische Freiheitsproblem*,[1] to Professor Rudolf Bultmann "in heartfelt gratitude." The gratitude of the student was later joined by the friendship of maturity and the solace of loyalty. This bond has lasted through a lifetime during which many another was broken and irretrievably lost in the dark abyss of our times. But apart from the personal bond which has thus grown through the years, there also stretches from that earliest witness of it to the present occasion a still unredeemed *theoretical* obligation, and I cannot honour the occasion[2] better than by redeeming that obligation at last. What I had obligated myself to was an existential analysis of the Pauline self-experience which finds expression in Rom. 7.7–25. The interpretative history of this chapter in the course of the Pelagian struggle served the study of 1930 as a key to the clarification of

---

This is the author's translation and revision of the German original, published in *Zeit und Geschichte. Dankesgabe an Rudolf Bultzmann zum 80. Gerburtstag*, ed. Erich Dinkler, Tübingen, 1964. The English version was first published with the title "Philosophical Meditation on the Seventh Chapter of Paul's Epistle to the Romans," in *The Future of Our Religious Past: Essays in Honour of Rudolf Bultmann*, ed. James M. Robinson (New York: Harper & Row, 1971, and S.C.M. Press, London).

[1] A second, revised edition was published in 1965 (Göttingen: Vandenhoeck & Ruprecht), with an introduction by James M. Robinson, and with the present study added as an appendix.

[2] Bultmann's 80th birthday anniversary, August 20, 1964.

Augustine's conception of certain crucial aspects of the Christian life, aspects that meet in the problem of free will. Two considerations determined the choice of just this key. One was the plain historical fact that this text more than any other happened to serve as the focus and exegetical paradigm of the debate between the combatants themselves; the other was the conviction that this happened by rights, i.e. that the Pauline statements in question are indeed entitled to such a key position. But they are so only if what they express are not contingent but necessary truths.

The statements would be contingent, in the sense here used, if the 'I' speaking about itself were Paul's own empirical person, i.e., if we were dealing with an autobiographical report (of which one part would describe the past, another the present). They would also be contingent if the speaking 'I' were meant to represent a psychological type—such a type of person, e.g., for whom the forbidden, when and because it is forbidden, gains irresistible attraction: widespread as the *fact* may be (but how is irresistibility ascertained?), its generality would be merely empirical and as such admit of exceptions from the rule, which then would also be excepted from the consequences of the rule, such as the need for grace. And again the statements would be contingent if the 'I' were historical mankind (or the people of Israel as its prototype), which 'must' pass successively through the phases 'before the Law' and 'under the Law' in order to reach the phase of Grace 'after the Law': necessary as this sequence might be for the progress of history, the individual's belonging to a particular phase of it would be contingent and, for his perspective, would make the contents of the others inactive—for the post-Pauline Christian, e.g. a matter of mere historical retrospect.

Contrariwise, the statements would be necessary if the speaker were Man as such, so that what is said in this I-form about the failure of the attempted fulfillment of the Law holds for the Christian no less than for the Jew and the pagan, and precisely for this reason constitutes a valid argument for the Christian alternative, even an integral moment in its own inner movement. This last assumption I made and expressed in the study of 1930, without proving it. I rather declared its proof to be a still outstanding task. Now 'proof' can here only mean: explication of the modality of existence where a plight like that described in Rom. 7 is intelligibly at home and is bound to emerge from its radical acting-out. The phenomenologically demonstrated necessity of such a plight in such a life would lend support to the thesis that *it* could be what Paul meant. No proof can go further where in the nature of the case, i.e. according to the condition of all hermeneutics, we work with a hypothesis of empathic understanding.

Plan and draft[3] of such an analysis indeed preceded the publication of the Augustine study and still provide the basis for the present, renewed attempt. It is the attempt at a structural analysis of that mode of human being in which the 'primal sin' spoken of by Paul and Augustine is inevitably committed and constantly renewed. The analysis aims at showing the genuine and dialectical necessity of the structure which here operates—genuine because rooted in the manner of movement of the human will as such, and dialectical because even as necessary it is yet the will's own deed, and thus the self-decreed fate of a freedom delivered up to itself. The philosophical analysis, tracing the necessity back to its existential ground, must show how the operative dialectic, which issues into the experience of insufficiency, in turn springs from the fundamental ontology of man's being. Only on this condition do the Pauline statements have the validity they claim. The essay thus experiments with a specific understanding of those statements, according to which they ought to have such a validity. For the purpose of this experiment we must dare to translate the content of Paul's statements into the language of existential form description—we might say 'translate back into', in so far as our preconception is correct.

We preface the analysis with the passage from the Epistle to the Romans to which it refers. What follows upon the quotation, however, is not an exegesis of the text but a freely philosophical reflection or meditation on the general existential phenomena which by hypothesis may be those that underlie the entire Pauline statement as its premise in the human constitution.

> Rom. 7.7–25. (7) What then shall we say? That the law is sin? By no means! Yet, if it had not been for the law, I should not have known sin. I should not have known covetousness, had the law not said 'thou shalt not covet'. (8) But sin, receiving impulse from the commandment, wrought in me all kind of covetousness. For without the law sin is dead, (9) and I once lived without the law: but with the advent of the commandment sin came alive, and I died, (10) and the very commandment given for life proved to be death to me. (11) For sin, taking impulse from the commandment, tricked me and through the commandment killed me. (12) Now the law is holy, and the commandment is holy and just and good: (13) did, then, what is good bring death to me? By no means! Rather it was sin, so that it might come to light as sin, which wrought death in me through the good, so that sin through the

---

[3]First laid down in a 1929 letter to Rudolf Bultmann, a copy of which, with great good luck, stayed with me through all the wanderings of my life—so that thirty-five years later, and with some lessening of the original diffidence about it, it could at last see the light of day in the developed form of this essay. (This is, therefore, I believe, the piece with the longest incubation of any I have ever published.)

very commandment might become sinful beyond measure. (14) For we know that the law is spiritual: but I am carnal, sold under sin. (15) For my own actions are beyond my ken: for not that which I will this I do, but what I hate this I perform. (16) Now if I perform that which I do not will, then I consent to the law and own that it is good. (17) But by that token it is not I any more who acts but the sin which dwells within me. (18) For I know that within me, that is, in my flesh, there dwells no good. For willing what is right is in my power, but doing it is not. (19) For I do not perform the good which I will, but the evil I will not, that I do. . . . (21) So I find in me, who wills to do right, a law by which evil lies close at hand. (22) For I delight in the law of God with the inner man, (23) but I see in my members another law at war with the law of my mind and making me captive to the law of sin which dwells in my members. (24) Wretched man that I am! Who will deliver me from this body of death? (25) Thanks be to God through Jesus Christ our Lord! So then, I of myself serve the law of God with the mind, but the law of sin with the flesh.

Man is that being who not only relates himself to the world in 'intend-ing' acts (*cogitationes*) but in so doing also knows about these acts and therewith about himself as performing them. Thinking is always and simultaneously an 'I think that I think' (*cogito me cogitare*): thus a being essentially self-related, and 'constitutively' so, because only in and through such self-relation it constitutes itself as an I. This most formal characteristic of 'consciousness' being always self-consciousness, its essential reflexivity, already provides the condition both for the possi-bility of human freedom and for the correlative necessity of its self-frustration. Both grow from the same root in the same act of realization. Not, it is true, from the innocuous iteration of a neutrally 'representa-tional' *cogito me cogitare*: the *cogito* as mere representational (percep-tual) reflection upon itself is not the originative seat of self-consciousness and freedom.

Rather it is the *will* in which the reflexive process relevant for free-dom is performed. To the abstract-formal sense of the *cogito me cogitare* (as mere neutral self-awareness), there corresponds in the field of con-crete existence the fact that willing likewise says, not only 'I will', but at the same time also 'I will that I will this' (*volo me velle*). Every willing wills itself and has at each moment already chosen itself. The will thus has in itself its own inherent reflexiveness in whose perform-ance it primally constitutes itself as what it is, and by which it is radically distinguished from any mere desire or impulse (*appetitus* of any sort): impulse, directive as it is, is non-reflective, appetition is not concurrently an *appeto me appetere* as volition is a *volo me velle*. It must be noted that the reflection of the will is itself volitional, the will is at once the wilful positing and affirmation of itself. The formula, therefore, reads not simply *cogito me velle* (after the Cartesian pattern), but *volo me velle*.

Thus understood the will is not just another and particular physical function among others, classifiable under wishing, desiring, striving, impulse and the like. Nor is it the same as explicit resolve or, in general, anything that appears and disappears, is sometimes present and sometimes absent. The 'will' is *a priori* always there, underlying all single acts of the soul, making it possible for things like 'willing' as well as its opposite—lack or renunciation of will—to occur as special mental phenomena. It precedes any explicit resolve, any particular decision, although it is in itself, in its essential nature, nothing but continuously operative *decision about itself*—that permanent self-determination from which the subject cannot withdraw into the alibi of any neutral, indifferent, 'will-free' state: for the primal decision of will is itself the condition for the possibility of any such state, be it indifference or its opposite.

The 'will' which performs this permanent decision, or rather, which exists as its performance, is thus nothing other than the fundamental mode of being of *Dasein* in general, and the word merely signifies the formal-structural fact that the being of *Dasein* is such that in each of its actualities something or other is its concern, and the final concern in all the variable ones is its own being as the ultimate task of this being itself. In brief, 'will' signifies what Heidegger explicates under the head of 'care'. The formula 'being an issue for itself' circumscribes what we here mean by the reflection of the will.

This activity of the reflection of the will is the primal deed of the self's grounding itself. In its process there is brought about the continual self-constitution of the moral person, which sustains itself through it as the synthesis—at work from moment to moment, but continuously integrating—of the moral self-identification of the ego. Only through this self-constitution in the reflection of interest—be it even in the mode of self-dissembling—can there be an identical subject of possible accountability. All the phenomena of morality—freedom, choice, responsibility, conscience, guilt—are rooted in this primordial reflexiveness. Its *a priori* presence is the ontological basis of freedom.

But how is it to be understood that this selfsame fact also accounts for the necessary failure of freedom, its inevitable ensnarement in itself? Any deduction of 'insufficiency' as culpable and answerable must conceive it as a necessary but none the less self-committed deed of freedom itself, however paradoxical, even absurd this may seem. The (volitional) reflection of the will is the site of freedom: the domain of the will in general is also that of unfreedom: it must therefore be a *mode* of its reflection in which the latter is generated—and an unavoidable mode at that, if the Pauline-Christian insufficiency-thesis is not to be a mere slander of man (which Nietzsche thought it to be).

When we first introduced the *cogito me cogitare*, we rejected its merely 'representational' (perceptual) modality as inadequate for the reflexivity of existence we are dealing with. But now precisely this objectifying, viewing mode must be considered. Its role too is fundamental for the very possibility of freedom. For only by objectifying the universe of the other to the 'world' of objects over against itself, by standing back from them as a subject, can freedom first create for itself its possible 'space': only from this generic 'distance' does the self enjoy freedom of movement and choice with respect to environing reality. Now this same objectification which man, as a primordial act of his being, performs *vis-à-vis* the being outside of him, setting it over against himself as 'world', extends necessarily and correlatively also to himself: he too becomes a *vis-à-vis* to himself. In the objectification he steps forth out of an 'original' unity with the all of being (the 'innocence of the creature') and opens up an essential distance that is henceforth interposed between himself and all-that-is. And across this cleavage the ego confronts not only that objectified universe but also itself as one of whom it can say 'I'—and must say it because, with the isolation once happened (this 'once' is the imaginary past of the Fall), it thereafter must hold its own in this apartness for better or for worse. Thus, along with the objectivation of world, there is already inevitably given the possible, viewing objectivation of self (which is essentially distinct from the 'reflection of the will')—and with it also the necessary possibility of that taking distance from one's self which forsakes the humility of unmediated creatureliness for the pride of mediacy in the relation to oneself.

Thus the reflection of the will is matched by an equiprimordial self-objectivation of 'intuition' (representation). In terms of our formula, the relation can be expressed thus: The *volo me velle* has in itself the essential possibility of changing into a *cogito me velle* (*cogito* here taken in the specific sense of object-thought). In this switch, freedom dispossesses itself: instead of living within the execution of its self-chosen action, it looks at it from without as its own observer and so has already become a stranger to it—has at bottom forsaken and betrayed it. Out of the pure futurity of unconditional engagement to which it had committed itself with the action, it has fallen into a 'present' of objectified 'data', in which curiosity finds the secure footing of a beholder against the totally exposed movement of the actor. In such self-objectivation freedom, shrinking from its part, assures itself again of that support of which in the venture of resolution it had just let go. *In concreto*, the objectivation can take a variety of psychological forms. Mostly, it will work with the side-glance of comparison with others (which means that the social sphere, the 'with-one-another', provides the horizon of objectivation, even if only in imagination). At any rate, it always substitutes me the observable actor for the action unconditionally living in the act itself. Shouldn't this be at least one meaning, perhaps the minimal as well as the fundamental meaning, of the Pauline concept of 'self-glorying' in one's work?

This peculiar obduration of temporality in itself, in its immanent performance, or, expressed in the formula chosen above, the inevitable, self-generating alternation from *volo me velle* to *cogito me velle*, can be regarded, so I think, as the trap in the Law that is not only consistent with its holiness but even directly caused by it, since the Law as such enjoins self-consciousness. It is a noble trap for it is nothing but the snare of freedom itself, prepared as well as dared by it, because 'Law' in the highest sense means nothing heteronomous but precisely freedom's demand upon itself. In other words, the dialectics here in force lies beyond the difference of heteronomy and autonomy. For the 'thou shalt not covet' in which Paul epitomizes the meaning of the Law, one might well substitute Kant's idea of duty as opposed to inclination—and the dialectics would remain the same in principle (see below).

However, with the turn from *volo* to *cogito*, from the reflection of the will to self-objectivation, the matter does not rest. A freedom that is in earnest about itself will not stop here; it is on guard against its own tricks and keeps its eyes open. The will in its living reflection will catch up with its own objectivation, find itself out in the appeased anchorage of looking-on and sweep it up in a new resolve that now encompasses this very situation together with the original object: this is thus, on a second plane, restored to its authenticity, and the congealing of the representational 'present' is re-dissolved into the flow of the volitional 'future'. But this new stage of 'reflection', in its temporal performance, will again lapse into objectivation—and so there ensues a ceaseless, self-mirroring back and forth, an elusive but highly real dialectic which is not even separable into successive parts. Driven by its own dialectic, the will modifies itself into the infinite spectrum of its inherent ambiguities, losing itself in it without ever attaining to a univocal condition—unless this, of itself endless, dialectic be halted from somewhere else. About this possibility philosophy has nothing to say.

Let us briefly treat the distinction, just touched upon, between 'heteronomous' and 'autonomous' ethics as it relates to our problem. In the form of heteronomy, especially in the religious context where it was first noted, the dialectic looks as follows: Since faith in the authority of the divine lawgiver (whereon hangs the obligatory force of his com-

mandments) includes faith in his justice, the observation of his commandments *must* go along with the *expectation* of reward and punishment,
even if no *wish* for them exists. But the certainty of this very faith,
morally necessary as it is, destroys the purity of fulfilling the Law by
giving it a utilitarian tinge: it thus protects divine morality and sanctity
of the Law at the expense of the possibility of human morality and
sanctity of the will. On the other hand, if the certainty of divine consideration of merit, positive and negative, is denied, then the seemingly
rescued possibility of human morality is once again destroyed, since the
Law of a God who is, if not outright unjust, at least incalculable,
capricious, or indifferent—in short, the Law of an amoral God—cannot
be holy and so cannot claim any moral authority. Thus fulfilling it cannot be moral either, except by error (lack of clarity) concerning the
dubiousness of its source; and error itself, or insufficient reflection, must
not be made the condition for morality. This means, then, that the possibility of human morality cannot be rescued at the price of waiving
divine morality, any more than the divine can be preserved without
perversion of the human; or, more briefly, human morality can no more
exist without divine morality than co-exist with it.

So it is under the condition of heteronomy. Kant thought he could
evade the dilemma by replacing the divine lawgiver with the self-
legislation of reason, that is, by making the moral law autonomous and
thereby detached from the idea of reward and punishment. But we have
shown above that pure inwardness also procures for itself, through the
mirroring of self-objectivation, a kind of self-recompense which (known
under the name of vanity) is no less corrupting than the counting on
return from outside—possibly more, since it can be enjoyed without
delay, in the very performance of the act, whereas the counting on later
reward from without demands the strength of a patient, long-sustained
faith. In truth, the alternative 'autonomous-heteronomous' is over-
arched by the more essential alternative of authentic and inauthentic.
For, obviously, the antinomy immanent in the act, which we have described, is more fundamental than that deriving from the consideration
of transcendent and future facts, and it is common to both the autonomous and the heteronomous positions; it represents the existential
antinomy of the moral realm as such, independently of all theories
concerning the ground of the moral norm. To put it at utmost brevity,
the antinomy means that under the condition of human ambiguity the
attempt at holiness of will condemns itself to an unholy will. It is my
opinion that this antinomy stands behind the despair of the Pauline
self-description.

But why should the slipping into 'objectivation' be necessary? Being
a possibility of freedom does not make self-objectivation a necessity. To

begin with, the self-objectivation is necessary, indeed morally demanded, *qua* examination of one's own action, which is first of all an examination of one's motives (what Kant called the maxims of the will); and in so far as this examination—the self-exploration of conscience—belongs to morality as such, it is inseparable from the doing of good. In other words, self-objectifying is *eo ipso* given with the fact that morality is reflexive by its nature, and its necessity is itself a moral one, quite apart from its being also a psychological one. For the *homo religiosus* this takes the form of understanding himself from the standpoint of God and asking 'how does my action look to his eyes?' He must try to look at himself through God's eyes: i.e., to turn his own eyes into those of God. The 'before God' becomes thus, of necessity, a 'before myself'. But this substitution can, under the condition of creatureliness, only be maintained if I put in place of the infallibility of the divine gaze, which is denied me, the uttermost distrust of my human gaze. That is to say, for the sake of the good, the self-objectivation must be evil-minded and anticipate all possible wickedness. The distrust must be malicious. The malice of distrust is to know all that is possible, and to suspect that it is actual. In order to be able to know all that is possible, and to miss nothing, the distrust must be inventive in evil. Armed with that inventiveness, the distrust of myself becomes the inevitable price for the absoluteness which I, at one and the same time, ask of myself as an agent and arrogate to myself as a judge, and it must turn into positive self-suspecting. The attitude of distrust which I assume as my own observer *in loco Dei*, with a preconceived partiality *in malam partem*, is the only substitute for the omniscient impartiality of God; it is the sole self-protection against my corruptibility as judge in my own cause— the sole guarantee of my integrity. But it turns against itself. The distrust extends not only to what the observer finds before him, but also to this very observing itself, which again, after all, is an 'acting' of this ambiguous human I that is here meant to play a divine role. And such a distrust cannot help discovering that its own performance is not safe against turning from a critical into a self-enjoying observation, commending itself for being so critical, even merciless . . . . Indeed the distrust must discover, if only it is sufficiently radical, that what it thinks, it also endows with reality: that the evil possibilities discovered, i.e. invented, i.e. created by itself, obtain with such discovery already a share in the realization of the will and thus as it were get their money's worth out of it. And it discovers that any purity of the will which may have existed in the naïve state, is lost in the cunning of a will schooled by distrust itself—in the endlessly opened manifoldness of a soul grown more 'profound' in that school.

But why is the inner temptation irresistible? The question is hardly

distinguishable from the other: Why can one never be sure not to have
succumbed to it? Here lies the deepest mystery of freedom, and the most
difficult to verbalize. It concerns the relationship of possibility and
necessity in matters of freedom; or rather, freedom's relation to its own
possibilities, which is a peculiar kind of necessity, namely that of a
necessary act of freedom. For its description I have nothing at my disposal but allusions and metaphors.

One might speak of a kind of giddiness of freedom in the presence
of its possibilities. Because those possibilities are left entirely to its
discretion, the giddiness befalls it as soon as it takes its stand on itself
alone and in the sole presence of itself, i.e., of its own possibilities-to-be.
And that giddiness causes it actually to plunge into every espied possibility of self-variation and try its taste, so long as this involves no more
than the internal self-interpretative definition of its 'How' and not yet
the choice of external action. Over the latter's 'What' freedom has, of
course, control; but not, paradoxically, over its own 'How', on which
the moral quality of the action depends.[4] Its not having control over
this is the paradoxical result of the power it equally has over all the
options. Not in spite, but because of its unqualified authority over
the 'How' of its being, freedom must be iridescent. As each actual state
of it does not simply exist but is an *ad infinitum* continued product of
its subjectively boundless self-determination (which as such is placed
amidst the dizzying offer of its possibilities), and because this self-
entrusted 'How' is *potentially* manifold—freedom in each of its concre-
tions is already *actually* many-faced, i.e. ultimately ambiguous.

As entirely left to itself, freedom in its being from moment to moment
is its own product, and from this being-entrusted-to-itself no thing-like,
unequivocal being, on which it could rest for support, relieves it at any
point. Nor does anything protect freedom, fully released to itself as it is
in reflection, from the lure of its own possibilities (as the unequivocal
biological order did in the state of nature). Giddy with their protean
phantasmagoria, it must itself glitter in their changing hues. And since
the possibility of spuriousness, without which genuineness would not
be that of freedom either, is positively its own, shrewdly self-seductive
freedom manages, along with each act of genuineness, somehow to

---

[4]The reader will note that this is the diametrical reverse of the Stoic position,
which held that the external domain is outside our power while we have clearly
control over the internal domain. The profoundly significant meaning of the reversal
cannot here be elaborated. The prevalent modern, counter-classical view of the
relation of man's outer and inner power, viz., his dominion over things and his impotence over himself, is the end-result of two largely independent historical developments in the one domain and the other (that of nature and that of man), whose
confluence shaped the modern situation.

realize the corresponding spuriousness as well. As freedom it enmeshes itself in its possibilities as absolutely self-owned. Thus the self-produced concretion of its How at any moment, ever continued by the unsteady-sovereign reflection of self-concern, is comparable, as regards its critical identifiability, to the iridescence of a mother-of-pearl or an oil-slick on the water: each place seems at first to possess its colour of the spectrum unequivocally; but the slightest change of my location shows me another, and I discover that no place owns any one colour definitively but each already contains them all in itself . . .

Therefore, when in the oscillating reflexivity of the will during the consciously moral act, it happens that freedom is offered the defection into self-objectivation—a possibility inherent in consciousness as such—then it has already made use of it, however concealed: for freedom cannot resist its own possibilities. And this is the true and supreme mode of temptation: not the lure of sense nor outward self-seeking; not calculation of profit or fear of loss; not the charm of the forbidden or whatever else may be the spiritual sweetness of sin—none of these is the ultimate snare, all these one can resist; but this: that freedom, even when successful in abstaining from unethical outward 'work', encounters in the ownmost sphere of its self-grounding this inward possibility of itself which always lies in wait and claims its mental enactment; and the fact that here, within the mind, the mere thought is the act, and the possibility to think it is necessity to think it, and willing not to think it means to have already thought it, and not-having-thought-it may be concealing it, and concealing it may be its most suspicious presence: this labyrinthine structure of subjectivity *per se* makes the self-temptation irresistible to freedom in its helpless dealing with itself. Prior to any explicit counter-resolve, even in the heart of any counter-exertion itself, it has already succumbed to it in some subtle way. For since it is entirely alone with itself and has nothing but itself, it will not pass over any possibility of outwitting itself, if only here too it remains the agent: in being left-to-itself it is tuned to relishing itself and thereby is 'sinful'. If lust is at work here, it is the very non-sensuous, spiritual lusting of the self for itself. All purity of the will stands under this shadow.

Only at the stage of conscious, explicit morality does this temptation to self-objectivation come into play: i.e., precisely when, and not before, freedom in the 'reflection of the will' has come to itself. But that explicitness of morality is brought about by the Law. As the Law through its Ought first makes freedom reflective and thereby morality possible, so through its compulsion to self-scrutiny it creates at the same time the condition for the plight of subjectivity and the perversion of purpose. This is the 'impulsion to sin through the commandment'. But the possibility of the Law in turn rests on the condition of 'knowing' as such, which originates with the primal objectification of the world and the split between self and world that goes with it. Since it is that split which first makes it possible for him who thus can say 'I' to *know* about himself, and thereby generates freedom *and* its inescapable snare at the same time—therefore the myth ascribes the Fall to the eating from the tree of knowledge.

Again, the objectivation of the world is from the first a function of the human being-with-one-another, constituted by it and continuously maintained in its discourse. More specifically, this same discursive collectivity also furnishes the general horizon and the particular references for the self-objectivation as this operates, e.g., in comparison and appraisal and may reach right into the inner recesses of the 'isolated' subject. This is the existential basis for the critical role which the 'cosmos' in the sense of the human-social world plays in the context of the Pauline interpretation of being. This role of the *Miteinander* in the objectifying of self is not to be confused with that of the *man* ('they') in Heidegger's analytic of existence, i.e., with absorption into the anonymity of the many, the taking over by public generality. On the contrary, it is the setting-off of the I from its background, i.e., the attempt at being-oneself in the moral purpose, where the described self-objectivation lurks and does its disturbing work. This of the two is the more central phenomenon and the more profoundly pertinent to the human condition. It is also, admittedly, the rarer phenomenon. Whereas proper will and watchfulness can gain mastery over the one, the other pervades the very exercise of will and watchfulness itself.

If, then, our interpretation is correct, the plight described by Paul is not the individual's submersion into the 'they', but his submersion into the solitary presence of his own conscience; and this plight becomes the greater, the more he withdraws from the 'they' to his self, and the more radically he demands of himself a purity of will. It is a plight, therefore, which the Law produces only when taken seriously, not when practised outwardly. It is the plight, not of superficiality, but of depth, not of the letter but of the spirit, not of legality but of morality.

Jesus, in his critique of 'Pharisaism', had intended to expose the bad 'piety of the Law'. Paul's critique strikes at all piety of the Law. Jesus' critique was intended as a reproof, Paul's as a confession. The former castigates, from without, a false and corrigible attitude; the latter describes, from within, a true and unavoidable experience. Jesus did not summon away from the Law, but called from outward to inward, from blind to seeing, from superficial to serious compliance with the Law. But where that call leads, there the real experience of the Law waits. Thus the Pharisee corrected by Jesus would find himself in the Pauline situation, still unredeemed but cognizant of it: from an inauthentic he would have become an authentic Pharisee. So the Pauline characterization of the condition 'under the Law', which leaves all caricature and merely empirical typology behind, can be understood as the epitome of an existential concept of 'Pharisaism' (taken in a broad, formalized sense of the word, not bound to the historical case). Accordingly the 'Pharisee' would be man as such *vis-à-vis* the Law whose just claim he strives to satisfy, *as he should*. This means that he would be a 'Pharisee' when at his most serious best; for precisely by assuming the 'holy Law of God' as a personal mandate he exposes himself to the supreme test of man answering for himself—and thereby enters the dimension where alone he can experience the valid defeat of his mere humanity. If he suffers defeat here—this is Paul's logic—then only one road is left to him: that which leads to the cross. 'Pharisee', then, is 'man before Grace' generally, but in earnest 'under the Law' and thus on principle open to the need for Grace, which need he will come to feel when he fully realizes the condition of the 'Pharisee'. But such realization can only grow out of the experienced dialectic of the 'condition under the Law' itself, and since this includes the recognized necessity of that dialectic, it is at the same time a recognition of the existential unsurmountability of Pharisaism so understood. According to that understanding, then, existential self-knowledge belongs to the complete wholeness of the Pharisee. In the image drawn of him by Jesus, this is surely not the case.

To Jesus, 'Pharisee' is a party or group name; the Pharisee is an empirically encountered type among others, one faction within the religious variety of his environment, characterized by a specific attitude which Jesus fights because it is wrong and avoidable. He can therefore contrast it with better attitudes of which his environment also offers examples. It has always been debated whether Jesus' typology was empirically fair. But whatever the historical verdict, his was the naïve, popular, as it were visually typified image of Pharisaism; and the 'type' was a polemical caricature: the Pharisee is in the crude sense a hypocrite and demonstrative bigot. The truly pious Jew never had reason to recognize himself in this picture. He could recognize it as the warning against a temptation by which the Torah piety is threatened and to which Jews (and others) have often succumbed, but which they also have time and again successfully withstood. Jesus himself did not have to search far for examples of true piety. He found them in simple, believing women, Samaritans, publicans. Contrasted with them the Pharisee, as the gospel paints him, stands already convicted by the plain standards of popular, moral feeling—which therefore may easily indulge in that sense of superiority in which the roles can become reversed again or the distinctions obliterated.

For Paul, on the other hand, the Pharisee is not a religiously inferior type, as he was for Jesus, but the ultimate position before Grace; and for him it is just the most earnest, most inward striving ('with the inner man') to fulfil the 'holy Law', conceived in its essential demand, that is doomed to that failure which signifies the defeat of man as such—of man who, in the attempt to fulfil the Law, exposed his humanity to the ultimate test and in its pursuit came into his ultimate possibility and impossibility before God. (So it is if one really must push things that far—which of course is open to question.) Jesus thus takes the lowest, Paul the highest mode of Law-piety for his critical object; and that is not just a difference in polemical method, but a difference in the anthropological premise itself. For the highest position comprises all others under itself, and with a verdict on the optimal the lesser is judged *a fortiori*. The lesser, on the other hand, leaves above itself human alternatives still eligible—namely, the non-'pharisaical'—and thus represents a specific corruption, widespread perhaps and typically human, yet capable of rejection and avoidance.

Accordingly, Jesus simply points to the true attitude towards God as the superior alternative and assumes it to be attainable, given genuine human willingness. That he holds that willingness to be more readily found among the poor and oppressed than elsewhere is another matter. But found it is in his view; and so his death on the cross, or generally, the redemption of a mankind, constitutionally sinful, through the suffering and resurrection of a saviour, has no rightful place in Jesus' own message. Men have immediate access to God and to genuine being before him, so long as they hear and heed his call. This statement only re-iterates the old, if much-disputed, proposition that Paul's message *about* Jesus as the crucified Christ signifies a decisive step beyond Jesus' own message—a step with which the paths of the old creed and the new really part.

Other Books by Hans Jonas

Augustin und das paulinische Freiheitsproblem: Eine philosophische Studie zum pelagianischen Streit. Göttingen: Vandenhoeck & Ruprecht, 1930; 2nd, revised and enlarged edition (with an Introduction by James M. Robinson), 1965.

Gnosis und spätantiker Geist. Vol. I: *Die mythologische Gnosis.* Göttingen, 1934, 1954; 3rd, revised and enlarged edition, 1964.

Gnosis und spätantiker Geist. Vol. II/1: *Von der Mythologie zur mystischen Philosophie.* Göttingen, 1954, 1966.

The Gnostic Religion: The Message of the Alien God and the Beginnings of Christianity. Boston: Beacon Press, 1958; 2nd, enlarged edition (paperback), 1963.

Zwischen Nichts und Ewigkeit: Zur Lehre vom Menschen. Göttingen, 1963.

The Phenomenon of Life: Towards a Philosophical Biology. New York: Harper & Row, 1966. Paperback: Dell Publishing Co. (Delta Books), 1968.

Wandel und Bestand: Vom Grunde der Verstehbarkeit des Geschichtlichen. Frankfurt: Vittorio Klostermann, 1971.

Organismus und Freiheit: Ansätze zu einer philosophischen Biologie. Göttingen, 1973.